W9-AQU-191

An Advanced Guide to Psychological Thinking

An Advanced Guide to Psychological Thinking

Critical and Historical Perspectives

Robert Ausch

LEXINGTON BOOKS
Lanham • Boulder • New York • London

Published by Lexington Books
An imprint of The Rowman & Littlefield Publishing Group, Inc.
4501 Forbes Boulevard, Suite 200, Lanham, Maryland 20706
www.rowman.com

Unit A, Whitacre Mews, 26-34 Stannary Street, London SE11 4AB

British Library Cataloguing in Publication Information Available

Library of Congress Cataloging-in-Publication Data

Ausch, Robert.
An advanced guide to psychological thinking : critical and historical perspectives / Robert Ausch.
p. cm.
Includes bibliographical references and index.
ISBN 978-0-7391-9542-0 (cloth : alk. paper) -- ISBN 978-0-7391-9544-4 (electronic)
1. Psychology. I. Title.
BF121.A88 2015
150.1--dc23
2015000332

Printed in the United States of America

Contents

Introduction   1

1   The Creation of Mind   11
2   A Multiplicity of Psychologies   29
3   Methods of Psychology   53
4   The Principles of Learning   65
5   Biology, Brain, and Behavior   113
6   On Developmental Thinking   143
7   The Cure of the Soul in the Age of the Therapeutic   187

Conclusion   237
Bibliography   241
Index   251
About the Author   259

Introduction

FOUNDATIONAL TENSIONS IN PSYCHOLOGICAL THINKING

Psychology has many lives. In addition to being a discipline in the modern university, it is a technology of healing and self-improvement and a pervasive language used to make sense of the self and others (Smith, 2013). At this point, it is almost a cliché to say that we live in a psychological or therapeutic society, but these expressions still capture something unique about the relationship between psychology and Western societies that developed over the past century, especially in postwar America (Furedi, 2004; Nolan, 1998). Even within the university, it is difficult to see psychology as a singular discipline (Koch & Leary, 1992). Besides the ever-present split between its experimental and clinical sides, there are in practice a host of disciplines that share surface similarities in that they all study something related to mind and/or behavior. The term "mind" itself is a bit imprecise, but is meant as a kind of summary term including all the various characteristics, abilities, and functions related to complex human thought and action (Mandler, 2007, p. 18). In terms of method, some of these model themselves after the natural sciences and some the human sciences. Sometimes these disciplines purport to study the same object—many look to the effects of the "environment" or the processes of "learning," for example—yet what they actually mean by these terms is quite different (Kagan, 2013). Psychologists might use the term "learning" to describe a rat finding its way through a maze, a child figuring out the meaning of a complex sentence in school, or a change in the synaptic pathways of the brain. Adding to the confusion is the everyday use of psychological terms that might still refer to something else entirely, as in "I 'learned' to be a better person," which reflects a shift in how the world is experienced. These disparate processes are said to refer to the same underly-ing phenomena.

Naturally, part of what happens in the university involves bringing preci-sion to everyday language, especially in the sciences. But psychology is unusual here in a couple of senses. First, as just noted, within the disciplines themselves, the same term often has different referents. Second, psychologi-cal language refers to both an expert language for studying mind and behav-ior as well as a public and shared language for talking about psychological properties. This language became more pervasive in Western Europe after around 1600 (G. Richards, 1992). This everyday psychological language is often a source for academic psychology, and academic psychological lan-guage can make its way into everyday language. One thing that both lan-guages share is the sense that the realm of the mental is a private and inner space (Graumann, 1996, p. 94). They also share the notion that the mental is connected with personhood. Even everyday psychological language has multiple uses. Cognitive psychologists often focus on "theory of mind," that is, an individual's means of inferring the mental states of others and referring others to their own mental states (Premack & Woodruff, 1978; Apperly, 2012). This is obviously important, but everyday psychological language can also be a rhetorical strategy to communicate authenticity (Searle, 1969) or personify an event, among other things. When it comes to psychological language, as with all language, the meaning and function of terms change very much with the context.

The objects of psychology are products of language, and even though this language is intended to represent entities or processes in the world and thus contain elements of natural groupings, they can never be wholly disentangled from each other (Rosch, 1973). Thus, there is arbitrariness or at least a relevant history to the divisions they bring (Harris, 2003). This language is often metaphorical, perhaps more often than is recognized if one does not attend to the history of the terms. Terms like "memory" or "intelligence"— the first derived from the Greek word for mindful and related to mnemonic techniques and the latter from the Latin meaning the capacity to discern or perceive—hardly seem like metaphors anymore (Danziger, 1997). These metaphors often work as models, offering a way to represent the abstract (Leary, 1990). What exactly are cognitive "processes"? The term "process" is a functional one, implying a relationship between an action and an end. Presumably they are similar to certain physiological mechanisms and per-haps those used in computing technology. Yet these have obvious material instantiations. But with the term "processes" we have not actually said much other than try to make a covert analogy (Robinson, 1985). One popular metaphor today is that of a "network," which seems to be replacing that of a "system" (e.g., memory system, attachment system), and both seem much preferable to the older metaphor of "states." These types of metaphor are reductive in an attractive sense as well as seem to offer explanation in the guise of description (ibid., p. 89).

Sigmund Freud, the master of metaphor, understood this well. As he put it, "In psychology we can only describe things by the helps of analogies. There is nothing peculiar in this. . . . But we have to constantly keep changing these analogies, for none of them lasts us long" (Freud, 1926, p. 195). Each age in psychology seems to have its master metaphor: in the eighteenth century it was the association; in the nineteenth, the reflex; and in the twentieth, the computer. These master metaphors capture the imagination of both scientists and the public, and as productive as they can be, they can also have limiting effects that are hard to see until the dominance of the metaphor has long passed. One such metaphor, as we will argue extensively, was the reflex, which is a causally conceived relationship between stimulus and response, a metaphor that in many ways has left an indelible mark on the discipline, especially with respect to methodology.

1. THE BASIC TENSIONS: INSIDE AND OUTSIDE/STRUCTURE AND FUNCTION/HIGHER AND LOWER/DESCRIPTION AND EXPLANATION

This book focuses on identifying some of the key conceptual foundations of psychology in Western societies, their origins, and how those concepts translate into institutions and practice. Looking at foundations in this way doesn't necessarily imply criticism, though it can, as conceptual confusion can arise from not considering these foundations carefully enough. We begin with the premise that a psychological and "therapeutic" sensibility has become pervasive, particularly in the United States, giving ideas emanating from psychology a kind of power and influence never experienced in the past (Imber, 2004). We will focus specifically on four areas within psychology and the academic disciplines that represent them: learning, neuropsychology, child development, and psychotherapy. These have been selected for several reasons. First, they will represent the areas that were the focus of late-nineteenth-century psychology, those years that psychology presented itself as a coherent, modern field and an important university discipline. These years were important in the spreading of a psychological sensibility as well (Cushman, 1995). Many basic psychological categories as we conceive them originated with the Greeks but were reworked in the nineteenth century and have not strayed far since. Daniel Robinson (1995, p. 259) describes contemporary psychology as a nineteenth-century enterprise, meaning that although the content of the field has obviously changed, it still remains, in some sense, beholden to nineteenth-century concerns. Thus, really making sense of how psychologists think requires a return to the thought of the nineteenth century.

Given this, we will lay out some of the conceptual foundations of psychology as they were built into the discipline itself. Second, these four areas nicely reflect the ways in which psychological ideas are given life and shape experience as they become embedded in the practices and institutions of a particular society. In our case, contemporary schooling, popular science writing/ medicine, child rearing, and mental therapy have all been shaped by conceptions originating in psychology. Finally, these areas represent some of the larger subdisciplines within psychology itself. Naturally, we could have selected others as well. The point of this analysis is not necessarily to be comprehensive. In fact, given its scope, comprehensiveness is impossible. As we make certain generalizations about how psychologists conceive what they study in the interests of identifying consistent themes across disciplinary contexts, it is important to acknowledge the rich tradition of critical psychologies that engage in a similar enterprise (Henriques etal. 1998; Fox, Prillel-tensky, & Austin, 2009; Teo, 2005)

This book will make the argument that psychology is grounded in several conceptual tensions. Sometimes they are framed as dichotomies, sometimes as continuums, and sometimes as just related terms, but regardless they are key to how psychology makes sense of the world. They can take different yet related forms and can also embody some of the confusion that sits at the very heart of the discipline itself. We will focus on three conceptual tensions— that between inside and outside, structure and function, and higher and lower—and one methodological—that between description and explanation. As we shall see, there are a myriad of other ones that derive from these basic ones. We will start with the changing boundaries between inside and outside because it was the seventeenth-century variant of this tension, specifically that between mind and body, that created the conceptual conditions which made the emergence of psychology possible. Sometimes this is described as "Cartesianism," but Rene Descartes was certainly not the only one working within this framework.

One example of this was the common notion among British Empiricists that as physics explained the laws of matter, the outside world, psychology explained the laws of mind, the inside world. The idea that the worlds inside and outside human beings might or might not operate by different principles was foreign to Greco-Roman thought as nature had only one set of principles (Kitto, 1950). Whether the principal object of study was reason, as it was for the eighteenth century, consciousness, as it was for most of the nineteenth century, or behavior, as it was for the twentieth, part of what psychology sought was a consistent means to define the inside as against the outside and vice versa, along with establishing a stable and self-evident boundary between them. In general, classical and Christian thought viewed truth as emanating from within and regarded the outside as a source of distortion. Thus, notions of inside and outside were related to those of higher and lower, and even more basically, those of reality and appearance. The revolution of the seventeenth century was to gradually reverse this relationship, making the inside a source of distortion, especially with respect to knowledge of the natural world.

The separation of mind and body created several unique conceptual problems for these new ways of conceiving the psychological. There were the obvious problems of how to bridge the realms of mind and body as well as how to correct for the distorting effects of mind on the natural sciences. These are well recognized (Burtt, 1932). Most psychologists, however, are not ready to give up the notion that mentality requires its own level of analysis, even if they suspect that mind is a product of more basic brain activity (Bruner, 1990). But a more subtle and often underappreciated issue was finding a space to locate the agent of reason. Reason, of course, is a product of human activity, but such a view was too holistic. Often it was simply assigned to some agent or element within the mind itself, what has been described as the homunculus fallacy. In the case of seventeenth-century thought, this was often quite literal, as was the case with what Daniel Dennett (1993) has termed the "Cartesian Theatre." Descartes assigned reason to a singular point of reflection within consciousness capable of scanning its contents. Here the idea of a little "man" inside the mind was most apt. John Locke and his followers assigned reason to a faculty of mind, and by the eighteenth century, not unlike today, it was viewed by French materialists like Julien Offray de La Mettrie and Pierre Jean George Cabanis as an emergent property of physiological activity. Over the course of the twentieth century, psychologists have assigned reason to various entities including a faculty of intelligence, a "conditioning" environment, DNA, computer program-like functions, and most recently, networks of nerve cells and synapses. These "explanations" simply hide what we do not understand (Deacon, 2012).

While many in the disciplines that make up today's psychology have pointed to the mystifying effects of the distinction between mind and body, they don't always recognize the confusing relationship between structure and function, a relationship that has created and that continues to create unique problems for the disciplines and often becomes another site to express the tension between mind and body. In general, the natural sciences tend to study things-in-the-world and view them through a language and a set of questions appropriate to structures. One of the consequences of shifts in biological thinking from the nineteenth century forward was that certain functions, including certain behavioral patterns, could be conceived similarly, especially with respect to natural selection. For instance, dam-building behavior on the part of beavers was viewed as a product of natural selection and is just as biologically "real" as certain anatomical structures. While "functionalist" approaches preceded the spread of evolutionary ideas—this is one way to understand the tension between faculty and associationist approaches to psychology in the eighteenth century, for example—Darwinism provided them with a broader biological framework that helped support the scientific status of psychological explanations (Boakes, 1984). Psychology, as a consequence of this, was able to turn away from a structural approach to mind, viewing it as a composition of mental entities, and instead describe mind as a series of functions, processes rather than elements.

This was the way many in the first few generations of psychology—Wilhelm Wundt, William James, Max Wertheimer, and even Freud—conceived the mind. Sometimes these functions had fairly obvious referents. There was not much debate about what made up the function of "vision"—although there was some related to where sensation ended and perception began (Turner, 2014). However, for various reasons—including the nature of psychological phenomena, their status as human kinds, linguistic and cultural variability, and their context-bound nature—sometimes those referents were less evident. It is not clear, for example, where the function of thinking begins and the function of feeling ends. It is not clear precisely which behaviors/mechanisms make up the function of motivating or even remembering. Figuring out functional referents is even trickier when we describe these processes using nouns like "personality" or "depression." And of course, many of these referents are then re-integrated into the structural languages of physiology or neuroscience.

Thus, most sciences—with some exceptions like physiology or evolutionary biology—study structure and use the language of structure to describe objects that they "see" using their instruments. Thus, they focus on identifying constitutive parts, measuring various properties, and detailing relationships with other structures. In contrast, for the most part, contemporary psychology is about function. Thinking, feeling, and remembering are things the mind does, not entities the mind possesses. Psychologists, following in certain philosophical traditions as well as everyday psychological language, can create linguistic havoc by gradually turning these entities into structures—they become thoughts, feelings, and memories. The consequence is a basic confusion between structural and functional language. Some of this is likely related to the fact that the so-called hard sciences typically employ the languages of structure and these are the types of science psychology has always struggled to be. Since its origins at the end of the nineteenth century, psychologists have sought the underlying "structures" that make mental functions possible. Various candidates, typically borrowed from other disciplines, have included: reflexes, ideas, psychic energies, drives, genes, neurotransmitters, hormones, modules, and so on. On the other hand, a wholly functionalist psychology, as variants of behaviorism represented, risked erring too far in the other direction—not simply ignoring physiology, as they were often accused of, but ignoring organization altogether. Human beings seem to be highly adept at recognizing and creating patterns (Kagan, 2013), and all functions require some level of organization, whether this organization is immanent in the processes themselves or imposed upon them.

Adding to this is the fact that in everyday psychologizing, people move from structural to functional language without skipping a beat, and this confusion spreads to academic psychology as well. Is intelligence a process the mind engages in or a trait the mind possesses? Is attachment a description of behavior or a force that causes certain behaviors? Is a cognitive structure or schemata a description of certain responses to a problem-solving task or an entity that generates certain responses to a problem-solving task? Are the objects of psychology best expressed using verbs or nouns? The English language often tends to play fast and loose with these distinctions especially when it comes to the realm of the psychological. There is always a temptation to employ structural language and metaphors in psychology simply because they ring true. Sometimes it is not clear whether one should use structural or functional language because it is not clear what is actually being referred to. Is the unconscious a thing or a process? What about a gene, as opposed to DNA, which is certainly a thing? All this confusion makes it even more likely that psychologists working in different subfields or even in different contexts do not share the same referents.

The notion of "structure" is an engineering metaphor, but since the nineteenth century has emphasized that internal relations are constitutive (Williams, 1985). This relates it to the classical idea of form. In fact, in the nineteenth century the relationship between the terms was more explicit, especially in morphology where internal and external structure was contrasted with each other (ibid., p. 302). Internal structures reflected the relationships between constitutive parts that made up the whole. The term function, on the other hand—a word that has its roots in notions of proper performance or action—is intimately connected with Aristotelian notions of purpose. When one assigns several pieces of wood the function of a table, one has clearly said something about its purpose. The verb "assigned" is important because functions are typically assigned from the outside (Searle, 1995). Often that "outside" is human consciousness. One of the functions of DNA is to assist in protein synthesis, though DNA does not know this. Only humans do. Thus talk of functions always involves making judgments, and it also involves imposing a purpose, both of which are too often ignored by psychologists whose notions of function were shaped by nineteenth-century evolutionary naturalism.

The distinction between higher and lower is much more directly a product of the Greco-Roman worldview. Like a similar tension between appearance and reality, it is the ground upon which all Western theories of knowledge are situated. After all, the simplest way to understand the purpose of science is to see it as a tool that bridges the gap between appearance and reality. In

the case of psychology, the tension allows psychological concepts and findings to present themselves as value-free while importing the values of a
particular time and place. Two areas within psychology where this becomes
very clear are in developmental and psychotherapeutic theories and practices
(Burman, 1994; Pickering, 2006). In both cases, terms like "advanced,"
"healthy," "primitive," and "instinctual" become markers for higher and lower forms. In general, notions of the good are pervasive in psychology.

Finally, the last tension we will focus on is a methodological one—that
between description and explanation—and gets to the very heart of what it
means for psychology to present itself as a science. This tension is related to
that between cause and reason as well as, once again, the more basic one
between appearance and reality. Since the rise of the experimental sciences,
explanations have involved the laying out of cause-effect relationships and
relating them to more general natural laws. Yet, the rise of a psychological
orientation turned this into a problem. Could there be certain knowledge
when knowledge was a product of the mind and imposed on the world?
Furthermore, as Immanuel Kant further divided the human world from the
world of nature, the question arose as to whether human phenomena could be
captured via the conceptual tools used to study nature. This led to the notion
that psychology be a science of description or "understanding" as opposed to
an explanatory one. These ideas made their way into twentieth-century
psychology in all sorts of ways, ranging to recognition as to the limitations of
logical positivism to the rise of a qualitative approach to methodology (Denzin & Lincoln, 2007; Parker, 1989).

The tensions we will describe are not "resolvable" nor are they wrong or
corrupt. In the age of postmodernism anything that feels like a dichotomy is
automatically suspect, but one must remember Jean Piaget's findings that
young children rely on dichotomous or "essentialist" thinking as a means to
make sense of more complex relationships that are still as yet beyond their
grasp (Piaget, 1929). The same is true of scientific thinking in general (Piaget, 1971). Our focus here is on the conceptual confusion generated by this
language, not necessarily that these terms can somehow be replaced in a
more sophisticated psychology, though at certain points we will make some
suggestions in this direction. As things stand today, there is no psychology
without a distinction between mind and body, no matter what the conceptual
cost. There is value, however, in making these problems explicit.

2. THE PLAN OF THE BOOK

The first three chapters examine the origins of these tensions in philosophy,
psychology, and methodology. Because psychological categories have a long
past in Western thought, we must begin by looking at the way in which

nineteenth-century psychology was shaped by the thinking of Aristotle, Descartes, Hobbes, Locke, Rousseau, and others. This will help us understand some of the assumptions psychologists make when conceiving the mind including its distinction from the body, its interiority, various capacities, and means for knowing, among others. We then turn to a "revisionist" history of psychology which contests the well-worn idea that psychology began in 1879 with the opening of Wundt's laboratory, followed by a "debate" between structuralism and functionalism, and then a series of "revolutions" including behavioral, cognitive, and more recently neuro-biological. We discover both that the first few generations of psychologists were much more explicit about some of the tensions we are outlining as well as their own ambivalence about whether a natural science of mind was possible. Finally, we explore the question that has haunted psychology since the nineteenth century: Is psychology a science? What are the appropriate scientific methods for psychology? Is psychology to be a science of explanation or description? And how has the discipline developed as a result of these tensions? One route was to find certainty in methodology, especially those that offered the possibility of quantification and measurement (Toulmin & Leary, 1992; Aronowitz & Ausch, 2000).

The fourth chapter focuses on psychology, public education, and nineteenth-century physiological thought, particularly the extension of the reflex concept into the psychology of learning. We trace the ways in which psychologists borrowed the question as to the source of reflexes from the study of animals and reconceived them as originating dichotomously, between either innate or acquired sources. American psychologists focused almost exclusively on the acquired and ended up using these ideas to rework traditional conceptions of learning. These conceptions were then imported into public education as educators were looking for new ways to assess students and bring order to a rapidly expanding system. We then turn to the German context where psychology and its place in schools took a wholly different direction. Next, we look at the critique of "mentalism" that comes out of the behavioral approach and try to extract some valuable cautions about psychology's dependence on unseen mental entities. Finally, we try to move beyond critique and offer an alternate framework for considering learning.

In the fifth chapter, we turn to biology. The developments in physiology in the early nineteenth century established the ground for a scientific psychology. Mind became a physiological problem as much as a philosophical one. Physiology offered psychology a language for the study of the relationship between structure and function that could be framed scientifically, especially after the spread of Darwinism. Early psychologists not only borrowed the methods of physiology but some of their key concepts. These concepts framed the ways in which the brain was studied and continues to be studied to this day. While it is hard to deny the advances of contemporary neuroscience, these same advances have created problems for psychology as many in the field turn to reductive models of the brain and nervous system in order to offer their own work physiological ground. For some, psychology is reducible to synaptic connections and neural wiring. However, as we argue, this is hardly an adequate language for making sense of persons and their lives. We also look at other frameworks for reducing psychology to biology and conclude with a less reductive account of brain development and its implications for psychology.

In the sixth chapter, we look at psychology's understanding of child development, both how the concept emerged from evolutionary thought and how it lays out a prescribed trajectory for maturation that fits with certain preexisting cultural values and assumptions. We focus on the origins and development of the idea of recapitulation and its relationship to psychology. We then look at the theories of some of the leading thinkers on child development in the late nineteenth and early twentieth centuries and their shared assumptions as well the recent turn in developmental psychology to nativism. Finally, we focus on language development in ways that try to understand change outside of the tight constraints of traditional approaches.

The seventh and final chapter looks at psychotherapy. We examine at the genesis of a psychological approach to both pathology and treatment as well as the emergence of the current therapeutic sensibility. While Freud is often characterized as central to these developments (Rieff, 1966), we will discover that this sensibility preceded his work, making much of it seem common sense by the time it appeared at the turn of the twentieth century, and that it has moved in directions Freud would likely not accept.

Finally, we conclude by trying to bring together some of the critical strands we have been developing and lay out some preliminary conclusions, particularly with respect to the problem of structure in the study of psychological functions.

Chapter One

The Creation of Mind

The West has inherited much from the Greek way of conceiving mind filtered through Christianity and Enlightenment rationalism. The years between 1637, the year of the publication of Descartes' *Discourse on the Method*, and 1781, the year of the publication of Kant's *Critique of Pure Reason*, were especially important in creating the notion of mind that became psychology's object of the study. In the nineteenth century this tradition was reconceived through evolutionary naturalism. All of this culminated in, as the standard history goes, the establishment of the first psychological laboratory by Wilhelm Wundt in Leibzig in 1879, and by William James at Harvard shortly thereafter. The world of academic psychology (that is, from the 1870s on) was the world of a mostly Protestant—at least where institutionalized psychology thrived—but secularizing, industrializing, urbanizing Europe and later the United States, and they were looking to develop new conceptions of the relationships between persons and authority, individual, and community as well as the interior world and the external one. It was a world of increasing wealth, an expanding state, and rapid technological change. For many, science was regarded as the source of much of this progress and thus, the idea of a science of mind was attractive to those who wished to understand and even modify human nature to meet the demands of this new world (Smith, 2013).

The Cartesian compromise had permitted much of what once reflected the spiritual nature of the universe to be moved onto the immaterial plane of mind. Some saw psychology, especially in the latter part of the nineteenth century, as repudiating that bargain (Rylance, 2000). Since then, the West has struggled with a conception of mind that is both inside of nature and outside it, a quasi-spiritual power that makes humans unique from other species, yet a biological organ, the result of natural selection like any other operating along mechanistic principles. From Greek thought forward,

11

psychology has been a moral discourse, never simply a description of mind or soul, but a value-laden vision of what people in a particular society should be like, a vision of good and evil, right and wrong.

The tensions that ground psychology, those between structure and function, inside and outside, higher and lower, and description and explanation, have their beginnings in the Greek worldview yet have been reconceived over and over again since then. They find their origin in a basic tension that organized Greek thought, that between being and becoming, a product of Pre-Socratic thought which was reconceived by Plato as that between reality and appearance. While not identical, the tension between structure and function is one variant of that between being and becoming. Similarly, the tension between inside and outside is related to that between reality and appearance as is that between description and explanation, though these notions emerge much later. Finally, all of these distinctions are invested with morality expressed as the tension between higher and lower. Christianity expressed the tension between inside and outside as that between spirit and flesh, which was reconceived as that between mind and body in Cartesianism. In early modern Europe the tension between structure and function was expressed as a conflict between a faculty and an associationist view of mind and was later reworked through the framework of nineteenth-century biology. The goal of this chapter is to take us through some of these shifts up to the nineteenth century, while the next two will focus on how they played out in the disciplines that made up psychology during the nineteenth and early twentieth centuries.

1. HIGHER AND LOWER: REASON AND APPETITE

There is a danger with looking to the sources of modern psychological concepts in Greek thought, and that is the tendency to read present concerns back on the past. The Greek interest in the soul evolved in a world different to the modern West. That being said, German philologist Bruno Snell (1953) had a point when he famously claimed that the Greeks discovered the mind. He meant that the Western conception of mind is an especially peculiar idea, especially in its link with personhood. For the Greeks, what eventually becomes the mind was tied up with two issues: human dignity/uniqueness as well as the acquisition of knowledge (Rorty, 1979). The Greek mind was both religious, part of a conception of a personal soul, and scientific, pure knowing reason (Leahey, 2005). It alone would bridge Plato's gap between appearance and reality as it alone offered access to the world of forms.

When one considers a Greek view of mind, one can begin with the term *psyche*, from which the discipline of psychology takes its name. *Psyche* is sometimes translated as either mind or soul due to the fact that in Greek thought these senses of the term were indistinguishable. There were several other Greek words for similar ideas. The word *pneuma* also referred to the soul, though it was meant in a more traditional sense, as in a breath of life. The term *noûs* can be translated as mind but also reason, as in the faculty of reason, but *psyche* and *noûs* are not the same. Technically, *noûs* resides in the *psyche*; but *psyche* does not survive the death of the body, *noûs* does. At least this was the position of Aristotle until the church assigned the power to survive death to the soul (Graumann, 1996). The *psyche* is the inner nature of the human being, something that can be divorced from any context or specific individual and made an object of study.

In Plato, one finds an influential division of the *psyche*. Before Plato, the soul was something like a "life breath." You see this in the Old Testament and in Homer. Again, this is represented by the term *pneuma*. Plato, following his teacher Socrates, turned the soul into the basis for human morality. It was distinct from the body and had primacy over it. The soul became the source of key human activities: fairly fundamental to what we consider the work of mind to be. The soul was divided into reason, appetite, and spirit. Reason [*Logistikon*—appreciator of the logos] was the source of knowledge and one's access to the universe of forms, a higher, spiritual world. Appetite [*Epithumetakon*], what we might also term desire, was responses to the world, thus the least stable. They were part of the "nutritive" soul shared with plants and thus the lowest part of human nature. Spirit [*Thymos*] was the more traditional sense of soul as a force. It carried plans into action. It was part of the "sensible" soul shared with animals. Later, in Augustine, spirit became the "will," whose freedom to choose or not choose sin was key.

What later becomes the mind was actually distributed across the body: reason in the head—the highest faculty and thus closest to God—spirit in the heart, and appetite in the gut. In the *Phaedrus*, Plato described a chariot steering two horses with reason attempting to steer appetite and spirit. The ideal life, for Plato and the Stoics who followed him here, was one where reason dominated spirit and appetite. This view goes back to at least Homer and played a large role in Galenic medicine. In fact, most philosophies/ psychologies to the present day tend to view human nature as dominated by one or the other of these. In the Greek and Christian view, reason tended to dominate, at least ideally. We find vestiges of this in the various cognitive psychologies and rational or humanist therapies. One way to describe the development of modern thought—that is, European thought since the Reformation—is the gradual ascendance of psychologies of appetite beginning with a much more depraved conception of human nature in many strands of Protestantism and continuing through the hedonism of Hobbes, Adam Smith, Utilitarianism, behaviorism, and Freudianism. It is also worth noting that the most influential psychological metatheories of the twentieth century—Behaviorism, Psychoanalysis, and Darwinism—view human nature more or less in a similar way, dominated by internal and/or external forces of which there is little control, including stimuli from the environment, drives, instincts, ancestral adaptations, and unconscious impulses. The Greeks recognized these but were clearly more optimistic about the capacity of reason to control them.

2. STRUCTURE AND FUNCTION: PURPOSE

Plato had introduced the distinction between the appearance of an object and its essence or form. Aristotle accepted this yet turned away from Plato's devaluation of sensory experience to the observational study and classification of nature. His biologically based system dominated the West until the seventeenth century and continues to shape basic psychological categories to the present. It was, however, a part of a broader worldview wherein the parts and functions of the soul were reflections of the larger moral logic of a universe in which everything had purpose and meaning. Aristotle accepted Plato's notion of the soul as the source of key human activities, but added that its properties were fundamentally connected with the material body. The affairs of the soul involve alterations in the body.

As Daniel Robinson (1995) put it, Aristotle insisted "that an understanding of human and animal psychology depends on and is informed by our knowledge of the material (biological) conditions of life . . . [and] was the first to specify the domain embracing the subject matter of psychology and, within the domain, to frame explanations in terms of the presumed biology of organisms" (47).

Yet, he was no materialist or atomist. At base, the Aristotelian soul was not a thing, but the first principle of animate life. Aristotle took the division of the soul further, introducing many more "faculties" that were arranged hierarchically. They included the faculties of nutrition (growth: possessed by all living things), locomotion, sensibility (sensation, desire, movement in response to stimuli, pleasure, and pain—which shaped action from infancy on and required education to alter), imagination (memory), and the intellect—what he described as a tablet upon which nothing is written. The intellectual faculty was unique to humans. It involved a conceptual space, not a literal one, and the power to form abstract judgments (Robinson, 1995, p. 48). These faculties were not only defined by what they were [form or structure] but by what they did or their purpose [function]. They were functionally but not structurally discrete. Aristotle opened the door for a shift in focus away from the study of pure forms as he sought to identify the nature of a thing through an understanding of its function. This involved his doctrine of the four causes. To know something, said Aristotle, was to know its cause. These included four: formal, material, efficient, and final. This meant that to fully understand an aspect of biological life, one needed to ask about the form and matter that made it up as well as its immediate cause and ultimate purpose. Although all these causes were relevant, Aristotle's teleological view directed him to focus on final ones. This shaped Aristotle's conception of biology. For instance, Aristotle rejected the idea of Empedocles that animal parts were the result of chance variation and a process of "natural selection" where those with unfit parts did not survive. He argued instead that all animal parts were part of an integrated whole and came into being with an end and purpose.

Aristotle also introduced a principle of development, a manifestation of an inner power toward growth and change. Objects move from a state of potentiality to actuality, becoming their essence or purpose. Thus, explanations of life and nature were teleological and required an understanding of purpose. To cite Robinson again, " . . . animals and human beings do something for the sake of attaining something or in order to achieve a given goal . . . processes and functions are understood according to the larger objectives or goals they serve" (Robinson, 1995, p. 50). Eighteenth-century Romanticism and nineteenth-century Evolutionism later transformed this into the idea of progressive evolution, in part, to replace the absence of purpose in seventeenth-century Newtonianism. Again, without imposing modern concerns on Aristotle, it is worth noting that his biological functionalism has become, in essence, the basic frame of modern psychology.

3. INSIDE AND OUTSIDE: CONSCIOUSNESS

There are equally compelling cases to credit Descartes, Hobbes, and/or Locke as the inspiration for the modern view of mind. Either way, it was in this period in the mid- to late seventeenth century that a new conception of mentality was developed to meet the challenges of the new corpuscular philosophy, experimental science, and the collapse of the Aristotelian system. Satisfactory explanations had long revolved around causality. What Galileo and Newton did, and Descartes defended, was lay out a more limited sense of what it means to be a cause (Robinson, 1985). Aristotle's "complete" account that included a notion of purpose was rejected, at least explicitly if not entirely. The culmination of this tradition for the purposes of this narrative was Hume and Kant, the former turning causality into a psychological category, and the latter essentially turning all of experience into a psychological construct. While the mind had no direct access to the world, the power of mind to shape experience placed psychology in a unique place among the sciences.

Working in a world where a century of religious conflict had undermined the self-certain and stable medieval synthesis, Descartes sought to ground knowledge in the science of Galilean mechanism (Toulmin, 1992). Gone was the purpose-filled and hierarchical medieval conception of nature, only to be replaced by an atomic, mechanical, mathematical, and inert one. Knowledge was no longer a moral vision but a "correct" picture of reality. While the Greek and medieval view of perception held that the sense organs received direct knowledge of the form of the objects perceived, in the new Cartesian version, ordinary experience was distorting and needed to be corrected by mathematics into an idealized world cleansed of the subjective (Leahey, 2005).

The division of the world into *res cogitans* and *res extensa*, the distinct substances of mind and extension, described in this century as "Cartesian-ism," has been so thoroughly discredited at the hands of its critics, it seems obvious that a dichotomy between mind and body was one of the least helpful legacies of Descartes' thinking as it, conventional wisdom argues, prevented the scientific study of mind for nearly three centuries. This is only partially correct. Descartes did leave a troubling legacy for psychology to deal with, but this was not it. For one, Descartes' philosophy was in the service of his physics and not the other way around. Reading Descartes one should be impressed by how much of what we would term "mental" was assigned to the realm of extension. The point of his separation of mind and matter was to provide the new sciences with the kind of certainty found in mathematics. This was the case because what was known through conscious-ness was not doubtable as only via consciousness can one have access to the reality behind appearance (Robinson, 2008, p. 66).

Descartes is rightfully credited with creating modern psychology's object of study taking Aristotle's soul (reflecting the totality of a person) and turn-ing it into the mind—that at its essence was a singular point of self-aware-ness (Rorty, 1979). He relegated many of the functions of the Aristotelian soul to the realm of body and introduced new language for talking about mind and its hidden operations. Mind, which had once simply been memory (e.g., re-mind), gradually began to reflect the unique capacities of humans (Smith, 1997). Furthermore reason, the traditional source of knowledge, was now a procedure, a method for knowing, and no longer simply a property of thought. This procedure, introspection of mind, offered a new vantage point from which to study the world. This point within the mind, or inner sense, was removed enough from the mind to view it as distinct—the so-called "Cartesian" theater (Dennett, 1993). Introspection revealed that the mind contained "ideas," which included sensations, perceptions, beliefs, desires, imaginings, and acts of will, most of which could be influenced by experi-ence. Descartes was then left with the infamous problem as to how these "mental" events caused physical ones. What distinguished the mental, aside from its incorporeality, were the powers ascribed to thought, which included self-awareness (not simply "awareness"), capacity to compel action, and language. These, therefore, distinguished humans from animals and left humans with freedom of will.

Descartes created a nature, and even a human body, cleansed of animism and vitalism, making its study through the mechanical sciences possible. He was able to demonstrate that "a number of psychophysical functions that had always been recognized as being corporeal could be accounted for in a way which did not render matter sentient" (Gaukroger, 1997, p. 278). This vantage also permitted the study of nature, distinct from the actual experience of nature. Descartes helped to create an objectified world, distinct from the actual experience of the world, a subject distinct from object. No longer were the forms of objects in the world perceived directly by mind, as was the case in Greek and medieval thought, but an intelligible world required "calculative" action taken by reason. These calculations distinguished the accidental qualities of objects, as they were experienced, now deemed "subjective," from universal or "objective" ones. Perception was distinct from sensation, and the action of mind was distinct from the nature of the world itself. Consciousness, a collection of mental entities and functions as well as the new object of psychology, was now independent of the experience of consciousness. This created the uniquely modern project of figuring out how to span the gap between consciousness and the world.

Descartes separated the realm of mind from body while embracing the physicalism of Galenic medicine. For him, animal spirits, which belonged to the realm of the body and operated mechanically, were capable of stirring passions and creating disturbances in the realm of mind. One of the key mechanisms for the actions of animal spirits involved the reflex. Descartes introduced the notion of a reflex, though the idea preceded Descartes, to explain the physiology of involuntary motion. Animal spirits, Descartes argued, travel through nerves and are "reflected" within the brain and eventually deflected by the pineal gland into nerve channels to produce motion. In the next generation, physician and founding member of the Royal Society Thomas Willis extended Descartes' reflex-mechanism to include many mechanical responses by the brain and body to sensory stimulation which became, in the nineteenth century, the basis for the reflex arc, which would view many of the functions once attributed to mind as mechanical responses to external stimulation. Descartes' critics, on the other hand, rejected not his dualism, which seemed sensible, but his thoroughgoing mechanism (Robinson, 2008). They argued that a sentient or vitalist principle must be present to explain living processes. Thus Descartes' critics, the neo-Platonists and Aristotelians, were the real "spiritualists," as they still required the traditional notion of soul to explain movement while Descartes didn't. His dualism was, however, the focus of Pierre Gassendi's attacks, who ridiculed the idea that mind and body could be distinct substances and was the inspiration for eighteenth-century French materialism and their "anti-Cartesianism." A more balanced view sees Descartes as laying the foundation for what today is termed "emergentism," the idea that mind emerges from the relationships between the physical properties of the body, a view that was commonplace by the eighteenth century and is not far from what many psychologists believe today (Robinson, 2008, p. 28).

What Descartes did bequeath to psychology is what we have previously described as the homunculus fallacy (Kenny, 1971). Sometimes, as was the case with the Cartesian theater, this was quite literal. There seems to be an intelligent agent inside mind "scanning" its contents. This was the sense that was taken up by Locke and British thought. Often, the homunculus fallacy has meant hiding properties of life that cannot be explained by the sciences of physics and chemistry in more cryptic forms (Deacon, 2012, p. 82). Descartes well understood that his new science required explaining life using the same principles Galileo used to explain the world of physics. Yet, he was not prepared to see thinking as a component of the reflexive mechanism with which he viewed the body, so he attributed to mind the power of reason. Without a properly physicalist explanation, he simply made the mind an immaterial substance. Psychology is replete with homunculi, what look like mechanisms but are actually stand-ins for incomplete explanations. In the past century alone, the inexplicable properties of mind have been hidden in reinforcers, DNA, computer-like programs, and more recently neural networks. In the century or two after Descartes, these properties were located in various forms of a life force. In part, this follows from the fact that life doesn't seem to be explicable without some notion of purpose, so purpose is simply reassigned somewhere else. One of the revolutionary elements of evolutionary thought was to introduce nonteleological notions of purpose, that is, to make purpose an accident or illusion. This probably helps to explain why it has been so influential in psychological thought, but as we shall see, more often than not, the homunculi are simply hidden better. This is the real legacy of Cartesianism.

4. INSIDE AND OUTSIDE: BODIES AND MOTION

Thomas Hobbes, Descartes' great adversary and fellow Galilean, extended mechanism to all of human nature, establishing the foundation of a thoroughly physicalist psychology. Like Descartes, he turned inward to find truth. But, instead of a theater of ideas, he found motion. The soul was composed of clashing atoms. The source of knowledge was not innate ideas like Plato but sense perceptions and perturbations of spirits caused by the motion of atoms. These motions, which in the case of bodily appetites were termed "desire," were the result of both native forces and experience (Robinson, 1995, p. 242). Passions, the result of sensory motions to the brain and heart, caused bodily motion. Here Hobbes has added something key. Gone was the Greek notion that the purpose of the soul was reason, or the Christian notion that the purpose was to be saved or draw close to divinity. The atoms of the soul had a much simpler calculus: drawing toward the pleasurable and away from the painful. Thus, self-preservation became their principal virtue. This was the foundation of good and evil. It was not that the Greeks did not recognize the motivating power of pleasure and pain, they surely did; but ideally these forces were to be controlled by reason. Even medieval Christians accepted that with Divine help, a life led by reason was possible. Hobbes is the father of the modern "selfish" view of human nature we find in behavioral theories, psychoanalysis, and evolution. Locke too recognized a role for pleasure and pain in the shaping of habits. By the eighteenth century, pleasure and pain were considered the primary sources of human motivation and behavior—as opposed to sin and a deformed will, which had been the case before. They were also the foundation of morality. Learning involved the shaping of behavior in the form of habits, using pleasure and pain. Educators were tasked with using pleasure and pain to shape character as Locke described in his influential *Treatise on Education*.

Hobbes, like many in his time, was seeking a new political foundation for the secular state. He rejected the medieval notion that sovereigns were appointed by God. He also rejected the classical notion that humans were innately political animals seeking an ideal regime. The problem, Hobbes argued, laying out a theory of the new seventeenth century "bourgeois man," was that humans were neither political nor social beings, but were directed toward their own narrow self-interests. In Hobbes, the individual came first. They did not, as the classical tradition implied, naturally desire government. This means that, against Plato, the state could not provide them with a path to perfection through the formation of character. The state must begin by accepting this aspect of human nature, from which one can derive natural law, and use institutions that are laid out along the lines of reason to help direct human passions. Human happiness came from satisfying desire. Because humans were directed toward self-interest, morality and self-interest must coincide. It meant, more broadly, that natural law and morality always coincide, supporting the search for moral sanction in the natural world (Smith, 1997). These ideas found fertile ground in the post-Civil War and proto-capitalist society of seventeenth- and eighteenth-century Britain, struggling to develop a new understanding of human nature that supported notions of competition, free trade, the pursuit of self-interest, and religious freedom.

5. STRUCTURE AND FUNCTION: FACULTIES AND ASSOCIATIONS

Locke and the British associationist tradition simply finished the work of Descartes, making the senses the source of knowledge, and further invested mental states with causal power. Locke used the term "consciousness" and made it central to the mind, though its essence lay in its operations (Walsh et al. 2014, p. 114). The term brought together the Latin term *consientia* and the French word *conscience*, the latter used by Descartes, blurring the distinction between mind as a natural object and mind as a moral one. Locke redefined the self or "I," not as the soul, but as consciousness over time, thus setting the stage for its eventual insignificance. Locke also followed Descartes in accepting that the contents of mind were immaterial ideas. He too distinguished between primary qualities—the Newtonian universe—and secondary ones—the "subjective" or simply the imposition of mind on nature. Again, the problem of knowledge, one that science needed to solve, was how to bridge the gap from a "subjective" mind to an "objective" world. Contrary to the accepted view, for Locke, mind was not completely "blank." While the contents of mind were empty at first, mind had innate faculties—perception, memory, combination, desire, deliberation, and will—that were the source of an "internal" sense, though this was often dropped by Locke's followers.

The idea that knowledge came from experience involved a new sense of the term "experience" which was tied to the term "empirical," one of the most difficult words in the English language (Williams, 1985, p. 115). The Greek term *empiriki* referred to a school of medicine that focused on observation and disdained theoretical explanation. Until the seventeenth century the term was typically a derogatory one, meaning ignorant. The terms "experience" and "experiment" were interchangeable until this time, both meaning to put to the test. During the seventeenth century the meanings of the two terms began to diverge with the former referring to a consciousness of what has been tested, and more broadly, consciousness of an effect or state, while the latter term maintained the simple sense as an actual test or trial (Williams, 1985, p. 116). The term "empirical," while no longer derogatory, maintained both senses, that is, based in observation and a-theoretical, which was also a synonym for practical. By the eighteenth century, the term "experience" implied a fuller and more active form of consciousness than simple reasoning and thus took on an aesthetic dimension as well, especially in Methodism where it became a firmer ground for religious truth than that of authority (Williams, 1985, p. 127).

The mostly British and later French sensationalist tradition sought to generate certain knowledge as a ground for social order, though this time in the associations of ideas, which became in Hume, a universal, attracting force, the mental equivalent of Newtonian gravity. But the skeptical Hume went further and made it clear that moral philosophy must begin with an understanding of mind and the limits of human experience, famously arousing Kant from his dogmatic slumber. Causality was a product of the mind, not nature. Even more importantly, by making ideas causally dependent on more powerful impressions and identifying the passions as a type of impression, he made reason a slave to the passions. What this meant, in essence, was that human beings were primarily creatures of instinct and feeling. It was the job of reason to serve them as they were the true source of human action (Penelhum, 1993). The leap to Darwin, Freud, and Skinner was no longer so far.

The idea of mind as a series of passive associations never appealed to German rationalism much more connected to a traditional conception of mind as the source of reason. The Germans, like the French, appreciated Locke's natural history of the soul, but unlike them, could not accept his grounding of the soul in experience and not reason (Smith, 1997). German thinkers in the eighteenth century established an alternative vision of science, not so much the recording of facts acquired by experience, but a systematic understanding of the rational soul. This would establish the kind of certainty the tradition stemming from Locke could not. This German tradition accepted that consciousness, or *bewußtsein*, was the object of psychology. The term was coined by Christian Wolff in 1719 and was meant as an equivalent of the Latin term *conscientia*. In the German use, the term had a rationalizing sense to it, but it still retained the Cartesian sense that mind referred to interior, self-contained states, and processes (Graumann, 1996, p. 86). A generation of German thinkers, from Leibniz and Wolff to Kant, described a mind that was active, unified, and possessed innate faculties that organized experience. For instance, Gottfried Wilhelm von Leibniz's atomic-like substance, monads, possessed self-action, unity, perception, and appetite, and when compounded, composed the human soul. The active intellect involved a process called "apperception," which united precepts in consciousness and subjected them to attention and thought. This was the ground for experience. Both perception and apperception were psychological events, neither explicable through mechanical principles. From this came the idea of a rationalist psychology that included the study of the soul's nature, unity, free will, purpose, and its relation to materiality (Vidal, 2011). Until the mid-nineteenth century, this was what was commonly meant by the term "psychology."

This rationalist tradition found its fullest expression in Kant who argued that experience was organized by a preexisting rational structure. Kant also distinguished between pure reason and practical reason, the latter depending on a self-imposed identification with a rational moral imperative. This was the source of freedom and autonomy, the recognition of which was the path to selfhood. Freedom came not from action but intention, again leaving a vital role for a psychological study of mind. Along with Kant's analysis of the structure of thought, his understanding of autonomy shapes notions of maturity and development in psychology to the present day (Schneewind, 1998). Kantianism left humans in two distinct worlds: a natural one governed by physical laws, a product of the basic structure of the human mind, and a moral one governed by intuitive moral principles. From Kant forward, the mind was regarded as being composed of three basic faculties—knowing, feeling, and will. These were conceived of as innate. Kant also developed his own idea of the study of humans and their world—anthropology—which included products of work, accomplishments, beliefs, language, what we would now describe as culture, as well as the bodily aspects of human nature (Walsh etal. 2014). By the turn of the nineteenth century this faculty approach and Hume's associational one competed to explain the structure and workings of the human mind, the former finding expression in phrenology, Scottish common-sense psychology and neurophysiology, and the latter in the work of James Mill and Alexander Bain. In the 1860s, Hebert Spencer sought to overcome this division in a new evolutionary synthesis.

6. HIGHER AND LOWER: NATURE AND CIVILIZED

Augustine made feelings and ultimately the will sovereign of the soul. Each person had knowledge of their own consciousness through an inner consciousness that provided an inner awareness of truth, morality, and personal identity (Robinson, 1995, p. 75). Perception involved the will as it was forced to deal with a mind in conflict with itself, the result of a sinful nature competing with reason. Augustine represents the beginnings of an emotionally dominated, conflict-ridden, autobiographical or "expressive" tradition in the literature of the West, which includes figures as diverse as Michel de Montaigne, the American Puritans, and Charles Baudelaire, all of whom laid the ground for the emergence of a therapeutic sensibility (C. Taylor, 1989). Charles Taylor argues that during the seventeenth and eighteenth centuries a new psychological sensibility emerged as a kind of interiority, a reflection of a person's inner nature and truth, which was later taken up by nineteenth-century Romanticism.

It was Rousseau, however, who offered a healing vision of human nature embraced by moderns that would eventually become the foundation of current therapeutic sensibilities. Like many who followed, Rousseau sat in an ambivalent relationship to the Enlightenment, using the tools of Enlightenment to explain its failings. Against the great *philosophes* of eighteenth-century France, Rousseau declared that rather than perfecting humans, civilization has corrupted them. It has taken humans from the freedom and vitality of a state of nature and transformed them into prejudice-driven dependents. Rousseau never imagined humans could return to this state of nature but they certainly could learn from it. In fact, here we find some of the impetus for the study of children (genetic psychology), savages (anthropology), the insane (psychiatry), and animals (comparative psychology)—those beings that had not yet been corrupted by civilization. Education of children needed to resemble the education of nature. This meant allowing pupils to engage "objects" directly—the foundation of every progressive theory of education in the West since 1762, the year *Emile* was published. Only such an education can awaken proper feelings inspired by nature.

Children, Rousseau proposed, are dominated by sensations and not yet ready to use their minds independently. Hence, development was a passage from immature to mature thought, from dependency to autonomy, from the simple to the complex. Education must follow this trajectory and keep to the capacities of the natural child. This gave psychology a very powerful place in shaping educational thought for centuries to come as well as created a developmental trajectory from immaturity to maturity which, framed through evolutionary thought, still dominates much of developmental psychology to this day. Education was no longer molding character or the imposition of reason, as it was for Locke, but nurturing an inner potential (R. J. Richards, 1992). The sources of this natural morality were not God nor society, but the self within which essential goodness lies. Humans were more than simply the transparent self of Descartes and Locke. Invoking a traditional Augustinian theme, the self was divided, complex with hidden elements. By discovering this self and knowing it authentically, humans could be liberated once again. Gradually, personal fulfillment replaced the harsher demands of traditional morality. This is the essence of the therapeutic path (Rieff, 1966).

7. STRUCTURE AND FUNCTION: ADAPTATION

Charles Darwin's recasting of the functionalist or "adaptationist" tradition was one of the key contributions of evolutionary thought to modern biology, and later, psychology. Given the ways in which objects in the world present the appearance of change, it is not surprising that societies concerned with eternal truths often sought the underlying essence or "form" of an object. This was true of living objects as well, and many societies have ways of talking about various biological forms or species. In some societies, for example, it is well accepted that certain plants and animals cannot go against their nature. In the Old Testament, all species are created according to their kind. Formalism was central to Platonic thought and the classical worldview as well as easily reconcilable with Christianity. The idea of fixed and clearly delimited species came out of this formalist tradition as well as a conception of nature that was permeated with sharp breaks rather than contiguity. This perspective continued to dominate Continental biological thinking well into the twentieth century. For a long time, a formalist approach was viewed as essential to making a discipline scientific, even after Darwin (Bowler, 1996). This is what made Darwin's blurring of the distinctions between species so difficult to accept and also what made genetics so attractive to early twentieth century science as, until the 1930s, it was believed that the new science of genetics confirmed that in the case of transmutation of species, nature must "jump" from one form to another. Even the idea of evolution, commonplace by the late eighteenth century, reflected an unfolding of innate patterns over time. In the late eighteenth century, this variant of formalism was revived by the German *naturphilosophie* of Johann Wolfgang von Goethe and Lorenz Oken, part of a larger romantic reaction against the rationalism of the Enlightenment, especially the *tabula rasa* of Locke. Form, in this tradition, was a manifestation of an inner unity, a *bildung* or an underlying unity of plan. Throughout much of the nineteenth century, especially in France and Germany, biology was a science of morphology, seeking the idealized essence or plan of a group's basic character, an essence that existed only in the realm of thought and the mind of God. For these thinkers, adaptation or environmental conditions were not very significant. Morphologists always had the advantage, especially as the idea of evolution spread, which the natural world appears to align more with the idea of distinct forms or species as opposed to continuous, blurry ones. For them, as we shall see in a later chapter, the laws of nature they discovered in evolution were the same ones at play in individual development, offering an analogy between ontogenesis and phylogenesis that often became literal.

In contrast to the continent, in eighteenth-century Britain, utilitarianism was the language of thought. All aspects of biological life were useful. While theorists of design on the European continent tended to be formalists, functionalism flourished in British biology. This tradition accepted that traits that satisfied similar needs in animals, even if very different and under different conditions, should be grouped together. Thus, functional groupings were legitimate. By the nineteenth century, Darwin's usage of the term "adaptation" to describe the functional relationship between organism and environment was well accepted. The term had been a seventeenth-century one used to describe the suitability of an object for a particular function. It was taken up by the British school of natural theology to illustrate God's wisdom by perfect fit of form to function. In this tradition, studying adaptations led one to the perfectness of design and communicated much about God's nature and character, not to mention, provided a model of harmony for society in general. One of the best-known examples was William Paley's *Natural Theology* of 1802. Decades later, Darwin borrowed much of Paley's language, formulations, and assumptions, though he notoriously "flipped them on their head."

For Darwin, like Paley, the world was filled with adaptations that were a consequence of a higher law. These adaptations were the key to survival and were always specific to local circumstances. Both saw beauty in adaptation. For Paley, on one hand, these adaptations were perfect; for Darwin, on the other hand, they were simply better in a specific context. In Paley, adaptation was linked with providential design; in fact, adaptations provided evidence for design. Like Darwin, he virulently rejected endowing nature with supernatural qualities or self-organizing principles. Where they differed was in emphasis. Where Paley would see design, Darwin would later see the work of selection or history. While Paley saw adaptations as a result of design, Darwin saw "design" as a result of adaptations. Darwin's recasting of the term adaptation, however, hid how much he still remained beholden to the Paley-ian tradition (Young, 1983, p. 97). The term retained its sense that there existed an ideal way which an organism could fit into its environment. Biological good and moral good bled into each other. It also suggested that there was a preexistent, predesigned environment that organisms adapt to, losing sight of the fact that identifying an "environment" only makes sense in relation to specific organisms in specific moments of time and also that organisms shape what counts as their environment instead of simply adapting to preexistent ones (Lewontin, 2002).

Darwin's "recasting" of functionalism borrowed a well-accepted distinction from the Cuvier-Geoffroy controversy of the 1830s between unity of type (formalism) and conditions of existence (adaptation). The formalism of a "unity of type" classification argued that beings with similar morphologies belong in the same class, regardless of conditions of existence, or functions (Appel, 1987). Cuvier used the term conditions of existence to refer to an organism's internal organization, but Darwin instead saw these conditions as a response to the environment (Russell, 1916). He rejected the idea that conditions of existence follow unity of type and instead argued that conditions of existence—that is, natural selection—explained unity of type through the principle of common descent (Gould, 2002). In other words, species shared morphological characteristics if they shared common ancestors. This shift changed biology forever but also created a new scientific ground for psychology later in the century. Like morphological characteristics, functional characteristics were also indicative of common ancestry. Functions too were a product of selection, meaning what were once God-given mental faculties could be reconceived as selected-for physiological functions and their study could be part of science.

This was how Darwin came to view instincts. In his early work, still working through a more Lamarckian vision of evolution, he viewed instincts as inherited habits—that is, adaptive responses in an organism's lifetime that would be passed on to future generations and become innately determined behaviors (R. J. Richards, 2009).

This was the way Spencer viewed instincts and was important to many nineteenth-century thinkers because it explained many of the complex behaviors that associationism could not. Later, Darwin continued to use the idea of passing on acquired characteristics, except that they became a source of variation for natural selection to operate on or an explanation for traits that could not be explained by natural selection (R. J. Richards, 2009, p. 98). He used this line of thinking to explain innate moral dispositions: what were once habits of parental nurture and group cooperation became the instinctual endowment of a species. Later he also used this to explain emotional expression. When he could not find an adaptive value in emotional expression, yet their similarities across species suggested they had an evolutionary history, he set aside the theory of natural selection altogether. What began as habits that brought some relief or gratification (e.g., wrinkling a nose) and were associated with a particular mental state (e.g., disgust) became instinctual over the course of time.

Thus, biological study involved the study of instincts. This was not new. But in order to understand evolution, one must study the environment as well. In fact, to put it a bit stronger, Darwin created a new understanding of the environment, one that was wholly distinct from the organism. Darwin's "environments" could be studied separately from the study of the structures and functions of the organisms that inhabited them, as had been the traditional focus of formalist biology, giving science a new object (Ospovat, 1981). Darwin was crafting a new vision of science. He undermined the distinction between the biological and the physiochemical world, between biology and physics. He extended the victory of Newtonianism to biology, establishing that a mechanical explanation of the origin of the species was possible, even if for many, Darwin's particular mechanism was not wholly convincing. Ironically, for Darwin, natural selection was not really a mechanism. Certainly he did not have a machine in mind when he described nature in *On the Origin of Species* as a model of selflessness, care, and industry (Richards, 2009, p. 104). Arguably, Darwin's language in the *Origin* was metaphorical, but so too was the term "natural selection." It was not a mechanism or process but the accidental consequence of biological activity and time.

Darwin offered a new methodological foundation for his science. He believed his principal theoretical induction, natural selection, was empirically verifiable, even though others did not see it that way. Most of his scientist critics argued that his theory was not inductive at all, a line of criticism that surprised Darwin. It was deduced from a preexisting theory and explained disparate facts, which only a generation later would have been considered completely acceptable in science. His science was to no longer focus on the nonliving (e.g., the fossil record) but on the living (e.g., geographical distribution, heredity) and study adaptation, the mark of selection. Such a science was easily moved inside as well, into the spaces of the laboratory, and was quickly taken up by professionalizing scientists looking to increase the authority of their work and push amateur theologian-biologists out of the field. Darwin well understood that natural selection was only a hypothesis, its fate determined by how well it explained the facts. Still, he allowed theory to play a far more important role in science than many of his colleagues did before, and a science permitting theory offered an infinitely broader scope than one limited to induction.

The spread of Darwinism helped to create new ways of thinking that were gradually imported into psychology, especially child psychology. These include (1) firmly establishing that humans were part of nature; (2) the methodological distinction between organism and environment which in turn promoted a distinction between nature and nurture; (3) the view that psychological functions were homologous to biological structures in their origins and are therefore proper objects of science; (4) the idea that mind must exist in simpler forms and that (5) its development was a passage from simple to complex, from instincts and reflexes to reason; (6) a focus on intraspecies variation suggesting the importance of studying individual and group differences; and (7) the idea that biological mechanisms did not always have to be reduced to their physics (O'Donnell, 1985). All this meant a fundamental reconceptualization in the relationship between function and structure. In the post-Darwinian world, in one sense structure was the product of function, a reversal of the classic view where function followed from structure. And yet, in a more basic sense, when it comes to life, structures and functions mutually create each other, perhaps even undermining the distinction itself. This can create problems for a psychology still struggling with the relationship between them.

Chapter Two

A Multiplicity of Psychologies

Most psychologists are familiar with the well-repeated notion that the discipline began with the establishment of "structuralism" in Wundt's laboratory in 1879 and the various "revolutions"—Functionalist, Behavioral, Gestalt, Cognitive—since then. The term "revolution" tends to imply the kind of paradigm shift Thomas Kuhn famously described, and likely originates in the 1960s as many in the field were reading his work, but this is not a particularly accurate reading of this history (Leahey, 1992). Even the idea of a singular history of the discipline misses how little in common different types of academic psychology had with each other. Looking at these various psychologies and the context within which they emerged allows us to get a sense of how these were translated into contemporary programs of research but more importantly, why nineteenth century concerns around the relationships between inside and outside, structure and function, and description and explanation are still significant.

The importance of 1879 was highlighted in E. G. Boring's canonical *History of Experimental Psychology*, first published in 1929 and then revised substantially in 1950. In an attempt to present psychology as a coherent discipline with a single start date, Boring played down the fact that there have been many competing "psychologies" both past and present. The late sixteenth century is a much better place to look for the start of something like psychology as Protestantism, with its replacement of the confession of sins with intensive self-examination, highlighted the importance of understanding mind and created the ground for a new type of study of it (Vidal, 2011). These new ideas along with the new mechanical philosophy helped to establish a new philosophy of mind, the first modern psychology of mind, in the writings of Descartes, Locke, Kant, and others as we reviewed. After 1879, one finds several psychologies developing, including at minimum the introspection of consciousness of Wundt and Titchener, the study of variation by Galton and Pearson, the clinical approach of Jean-Martin Charcot and Alfred Binet, and the functionalism of William James and James Angell. These came out of different national traditions—German, British, French, and American respectively. And, by the early twentieth century, one could distinguish, at the minimum, between a behavioral approach, a psychometric approach, a clinical approach, and an introspective one. Thomas Leahey (1992, p. 312) makes a similar case, except divides what we are characterizing as the behavioral and introspective approaches into several broader research traditions beginning in seventeenth-century philosophy: the representational, realist, connectionist, and reductionist. These distinctions highlight the diverse ways in which psychologists conceived their objects of study (e.g., mental entities vs. behavior vs. mental relationships vs. physiological entities) and the paths to understand them.

The academic disciplines of psychology were born in ambivalence, especially in the case of some of those who are still held up as heroes by the discipline. As we will argue, early psychologists were struggling with the same tensions that have been our focus this far. In the eighteenth and early nineteenth centuries, psychologically oriented philosophers struggled to define the relationship between a mechanical body and an immaterial mind. This involved a reconfiguration of the relationship between inside and outside—the body operated via the same principles as the external world—as well as protecting the higher, spiritual world of mentality from the lower, material one. The latter issue played out among the educated public in mid-nineteenth-century Europe, until the turn of the twentieth century, at which point only professional psychologists could participate in these conversations (Rylance, 2000). The second psychologies, those of Wundt, Galton, Binet, and James, were more clearly sites of tension between structure and function, and as we shall see in the next chapter, between description and explanation. Although technically, at least in the United States, "functionalism" and its behavioral offshoots came to dominate psychology, questions as to the relationship between structure and function were only temporarily set aside, until they returned to the fore in the second half of the twentieth century with the increasing influence of cognitive approaches. The same case can be made with the tension between inside and outside. For a few decades, the "inside" was off the table, though it always remained as a set of unspoken presuppositions or vague references to constitutional differences, until it too returned to the foreground after the Second World War.

1. HIGHER AND LOWER: THE FIRST PSYCHOLOGIES OF THE SOUL

The term *psychologia* was first used in the writings of German Protestants after 1570 (Vidal, 2011, p. 21). It referred to a science of the soul that combined natural philosophy—the antecedent of the natural sciences—and Christian moral philosophy. In the Aristotelian scheme of late medieval scholasticism, the soul explained the form and function of all living beings, not simply humans. In the late medieval university, the vegetative and sensitive souls were the subject of physics, and the rational soul was the subject of metaphysics; but those studying medicine, theology, and rhetoric also covered these topics. The principal text of this science of life, as it was called, was Aristotle's *De Anima*. Even before Descartes split off an immaterial mind from a passive and mechanical body, Protestant reformer Philipp Melanchthon had already attributed the vegetative and sensory functions of the soul to the body and rational functions to the mind. In his quest to move away from Aristotelianism, Melanchthon suggested philosophy focus on the operations of the soul rather than its substance and that its findings could be used as a guide for conduct (Vidal, 2011, pp. 37–45).

Thus the study of mind was to be part of moral philosophy, that is, the branch of philosophy focused on the rules for everyday conduct as distinct from natural philosophy. As Aristotelianism began to collapse, so did the traditional *scientia de anima*. This was replaced by a new science of the human soul grounded in the body. As Vidal (2011) explains, by the early 1700s, a new sense of the term "psychology" emerged that described a field that had moved away from studying the soul in general, the form of all living beings, to the human soul exclusively (p. 74). Descartes was a key figure in this shift. By ridding animals of their souls, he established a domain of life that could be described mechanistically. By separating the soul from the human body, he created the possibility of a study of humans using the principles of mechanism with the kind of cause-effect relationships found in physics. Galileo's corpuscular philosophy replaced the substances of Aristotle, allowing the properties of the body to become simply a result of the movement of atoms. Not only were these analyses gradually extended to mind, but the mind itself became limited by the body—that is, the capacities of mind were limited by the nature of the senses (Vidal, 2011, p. 76). Psychology's object was restricted to mind, while other sciences took up the study of the body.

By the late eighteenth century there were individuals who referred to what they studied as "psychology" and sought to teach courses in this discipline. In this new psychology of mind, the soul was an entity whose operations and content needed to be understood as a psychophysiological entity. Because the study of the soul laid out the operations of thought and action,

Chapter 2

eighteenth-century Enlightenment thinkers regarded psychology as the most useful of the sciences (Videl, 2011, p. 102). The new psychology was conceived as a science grounded in experience that was said to repudiate Descartes' immaterial mind in favor of one united with the body. Locke's "analytic" model—the breaking up of mind into ideas and ultimately sensations—was regarded as the foundation of the discipline. In France, Étienne Bonnot de Condillac and Charles Bonnet used Locke's method to call for the study of the sensationalist sources of knowledge. They traced all higher functions of mind to their source in sensation, sometimes even to specific nerve fibers. In Germany, in contrast, Christian Wolff called for a rationalist psychology based in deductive principles in contrast with Locke's empiricist one. The mind had the capacity for apperception and thus the chance to become aware of itself. Wolff's mind was grounded in a reflective activity. This contrasted with the passive notions of mind that tended to dominate British and French psychology and somewhat accounts for the different directions psychology took in the late nineteenth century as the United States was influenced by the British version and Continental Europe by the German version. By the close of the century, Kant insisted that both a rational and an empirical science of psychology were impossible (Teo, 2005), though psychology should be an autonomous discipline anyway, and he went on to lecture in psychology, or as it was called then, anthropology, for many years.

A central question in this first psychology involved appropriate methods. One of Kant's students, Jakob Fries, argued that although inner experience was different than outer experience, it was amenable to rational study via introspection. But this study was not to be a mathematical one, as the units of mind were qualitative and not quantitative. One of Kant's successors at Konigsberg, Johann Friedrich Herbart, disagreed. He focused on consciousness, which he described as a dynamic unity, made up of mental units that could be measured—though some existed outside of awareness, an early version of the unconscious. He sought to develop a mathematical model of mental action and turn psychology into a quantifiable science. To many in a new generation of experimentally minded thinkers, representing the mind mathematically was key to turning psychology into a science of the Newtonian variety. By the middle of the next century, this possibility inspired Gustav Fechner as he sought to measure just noticeable differences in psychic experience and conclusively demonstrate that mental activity could be expressed mathematically.

The first empirical psychology journals appeared in the 1780s. They focused on medicine, physiology, and especially education. Filled with personal narratives and cases of the normal and pathological, they established a moral medicine helping to better people through self-knowledge (Teo, 2005, p. 113) A common topic was the physiognomy of Lavater, the first popular psychology, which paved the way for Gall's phrenology and later, psychoanalysis in the sense that it was practical and allowed ordinary folks to practice psychology. The relationship between academic and popular forms of psychology was a fluid one. In the 1770s, Swiss philosopher Jean Trembley presented an extensive vision of psychology. He argued that in addition to the traditional topics of rationalist psychology, empirical psychology could study actions of people in society, animals, and the history of childhood. Trembley insisted presciently that specialization was necessary for progress (Teo, 2005, pp. 148–150). In 1786, Jacob Friedrich Abel produced the first comprehensive psychology textbook. It focused both on the immaterial soul as well as the operations of sensation, imagination, attention, thinking, feeling, willing, and motion. Psychology texts continued to appear throughout the first half of the nineteenth century, often influenced by the proto-evolutionary writings of German Romanticism, which paved the way for the integration of Darwin and psychology at the close of the century (Himon, 1979).

British psychology developed along a slightly different path, and the transition from first to second psychology reflected shifting notions as to the object of psychological study. In this case, a transition from first to second psychology is not as clear-cut, though Hartley and Bain probably belong to the more philosophical first psychology and Galton and Pearson the second professional-scientific one with Spencer somewhere in between. By the end of the sixteenth century, the English language was far better equipped to explain the psychological in a novel way than it had ever been, especially as linked with the body (R. J. Richards, 1992). Gradually, for example, the English term "human nature" began to refer to both the essence of the human soul and the physical reality of the mind. Nature, not God, was seen as the source of this essence, and thus natural science, as opposed to religion, provided the means to understand it. As Roger Smith (1997) points out, this was a marked contrast even from the 1600s, when law went from human affairs to nature; now law went from nature to human affairs. This gave natural science a new authority. Dominated by the philosophy of Locke and later Hume, British psychology extended to logic, morals, social criticism, politics, and religion with associationism at its core (Vidal, 2011). Thomas Reid introduced the term "psychology" in the eighteenth century, and John Stuart Mill used it to describe a science of mind in 1843 (Hearnshaw, 1964). This psychology, sometimes known as "pneumatology," flourished in Britain during the Victorian era and was an object of popular and cross-disciplinary conversation and debate. It was mostly replaced by a version exclusively for specialists after 1900 (Rylance, 2000). This new specialist version was described as "scientific," a word that came into popular use around the same time (Rylance, 2000, p. 7).

One source of evidence of the popularity of this first psychology in British society broadly, even as some were criticizing it, was the sheer number of new words created to talk about it in the period from 1830 to 1890. A short list of these includes: psychologize, psychiatry, psychosis, psychopathic, psychotic, psychical, psychotherapy, psychosomatic, psychophysical, psychomotor, and psychoneuroses (Rylance, 2000, p. 18). Psychology was a popular subject for debate because it offered a way to consider broader social and intellectual changes, some of which were associated with the move from a Christianized worldview to a more secular and materialist one. Mid-nineteenth-century psychology in Britain still regarded its object as the study of the soul. Debates raged about whether the goal was best achieved when mind was viewed as a collection of innate faculties or a series of associations resulting from experience, but all agreed that the soul was not amenable to a materialist analysis in the way the body was. Yet, it was obviously amenable to philosophical study. As Rylance (2000) explains, it was appropriate to talk about the operations of the soul as a means to appreciate the work of God; it was not appropriate, however, to study it in such a way as might disturb this theological worldview (p. 25).

An exclusively physicalist analysis presented such a threat. The immaterial soul was understood as containing lower faculties or powers like sensation, appetite, and desire as well as higher ones like reason and attention, but also love and faith. Typically the relationship between higher and lower powers was viewed as antagonistic. A moral life involved the subduing of the lower powers on the part of the higher ones, a moral view that would soon be reconfigured in biological terms by the neurologist John Hughlings Jackson. Even associationists managed to agree that these powers were somehow built out of experience, a position that became increasingly untenable as the century progressed. One of the problems with psychology, as viewed by Victorian society, was that it sought to narrow the gap between these higher and lower powers (Rylance, 2000, p. 28). The power of the faculty psychology approach was that it jibed with "commonsense" language for talking about the mind. To many Victorians, the materialist approach of the second psychology, which began to spread in the 1880s, especially its mechanism, simply felt wrong (Rylance, 2000, p. 38).

The gradual shift from first to second psychology in Britain is evident if one looks at the changing ways psychology was defined over the course of this period. In an encyclopedia of 1830, psychology was "the science of the soul or spiritual principles in man . . . the scientifically conducted observations of the operations and changes of the human soul . . . [which] takes for granted the distinction of spiritual subject . . . from the body" (cited in Rylance, 2000, p. 28). In a popular textbook in 1842, psychology was defined as "the history of mental faculties" (Pritchard, 1842, cited in Rylance, 2001, p. 14). An 1865 definition described a mental event as ontologically autonomous and "cannot be resolved into simpler elements as it was not material" (Rylance, 2000, p. 24).

One finds evidence of a new view, influenced by Spencer and Darwin, in the writing of T. H. Huxley who defined psychology as "a part of the sciences of life or biology, it deals with the psychical instead of the physical. . . . As there is an anatomy of the body, so there is an anatomy of mind; the psychologist dissects mental phenomena into elementary states of consciousness as the anatomist resolves limbs into tissue and tissue into cells" (Huxley, 1879, p. 50, cited in Rylance, 2000, p. 79). Huxley's position was still radical in the 1870s, but by the 1890s, even in mainstream writings, the view had changed and the basic framework of the first psychology no longer fit with the changing times. An 1891 definition in a British Encyclopedia insisted, "the view that the mind is a . . . [composition of] distinct faculties and psychology is a process of labeling facts and putting each into their proper components . . . is to mistake a name for an explanation" (cited in Rylance, 2000, p. 39). In 1897, one of Wundt's students, the American Edward Wheeling Scripture, in one of the first histories of the new psychology, defined it simply as the study of "the generalized, human, normal, adult mind as revealed in the psychological laboratory" (Scripture, 1897, p. vii, cited in Rylance, 2000, p. 6).

This "first" psychology was prevalent in the thinking of the French *philosophes,* especially as read through Locke, but it was the new "moral" therapies of Pinel and Esquirol that dominated original French thinking on psychological matters for most of the nineteenth century with the exception of the "spiritualist" psychology of Maine de Biran. In the United States, like Britain, psychology was part of moral philosophy. Moral philosophy included studies of the soul, human nature, and conduct, both practically and theoretically. It was associated with the Scottish thinkers like the Earl of Shaftesbury and Francis Hutcheson who had argued that humans have an innate moral sense which should be a necessary guide for conduct. Psychology was a key part of Scottish philosopher Thomas Reid's philosophy of "commonsense," highly influential in the United States, which argued that all humans share a common sensibility present in ordinary language that allows them to judge sensory knowledge, a response to the skepticism of Berkeley and Hume. This common sense provided a shared moral foundation. Such study embraced science, but of a particularly Baconian variant. It simply sought to collect facts, the results of which would reveal God's design. One of the most influential texts of the period was Thomas C. Upham's *Elements of Mental Philosophy,* published in 1827, which dominated the American college curriculum until the 1890s when a new generation of German-trained psychologists insisted on changes and William James published his *Principles of Psychology* (Fuchs, 2002).

2. STRUCTURE AND FUNCTION: THE SECOND PSYCHOLOGIES

The second psychologies were filled with unresolved tensions from the start. There was the well-known tension between the European "structuralist" approach and the American "functionalist" one, but there was also ambivalence about whether a scientific psychology was possible outside certain proscribed limits. There was also a tension between the field's academic and public goals (Smith, 2013, p. 71). The Galtonian study of populations as well as the French-based study of pathology never quite fit into the story of this divide, though both turned out to be quite influential in the development of twentieth-century psychology. The most influential history in the field, E. G. Boring's 1929 *History of Experimental Psychology*, substantially revised and republished in 1950, was an attempt to create an impressive but singular pedigree for a floundering experimental research tradition in psychology. Moreover, Boring, like his mentor E. B. Titchener, sought to prevent psychology from becoming an applied discipline (Toulmin and Leary, 1992) as he also sought to divorce it from philosophy. He laid out an intellectual lineage for the new psychology, what we are describing as the second psychology—a fusion of British associationist philosophy, evolutionary thought, and German experimental physiology developed during the period from 1850 to 1890. The new experimental psychology, Boring explained, borrowed the methods of physiology and employed them to take over the study of the mind that had once been the province of philosophy. The task began with Gustav Fechner's "psycho-physical parallelism"—which indicated that mental activity could be measured—in the context of advances in sensorimotor analysis and the neurophysiology of Ernst Heinrich Weber and Hermann von Helmholtz. It culminated in the establishment of Wundt's Leipzig laboratory in 1879. There, the soon-to-be autonomous science of psychology was inaugurated, based in the introspection of consciousness.

And yet, Wundt would have likely been uncomfortable with this narrative. Introspection and the experimental study of consciousness, for Wundt, was part of the work of philosophy. It involved testing the claims of philosophy in an empirical setting, so as to develop them further. Experimental psychology was never meant to supplant philosophy. William James was assigned the role of developing this tradition in the United States, developing his own "functionalist" version. Yet James hardly saw himself as an experimental psychologist. His quip in his *Principles of Psychology* that the experimental psychology of Wundt, so focused on recording the minutiae of conscious experience, could never have developed in a country where its inhabitants could be bored, suggested that he had mixed feelings about this tradition as well (James, 1890, p. 192). The quote was taken up by critics of James, especially Scripture, and used as evidence of James's lack of an experimental sensibility.

There was a reason for Boring's choices, especially in the first version of his history published in the 1920s; by the second version he toned down his opposition to all things applied. Laboratory psychology was competing with applied variants including mental and personality testing, industrial psychology, and clinical psychology (Herman, 1995). These were slowly coming to dominate the field and, in Boring's mind, risked psychology's precarious status as a science. Unlike those who sought to turn psychology into a science of behavior, Boring understood the centrality of introspectionism in the development of his version of psychology. By focusing on the experimental study of the basic contents of consciousness via introspection, psychology ended up carving a domain for itself that was distinct from physiology, yet allowed it to apply physiological methods to philosophy (O'Donnell, 1985). Introspection was not some naïve methodological mistake. It was a means to distinguish what psychologists did and studied from what physiologists did and studied. Even the label "introspection" is itself a problem because it neglects that Wundt worked hard to distinguish his "experimental" introspectionism from the "armchair" introspectionism of traditional philosophers. Many philosophers appreciated the opportunity to study psychological phenomena in laboratories, the results of which they could integrate into broader speculative theses, but they still viewed all this as the work of philosophy. This was certainly true of Fechner, Helmholtz, and Wundt.

In the United States, because philosophy was part of a broader curriculum in character and the fight against a godless materialism, psychologists fought for their own departments to escape the oppressive oversight of college presidents. The psychological laboratory, no longer located in philosophy departments, allowed them to pursue a materialistically focused study of mind without incurring the wrath of the still very religiously minded administrators (O'Donnell, 1985). These administrators remained sympathetic as long as psychologists refused to reduce the mind to simple matter. This approach provided psychologists with autonomy and job security as well as staved off the threat of Darwinism by extricating mind from Darwinian materialism while borrowing its insistence that science focus on physical mechanisms (O'Donnell, 1985, p. 89). By the second decade of the twentieth century and the rapid spread of a "third" behavioral psychology, the climate of the university had changed so much that a science needed only ground itself in utility and social reform to prove successful.

The spread of the second psychologies took place across very different national contexts that shaped the way they developed in each of these countries. In Germany, it took place against the backdrop of the development of a strong industrial base and a resurgent nationalism (Mandler, 2007). Many Germans had turned to nationalism after the humiliations of the Napoleonic Wars at the start of the nineteenth century. While Germany was not yet able to unify itself politically, it was able to do so culturally, especially through education. In 1803, Alexander Humboldt established a new university in Berlin, which developed new standards for the fusion of teaching and research. By the end of the nineteenth century, this new German model became the model for all higher education across the West. In the Humboldtian University, philosophy was king. In fact, a better "official" date to describe the beginnings of institutionalized psychology is August 21, 1824, the year the Prussian State required future teachers be tested in psychology, which required that it be part of any course of university study (Walsh etal. 2014). By 1833, Friedrich Eduard Beneke already described psychology as the natural science of inner experience apprehended through internal perception.

These developments coincided with a revolution in physiology, particularly in the work of Johannes Müeller and his students. His *Handbook of the Physiology of Man*, published over the 1830s, shaped the study of physiology until Darwin. His students included Theodor Schwann, Emil du Bois-Reymond—who gathered evidence for the electrical basis for neural action—and Hermann Von Helmholtz. The latter two founded the "Berlin School" and, rejecting the vestiges of vitalism in Müeller, required that all explanation in physiology be of a physio-chemical nature, ridding physiology of the last vestiges of vitalism. One can make the case that the appearance of their materialist oath, first laid out in a letter written by du-Bois Reymond in 1842, was the real beginning of the "second" psychology. It also left the discipline with a dearth of non-physicalist explanations, requiring that the unique properties of mind be projected onto various homunculi for the next century and a half.

Müeller combined the sensory perspective of British associationism with a new motor perspective that was developing in physiology, particularly the role of nerves in muscle movement. He applied this analysis to the functional organization of the nervous system (Young, 1970, p. 90). Müeller's research focused on basic sensory and motor functions rather than dealing with the kinds of higher mental faculties that remained the province of philosophy. He traced volition to the spontaneous movements of the fetus and argued that over time and practice, these movements turned into complex motor associations, thus practice turned involuntary action into voluntary action. These "habits" united sensory and motor activity and were traceable through specific pathways in the nervous system. This model—the path from environment to sensory organs to sensory nerves to brain to motor nerves to muscles to behavior—became the basis for the "reflex arc," which came to dominate psychological thinking for well over a century.

In post-Boring accounts, Fechner, Helmholtz, and Wundt are regarded as the heroes of the new experimental psychology. The case, though, is a bit more complex. Gustav Fechner, for instance, sought to combine the new experimental methods of physiology with German *Naturphilosophie*, a school of nature-study/biology originating in Goethe that dominated German universities in the first few decades of the nineteenth century. It saw nature as a living, dynamic force undergoing progressive development that had to be understood holistically. In 1850, Fechner developed a way to represent the relationship between the mental and the physical mathematically, what was later termed Weber's Law, though he was careful not to regard this relationship causally. This was Fechner's central contribution, demonstrating that consciousness could be measured and creating the conditions for a science of psychology in Kantian terms.

Mathematics allowed Fechner to express unobservable mental relationships in observable terms as a physical unit of measurement corresponded with a mental one (Adler, 1998). Both he and Helmholtz adopted the principle of the conservation of energy, which allowed them to regard physical energy as capable of being transformed into mental energy, an idea that in essence opened the door for analogies from the study of the physical world. Critics accused him of confusing psychological sensations with physical stimuli presented in experience (Walsh etal. 2014, p. 536). The influence of *Naturphilosophie* led Fechner to see consciousness as a unitary phenomenon, yet subject to determinable laws. He often described the universe as a being with consciousness (Smith, 2013, p. 82). Most of this speculative "excess" was dismissed in Boring's account.

Helmholtz represents a slightly different case, much more an exemplar of what we might view as a traditional scientist though no less aware of the philosophical issues at stake. He built his reputation in the 1840s and 1850s by identifying the principle of the conservation of energy and measuring the speed of the transmission of nerve impulses. His discovery that the speed of nerve impulses was slower than believed meant perception was not "immediate" and suggested a larger role for psychology in perception (Lenoir, 1993, pp. 120–121). He was also involved in reforming medical education so that physicians were required to perform research. But these scientific findings obscure an underlying philosophical project that can be best grasped by looking at his well-known controversy over nativism/empiricism in the study of vision with Ewald Hering in the 1850s. While Helmholtz framed the conflict as a debate over whether innate mechanisms determine perception, the essence of the controversy was about where sensation ends and perception begins. What exactly were the boundaries between mind and the external world, a question just as relevant today as it was in the 1850s?

By making perception "innate"—that was never Hering's position anyway but Helmholtz's caricature of his position—Hering gave a reduced role to "psychology" and a more prominent role to physiology. Helmholtz described Hering's view as too physiologically determined and instead argued that perceptual structures were generated in experience, making them the province of psychology. Even though Helmholtz proved victorious over Hering in the short run, in the end, Hering proved correct in the sense that the physiological structure of the senses tend to shape the ways in which the world is perceived, especially those structures that are a product of selection pressures. On the other hand, Helmholtz proved correct in the sense that he argued positing innate mechanisms without understanding them typically explains nothing, though this was never Hering's position. In any case, this was a struggle over defining the extent of the psychological as well as the relationship between structure and function. It was not a question that could be settled empirically.

Like Fechner, Wundt also sought to combine his experimental work with a grander philosophical project. He was not particularly well known before the publication of his *Principles of Physiological Psychology* [*Gr ü ndzuge der Physiologischen Psychologie*] in 1874. He had been a research assistant to Helmholtz, but they did not have a good working relationship (Diamond, 2001). Wundt's research focused on the measurement of reaction time. In *Principles*, he combined the disparate research of physiological psychology into a coherent whole. In 1876, Wundt was given a small room at the University of Leipzig in which to store his research demonstration apparatus. Toward the end of 1879, two of Wundt's students, Max Friedrich and G. Stanley Hall, began to use the space for reaction time experiments, thus the so-called establishment of the first psychological laboratory (Koch and Leary, 1992). In 1882, this officially became a research institute, but because Wundt was no longer interested in doing much experimental research himself, he appointed Hugo Munsterberg as director. While he did support the development of an experimental tradition in psychology mostly through his students, the range of topics he considered appropriate for experimental study was fairly narrow: sensation, perception, attention, and reaction time. For him, higher mental functions like memory and thought were simply not amenable to experimental study. A more extensive vision was developed at Würzburg by Oswald Külpe and his group. Still, most of the influential figures in the early years of the new psychology made their way into Wundt's laboratory at one point or another. Wundt viewed his work in psychology as part of the development of philosophy (Diamond, 2001, p. 60). Like many in Germany, he opposed associationism because it turned the mind into a passive entity and it supported an incorrect view that the contents of mind could be decomposed into elemental units. For Wundt, active synthesis was a key feature of the workings of mind. He regarded the contents of mind as "events" rather than "ideas" and rejected borrowing methods from the study of nature employed by physics (Danziger, 2001, p. 76). The only appropriate empirical method for psychology was introspection.

Wundt also rejected the implied intellectualism of associationism and instead viewed the events of mind as affective in character. He used volition as prototypical of psychic processes (Danziger, 2001, p. 80). For him, volition had both consciousness and direction. It was both physical and psychical. Its basis was *trieb* or impulse, which were primarily affective and motivational currents. They were psychic but depended on a "supply of innervation energy available in our nervous system" (Wundt, 1887, p. 483, cited in Danziger, 2001, p. 106). Wundt, like many in his generation, viewed energy, whether physical or psychic, as a central force in movement and thought. Wundt turned Christian Wolff's object of psychology, *Bewußtsein* or consciousness, into *erleben* or immediate experience, with the latter being more personal and subjective (Graumann, 1996, p. 87). This moved psychology beyond simply the study of inner experience, as immediate experience also referred to the outer world, meaning psychologists could refer to a world beyond perception. Yet, in immediate experience, one did not encounter the objectified representations that made up the study of physics. One instead encountered acts of consciousness that were intermixed with each other (Danziger, 2001, p. 82). Even the basic categories of psychic processes—thinking, feeling, and willing—should not be confused with actual psychological events. They did not exist independently, nor independent of each other. They were reifications of lived experience. When they are confused with each other, psychologists are guilty of what William James later termed the "psychologist's fallacy" (Danziger, 2001, p.83). As Kurt Danziger (2001) points out, Wundt would have rejected the decomposition of behavior or mind into interactions between its components parts (p. 85).

Wundt's ideas extended to the relationship between individuals and culture as well. There were no minds in isolation, and a social component could not simply be added on later. This type of study, which was not experimental, constituted the basis for his *völkerpsychologie*, which occupied him after 1900. There he focused on common mentalities as expressed in cultural forms like language, myth, and customs. *Völkerpsychologie* highlighted the universal aspects of these expressions as opposed to the science of ethology, which highlighted these expressions in particular societies. Like the mind, these social forms were not reducible to the actions or thinking of individuals but operated as wholes wherein interpersonal influence was a function of the interconnectedness of immediate experience.

Wundt's understanding of methodology was also very different than is recognized today. Initially he viewed psychology as occupying a middle ground between the natural sciences [*naturwissenschaften*] and human sciences [*geisteswissenschaften*], though by 1883, he came to regard psychology as the foundation of the *geisteswissenschaften*. Its method was the structured introspection of immediate consciousness with control and variation of stimuli. This was not to be the introspection of the philosophers who naively believed they could examine the contents of their own consciousness, but a new method of self-observation that sought objectivity and replicability (Blumenthal, 1998, p. 81). To shield the results from distortion on the part of consciousness, Wundt required an immediate response. The experiments of

Wundt and his students looked very different from the experiments in to-day's psychology as a result of this. For one, Wundt and his students alternat-ed between the roles of experimenter and what was often described as the "reactor." Only later, when the roles of experimenter and experimented be-came more fixed, did the term "subject" emerge (Danziger, 1990, p. 54). In fact, in the early days of experimental psychology, journals tended to publish the initials of the reactor, as the role of a trustworthy and well-trained reactor was just as important as a reliable and well-trained experimenter.

Consciousness for Wundt was not a thing, but a series of events, not unlike what William James meant by "stream of consciousness." This is part of why he was skeptical of the category of memory as it implied that some-thing in consciousness endured over time. It was forever undergoing trans-formation (Blumenthal, 1998). The job of experimental psychology was to measure its rates and flows. What philosophers had once described as the faculties of mind were, according to Wundt, different ways of looking at the same basic process (ibid. p. 83). Such study required unique methods and could not simply be those borrowed from physics, chemistry, or physiology. In fact, it precisely studied the elements of experience that physics left out (Danziger, 1990, p. 38).

In Britain, in contrast, the second psychology was shaped by the fact that most of its development took place outside the university and that it quickly took on an evolutionary frame. The two major institutions of higher learning in Britain, Oxford and Cambridge, remained training grounds for a gentle-manly elite during this period, and the most influential figures in the develop-ment of psychology were either outside the university altogether, like Darwin and Spencer, or were appointed in some of the newer ones. The key steps in the formation of a "second" professional psychology in Britain were laid out in the "first" psychology of the 1850s by Alexander Bain and Herbert Spen-cer both responding to these dramatic developments in German and British physiology and are also the real architects of the "third" or behavioral psychology, much more so than Ivan Pavlov or John Watson. Both Bain and Spencer helped to turn the moral category of "effort" into a physiological and involuntary one, a motor discharge that reframed the relationship between individual and environment in biological terms (Smith, 2014). This was, in its essence, the foundation of later behavioral thinking.

Alexander Bain, one of the few influential mid-nineteenth-century British thinkers to have an academic position, attempted to integrate the new sensor-imotor perspective from physiology with the associationist tradition in Brit-ish philosophy (Young, 1970, p. 111). However, unlike many in this tradition who tended to view learning or the creation of associations as a passive process, following Müeller, Bain made spontaneous activity the basis of learning (Boakes, 1984, p. 101). By the 1820s, James Mills had already extended an associationist analysis to so-called higher mental functions including affect and will and traced them to various sensory experiences including the senses themselves, the muscle sense, and pleasure/pain. But Mill's analysis had only highlighted the limits of associationism. The problem was its passive conception of mind. How could it account for novel thought and creativity? How could it explain mental powers that appeared to be more than just a sum of sensations? If all knowledge came from the same external environment, how could there be disagreement? These were the central problems with the associationist view of mind in the second half of the nineteenth century, and Bain tried to solve them.

To start with, according to Bain, the mind had to be viewed as an active power and not a passive receptacle. For Bain activity involved the transfer of energy via the nervous system. Bain, encouraged by John Stuart Mills, accepted the idea of the independence of sensation and muscular motion. Volition began with "spontaneous movements" due to nerve force which, when shaped by pleasure and pain, directed those movements toward a purpose. Complex motor associations were developed through practice. Thus practice turned involuntary motion into voluntary motion (Boakes, 1984, p. 11). These motions along with external sources of reward and punishment constituted the will (Rylance, 2000). Following Müeller, Bain argued that habits connected sensory and motor activity and that these played out along specific pathways in the nervous system. Although Bain was vague about physiological specifics, after Bain, all psychological explanations had to take into account the physiology of the nervous system. Bain extended the reflex arc from a specific physiological concept to a broader psychophysical one, thus keeping psychology grounded in physiology. After Bain, motor activity was central to learning, as opposed to simply mental activity, and hence knowing was to be a result of doing (Young, 1970). This model opened the door for animal psychologists in the 1880s to argue that mind could be studied via the observation of behavior.

Due to the spread of evolutionary ideas after 1860, it was not Bain's psychology but Spencer's that dominated the second half of the nineteenth century. Spencer dealt with the limits of associationism by uniting sensorimotor associationism with a theory of evolution (Young, 1970, p. 169; O'Donnell, 1985). This provided the biological ground for behavioral theories well into the twentieth century. It also precipitated the beginning of the end of faculty psychology by turning the faculties into convenient abstractions for describing various modes of adaptation (Rylance, 2000, p. 212). Spencer's evolutionism was pre-Darwinian. He was influenced in the 1830s and 1840s by phrenology, specifically the idea of cerebral localization, and by romanticism—the idea of evolution as a universal tendency toward individuation and the specialization of functions. Reading William Carpenter in the 1850s, he discovered Lamarck and the notion of the inheritance of acquired characteristics. He integrated his conception of progressive evolution with associationism. The principle of utility, what he now termed adaptation, united all of life.

This led Spencer to view mind as an adaptation of organism to environment wherein "learning" during life was passed on to descendants through use-inheritance. Intelligence emerged from ancestral sensory experience but was eventually passed to offspring in the form of instincts. One could now explain the source of higher mental faculties by referring to the experiences of ancestors as opposed to simply the experiences of the individual, which is in the terms of critics, how mind started with so little but ended up with so much (Rylance, 2000, p. 220). This made associationism tenable again. Learning involved the coordination and modification of individual action so that inside corresponded with outside. After 1860, Darwin made these ideas scientifically respectable by grounding them in vast amounts of evidence, though he remained ambivalent about the inevitability of progress and use-inheritance. In the 1880s and 1890s, students of Darwin and Spencer followed them in accepting the continuity of animal and human capacities and developed techniques to study mind in animals, which would become the methods of the nascent third psychology.

For Spencer, use-inheritance guaranteed the inevitability of progress in evolution and provided Victorians with a new, scientifically respectable, all-encompassing worldview (Houghton, 1957). Learning, now seen as the source of adaptation, was essential to the progress of the species as it was passed on to future generations. It also explained the development of morality (Richards, 1987, p. 246). In a general sense, this relationship between learning and progress was fundamental to Anglo-American psychology, even after it was widely accepted that natural selection not use-inheritance was responsible for evolutionary change. It remained a background assumption in all U.S. behaviorisms that tended to take the importance of "learning" in biology for granted.

The case of France was different. The French too reformed their universities, this time after their humiliation by Prussia in the 1870s. Yet, even still, the French universities never fully recovered from the specter of the French Revolution during the nineteenth century (Jahoda, 2007). This was reflected in a concern for "crowd" or group psychology. The second psychology in France also developed in relation to psychiatry more than philosophy, and this was reflected by the influence of the therapeutic techniques of Jean Martin Charcot, Pierre Janet, and Hippolyte Bernheim. This focus also shaped the work of the two leaders of French psychology during the late nineteenth century, Theodule Ribot and Alfred Binet. Ribot sought to make French psychology experimental and looked to the Germans and British for guidance. The spirit of the natural sciences has invaded psychology, he famously predicted (cited in Koch & Leary, 1992, p. 16). Ribot rejected the French version of moral psychology, and influenced by the positivism of

Auguste Comte and Hippolyte Taine, sought to focus a naturalist psychology on heredity and racial differences (Staum, 2011). His contemporary, Binet, began his career looking for anatomical correlates of mental traits using head measurements. He gradually abandoned this approach to trait measurement for a more psychological one, which he developed for the sake of educational reform in order that each individual be educated according to his or her capacity (Staum, 2011, p. 138). These measures were imported into the United States and became the framework for Lewis Terman's IQ tests (Chapman, 1988; Rogers, 1995). Ribot's tenure at the Collège de France was followed by that of Pierre Janet, who continued the focus on disturbances of the mind and a clinical approach.

In the United States, Wundt was read through Titchener. Titchener did not agree with Wundt as to the strict limitations of the experimental methods, nor did he relate his introspective methods to broader philosophical themes. He also sought to rid Wundt of his "volunteerism" or focus on the will and his doctrine of apperception. Instead, Titchener tended to read him as an elementalist in the tradition of Locke (Koch & Leary, 1992, p. 12). Like Wundt though, he adopted the typically German academic disdain for application. Although the text of Titchener's student, E. G. Boring, was highly successful, his battle with application was not. Neither he nor his mentor thought psychology could explain everyday conduct, and they both agreed psychology should remain a narrow experimental field, though more extended than the range that had been advocated by Wundt (Danziger, 1997).

The leading voice of psychology in the United States during this period was William James. James had discovered Herbert Spencer's evolutionary system in the 1870s and used his work as the principal text of his seminar on psychology at Harvard, the first of its kind. The seminar was so popular Harvard allowed James to open its first psychological laboratory; like Wundt, he was given a room to store his equipment. James objected to Spencer's assumption that evolution was directed by necessary responses of organism to environment. This turned adaptation into a passive response, he argued. Especially with respect to mind, James regarded it as actively generating solutions—some of which survived due to natural selection. James insisted that every idea of action is related to an action—knowing is doing—and that many of these ideas of action, particularly willed ones, can be described as instincts selected by consciousness. Thus intelligence, for James, always triumphed over biology (James, 1890). He objected to the introspectionist's decomposition of thought into elemental ideas as well as what he saw as the misguided environmentalism of empiricism. Instead he described a host of instincts (e.g. curiosity, modesty) that guided human behavior, though consciousness ultimately selected which ones were turned into action, thus the principle of natural selection applied to the mind.

These ideas made up James's pragmatism. But there was more than this to James. For James, all mental activities were perceived through someone's consciousness. These included scientific laws as well (Taylor, 1998, p. 106). James (1912) called this approach "radical empiricism." Like Wundt, he focused on immediate experience as perceived in consciousness, Unlike Wundt; however, he became more and more skeptical of whether experimentalism could achieve this. After the publication of the seminal *Principles of Psychology*, James began to study other modes of consciousness, including religious conversion, psychic phenomena, and psychopathology. The purpose of this was to understand consciousness in all its manifestations. Ironically, this work ended up becoming an embarrassment to the next generation of psychologists and much of this work has been omitted from this history of the discipline (James, 1912, p. 107). Some psychologists even began to view James as a disaster for psychology's reputation.

By the turn of the century in the United States, this variant of a second psychology was well on its way to becoming an applied discipline and would continue to be so as it pushed itself into universities, now controlled by a new generation of more practical-minded managers (O'Donnell, 1985, p. 212). Psychologists offered their new practical technologies (e.g., tests, findings) to various reform-minded groups all the while describing them as grounded in scientific research, thus politically neutral. Take the case of G. Stanley Hall, much more central to the institutional development of U.S. psychology than William James. Hall was James's student and was influenced by his evolutionary pragmatism—ideas were adaptive responses to the environment. Both borrowed a model of psychology from the disparaged science of phrenology—psychology could develop into a science for the prediction and control of human behavior. After returning from graduate study in Germany and securing a position first at Harvard and then at the new Johns Hopkins, Hall established laboratories to focus on experimental study.

A great majority of his students, however, did not go on to become experimentalists. They followed Hall's path. His appointment was a joint one in pedagogy, and when he moved to Clark, Hall devoted his time to building alliances between psychology and education. For Hall, this was an important way to secure the independence of psychology and the attractiveness of it as a discipline. To many of his students, education became the primary site for the exploration of psychological ideas. Often laboratory training allowed them a level of expertauthority yet did not often affect the much looser requirements of methodology in educational research. Just to give a sense of Hall's influence by 1898, fifty-four PhDs had been awarded in the United States, thirty by Hall himself, and most of them ended up in teacher training colleges or in child study (O'Donnell, 1985).

3. INSIDE AND OUTSIDE: THE THIRD PSYCHOLOGIES

There were at least two alternatives to introspectionism in psychology by the turn of the twentieth century: the comparative study of animal behavior developed by George Romanes and the study of variation pioneered by Francis Galton. The first was regarded as experimental and the latter applied, and both would come to ground a "third" psychology justifying itself as both the experimental study of mind and a practical technology of social and behavioral change. This was not an easy balance. Both also developed a model of psychology that rejected the direct study of the internal world of mind but claimed to study it through its external manifestations, the former in behavior and the latter in statistical descriptions.

After Darwin published *The Descent of Man* and the human mind was accepted as a product of evolution, the door was opened for comparative studies of humans and animals as a means to trace the ancestry of mind. In fact, during the 1860s and 1870s, the question of whether or not animals had a mind was a widely debated one among Victorians, especially among non-scientists (Curti, 1980). And yet, as much as Darwin's peers respected him, they also criticized him for relying exclusively on inductive evidence. To correct this, Darwin's students moved comparative psychology into the laboratory using experimental methods. But, it was mostly Spencer, not Darwin, who represented evolutionary ideas in the Anglo-American world in the late nineteenth century. In his variant of progressive evolution, reflexes were transformed into instincts, memory, and finally reason-based behavior. Because the inheritance of acquired characteristics was Spencer's primary mechanism to explain evolutionary change and his belief in Bain's principle that muscular movements followed by success were likely to be repeated, he regarded instincts as inherited conditioned reflexes. Both Spencer and Darwin saw the resemblance between instincts and learned acts that had become habitual, and neither made a sharp distinction between learned and inherited acts—a distinction that only became more widely accepted after 1890 and the influence of August Weismann. Thus, there were two possible sources of instinct: use inheritance and natural selection.

Darwin's friend and younger colleague, George Romanes, established the post-Darwinian comparative psychology tradition by making the genesis of mind in animals his focus (R. L. Richards, 1987, p. 347–353). Because introspection was impossible in animals, he sought to identify "outward" manifestations of mind. He regarded instincts as more evolved forms of reflexes as they included mental perceptions and thus some level of consciousness as opposed to Spencer who saw instincts as simply compound reflexes. He introduced the term "intelligence" to explain behavior that showed the beneficial effect of past actions, thus intelligence could be inferred if one witnessed modifications in behavior, the outward manifestation of mind (Boakes, 1984, p. 23–27). Furthermore, according to Romanes, one could infer consciousness from evidence of choice, thus certain animals possessed consciousness. He also distinguished between perfect instincts—those that were fully organized at birth—and imperfect instincts—those that required further development and thus some type of learning. Interestingly, European ethology tended to study perfect instincts in animals and therefore focused more on what was inherited, while North American comparative psychology tended to focus on "imperfect" ones and thus turned to the study of learning (Burkhardt, 2005).

Romanes's contemporary, Conway Lloyd Morgan, objected to the attribution of the experimenter's complex mental states to animals—he did not reject talk of mental states altogether as he is often interpreted and, in 1894, articulated his influential canon: in no case may we interpret the action as the outcome of the exercising of a higher psychical faculty, if it can be interpreted as the outcome of one that stands lower in the psychical scale (Morgan, 1894, p. 53). For instance, Morgan argued, one could explain animal behavior that seemed purposive and guided by simply using Bain's trial-and-error learning—that behaviors with satisfying consequences were repeated—which for him became a correlate of natural selection. In other words, nature selected those organisms that had stumbled upon adaptive solutions. Morgan distinguished between basic reflexes or specific responses to external stimuli, instincts, or the inherited habits of a class of animals and intelligent acts or conscious adaptations to the environment (R. J. Richards, 1987, p. 386). He distinguished a psychology focused on the study of consciousness and a psychology that studied observable behavior, which later translated into distinction between structuralism and functionalism in U.S. psychology.

In a view that later influenced Edward Thorndike, Morgan regarded trial-and-error learning as biological as well as behavioral. It reflected an association between a neural representation of action and a consequent event. Sometimes this sequence was triggered by an innate response to an eliciting event (instinct) and sometimes by an arbitrary response to an eliciting event (learning). As was the case with Romanes, Morgan accepted that instincts could be "perfected" through an associational mechanism, and this flexibility of instinct allowed him to explain a great deal of adaptive behavior without attributing consciousness to animals. In the case of humans, further evolved intelligence allowed the perception of relations between actions and events that followed as well as between abstract entities, but these too were grounded in association (Boakes, 1984, p. 39). Thus human intelligence could be explained using the principles of association and trial-and-error learning. By 1894, Morgan had moved to study trial-and-error learning almost exclusively, as this allowed for more experimental control, but he continued to recognize the interrelation between instinct and learning. For instance, he accepted that some "instincts" only express themselves fully if exposed to specific environmental conditions (Boakes, 1984, p. 43). Comparative (animal) psychologists—who clearly could not study the contents of consciousness—tended to try and modify animal behavior in their laboratories in order to compare instinctual and modified behavior. As these methods were integrated into other fields, especially child study, the focus shifted exclusively to adapted or "learned" behaviors.

James's other influential student, E. L. Thorndike, coming directly out of comparative psychology, focused exclusively on this type of learning and the development of tests to measure it. Watson too worked with this type of learning in rats and by 1913 was ready to insist that all psychologists employ the methods of comparative psychology. Both cleverly borrowed metaphors from physiology: stimulus, reflex, connections; and both tended to ignore one of the key lessons of Darwinism: that adaptations are reflections of a particular relationship between specific organisms and their environment, that is, learning, as they characterized it, was context and species-specific. While the influence of comparative psychology itself waned, its central methodological requirements were transferred to the study of learning and applied to the exploding fields of educational psychology and mental testing. We will focus on the rest of the story of the third psychology, the fusion of learning, psychology, and education, in a later chapter.

In Britain, the seminal figure in this period was Francis Galton's student Karl Pearson, though the study of individual variation that he initiated was very different from what was developing in Germany. For one, it was non-experimental and applied from the start. It required a sharp distinction between researcher and subject, and in fact, the researched were not really even subjects, but only statistics (Danziger, 1990, p. 55). Results were reported as averages rather than individual responses and aggregate groupings could be compared. This opened the way for people to become objects of intervention rather than subjects of experience (Danziger, 1990, p. 67). Galton had focused on measuring individual variation mathematically, borrowing the terms "heredity" and "inheritance" from a legal context. Galtonians sought to measure human intelligence through assessments of sensory and other simple functions. Galton had set up a small anthropometric laboratory at the International Health Exhibition in 1884, taking various measurements of random individuals and generating wider interest in his research, and his most influential work, *Hereditary Genius*, inquired whether talent clustered in families.

While Galton's measures were crude, his idea of linking ability to inheritance spoke to Victorian society, especially those influenced by his cousin Charles Darwin's ideas (Bannister, 1979). Unlike Darwin, who assumed the fittest go on to reproduce more, Galton feared that the most able would reproduce less. This led him to "eugenics," a term he invented to describe his project of making sure to breed the "best" of each class, recognizing that industrial societies needed laborers as much as it needed intellectuals. Galton doubted whether his methods could distinguish the effects of inheritance from upbringing and turned to the study of twins. This moved him to conclude that, for the most part, nature prevails (Forrest, 1974, p. 130). In the 1870s, Galton began to quantify inheritance through the study of pea seeds and developed the idea of "reversion" to the average (or regression to the mean—that is, over time the contribution of the genius to their descendants becomes less and less significant. His student Karl Pearson called this the "law of ancestral inheritance." Galton also developed the idea that one could measure the way in which the variation of one variable relates to the variation of another. This became the technique of correlation. His student Karl Pearson developed these techniques further, establishing the field of biometry, or the measure of small changes in populations.

Galtonianism contributed three important ideas to psychology. First, mental traits can be inherited like physical ones. Second, the ways in which certain characteristics run in families can be measured and separated into the inherited and the acquired. And third, that one could measure populations using distinct yet relatable measures to those used to measure persons. This gave psychology, particularly applied psychology, a new mission: explain individual differences using measures of population. These techniques were integrated into the study of education, intelligence, personality, and psychopathology fairly quickly. By the 1890s, European thought had moved away from its mid-century liberalism, and this along with the influence of Weismann reinforced a nativist perspective. Galton's message of selective breeding fell on receptive ears. The case was different in the United States.

The Galtonian tradition was imported into the United States through his student James Mckeen Cattell whose "Mental Tests and Measurement" published in 1890 argued that all students should be tested using Galtonian measures. Cattell objected to lack of focus on individual difference or "variation" in Wundt's paradigm (O'Donnell, 1985). He also introduced the use of statistics in all of his courses (Diamond, 1998, p. 92). Cattell tried to broaden the definition of experimental psychology so that it also included mental testing, but he faced much resistance from Wundt's principal representative in the United States, Edward Titchener. Boring barely mentions Galtonianism in his 1920s text (Diamond, 1998, p. 95). The neo-Galtonian approach was far more attractive to the new class of manager-administrators in universities as well as the new philanthropic sources of funding for research. Its results could be used to rationalize administrative decisions and partly as a result, psychology's growth was explosive.

The gradual fusion of the behavioral and Galtonian approaches created a fundamentally functionalist psychology that was able to express certain structural components of mind in mathematical terms. This was obviously the case with concepts like intelligence and personality. In education, this approach captured seemingly structural entities like student understanding and aptitude. More broadly, as psychology became that study of groups rather than individuals, these structural entities became abstract properties of groups rather than entities inside individuals. For experimentalists, variations between treatment conditions became the data itself, rather than a source of error (Walsh etal. 2014, p. 524). Ultimately, the consequences of this integration allowed a blurring of the distinction between structural and functional language and the metaphors associated with them. The demise of exclusively behavioral explanations in the second half of the twentieth century left psychologists with two options. The first option was to turn psychology into the study of functions as distinct from structures, and this was the approach taken by cognitive psychology. The second possible approach was to turn psychology into the study of structures and the functions correlated with them, which was the approach of neuropsychology. What was missing, with a few exceptions we will review in a later chapter, was a better integration of notions of structure and function as well as recognition of their complex relationship.

Chapter Three

Methods of Psychology

The question of whether or not psychology can be a science hinges on the definition of science. In the case of psychology, this issue is related to the tension between sciences that are descriptive and sciences that are explanatory as well as the distinction between causes and reasons. Ever since Kant declared that psychology could be neither a rational science, because it could not produce knowledge of that which precedes experience, nor an empirical science, because its objects are studied via introspection and cannot be expressed mathematically, defenders of psychology have struggled to articulate exactly what kind of science psychology could be (Robinson, 1995). By the late nineteenth century, many of those that did "psychology" in universities—which included folks who saw themselves as either experimenting philosophers or psychically oriented physiologists—adopted some of the tools of the natural sciences as a means to access the growing authority of science (O'Donnell, 1985). These were both methodological tools—the laboratory, experiment, measurement, quantification—as well as institutional ones—separate departments, scientific societies, journals, peer review, exclusion of amateurs, and the like.

The problem with definitions of science is that the meaning of science tends to depend on the context. To the general public, to describe something as a "science" connotes that the knowledge they produce is objective. And objectivity in this case means that its results are free from bias and prejudice. As Stephen Gaukroger (2012) notes, the nonacademic view of objectivity vacillates between knowledge that is free from overt bias, which psychologists certainly seek, and knowledge that is free from any presuppositions, which is impossible. Allan Megill (1994) distinguishes between the absolute sense of objectivity and the disciplinary sense of objectivity. While the latter does not offer universal criteria of validity, it does attempt to offer authoritative criteria usually related to methodology (Megill, 1994, p. 5). For psychologists, however, one might speak of sub-disciplinary objectivity, as it would be impossible to generalize those criteria across the discipline.

1. EXPLANATION AND LAW

In a basic sense, the terms of science were set by Aristotle but became a major concern for European society in the nineteenth century. To understand something, said Aristotle, one must understand its cause. Until the seventeenth century, this implied cause in the sense of teleology or final cause. What was its purpose? With the rise of the experimental sciences, the search for final causes was replaced by the identification of efficient ones. To understand something scientifically was to know its immediate cause. This meant identifying a phenomenon as part of a network of cause-effect relationships and, ideally, seeing it as an expression of a more general law. This was called an "explanation." Newton offered a powerful example of this, and since the eighteenth century, psychologists have looked to find the kinds of general laws of mind that Newtonianism found in nature. Candidates in the nineteenth century alone included the laws of association, psychophysics, behavior, and development.

This was not yet the dominant conception of science. Until the mid-nineteenth century, science was a well-ordered body of principles obtained deductively. The key to making something a science was order, organization, and a focus on general laws. Much of this involved what we might term "description." An inductive, observation-based "empirical" approach was practiced but, at least outside Britain and the United States, was considered inferior because it was difficult to pull together into an organized whole. This was, as the Germans in particular understood it, *wissenschaft*. It was based in speculative principles primarily. This version of science was encountered by those U.S. students who went to Germany for graduate study during the period from 1830 to 1880, many of whom would go on to become the founding generation of American psychology. By the second half of the nineteenth century the term "science" tended to refer more and more to the study of matter (Williams, 1985). It gradually began to refer to the inductive/empirical study of the natural and human world and was viewed independently of philosophical speculation.

But what exactly made this new form of knowledge special? At first this variant of knowledge acquisition was understood through Francis Bacon and John Locke; that is, science was distinct because it required careful, unprejudiced observation. Robert Boyle's original vision of the laboratory was that it could ensure the objectivity of such observations and facts by controlling who participated in it as well as the forms of that participation (Shapin and

Schaffer, 1985). The key was that such knowledge was "unprejudiced" (Daston, 1994). Over the course of the seventeenth century, the idea that objectivity determined where science should end was replaced by the idea that objectivity guided how science should proceed (Gaukroger, 2012, p. 59). Both Hume and Kant in their own way undermined the foundations of these procedures, both turning causality into a product of the mind. The question for some was how to correct for this.

One solution was phenomenological. From the 1870s to the 1890s, Richard Avenarius and Ernst Mach laid out a vision of science that rejected metaphysics and limited itself to immediate experience. Thus, science was to be descriptive not explanatory. This shaped Wundt's vision for psychology: focus on immediate experience before the mind can impose its own categories. Wundt believed his experimental introspection accomplished this. Following Franz Brentano, he accepted a distinction between inner perception and inner observation. Inner perception was immediate, inner observation was not. As William Lyons explains, "Wundt believed that one could mold inner perception into a scientific method by so ordering and controlling the conditions that the process of inner perception came to resemble in all important respects external, ordinary perception while steering clear of becoming overblown and useless internal observation" (1986, p. 4). This required well-trained subjects. E. G. Boring estimated that subjects who performed less than ten thousand of these introspectively controlled reactions were deemed too inexperienced to provide data for published research from Wundt's laboratory (Boring, 1953, cited in Lyons, 1986, p. 5). Because Wundt believed more complex mental phenomena could not be controlled in such a way that made them amenable to inner perception, they were excluded from experimental study. In the next generation, behaviorists turned inner perception into inner speech making these experiments the study of behavior not mind.

An alternate solution was to replace simple induction with a hypothetico-deductive model that could offer predictions. Thus, the answer lay in experimentation: the adequacy of facts could be determined by deducing specific predictions from accepted theories, ideally controlling other factors, acting on the world and seeing if the world responds in the way predicted. This approach had been utilized since the seventeenth century but was widely discussed by philosophers in the mid-nineteenth century, especially those that were critical of John Stuart Mill's inductivism. Darwin, for example, described his work as inductive, especially to the public, but in reality, he was clearly developing a range of hypotheses across diverse fields and testing them against multiple sources of evidence. This is typically why natural scientists hold him in the esteem that they do. But, by the 1920s, World War I brought with it a crisis of faith in the institutions and practices of modernity, and the exceptionality of science was once again in question.

One response to the rise of skepticism that followed as well as the influence of neo-Kantianist talk of ideas presupposing experience was the logical positivism of the Vienna Circle led by Moritz Schlick, the chair of the philosophy of inductive sciences at the University of Vienna during the 1920s. Other members included Otto Neurath, Rudolph Carnap, Carl Hempel, and occasional critic Karl Popper. The logical positivists sought to restore the goal of explanation for science. They moved away from Machian phenomenalism toward physicalism or the idea that scientific statements had to be directly related to verifiable physical conditions. Influenced by developments in British logic and philosophy, logical positivists regarded science as consisting of two types of statements, formal and factual, the latter generated empirically and was testable. Their point was to offer new criteria for "demarcation" or distinguishing science from metaphysics. Ultimately, for the logical positivists, all sciences were reducible to physics. But with their restrictive conditions, critics argued, the logical positivists excluded too much from the sphere of science (Polkinghorne, 1984). Popper was skeptical of the group's inductivism and in *The Logic of Scientific Discovery* of 1934 moved toward falsification as the criteria of demarcation. Popper cleverly tried to build skepticism into the heart of the scientific method. Truth was always provisional. But there were problems with this too. Was the distinction between formal and factual statements tenable? Wasn't the identification of variables as distinct from each other itself theory-driven? Don't empirical statements always depend on untested and even unfalsifiable propositions? This criticism became known as the Duhem-Quine problem.

The path for the human or social sciences was similar. In 1848, John Stuart Mill sought to correct the backwardness of the "moral" sciences by encouraging them to adopt the methods of the natural sciences (Polkinghorne, 1984). Those in the social sciences who wished to follow this path sought to identify causal relationships as instances of universal laws, or perhaps generalization-like laws (Rosenberg, 1988). Since the nineteenth century, solving problems of method has meant emulating the most successful sciences, though this tends to be meant more didactically than practically (Gaukroger, 2012, p. 49). One influential idea was that of an "operational definition" coined by physicist P. W. Bridgman in his *The Logic of Modern Physics* in 1927. Here phenomena that are not directly measurable but can be inferred from other phenomena are defined by the procedures used to measure them. The work of operationalization is to identify exactly what is and what is not part of the phenomenon to be studied. For psychologists, if offered a means to turn inaccessible mental states into a concrete and measurable process, all as if sidelined questions of validity. Years later, Bridgman criticized psychologists for their dependence on rigid operational definitions, much more so than in physics. Also influential was Carl Hempel and Paul Oppenheim's (1948) nomological-deductive model. It allowed social science phenomena to be viewed as instances of universal law or fairly regular lawlike generalizations, which once certain preliminary conditions were met, could be used as a source for predictions. This was attractive as its basis was in probable outcomes not necessary ones, as in traditional causal notions, and hence it could be applied to nonexperimental sciences as well (Robinson, 1985, p. 110). Thus the notion of an "explanation" moved beyond an exclusive focus on cause-effect relationships, though critics argued that the identification of such relationships were the point of science in the first place.

During the years following World War II, faith in science was renewed as it came to occupy a broader and more ideological role in liberal-democratic societies. Beside a massive influx of government spending there was also the widespread sentiment that science could offer itself as a model for democratic societies. This was an idea that influenced Thomas Kuhn. Kuhn read Polish biologist Ludwik Fleck's *Genesis and Development of Scientific Fact*, written in the 1930s, which convinced him that the development of scientific knowledge had to account for the sociology of the scientific community (Nye, 2011, p. 238). Kuhn worked out these ideas during the 1950s and, along with Norwood Hanson, Michael Polanyi, and Stephen Toulmin, developed the idea of shifting "paradigms" to explain changes in scientific knowledge. These occurred, argued Kuhn (1962), during periods of "revolutionary" science. Typically "normal" science did not offer much opportunity to falsify the basic ideas of a paradigm. Something about Kuhn's less than radical politics made his ideas so successful, as opposed to others with similar theses (Nye, 2011, p. 256), and today most psychologists accept at least a limited form of Kuhn's thesis (Robinson, 1995). In a sense, both the logical positivists and the post-logical positivists accepted the idea that the world was "constructed," the former from the data of sensory experience and the latter from that data as filtered through conceptual categories (Hacking, 1999, pp. 42–43). Both rejected the idea that science can simply represent the world as it is, even though this vision of science persisted in the public imagination, yet both left traditional conceptions of explanation in doubt.

2. DESCRIPTION AND INTERPRETATION

All sciences begin with description. For the explanatory sciences this is simply the first step in identifying explanations. Put simply, description answers the what and explanation the why. There is typically a value dimension to this, as the phrase "mere description" implies, though there is also a historical dimension to this distinction. In other words, the distinction between a description and an explanation is determined by the context. Since Aristotle, the work of description involved classification and categorization.

These classifications were typically integrated into a broader system of principles. As we discussed, this was the sense of much of what was termed science until the nineteenth century. There was an aesthetic dimension to this as well, as there always is—that is, successful science organized disparate knowledge in a more useful way, but also in an attractive way, as was the case with Carl Linnaeus's *Systema Naturae* and Antoine Lavoisier's *Elementary Treatise on Chemistry*. Even as the experimental sciences grew in influence in the nineteenth century, Hume's problem was never fully resolved. As we noted, both phenomenological and logical positivism attempted to address this. And yet, by undermining the validity of causal claims, positivism made description the heart of science, whether these were descriptions of the contents of consciousness or descriptive statements that required confirmation. For them, explanation required metaphysical speculation, and description was by far the superior goal. Still, these debates in the philosophy of science didn't necessarily impact the practice of science, and especially in the case of the natural sciences, the search for causes continued.

As the term "science" began to refer more and more to the methods used to study matter over the course of the nineteenth century, critics sought to introduce an alternate notion of science that they felt better understood human phenomena. Such a science often involved *verstehn* or interpretation. The term was borrowed from Kant who had left humans in two worlds, a world of nature explicable through the natural sciences and a human world explicable through reason. This gradually led to the idea that the natural and human worlds needed to be studied via different methods. By the late nineteenth century, this became the distinction between the natural sciences [*naturwissenschaften*] and the human sciences [*geisteswissenschaften*]. This was a distinction embraced by Wundt and goes back to alternative conceptions of science in Liam-Battista Vico and Joham Herder. Both of these thinkers, in their own way, recognized the problems with using the methods of the natural sciences to study human phenomena (Polkinghorne, 1984). Vico argued in *The New Science* of 1725 that a true understanding of human phenomena required history and that people are always in a better position to understand the products of their own making. He stressed the limitations of observation and verification for the human sciences, as they tended to make human phenomena illusory, whereas the goal should be to make them intelligible. Influenced by Vico, Herder stressed the dependence of thought on language and the importance of feeling and subjectivity in historical analysis. He focused on the nature of different peoples—the *volk*—and asserted the importance of acknowledging their dignity and allowing them to come to self-realization as a people. This led to this first *völkerkunde* or ethnographies and the idea that cultures help to frame individual experience. Given the differences between people across history and culture, making their experiences intelligible required "interpretation," which allowed one to understand the world as others see it. This principle was borrowed by theologian Friedrich Schleiermacher and became central to his method of biblical criticism. The *völkerkunde* were developed further in the *völkerpsychologie* of Moritz Lazarus and Heymann Steinthal in the 1850s and 1860s who focused on shared thought and behavior patterns in groups and went on to influence Wundt.

Schleiermacher inspired Wilhelm Dilthey who sought to combine the broad scope of German idealism with the rigor of Kant's critical method, though he eventually rejected the Kantian notion that inner experience was merely phenomenal. Dilthey laid out his position in his *Introduction to the Human Sciences* of 1883 and his *Ideas for a Descriptive and Analytic Psychology* of 1894. In the latter work, Dilthey adopted the Kantian distinction between "*explanation*" (*erklären*) and "understanding" (*verstehen*) in order to distinguish between the natural and human sciences. Kant had already established that a human science could not be explanatory or universally valid and objective the way a natural science could because universality and necessity were products of the mind. Dilthey accepted this basic difference. While the natural sciences were oriented toward explanation, they focused on invariant causal laws; the human sciences directed themselves toward understanding, a kind of comprehension of particularity, which required an empathetic identification with one's object of study as well as the ability to interpret phenomena. The object of analysis for the human sciences was "lived experience," moments of living where the distinction between subject and object had not yet been imposed. From Dilthey's perspective, lived experience was eventually expressed outwardly in historical objectifications like culture or language, even in the "natural" world, or inwardly in subjective and intrapersonal experiences. The final goal of the human sciences was not to produce representations of lived experience, per se, but to understand a specific sociohistorical world through a study of its expressions.

Dilthey argued that the human sciences must ground themselves in an understanding of human psychology, meaning an alternate psychology from experimental versions, which generally modeled themselves after the natural sciences and analyzed the contents of a universal mind. Instead he imagined an interpretive and historical science that began from the premise that all psychological processes were mediated through history. Many European psychologists including Wilhelm Wundt, Eduard Spranger, and William Stern were influenced by Dilthey and focused on the development of the interpretative method or specifically on the relationship between culture and thought. In the 1930s, Stern's American student, Gordon Allport (1937), attempted to introduce these ideas into the study of personality through his distinction between an idiographic and nomothetic approach. Allport's notion of an "intuitive" approach alongside a generalist one was aggressively criticized by his American peers, and he eventually gave it up entirely (Lamiell, 2003). During these years, many of Dilthey's ideas made their way into U.S. anthropology through the influence of Franz Boas, though they did not affect U.S. psychology until much later.

3. EXPLANATION AND DESCRIPTION IN PSYCHOLOGY

Because science does not take photos of the world, but expresses its facts in language, it is impossible for us to completely distinguish between the world itself and our ways of perceiving and making sense of the world. We cannot "observe" reality directly. As Gaukroger elegantly puts it, "unmediated perception is not objective perception, it is not perception at all" (2012, p. 43). Part of what science does involves generating new ways of seeing the world via categorization and instrumentation, but these categories and instruments help to create the world they discover. In these cases, it becomes more difficult to separate the science from its context and the scientist from their world. The same is true of psychology. Psychology too helps to create the world it studies. The core problem that arises with psychology is not that its objects are unobservable. This is the case in chemistry and physics as well. The problem is that although the objects of psychology often have the same name, they do not necessarily have the same referent (Kagan, 2013). Theories are developed to explain facts, as in the natural sciences, but many of these facts are artifacts of the theory itself. Take a term like "affect." The problem is not that it is not observable, but that it can have a very different meaning or refer to very different experiences, depending on the context and the way it is measured. This means that for much psychology, anything like "falsifying" theories in the Popperian sense is impossible, as understanding is grounded in a network of assumptions and values that mostly remain unarticulated. Even when psychologists try and make their theoretical concepts clear, by borrowing these categories from everyday psychology, much of the theorizing has already happened by the time those categories are encountered (Danziger, 1997, p. 8). Some psychologists are constrained by the belief that psychology must yield explanations to be scientific—that is, identify relations of cause-effect—yet often the nature of the objects themselves yield only descriptions at best, though certainly not "unprejudiced" ones.

As a result of this, many psychological studies seek out correlations— predictable relationships among variables—and treat them as if they were akin to cause-effect relations, relations that would be impossible to identify given the limited capacity to control for other variables. In fact, the term "variable" itself arose as a means of conflating statistical entities with objective natural forces (Danziger, 1997, p. 172). In lieu of control, psychologists attempt to account for variation through various statistical techniques. As is easily recognized, the more variables one includes in an analysis the more likely one will discover correlations, especially when most of the variables are already part of the same semantic networks. Yet, when controlled experiments are utilized, the conditions tend to be so artificial and the measurement of variables so arbitrary, it is difficult to interpret findings. Measure a variable in a slightly different way and the results can change dramatically (Kagan, 1998). The issue is, methods of measurement create the objects that psychologists then go on to study, so that, for example, a score on a depression scale becomes depression, responses measured on a likert scale become an attitude, or changes in a measure of a response become learning. These artifacts can then be analyzed or manipulated as if they were identical with those objects in the world that are the basis of the study in the first place (Ziman, 2000, p. 89). Psychologists then seek out the causes of these artifacts standing in for objects-in-the-world or study how they vary in relation to other artifacts. Can one alter depression or learning with this type of intervention? Does attitude or intelligence relate to this other artifact (e.g., class, identity, schooling) standing in for other objects-in-the-world? Can one find relationships between one kind of artifact—attachment style, for example, a product of an observation, and another, say self-efficacy—the product of a scale? What about an image-based representation of a brain state—an artifact of fMRI technology—and anxiety—an artifact of yet another scale? Some psychologists argue that this is the price of operationalization, turning phenomena into things that are measurable. The price of science is loss of validity. Jerome Kagan (2013) suggests that psychologists use multiple approaches to measure the same variable in an attempt to deal with the problem of validity (p. 25), and this is helpful but probably not enough. It is certainly not a substitute for knowing where these concepts come from in the first place and how they have evolved. There are undoubtedly times in which controlled studies with measurable variables in limited contexts can yield fruitful results. This is probably most true in cases of physiologically oriented psychology. It seems Wundt was probably correct about the limitations of experimental psychology.

Over the course of the twentieth century, statistics became a necessary ingredient in validating psychological knowledge—essentially turning psychology into the study of variation and a quest to identify statistical differences (Starbuck, 2006). Often, variables are too similar to each other and overlapping to parcel out individual effects in a meaningful way, especially if statistical differences become a substitute for meaningful differences. In addition, the tendency to treat statistical errors as if they were all random, thus canceling each other out, as opposed to correlated with each other, calls into question the meaning of those analyses (Kagan, 2013). Most mathematicians have long recognized the problems with null hypothesis testing, as does the APA, yet psychologists continue to make this a primary form of statistical analysis (Rozebaum, 1960; Yates, 1951). Given the convention of looking for significance at the .05 level, a finding which would be considered too unreliable to have any meaning in most other sciences, many findings have little meaning (Uttal, 2007). At first glance, a one in twenty probability that successful findings are due to chance seems impressive, but once one takes into account all the failed studies that go unpublished and the tendency of experienced psychologists to develop explanations and theories after they already know what the data reveals, it turns out that the 5 percent figure likely includes a lot of questionable results.

In a way, psychology is very much of a science if we understand that all university-based scientific disciplines legitimize knowledge in similar ways: original research usually requiring intensive specialization—otherwise originality would be impossible—publication, communal standards of research, assessing the work of others, limited teaching, fund-raising, attending conferences, shared specialized language, and so on (Ziman, 2000, p. 30). Knowledge becomes conventionalized in science when it is published by a reputable journal, which naturally tends to prefer results which confirm the underlying assumptions of the discipline and cited by the right people in later publications (Ziman, 2000, pp. 33–36). Because the acquisition of university positions and job promotion is tied to publishing, there is no set limit on what needs to be produced. Academia is highly competitive, and there is a lot at stake economically, professionally, and personally (Ziman, 2000, pp. 49–52). Typically, the study of a specific phenomenon is never complete, at least until a particular topic is no longer in vogue for editors of journals or funders. Naturally, reviewers tend to prefer perspectives that support their own, especially the type of reasoning valued in their own research or research they are familiar with, so the range of ideas developed and forms of thinking supported tends to be fairly narrow, more so in that research which defines itself as experimental (Peters and Ceci, 1982). The establishment of an APA style in 1952 conventionalized language used in writing up research, and the adoption of a "problem-cause-solution" approach brought with it more standardization (Walsh etal. 2014, p. 542). Today, because operational definitions differ across subfields, findings tend to reveal more about the researcher's assumptions than the topics studied, especially in the case of excessive generalization (Starbuck, 2006; Kagan, 1998).

In recent years, some psychologists have tried to circumvent these problems by arguing that psychology is not a natural science but a human science. Psychologists influenced by this distinction eschew the laboratory and experimentation. They embrace more appropriate methods like ethnography and hermeneutics (Denzin & Lincoln, 2007). Rather than search for explanations, they focus on *verstehen* or interpreting phenomena and what they mean for people in their lives. There is much value in this approach, what Clifford Geertz famously termed "thick description," but there are also problems with the underlying distinction between the natural and human sciences. For one, it retains the notion that the Kantian gap between subject and object needs to be bridged methodologically (Aronowitz and Ausch, 2000). It also depends too much on a rigid distinction between nature and culture, when the meanings of these terms and their referents are historically and culturally variable (Geertz, 2000). What sounds like a way to distinguish between different kinds of objects of study actually ends up as an academic division of labor, more often privileging the natural sciences over the human ones.

There might be better ways to conceive this distinction. For one, there is the distinction between those objects for which context matters more or less. John Searle (1995) distinguishes between "brute" and "institutional" facts. A similar route involves a distinction between natural and human kinds, where the latter includes many objects currently studied by the natural sciences. Psychological categories are human kinds in the sense that using them changes people's conceptions of themselves. They have, what Ian Hacking terms, "looping" effects (1999). To be identified as having high intelligence or an extroverted personality, changes one's experience of the world. The same is not true when one is described as being made up of molecules. They deserve special attention when people put them to work in institutions and lead people to modify their feelings and behavior because they are so classified (Hacking, 1999, p. 104). Hacking suggests this language is more useful to the human sciences than the one-way metaphor of "social construction" where the world is passively created by human categories. Psychological categories appear "natural," but only to specific speech communities sharing a tradition of language use (Danziger, 1997, p. 191). They are also fundamentally normative. This is especially true in the clinically oriented branches of psychology whose goal is to identify correct and incorrect, sometimes called healthy and unhealthy, behaviors and mental processes. But this is also true in a broader sense. Here is just a short list of virtue in psychology: well organized personalities, secure attachments, rational thinking, developing, neural growth, achievement motivation, resiliency, lack of conformity/obedience to authority, learning, and a bit of stress but not too much stress.

The desire to emulate the natural sciences lead some psychologists to confuse causes and reasons, and in the end, all historical and social events are inexplicable except through reasons (Robinson, 1985). Reasons require that we mostly depend on the explanations of everyday psychology. They involve talk of motives, beliefs, thoughts, feelings, desires, and so on as these intentional states are the source of action. To explain the reason for an action is to assume the basic rationality of the agent involved, whether the agent is a person, an institution or a society (Dennett, 1978; Rosenberg, 1988). Reasons cannot be viewed as determining causes of action as a sufficient reason to act in one context might not be sufficient in another (Bouveresse, 1995). Unlike causes, reasons are often supplied from sources outside the agent, as their activity is interpreted and rationalized. And one doesn't necessarily preclude the other. We can explain events causally, in a deterministic way, and yet still assign reasons to the agents involved (Bouveresse, 1995, p. 74). Reasons are judged differently than causes. They are not judged so much as right or wrong or whether they predict with some likelihood the occurrence of some event as much as whether they correspond to a standard of good reason (Bouveresse, 1995, p. 76). Reasons are teleological in the sense that they reveal the agent's purpose, but those reasons do not necessarily have to reside inside people. Reasons might be hidden in action that has become habitualized or "second nature," yet they still reveal intelligibility when interpreted. A successful interpretation involves an appeal to common understanding, which themselves appeal to other common understandings. This is no escape from this hermeneutic circle. Interpretation involves *versthen* or empathic identification with the perspective of another. The question of whether the mind contains a rational structure which it imposes on reality (reasons) or simply copies the mechanical relationships found in nature (causes) is yet another variant of the debate between rationalism and empiricism, between Kant and Hume. It's hard to argue with the rationalist contention that limiting talk of what we conceive as the "psychological" in the West to the kinds of cause-effect relationships found in physics leaves out too much. Yet, it is also understandable why some psychologists would be drawn to the idea that psychology can replace everyday intentional mental language with physics-like mechanisms or an entirely physiological language, no matter how unlikely. But explanations, like descriptions, must be coherent to be successful as well. Both depend on narrative (Robinson, 1985, p. 117). They are not as different as the distinctions imply. It might just be the case anyway that detailed cataloguing and interpretation of the categories that shape the psychological in modern Western societies with an attention to context, language, culture, and history proves more valuable in the long term than explanatory mechanisms which parse up mind through artificial categories and divorce the psychological from its ground in human consciousness and experience.

Chapter Four

The Principles of Learning

Theories of learning occupy an important place in psychology, both histori-cally and as well as in its longstanding relationship with education, though learning has always been a concern in the West going back to the Greeks and before even if typically something radically different was meant by the term. The psychology of learning presents us with a great example of some of the issues that we have pointed to in the field. It has multiple referents, a subtle moral undertone—learning is clearly a "good" thing—and a ready-made au-dience looking to consume findings on the topic—schools, teachers, adminis-trators, and parents. It is easily represented as a singular "mechanism" or "process," both metaphors of course, bridging various contexts. And finally, it presents an illustration of the ways in which tensions between inside and outside as well as between description and explanation play out in psycholo-gy. In this chapter, we take the perspective we have been developing in the first few chapters and focus it more specifically on the relationship between a psychological concept, in this case learning, and its circulation into the worlds of modern life.

What made the psychology of learning attractive to early twentieth centu-ry psychology was that it allowed for a new relationship between a person's external and internal worlds in several senses. The first was methodological. Gone was the assumption that the only route to mind was introspection of consciousness with all its philosophical baggage as well as ground in philos-ophy departments (O'Donnell, 1979). This was not only because behavior was easier to observe, but also changes in behavior were viewed as concrete expressions of evolutionary activity. Second, it turned a traditionally episte-mological question as to the origins of knowledge into a biological one: Are higher forms of mind native to human beings or acquired through experi-ence? If they were acquired, as the behaviorists argued, then one could posit similar mechanisms for that acquisition across species, demonstrating once again that humans were part of nature. It is easy to underestimate the effects of this new way of thinking about the relationship between inside and outside, biology and environment, nature and nurture, on twentieth-century American thought. It became a language for addressing sociopolitical questions, all the while, couching them in the vocabularies of biology. The optimism that ran deep in American culture about the possibility of building a new type of society was translated into the liberal belief that the right social and educational institutions could properly socialize, even modify, human nature.

The intense focus on learning in early-twentieth-century psychology sat alongside notions of that which could not be learned, in other words, innate in some sense. Historically, there have been a myriad of ways to express this, starting with Plato's notion of innate knowledge of forms to Kant's transcendental categories. With the debates inspired by Cartesianism, notions of mechanical yet complex and ultimately divinely inspired behaviors were understood through the category of "instinct." The idea of an instinctual human nature, in some sense, was a corrective to the radical sensationalism of British and French philosophy in particular. By the end of the nineteenth century, instincts, now understood as prior adaptations passed on via natural selection or use-inheritance, continued to explain what association could not. It was widely accepted that psychology had to address this underlying instinctual nature. The prevalence of nature-based versus nurture-based explanations in psychology tended to reflect the political zeitgeist more than the findings of research. By end of the twentieth century, notions of instinct, though not the term itself, were revived by evolutionary psychology as well as by the influence of John Bowlby's attachment theory, even though the firm distinction between nature and nurture has always had a tenuous physiological foundation. More often than not, the language of instincts simply described early appearing and seemingly species-wide behaviors that could not be explained through available theoretical frameworks. It was a description of what was observed in animals framed in a term that implied an explanation.

Learning, in psychology, is typically conceived as the modification of behavior as a consequence of external stimulation. It is a technical definition of the more common term "habit," the importance of which clearly presaged early-twentieth-century psychology. This definition of learning was widely accepted during the years that variants of behaviorism dominated the field, roughly from the 1920s to the 1960s, and is still prevalent in most psychology textbooks for undergraduates and teachers-in-training. In these cases we find that the traditional objects of psychological study—psyche, soul, mind, consciousness, immediate experience—have been supplanted by a new one, behavior. Often one finds references to psychology as the science of "behavior," and the ideas of learning and behavior are intimately connected. Like learning, the term "behavior" is a fairly versatile one. It combines a descriptive category, the way an organism acts, with a prescriptive one, as in, to act in an acceptable way (e.g., behave!), which is the origin of the term in the first place (Williams, 1985). It is easy to add it to any term to make it "observable"—depressive behavior, intelligent behavior, aggressive behavior—but was borrowed directly from nineteenth-century physiology as a way to talk about organismic activity that may or may not have been volitional or conscious but had no moral sense (Graumann, 1996, p. 88). Most importantly—and this was a methodological point—behavior, unlike consciousness, could be observed, even broken into its component parts, extracted from its context, measured, and experimentally manipulated.

Another nineteenth-century metaphor that became part of the same semantic network as learning and behavior for psychology, perhaps more evident in the first years of the twentieth century, was "organism." The term "organism," like the term "organic," implies a relationship between parts and whole that is omnipresent in all forms of life where constitutive parts can be explained by their relationship to the whole. This is an obvious contrast from entities with mechanical properties. The term arose in the seventeenth century, adapted from the term "organize," to refer to the structural properties of life; though when it first appeared in the sixteenth century, it simply meant engine or tool as in the mind is the "organ" of intelligence (Williams, 1985, p. 227). Romanticism stressed the oppositional nature of the organic and the mechanical. The term "organism" was first applied to living beings in the 1840s and eventually became linked with the spread of evolutionary thought. Behavior and hence learning were activities of organisms and therefore part of evolutionary processes, arguably at the core of life. This made the study of learning and behavior an adjunct of biology and the work of psychology part of the scientific study of evolution. Organisms must adapt to their environments to survive, humans included, where adaptations were reconceived as changes in behavior. Hence, learning was a trans-species activity.

In many ways, investigating notions of learning in psychology gets to the heart of what the discipline is supposed to be about. What is its principal object of study: mind or behavior? Most definitions of psychology referenced mind or consciousness as opposed to behavior until about 1930 (about 70 percent for mind and 14 percent for behavior). From then until around 1970, nearly 70 percent referenced behavior, while only about 7 percent referenced mind. By the 1980s, while references to behavior remained roughly the same, references to mind increased to about 30 percent (Walsh etal. 2014, p. 3). Even many nonpsychologists know something about a period of time in academic psychology that was dominated by behaviorism, when the mind itself was deemed beyond scientific investigation and psychology was limited in its object of study to the behavioral correlates of mental processes. Some went as far as denying the existence of mental states altogether. Given that mental processes are not observable, the logic at first glance makes a certain amount of sense when paired with a naïve Baconian vision of science as a collection of observed facts.

The figure that probably took this most seriously was B. F. Skinner. He understood some of the problems that come with what he termed "mentalism" and tried to respond to them. His work has helped to create a multitude of practices—CBT, token economies, and reward-use in education—that seek to modify human behavior using the principles of conditioning. While there are conceptual problems with Skinnerianism, as we shall review, especially confusion between explanation and description, there is also a warning about the danger of relying on assumed mental entities that is still worth taking heed of. Today, this repudiation of the study of mental activity is understood as an "error" or having gone too far, but as we already noted, it was also part of a strategy for the institutionalization of psychology in the university. Even during those years, most psychologists were not "behaviorists" except in a very general sense. They were often actively involved in applied settings, particularly education and still considered mental processes in their work but tried to turn them into observables and ultimately measurables. This meant lots of behavioral translations of mental processes, particularly in various forms of measurements, assessments, and scales. Some of this was part of a broader generational conflict as the psychologists who still considered their work part of philosophy or physiology were replaced by a new generation of psychologists who were drawn to John Watson's virulent rejection of introspective methods and viewed the new behavioral methods as a means to protect the scientific authority and status of their work (O'Donnell, 1985). These behavioral psychologists tended to share many assumptions: a stimulus-response orientation, peripheralism and focus on sensorimotor activity, associational linking, and environmentalism. But what behaviorists really shared was a methodological commitment to "objectivism" (Kendler, 1992, p. 124). This commitment extended beyond the collapse of strict behaviorism in the 1960s and continues today in most psychology that describes itself as "experimental." This theory of method, what we can describe as methodological behaviorism, persists in much psychological research today, though rather than seeking relationships between stimulus and response, it seeks relationships between independent and dependent variables and allows for certain mental mediators (e.g., schemas, representations, maps, etc.) between stimulus and response.

Part of the story of learning in psychology is tied up with the story of U.S. public education, specifically around the development of new forms of teacher training, educational research, and assessment, all of which were tied together in turn-of-the-century America (Langemann, 2002). Early educational research was used to develop materials for teachers to use in their classroom, create novel ways to assess students, and as a rationale for the centralization of public education, especially in large urban areas like New York City and Chicago. From the 1890s to the 1920s, educational research emerged as an empirical and university-based science built primarily around behavioral psychology dependent on technologies of measurement and quantification (Langemann, 2002, p. 16). The category of "achievement," as in student achievement, gradually emerged as the quantifiable product of learning that could be used to measure students, teachers, novel curriculum, even schools against each other in a rationalized way. Since the turn of the twentieth century educational administrators, curriculum writers, publishing companies, test developers, and others involved in U.S. public education have turned to academic psychology to make sense of this principal activity that is supposed to take place in schools (Joncich, 1968). The influences of psychological conceptions of learning are still with us especially in the pervasiveness of standardized testing and certain types of educational research. One assumption still prevalent is that "learning" and even "understanding" can be measured by objective and standardized means wherein students, teachers, and schools can be compared against each other. Today's testing regime is oriented around measuring student achievement, while much educational research, especially in post-No Child Left Behind education, is oriented around increasing it. A second assumption still prevalent is that the training of teachers involves the breakdown of "teaching" behavior into its component parts. Today this is termed "methods"—as well as reducing the content of education into its component parts; today this is termed a "common core." This approach turns teaching into a technically subordinate task that requires management by administrators in terms set by the science of education (Langemann, 2002, p. 60).

U.S. public education at the turn of the century evolved in a tension between the egalitarian impulses of the progressive movement which sought to provide a proper education to all children and the reality of the need for a stratified and unequal workforce in industrial societies. How to create equality and inequality at the same time? How to balance the vocational needs of an industrial society, the socialization requirements of a pluralist society, and the equalizing requirements of a democratic society, all the while producing something one can term an education. While these tensions have never been resolved, one answer lay in the idea of "equality of opportunity." If all public students had an opportunity for uplift and success, then the fault of failure would lie with psychological or biological variables like lack of motivation or constitutional differences. This allowed schools to act as sorters and rationalized the development of a graded and later differentiated school system (Chapman, 1988). Today linking differences in inborn capacity to specific racial or socioeconomic groups is politically unacceptable unless one does it through the languages of medical pathology or environmental deprivation, but at the turn of the century this seemed a sensible way to explain the success of certain groups in American life. A language for talking about "instincts" was borrowed from comparative psychologists and evolutionary biologists and suggested a way to explain differences in constitution, and particularly after 1900, differences in intelligence. The notion that different children require different types of education, all within the public school system, became part of accepted wisdom. Furthermore, as we shall review, some of the relationship between conceptions of learning and U.S. education can be better made explicit by looking at how differently this relationship played out in the German context. For one, educational research was designed for teachers and not for administrators (Drewek, 2000). More importantly, the development of educational research took place in the context of the spread of Gestalt psychology, with its emphasis on wholes and synthesis rather than elementalism and decomposition, all of which was related to broader social and political currents in German society especially during the Weimar years (Ash, 1995).

Outside of psychology when individuals use the term learning, they are typically referring to the process of acquiring new knowledge and skills or modifying existing ones. This is also the sense that teachers use the term when they describe a student as having "learned" something. Most people work with what psychologists unfortunately term a "folk" theory of mind that views it as a container filled with various kinds of stuff: thoughts, knowledge, beliefs, feelings, and so forth. The term "folk" theory of mind is unfortunate because it removes such views from history and universalizes them. In fact, as we discussed previously, this view of mind was linked with the spread of Cartesianism and British Empiricism, and thus, linked with the spread of experimental science. Related to this, sits a view of learned behavior as acquiring "skill," again very much in line with the notion of habit in British philosophy. As David Olson and Jerome Bruner (1996) note, such theories of mind bring with them folk theories of pedagogy. In these cases, learning becomes the acquisition of propositional knowledge or the acquisition of "know-how" (Olson & Bruner, 1996 p. 16). The former seems to dominate education, becoming what Paulo Freire (1968) famously described as the banking concept of education or John Dewey, the dead weight of facts.

As Olson and Bruner also note, there really is no reason to damn this model of pedagogy. There is no reason why the acquisition of propositional knowledge should not be a part of education other than the bias of romantic and progressive sentiments, ultimately stemming from Rousseau. The behavioral view of learning acquired from psychology sits well with this view as it allows for the identification and measurement of propositional knowledge via assessments and standardized tests. This view also holds, again as noted by Olson and Bruner, that the ability to acquire new propositional knowledge requires the aid of certain mental abilities. Sometimes this was described as "intelligence" and conceived as fixed, while at other times it was conceived as something that could be improved through education. Either way it accounted for individual differences in learning, rationalizing differential educational paths. Further, "its principal appeal is that by virtue of its clear conception of what is known it purports to offer a clear specification of just what is to be taught, and equally, it purports to offer standards for assessing its achievement" (Olson & Bruner, 1996, p. 17).

In contrast, we can identify at least ten different types of learning that psychologists might be referring to when using the term. Psychologists distinguish between two major subtypes of learning: simple nonassociational learning and associative learning. In most cases, when psychologists refer to learning they are referring to the associative type. There are two types of simple learning, habituation—a decrease in response with stimulus repetition—and sensitization—an amplification of response with stimulus repetition. These operate in almost all life-forms including unicellular ones, hence they are termed "simple." Associative learning also has two types, associational or classical conditioning—wherein a linkage is created between two stimuli or a stimulus and response—and instrumental or operant conditioning—where a response becomes more or less likely as a result of its consequences. The latter is also referred to as trial-and-error learning. Both types of learning are only found in more advanced life-forms, thus they are presumed to require higher forms of intelligence and more complex brains than those required for simple nonassociative learning. All this clearly integrated into evolutionary thought.

There are, however, other variants of learning that come up in psychology. Ethologists will sometimes talk about phase-specific learning or critical-period learning, which they also term "imprinting" (Lorenz, 1970). Social psychologists influenced by Albert Bandura (Bandura etal. 1963) sometimes describe imitative or observational learning, but imitation was also a very important mode of learning for Darwin and early developmental psychologists. Other types include episodic learning—learning in response to a specific event; rote learning—learning "mechanically" by repetition; formal vs. informal learning—learning in school as opposed to learning outside of school; cognitive vs. psychomotor vs. affective learning—this is a distinction from educational psychologist Benjamin Bloom (1956) between learning that involves thought, behavior, or emotions; assimilative vs. accommodative learning—learning by addition vs. learning by breakdown and synthesis; higher-order or conceptual learning—learning abstract organizing principles; and finally situated learning—learning to participate in sociocultural practices (Lave and Wenger, 1991). All these variations reveal the flexibility of the term, yet the generic term "learning" still refers to associative type, especially in recent years in the context of looking for its neural correlates.

Similarly, what is counted as "learning" in education has always been historically and culturally variable and typically understood through various metaphors. Plato's notion of learning as a kind of remembering no longer speaks to many, with the possible exception of the followers of Noam Chomsky, nor does Locke's association of ideas. The behaviorists' "conditioning" of behavior is no longer as influential as it once was either, though it still occupies a prominent place in psychology texts and educational ones concerned with the management of student behavior (Kohn, 1992). Even the kinds of "processing" and "informational" metaphors ushered in during the 1960s with the spread of cognitive science are gradually being replaced by ones popular in today's neuroscience like "network" and "wiring." While these metaphors are helpful in that they speak to psychologists working in a specific time and place, they all tend to bring with them a similar problem. Today this involves assigning certain human qualities to the brain or networks of nerve cells; earlier this century similar qualities were assigned to other species or onto machines. These are all versions of the homunculus fallacy. And yet, the brain does not learn (Coulter and Sharrock, 2007). Synapses do not learn. It is even arguable whether animals learn. Human beings learn, at least in the way educators have been using the term for a long time, and that has relevance for most of people in their lives. At the very least, learning is a property of organisms and the worlds in which they reside. We consider learning a human activity, most often an interhuman activity, neither a brain activity nor a behavioral activity, though it involves both. It is properly described in people language, not molecular or organism language (Harre, 2005). One can metaphorically extend it to molecular language, using it to help understand neurological processes, just as was done with animals in the nineteenth century or computers in the twentieth, but one must never forget that these are metaphors. Learning requires consciousness and typically more than one. Even the mechanical-associationist version of learning, which was conceived by Locke as habit-formation, required consciousness.

In the 1870s and 1880s, comparative psychologists modified the meaning of learning so as to make the case for continuity of mind with other species. This meant leaving consciousness out. This was a useful methodological tool at the time, except that as it was imported into psychology to describe human activity, the original sense was marginalized, especially as translated into education, even given that it was fairly obvious that the most important forms of human learning required consciousness. The exclusion of consciousness was based in a methodological principle. It was in no way a result of a consensus that this better described what was actually taking place when human learning was occurring. It was easy to forget this as behaviorists focused on rats and cats in the artificial conditions of the laboratory. They transformed learning from a process involving persons to a process involving organisms and changed the type of language appropriate to talk about it. Interestingly, the same is happening today as learning is being transformed into a molecular activity, using the language of neurons and synapses exclusively. Too often, psychologists simply borrow from the scientific and technological metaphors that are in vogue and abstract the process from the rest of experience.

1. INSIDE AND OUTSIDE: LEARNING IN SCHOOLS

Learning in psychology was a solution to a methodological problem. How does one study consciousness if it is not observable? How does one study an "inside" if one only has access to an "outside"? The solution involved a specific interpretation as to the relationship between inside and outside, as to what precisely constitutes behavior as distinct from mind, all the while conceiving this distinction as self-evident. Often psychologists locate the inspiration for this approach to learning in the work of Russian physiologist, Ivan Petrovich Pavlov. Next to Darwin and Einstein, he is perhaps one of the most famous and respected scientists of all time. He has become a hero of psychology, demonstrating the power of experiment to generate general laws of behavior. Pavlov earned his reputation studying digestion. Influenced by Claude Bernard, he viewed organisms as purposeful, complex, biological machines governed by deterministic relations (Todes, 2001, p. 218). In the 1890s, he was working in the Russian physio-medical research tradition established by Ivan Sechenov in the 1860s. Sechenov had insisted on the importance of experimental research and that all explanations are grounded in the activities of the nervous system. Sechenov also used the principles of the sensorimotor reflex as the basic model for all behavior and analyzed all reflexes in terms of their biological functions or purpose (Yaroshevski, 1968, p. 89). Pavlov accepted all of this.

Pavlov won the Nobel Prize for his work in digestion, which gave him the prestige and financial resources to study conditioning after 1900. His original focus was on gastric stimulation as it was easily measured and the juices secreted were valuable as they were used for certain treatments in Russia (Boakes, 1984). Throughout the 1890s, it was well known amongst Pavlov and the students in his laboratory that the dogs salivated in the company of anyone who had food, but no one thought to study it directly. Two of Pavlov's students first sought to measure this salivary response in relation to what they called "natural" and "artificial" stimuli (Boakes, 1984, pp. 120–121). After Pavlov became involved, he and his students disagreed about the subjective states experienced by the dogs, and as a result, Pavlov decided to reject all subjectivist explanations (Todes, 2001, p. 224). He initially supposed that secretion was directly a result of information from the senses and part of a physiological reflex. Deciding against this interpretation, he began to describe it as a "psychic" reflex, which he only later termed a "conditional" reflex—poorly translated as a "conditioned" reflex (Todes,

2001, p. 228), giving the response a permanence that it obviously didn't have. He began to publicly discuss his findings in 1903, but was not well known in the West until after 1909. For Pavlov, this work was always a means to better understand neurological processes, not an end unto itself.

Pavlov's "discovery" of conditioning was not revolutionary—others working in physiological research at the time were well aware of it. Pavlov's contribution was figuring out the conditions that made conditioning hold. He was interested in the process by which neutral stimuli became "signals" for those that naturally elicited a response and the ways in which those signals were inscribed into the central nervous system, viewing it as a kind of physiological warning system (Anokhin, 1968, p. 141). Also, in sharp contrast to an Anglo-American tradition focused on learning new behaviors, he was interested in the "extinction" of conditional associations. His focus was always much more on the neural activity involved than on managing responses as would be the case with the American tradition. As his work became better known in the United States, he warned that the scientific component of the work was the ability to ground conditioning in the nervous system and not the method of conditioning itself, but to no avail; by this point he had become a hero to U.S. psychologists looking for objective, experimental, laboratory-based methods, especially as popularized by Watson. Pavlov's great contribution was not so much the idea of acquired conditioning itself, but a language that could describe it and be translated into laboratory activities. The term "conditioned" reflex implied both the passivity of the organism in relation to the stimulus and that the process mirrors the kind of sensorimotor reflexes one finds in the nervous system. Pavlov refused to tolerate any subjectivist terms or those terms that implied that the organism was active. In the end though, Pavlov's lasting contribution was his own personality—austere, meticulous, modest, though ambitious—a classic scientific personality which psychology could claim for its own.

Although Pavlov was one of the first to study acquired conditioning in his laboratory, the idea that various temporal events can become associated and modify behavior was well known in the nineteenth century, and the genesis of these ideas goes much further back. For instance, Aristotle noted the way ideas could become associated with each other, but this was not a conception of learning that had much impact on the Greek education. A new conception of learning emerged in the seventeenth century that did impact education, this time revolving around the notion of habit. Again, the importance of habits was well known in the Greco-Roman World. Aristotle, for instance, recognized them as a product of repeated voluntary performance, but Franciscan William of Ockham developed a new sense of the term in the fourteenth century. Ockham denied the reality of universals. They were simply representations of mind as all that existed were individuals. Ockham was also a defender of theological voluntarism as opposed to intellectualism, meaning the essence of God was will and not thought. He used the Latin term *habitus* to describe an acquired disposition toward specific objects resulting from repeated acts of will. Like Aristotle, he rejected the Platonic notion that habits were already formed at birth (Robinson, 1995, p. 110). Thus, habits were acquired as a result of experience. The same was true of moral habits and behavior in general as passions, the source of behavior, became linked with specific habits. All habits were directed toward specific objects, thus could not be innate, as one required experience to develop those links. Habits were strengthened by repetition. Because they were products of will, they could be moral or immoral. Over time, the mind could relate habitually to similar objects, thus creating general categories. This eventually became the foundation for a new epistemology and theory of education in the seventeenth century.

With the rise of the mechanical paradigm, the new experimental sciences, and the crisis of authority following the Reformation, an empiricist conception of knowledge arose to support the new authority given to experience. Two conceptually distinct but integrated variants of learning developed, both based in the new atomic theory—the first applied to mind and the second to bodies. The first began with the Cartesian premise that the mind contained ideas and Locke's suggestion that these ideas can be combined together and, though in a slightly different context—he actually identified the ways custom can distort knowledge—his idea of mental connections or "associations," a metaphorical extension of fraternities between people who were drawn to each other. The second variant was directly related to the atomic theory of the Epicureans and the long accepted relationship between habits and the power of pleasure and pain. In Hobbesian materialism, all life was composed of colliding bodies, drawn together and apart by attraction and repulsion. For humans, this was translated into the subjective experiences of pleasure and pain. Locke too recognized a role for pleasure and pain in the shaping of habits. These related but conceptually distinct theories of knowledge and behavior—technically, one belonging to epistemology and the other to moral philosophy—were united in the work of David Hartley.

Hartley applied the idea of association to all elements of experience and action. Following the work of moralists who used associations of pleasure and pain to explain the origins of a moral sense, Hartley developed a general psychology of thought and behavior. In his *Observations on Man* of 1749, Hartley offered a material basis for an associationist psychology grounded in the science of his time. Objects in the world released vibrations that caused sensations. These vibrations travelled along sensory nerves to the brain and travelled back to the body through motor nerves. Some were experienced as pleasure and some pain. Previously, Descartes had introduced the notion of a reflex to explain the physiology of involuntary motion. Animal spirits, Descartes had argued, travel through nerves and are "reflected" within the brain and eventually deflected by the pineal gland into nerve channels to produce motion. Hartley extended this to all motion including voluntary activity (Boakes, 1984). For him, voluntary behavior began from the kind of reflexive behavior described by Descartes which, when repeated enough, generated a will. Hartley argued that "learned" habits have the same basis in physiology as inborn reflexes, a notion that would have to wait for Pavlov to "discover" one hundred and fifty years later (Boakes, 1984, p. 94). One individual who saw the implications of these ideas for a theory of evolution was Charles Darwin's grandfather, Erasmus Darwin. It suggested to him continuity between animal and human minds. Due to the dominance of sensationalism, Hartley was more interested in the physiological aspects of sensation as opposed to those of motion.

This bias was corrected by the revolution in physiological thought in the period from 1820 to 1850 following the influence of Johannes Müeller as traditional sensation-based associationism struggled to integrate these new findings. This involved a reconceptualization of the idea of stimulation. The term "stimulation" comes from the Latin meaning to goad or incite to action. The term was used in eighteenth-century vitalist biology in order to overcome the Cartesian split between mind and body by uniting human will and mechanical action (Danziger 1997, pp. 54–57). In other words, because stimulation did not require the transmission of external force, as Newtonian matter did, it allowed for talk of intelligent yet involuntary and nonmechanical causes. Thus, the uniqueness of humans could be preserved while studying physiological processes that seemed automatic. The notion of "internal" stimulation was central to the new physiology. It eventually allowed for the extension of physiological concepts to psychology as internal stimulation characterized the causal power of mental activity. Behaviorism later transformed the notion of stimulation into a "pattern of energy" received by the senses that evoked behavior. One finds similar patterns in the case of terms like "organism" and "energy," categories that bridged human and animal life, and in the case of the latter, the living and nonliving, allowing the extension of Newtonian physics into the study of life (Danziger, 1997, p. 53).

Emerging from these new syntheses was the idea of a linear and direct path from environment to sensory organs, sensory nerves, brain, motor nerves, muscles, and behavior. This became the basis for the "reflex arc" which came to dominate psychological thinking for well over a century. The key thing about the reflex was that its parts were decomposable, not part of a broader whole as had been the case in vitalist biology. It also did not require "higher" forms of intelligence. The term was first introduced by British physiologist Marshall Hall in 1832 and specifically referred to a unit of neural function. While it had blurred the distinction between body and mind in its eighteenth-century usages, by the early nineteenth century, the reflex was regarded as a purely physiological mechanism. This was the sense that

Hall used the term. It was gradually broadened one again in the 1840s and 1850s to describe psychological units as well (Yaroshevski, 1968). The first explicit use of the reflex in this broader sense was by British physiologist William Benjamin Carpenter in the 1840s who first coined the term "ideomotor" reflex as a way to integrate the physical and psychological and whose popular textbook influenced Herbert Spencer and a generation of British thinkers. The expansion of the reflex concept was not on evolutionary terms, as it would be after 1860, but based in the idea of a Great Chain of Being (Young, 1983, p. 62).

These ideas also made their way into Russia during this period. Influenced by the German physiological tradition, the Russian medical researcher Ivan Sechenov laid out, in his *Reflexes of the Brain* of 1863, an entire psychology based in the physiology of the reflex. His crucial contribution was that reflexes can be both excitatory and inhibitory and the brain was organized along both of these types of reflexive paths. For example, in thought, the motor component of the reflex was simply inhibited. Sechenov consistently rejected any notion of the kind of "spontaneous" activity that was found in the work of Müeller and argued that all events in the nervous system have an immediate cause outside the nervous system. He turned all neurological and psychological activity into passive responses to stimulation. This was the tradition, as we noted that Pavlov would later find success in.

By the middle of the nineteenth century Victorian readers of Spencer began to see that reflexes were part of a broader worldview. For Spencer, use-inheritance or learning, simply a more complex form of the reflex, guaranteed the inevitability of progress in evolution. Learning, now seen as the source of adaptation, was essential to the progress of the species as it was passed on to future generations. It also explained the development of morality (R. J. Richards, 1987, p. 246). In a general sense, this relationship between learning and progress was fundamental to Anglo-American psychology, even after it was widely accepted that natural selection, not use-inheritance, was responsible for evolutionary change. It remained a background assumption in all U.S. behaviorisms that tended to take the importance of "learning" in biology for granted. Adaptationism provided psychologists with a biological framework with which to ground psychological research, one that was to be taken up by William James and other early members of the functionalist school. But as psychology became more interested in studying "learning," especially as it pertained to education, references to biology were dropped with the exception that the basic framework remained the reflex. For evolutionists, the distinction between an instinctual and a learned behavior was never very clear, but gradually, psychologists began to see behavior as emanating from two distinct sources: instinctual and environmental and more often than not, ignored the instinctual in their research, especially after 1900. After all, how could one generalize the principles of learning from the study of white rats if they possessed species-specific instincts? This was especially odd given the general embrace of evolutionary theory among psychologists and the importance of "variation" in Darwinism. There had to be variation in a population for selection to operate.

But, human variation, particularly when related to learning mechanisms as opposed to learning capacities, could call into question the validity of studying "general" laws of behavior divorced from specific species or settings. If variation was studied, it tended to be the focus of applied rather than experimental research. Again, the framework for understanding learning in the critical years from 1880 to 1910 tended to see it as related to but not necessarily the opposite of instinctual behavior as we might see it today. This began to change after 1910 when U.S. comparative psychologists, who had first focused on the way instincts could be modified by learning, turned exclusively to the study of learning and began to downplay specific questions of inheritance. Their study of animal behavior without reference to consciousness gradually moved them to argue that all psychology needed to be the study of objective behavior, meaning without reference to consciousness. As we noted previously, this does not necessarily follow. Wundt and his students at Leipzig also believed they were developing methods to study consciousness objectively. But in the United States, for the most part, it was gradually accepted that a focus on consciousness made objectivity impossible. Some of this was a function of U.S. psychology's applied nature from the start, meaning that the study of behavior was more likely to yield findings that could be useful in settings outside the laboratory. Many of this generation who trained in comparative psychology turned after 1910 to the study of education (O'Donnell, 1985). Edward Thorndike and John Watson are two of the most influential examples.

After 1910, both Watson and Thorndike hardened their opposition to the use of mentalist language in psychology. Watson especially was influenced by the mechanist physiology of Jacques Loeb—who insisted that all activity on the part of the organism was a consequence of external or internal stimulation. Watson (1913) sought to reform psychology by rejecting all talk of consciousness and creating a science of prediction and control. Watson's model of behavior, an extension of the concept of the reflex, one that initially acknowledged both inherited and acquired responses, now focused exclusively on acquired responses to external stimulation (Boakes, 1984). All of this was framed in broad but vague evolutionary terms, as examples of "adjustment" by organisms to their environment—as opposed to, for example, "transformation" of the environment by organisms, which would have been far too active. By taking the kinds of movements that physiologists had identified and demonstrating the ways they were established by isolating stimuli and observing stimulus-response (S-R) connections, this early generation of behaviorists developed the sense that they could eventually control behavior regardless of context or species involved. A psychology that could predict and control behavior, particularly learning, was not surprisingly, very attractive to school reformers in this period, particularly those progressives who dreamed of remaking human society by reforming education (Danziger, 1990; Ward, 2002, p. 79). Mind was transformed into an extensive series of connections between stimuli and response, connections that could be measured and quantified by various tests of performance and altered through the remaking of the environment.

Thorndike combined trial-and-error learning—what he termed "selecting and connecting"—with Galtonian measures of variation to develop an extensive testing operation in schools. He rose to prominence with the publication of his dissertation *Animal Intelligence* in 1898 where he applied the quantitative techniques of the Galtonians to the study of animal behavior and inspired the rise of comparative psychology in the United States. Thorndike grew up in a strict Methodist household and, like many in the first and second generation of psychologists, seemed to import the sober religion of their childhood into science, eschewing the decadence of philosophy and its lack of methodological rigor (Boakes, 1984). Thorndike's early research studied movement in response to various stimuli—light, gravity, and temperature—which he could control in the laboratory. He used a learning curve—a graphic representation of changes in retention of behavior over time—to measure learning as well as compare learning across species (Boakes, 1984, pp. 70–71). He "found" that learning progressed gradually and there was no "insight" or thinking (Thorndike, 1898, p. 45). The simplicity of the graph allowed researchers to compare learning across different contexts, without regard for the specifics of the organism or context involved. He focused on trial-and-error learning as he studied cats attempting to escape from his puzzle box. Although his results were only moderately successful, psychologists looking for nonintrospective methods quickly adopted the basic paradigm.

Thorndike used the term association interchangeably with "connection" or "bond." These connections, Thorndike argued, had a neurological foundation. He later described a child's development, presumably augmented by schooling, as a passage from practical, general, and limited associations to more abstract, complex, and specialized ones, perhaps confusing a temporal and logical sequence. In *Animal Intelligence*, Thorndike's notion of an "impulse to action" had mentalist undertones—he had not yet completely excluded consciousness from psychology (Joncich, 1968, p. 140). The associations were formed, borrowing from Alexander Bain and C. Lloyd Morgan, through trial-and-error learning. The key was that the organism's initial responses were spontaneous, thus not requiring mind. They became habitual as a result of satisfying consequences. Thus neither ideas nor imitation were involved in learning. Thorndike described this type of learning as establishing a connection between an idea, the perception of a situation, and a motor impulse, a connection that had become stamped into the organism's nervous system. This meant that knowledge of the consequences of behavior or intelligence was not required for learning. Thorndike argued that these connections reflected changes in the conductivity of various synapses and that the brain itself was a huge network of these connections that competed for survival, a position not so far from the position of contemporary neuroscientists. The further use of these stimulus-response connections strengthened them, what Thorndike termed the "law of practice," an idea that became much more popular than Thorndike's "law of effect" or his hedonistic principle that responses followed by "satisfying" states tended to be strengthened through a nervous system response. He was criticized for talking of "satisfaction" as it was too subjective. By 1910, Thorndike had moved completely away from animal research and exclusively focused on the application of trial-and-error learning to education.

Watson too began his career in psychology studying animals, specifically the behavior of rats. Watson's dissertation focused on testing learning at various stages of the myelination of nerve fibers, which he found did not increase learning, by measuring performance on various mazes (Boakes, 1984, p. 145). In 1907, Watson joined Robert Yerkes research on primate behavior framed in more traditional terms, as the study of primate subjectivity. Watson gradually became more scornful of this tradition as he believed it relied on too much subjective data. All this culminated in Watson's infamous lectures at Columbia published as "Psychology as the Behaviorist Views It" in 1913 where he called for a psychology that focused exclusively on behavior using the methods of comparative psychology. In contrast to Thorndike, Watson turned to study "classical" associations of the Pavlovian variety and even attempted to turn psychoanalysis into a study of conditioned associations. He tried to create "neuroses" in dogs through conditioning which earned the ire of his psychiatric collaborator, Adolph Myers, for minimizing the condition. After this he turned to the study of infants and began to place more and more importance on the role of education. His infamous study with Little Albert—oft repeated as an example of successful research—was hardly a success. Contrary to the received version, Albert did not end up with any "rat-phobia." In fact when he returned for a follow-up, the rat only upset Albert when Watson placed it directly on his chest (Boakes, 1984, p. 223). Within a few years Watson was forced to leave John Hopkins and entered the most successful phase of his career. His most influential publication, *The Psychological Care of Infant and Child* published in 1928 turned him into one of the leading childcare experts of his day. There he warned of the dangers of too much mother love and reassuringly told Americans that their offspring's path in life was not determined by innate instincts but could be molded by good parenting and education. Neither Watson nor Thorndike denied the importance of human instincts, only rejected that they could not be modified.

One of the consequences of the introduction of the reflex paradigm into education was that it offered schools a way to identify whether learning was occurring or not, key in an age when schools were responding to the challenges of mass immigration, urbanization, and industrialization. Thorndike's science of education offered a new class of administrators "data" which they could use in the transformation of education. James Cattell, the leading popularizer of psychology of the time and one of Thorndike's mentors, had argued that psychology could never attain the status of physical science if it could not rest on a foundation of experiment and measurement and was the first in the United States to develop mental testing. Cattell brought Thorndike to Teacher's College in New York City. Thorndike accepted Cattell's call and from 1905 until 1949 stood as the architect and dean of a psychology of education grounded in experiment and measurement. All that exists, exists in some amount, he famously argued (Thorndike, 1918, p. 16).

When Thorndike came to Teacher's College, teacher training was in the middle of a revolution. In 1906, less than 20 percent of teachers received any special training for teaching, much of which came from "normal schools," a subpar alternative to the high school (Thorndike, 1918, pp. 160–161). Teaching itself was often a temporary career for high school graduates lasting until they moved into another profession. Selecting teachers involved looking for those with "natural" teaching abilities. All this changed under Thorndike, as Teacher's College became a leading example of a new type of teacher education, one that required extensive training in methods and original research. By 1914, Teacher's College was the fourth largest graduate program in the country in any field and emulated by many schools of education across the country. From the beginning Thorndike was fairly critical of the dominant approach to the study of children, the child-study movement founded by G. Stanley Hall, and especially its dependence on a "questionnaire" method. Hall (1893) had interviewed children about what they knew and used the results to make generalizations about normative development. These studies were designed to be useful to teachers as well as parents. In contrast, Thorndike's research was aimed toward administrators and focused more on aggregate data. His early publications in education still took the form of child-study but criticized it for taking its results at face value (Thorndike, 1901, pp. 13–20). Psychology in education matters, Thorndike argued in his first version of *Educational Psychology* (1903), as it focused on key topics for educators: instinct, habit, memory, and reasoning. Here, Thorndike began to articulate his program for educational research: "We conquer the facts of nature when we observe and experiment on them. . . . When we measure we make them our servants" (164). Thorndike gradually turned to the study of Galtonian statistics as a way to design research framed in measurement.

One of Thorndike's first education-related studies established his long-standing opposition to the classical curriculum, in this case the study of Latin, as he found that, against the arguments of faculty psychology, the skills acquired during Latin education did not transfer to other contexts (Thorndike, 1900, cited in Joncich, 1968, p. 272). His study undermined the premise that a classical education "sharpened the mind." Mind, he argued, was not a general reasoning organ, nor a muscle that needed to be sharpened, but a multiplicity of specific associations and responses grounded in particular neural associations. His approach was soon described dismissively as the "dogma of specific training" because it rationalized the notion of subject-based and skill-based testing in education (Joncich, 1968, p. 275). Thorndike rejected the traditional mind of faculty psychology with "mystical" properties like attention or memory. For him, there were only associations; although ironically, he continued to use much of the language of faculty psychology, as did many behaviorists, until Skinner vanquished all mentalist talk. Thorndike studied spelling in a similar manner, creating his own spelling tests and introducing the test-retest method and some limited control of extraneous variables into educational research as a means of drawing causal inferences, techniques which became central to twentieth-century educational research. His magnum opus, the three volumes, *Educational Psychology*, published in 1913–1914, came to dominate the field for over half a century. William McDougall, critic of the dominance of environmentalism in education, wrote in the 1920s scornfully about the psychology they teach in New York and pointed out that there were "two schools of psychology, one that is Thorndike and one that isn't" and that his theory was a "theory of morons, by morons, and for morons" (cited in Hergenhahn, 2005, p. 74)— an overstatement perhaps, but it suggests the influence of Thorndike's connectionism during these years.

The other important argument Thorndike made was the importance of studying individual variation. This reflected his time in schools, as opposed to laboratories. For progressives, the hierarchical ordering of students resulting from testing often reinforced hereditarian theories of aptitude. We cannot know what a species is capable of, argued Thorndike, unless we study individual differences in responses or intelligence (Thorndike, 1911). Thus creating tools for the study of variation among children—tests, measures, scales, etc.—became a technical problem for educational research. General statements about students were false. There were only individuals and variation among individuals that could be tracked by measures of deviation and central tendency. Learning began with a state of "readiness," which when measured, revealed the state of an individual learner's mental maturation. The goal was to be able to use these measurements to make predictions about what students were capable of. General "laws of teaching" also needed to be applied with particular persons in mind. It is not "what teachers give but what students get that counts" said Thorndike, his version of what we might term today "learning styles" or "differential teaching" (Joncich, 1968, p. 325). Thorndike argued that teaching required a focus on those "bonds" a teacher sought to create (1922, p. 101). Thus, the job of the teacher was to create desirable bonds and break undesirable ones using the principles of habit formation. This process was different for different learners. All this attention to variation, which was common in applied settings, sat in tension with the behaviorist quest for universal laws of learning, which was common in laboratory settings, a reflection of the fact that, by the second decade of the twentieth century, the psychology of learning had become at least two distinct fields with fundamentally different assumptions.

In 1901, Thorndike had first offered to record student scores on various tests including muscle control, perception, association, memory, practice, and judgment so that educators could use the results to make their teaching more effective and administrators could use the results to reorganize schools effectively (Joncich, 1968, p. 286). Thorndike's goal, like many progressives during these years, was to turn educational reform from a political issue to a scientific one. This required the professionalization of school administrators, who had long been political appointees, as well as teachers. As Thorndike continued to develop subject-specific tests—his most successful were those in arithmetic, handwriting, and reading—they became sources of the development and centralization of curriculum (Joncich, 1968, p. 394). Curricula were literally developed to "teach the test." Thorndike moved away from the popular Binet-inspired tests that measured general intellectual capacities and developed differentiated ones. However, he did follow Binet in moving away from ordinal scales, which had low reliability, especially between mental and motor tests, and toward interval and ratio scales, all the better to perform statistics on. By 1923, half of all Teacher's College publications were tests and scales. Thorndike published many of these scales, framed as "in-service" training for teachers, and they were often relied on by teachers to plan lessons, especially by those without much training in the new scientific education. Even great teachers need psychologists, Thorndike insisted, not to be wasteful (Joncich, 1968, pp. 403–404).

Thorndike's views on the importance of variation led him to support eugenics until 1939. Unlike traditional societies, Thorndike argued, industrial societies required the means to differentiate between individual capacities and control them. After 1910, Thorndike began to argue that heredity was a prime determinant of intelligence and took up the study of twins first pioneered by Galton to support this case. He believed brighter children benefited more from training and practice than those who were not and even suggested that the children of the rich tended to be the innately brighter ones. What inherited differences do, argued Thorndike, was effect the capacity to make connections. Some critics of progressivism in education, like H. L. Mencken, saw this as a useful corrective to the idea that schools can "make intellectuals of peasants" (cited in Jonich, 1968, p. 320). Thorndike accepted the importance of instincts but insisted that because "unmodified" instincts have no notion of ends attached to them, experience can provide those ends, helping to select among available responses. His well-known "law of exercise"—essentially that the repetition of a situation-response bond strengthened it, an idea that sat well in an educational context that still valued repetition—was intended to play down the mechanical implications of his associationism. It gave humans the power to shape those associations. Less popular, particularly among behaviorists, was his law of effect, his version of the Hobbesian hedonistic principle that learning can be modified by satisfaction and dissatisfaction. Thus educators could manage learning through the "selection" of connections using repetition and satisfaction. By the time Thorndike died in 1949, his system of testing had supported the standardization of education for nearly half a century and promoted the belief that learning could be studied and measured, helping to bring order to a system dominated by political, regional, and economic conflicts.

That being said, Thorndike's influence and power put into practice and institutionalized some assumptions about education that have long gone unchallenged. First was the acceptance by educators of subject-specific assessment, now a technical problem rather than a philosophical one. Second was the idea that education could be improved through experimental/measurement-based assessment and research whose results allowed politicians, administrators, and the like to track the successes and failures of participants across the school system. In both cases, this meant education would be measured in outcomes or in performance. After all, in the current era of the common core curriculum, most educational research still studies reflexes: how does intervention X (stimulus) influence test scores (response)? Finally, Thorndike's message about individual variation has always posed a problem for public education. How to provide the same education to students who are different from each other? As Paul Chapman (1988) notes, Thorndike, along with Lewis Terman, Robert Yerkes, and Henry Herbert Goddard working with the NEA, public school administrators, educational publishers, and philanthropic foundations were central to the transformation of public education in a mechanism for "sorting" students. By the 1920s, terms like "ability grouping" and "tracking" were part of the everyday vocabulary of education (Chapman, 1988, p. 2). Faith in "scientific" assessments ran deep among the American public and was even advocated by Horace Mann in the 1840s. The first mental tests were developed by James McKeen Cattell. They tended to focus on simple sensory-motor tasks until Terman reworked Binet's tests at Stanford. With developing standards to deal with what Spearman had termed "errors of observation" or reliability, and a bit later, "trustworthiness" or validity, faith in the scientific value of testing grew (Rogers, 1995). For educational reformers, standardized assessments were viewed as the only way to remove the "subjective" element from evaluation, but also create standardized instructional materials (Giordano, 2005). Especially after World War I and the use of testing by the army, the small testing movement grew rapidly as politicians and the public demanded that schools be held "accountable," which essentially meant improvements in what was now termed "student achievement." While many are familiar with the role of IQ tests in this history, the subject-specific tests, which today make up statewide, standardized assessments, have managed to retain their place in schools in a way that IQ tests have not. It was Rousseau who first insisted that education required an understanding of children's nature, thus grounding curriculum in the study of psychology. But it was Thorndike who helped to institutionalize it. This new view asserted that designing schools and curriculum required an understanding of the psychology of learning and teaching as well as the sciences of assessment and psychometrics. Yet, there have always been other models of educational assessment and research. One that developed contemporaneously was John Dewey's "child-centered" one.

Dewey's work in education followed a different path than Thorndike's. For one, it was much briefer. About the only thing they agreed on was their distaste for the work of G. Stanley Hall (Langemann, 2000, p. 57). Dewey came to the University of Chicago in the 1890s and established an experimental school whose population was composed mostly of the children of other university faculty and staff. Dewey intended the school to function as a laboratory for educational research, and most of his ideas on education were developed during the years he was involved with the school from 1896 to 1904. There, he developed his notions of a child-centered education, which he described in *The School and Society.* Dewey's conception of education, one that was radically different than the associationist one taken up by Thorndike, required a conception of educational research that moved beyond assessment and measurement. He refused to view educational researchers as the middlemen between psychology and teachers as Thorndike did (Langemann, 2001, p. 50).

Because the school, for Dewey, was a totality of social relationships as well as a part of a larger community, one could not simply abstract something out of those relationships, say a score or measure, in any meaningful way. Therefore, unlike the case with Thorndike's work, the study of education had to take place in schools and remain within schools if it wanted to say anything intelligible. Furthermore, because Dewey's notions of education were more focused on the processes of learning as opposed to the products, a key tenet of his child-centered education, the success of the school or curriculum was more adequately reflected in the level in which it engaged children rather than how it affected any abstract notion of achievement. The goals of such a science were such that the organization of schools could be conducted in ways that increased intelligent control and understanding. Dewey was quite explicit about his distaste for some of the other paradigms in educational research he witnessed, especially when they used the vocabularies of science to establish their own legitimacy.

> There is a strong tendency to identify teaching ability with the use of procedures that yield immediately successful results, success can be measured by such things as order in the classroom, correct recitations by pupils in assigned lessons, passing of examinations, promotion of pupils to a higher grade. . . . Prospective teachers come to training schools . . . with such ideas implicit in their minds. They want very largely to find out how to do things with the maximum prospect of success. Put baldly they want recipes. Now to such persons science is of value because it puts a final approval upon this and that specific procedure. . . . It is prized for its prestige of value rather than as an organ of personal illumination and liberation. It is prized because it is thought to give unquestionable authenticity and authority to a specific procedure to be carried out in the schoolroom. So conceived, science is antagonistic to education as an art. (Dewey, 1929, pp. 15–16).

Dewey's scientific education was not intended primarily to train teachers or improve school methods, but to create new standards and ideals leading to social change (Langemann, 2001, p. 48). For him, the school was to educational research as laboratory was to scientist. Because student work was imbedded in nested sets of social and technical relationships, it made no sense to talk about a particular student's level of achievement, and thus, research that compared the results of one student against others made little sense. For Dewey the application of statistics of education was a problem because it did not allow for gradual independent growth of theories. New ideas around education, learning, and curriculum were supposed to be tried out in Dewey's school without the pressure of promising immediate improvements in student achievement. The job of school was simply to direct attention. If there was assessment, it had to be organic to what was already occurring in the school. For Dewey, however, schools were far more important than simply sites of education, but they were sites for the preservation of democracy. Dewey firmly believed that his kind of education would help heal some of the class and interethnic strife that was becoming more and more apparent in American life. But for the most part, U.S. public education in the twentieth century belonged to Thorndike, not Dewey.

2. INSIDE AND OUTSIDE: INSTINCTS

Given the conceptual dependence of notions of "outside" on those of "inside," of notions of the external "environment" on that which is interior to the organism, as a new conception of learning developed in psychology so too did notions of its opposite, that which was innate. In the twentieth century this was framed as a dichotomy between nature and nurture, but starting with Plato, the question of whether important qualities emanate from within or without has been fairly central to Western intellectual traditions. For most of the second half of the twentieth century, especially in United States, there was a shift toward nurture-based explanations. Yet, in the last few decades, this seems to have shifted once again, and nature-based explanations have returned to academic and popular discourse. What was once a conservative position associated with racism and eugenics is now a liberating one that ensures individuals are not held unduly responsible for certain behaviors or traits that are beyond their control. What was once a position that reflected despair and the impossibility of change is now an opportunity for medicine and pharmacology to perfect human nature. Sometimes there is an acknowledgement of the complexity of all this with claims like it's "both" or an "interaction," but this so-called compromise obfuscates more than its reveals. What does it mean that the source of trait X is nature? What does it mean that the source of behavior Y is nurture? What does it mean that they interact with each other? From a physicalist vantage point one might ask What are the precise mechanisms by which some endogenous or exogenous structure or force is translated into a specific behavior, mental process, or characteristic? Often this kind of specificity is lacking with the exception of a vague sense that it has something to do with genes and temperament or the environment and family.

Conceptually, the term "nature" in this sense and those semantically linked to it as they are used are fairly ambiguous. They can be used as synonyms for innate, early appearing, genetic, inherited, biological, inevitable, not a person's fault, moral, not learned, not constructed, or impervious to environment—which are all assumed to mean the same thing. The same ambiguity applies to the term "nurture." It can be used as a synonym for the physical environment, family, parents, outside the body, culture, not inherited, unrelated to biology, is a person's fault, immoral, or amenable to change, and so on. Behaviorists were convinced that the "environment" could cause changes in behavior, but for all their talk of reflexes and connections, they had very little sense of the physiological mechanisms involved. How exactly does the external world impinge on or modify the internal one? Today's social constructionists often argue something similar. What does it mean to say that a behavior or trait is socially or culturally constructed? Does it mean culturally variant, non-natural, malleable, or created by culture? How can "culture" create a behavior or psychological process? Similarly, behavioral geneticists like to talk about the "heritability" of a behavior or characteristic but are typically unwilling or unable to distinguish between "innate," "inherited," and "genetically determined," all of which mean different things. They have very little to say about how a gene "tells" the body or brain how to function.

We can trace these categories back to Plato's question at the start of the Meno, maybe the most influential question in all Western thought: is knowledge acquired by teaching or by nature? But we must keep in mind that this question was a moral one just as much as an epistemological one. Interest in this question in the nineteenth century was tied to the case of the wild boy of Aveyron (Rose, 1985). Also key was the influence of Darwin's cousin, Francis Galton, as well as the nineteenth-century science of comparative psychology, which came to regard learning and instinct as distinct sources in the first place. The past century's framework of making sense of nature and nature views them as distinct forces in the development of an organism. Sometimes one is said to be dominant, sometimes they are said to interact with each other. There are not many contemporary scholars who do not acknowledge that both of them are involved in development, no matter in what trivial fashion. We describe this framework as "mechanistic" because each is regarded as an independent entity that adds up to create a developed organism. Each can be added or subtracted from the process so that the effects of each can be studied separately.

This is the intention of the idea of "heritability" borrowed from behavioral genetics. The function of calculating heritability is to parse the effects of genetics and the environment. So one might hear, for example, that 70 percent of a trait is due to genes while 30 percent is due to the environment. The problem is this statement is misleading. Heritability is a means for explaining variation in a population. It is calculated by breeding to change the percentage of a trait in a population. It actually says nothing about individuals. Heritability is not the same thing as inherited. A trait can have high heritability, yet be highly influenced by environmental conditions (Lerner, 2002). In fact, heritability is measured under a specific set of conditions. It has no meaning out of those conditions. Unfortunately, it is often used to make the case for the genetic basis of behavior. Thus what began as a description of variation in a population changes into an explanation of a trait, even though heritability is not a property of traits.

The basic problem with all of these conceptual frameworks is that they have little biological validity. Bodies simply do not operate in this way. As Richard Lerner (2002) explains, there is no organism unless nature and nurture are both 100 percent involved (p. 250–255). Nature actually does nothing directly. Neither does its principal agent, the gene. Its effects are always indirect. Proteins do the actual work of cell production, not DNA. There is no heredity without internal and external environments within which proteins are synthesized and bodies develop. It is correct that sometimes genes act more directly on behavior (i.e., in certain chromosomal abnormalities), but even here an environment is necessary for genes to operate within. In most cases, the same set of genes in different environments is involved with different characteristics or behavioral outcomes. Likewise, the same environment, with different genotypes, results in different characteristics or behavioral outcomes. Finally, the same characteristic or behavior can be the result of different genotypes, different phenotypes, or any combination thereof.

There is so much redundancy within human DNA the possibilities are, if not endless, very extensive. Similarly, the "environment" cannot do anything without a physiological body, and there is no physiology without proteins, and there are no proteins without genes. DNA determines the limits of what's possible. No matter how powerful culture is, if it is genetically or physiologically impossible for a certain body, it will not happen. Sometimes the effect of the environment is also quite direct, as in the case of injury. More often, the environment works through ongoing developmental processes. Moreover, organisms actively modify their environment. They are not passively shaped by it. Nor is it correct to conceive the environment independently of the organism, as the environment is meaningful only in relation to a specific organism. The same environment is very different dependent on one's relationship to it.

Since Greek and Medieval thought were dominated by variants of idealism and Locke's empiricist critique of idealism was not developed until the close of the seventeenth century, the balance for most of Western intellectual history clearly lay on the side of nature. For the Greeks and Medievals this was because the source of reason and action was the soul, implanted within humans by God. Typically, it was accepted that humans also had a will, which could be affected by external forces via the passions and desire, but this was regarded as a baser or less noble source of motivation. Ideally, human motivation came from within, as was the case with proper knowledge. However, there was some question as to the source of animal behavior. In Aristotle, all beings strove to express their purpose. This was true of both the animal and plant worlds. As animals had both nutritive and sensible souls, their nature involved the functions of nutrition and sensation. The function of sensation certainly opened up opportunities to be affected by the environment, yet their fundamental nature was still determined by an internal source.

Making sense of endogenous animal behavior involved the notion of an instinct, derived from the Latin term *instinguere* meaning "to impel" and was first used to describe animal perception in the 1400s. The Stoics had regarded "instincts" as a lower source of behavior as compared with reason and this hierarchy stuck. Descartes undermined Aristotelianism by turning animals into machines. They had no souls, but only operated along the same mechanistic principles identified by Galileo and the new atomic philosophy. The fact that they operated according to automatic principles meant that they required an immediate external stimulus. Mind, which did not require external stimulation, was limited to humans exclusively. This was—and this is key—a pivotal way to distinguish between inside and outside.

Animals had fixed bodies that could only respond to stimulation in particular ways, and this determined their behavior. Not everyone accepted Descartes's demotion of animals to the realm of extension exclusively, and there were vigorous debates about whether or not animals were indeed machines all in the context of a search for vitalist principles to explain life (Boakes, 1984, p. 85; R. J. Richards, 1987, p. 22). For instance, Hieronymus Rorarius criticized Descartes' thesis and described animals in very human terms, arguing they were sometimes smarter than humans (R. J. Richards, 1987). This anthropomorphic impulse turned up frequently in the study of animals and even made its way into the writing of Darwin. One way to explore this question was through the study of complex instinctual behavior. This reflected a new way to conceive animal nature without recourse to Aristotelian categories. These instincts were placed in animals by God and came to reflect the perfect adaptation of creatures to their environment. With the spread of sensationalism in the eighteenth century, humans and animals returned to more similar footing. Both acquired knowledge and behavior from the environment. As we have discussed extensively, this meant either, that "ideas" representing objects in the world entered the mind through sensation and linked with other ideas to become complex ones or more likely that habits were formed due to repetition and the pleasurable and painful feelings associated with certain behaviors. Perhaps animals had less complex ideas or habits than humans, but the differences were ones of degree rather than kind.

Those that actually studied animal behavior were not satisfied with this. It was clear that animals within a species engaged in similar types of behavior that could not be traced back to sensation. It was also clear that many of these behaviors emerged early in life. In the 1730s the philosopher and deist Hermann Reimarus established a novel German approach that rejected the Cartesian reduction of animals to machines and view of behavior as a product of fixed corporeal structures and immediate external stimulation (Wilm, 1925). But Reimarus also rejected the sensationalists' focus on learning exclusively through sensory experience, as it could not explain uniform behavior across a species. Instead, Reimarus argued that "representational drives" which affected the senses directed "intentional" drives to action that promised pleasure (R. J. Richards, 1987). The most important of these drives were "skill" drives or instincts, which helped to preserve animals and their progeny. These "instincts" explained the seemingly automatic nature of animal behavior but also revealed their purpose. These inborn natural impulses—Reimarus used the word *trieb* to describe them, which is better translated as "drive"—were accomplished perfectly without reflection or experience and typically served preservationist or reproductive ends. Some could be identified at birth, some were delayed, and many of them could be transformed through domestication and training.

From then on, students of animal behavior were forced to work within Reimarus's frame and explain animal behavior that is unlearned and uniform in a species, yet too intelligent to be described as mechanical. This would become a key problem in the generations following the spread of evolutionary ideas. In philosophy, Arthur Schopenhauer utilized the language of drives to explain the source of activity in animals, alongside perception, and Hartmann viewed them as products of cerebral mechanisms performed unconsciously, though not mechanistically. These ideas went on to influence Nietzsche and later Freud. As we discussed extensively, the post-Darwinian search for more primitive variants of mind helped the idea that reflexes and instincts were simpler forms of thought gain acceptance. Most recognized the resemblance between instincts and learned acts that had become habitual and did not sharply distinguish between them. Only after the spread of the notion that the path of hereditary transmission from gene to body was unidirectional in August Weismann in the 1880s did the idea develop that there were two distinct possible sources of instinct: use inheritance or natural selection, standing in for nurture and nature.

Early twentieth-century thinking in the United States was dominated by a contradictory mix of hereditarian and environmentalist explanations of difference, especially with the rise of the Progressive Movement. Progressives sought to ameliorate the harsh conditions that followed industrialization, mass immigration, and urbanization through social reform. They firmly accepted the power of the state, science, and other institutions to help modify human nature. One popular nature-based framework was that of British psychologist William McDougall, who was skeptical of progressive environmentalism and developed his own instinct theory. Many American behaviorists accepted the basic idea that humans had an instinctual nature; they only refused to accept that this nature could not be modified or that this nature was the primary drive behind behavior (Curti, 1980). This included William James, Edward Thorndike, and John Watson. McDougall was different. He regarded instincts as the exclusive drive behind behavior as he attempted to reintegrate notions of purpose into psychology (McCurdy, 1968, p. 111). He defined instincts as inherited dispositions to attend to certain objects and act and feel around them in a particular way in order to provide goals for action (Boakes, 1984, p. 207). Most importantly, he rejected that they could be modified by experience, though he did acknowledge that in advanced societies they could be combined in novel ways. In *An Introduction to Social Psychology* of 1908, McDougall identified seven primary instincts: flight, repulsion, curiosity, pugnacity, self-abasement, self-assertion, and parental—all connected to specific emotions, though the list changed over time. For many American psychologists, this language was simply too teleological

(Danziger, 1997, p. 118). For others, it smacked of superstition and a pre-Galilean cosmology (McCurdy, 1968, p. 123).

McDougall's influence did not survive the rejection of nativism in the United States in the 1930s. Instead the notion of instinct was replaced by Robert Woodworth's "drive"—a result of hypothetical energy released by nerve and muscle cells due to specific stimulation, though very different from the German term *trieb*, which it is often confused with. One key difference was that drives were not goal directed but only directed to specific ends through a stimulus-response mechanism, meaning they could be modified by identifying drive-triggering events for various actions (Binde, 1992, p. 342). Another difference was that drives acquired energy from the nervous system; there was no distinct source of instinctual energy. Drives became the "biological" foundation of Clark Hull's neo-behaviorism in the 1930s. U.S. psychology remained a mostly "nurture"-based one—even in its interpretation of Freud—until the migration of European psychologists and ethologists to the United States during and following the war years.

Two of the most notable defenders of the centrality of instinct in the post-War period in the United States were German ethologist Konrad Lorenz and his longtime collaborator Niko Tinbergen. Lorenz, like his mentor, curator of the Berlin zoo, Oskar Heinroth, regarded species-specific behaviors just like any other morphological structure. This extended to all sorts of functions and allowed for comparisons of instinctual behavior across species (Burkhardt, 2005). He recognized that instincts could change behavior directly, or indirectly, through learning. This was due to the distinction between instinctive activities with inherited nervous system pathways and intelligent behavior acquired over the course of life. Lorenz (1970) rejected mechanistic descriptions of animal behavior and refused to view animals as "reflex machines." He recognized the vagueness of the term "instinct" and preferred Heinroth's "species-specific drive categories." He identified several conditions for identifying instinctive behavior: (1) evident in animals raised in isolation, (2) performed by all individuals in a species, (3) in excess of intellectual capacity of a specific animal, (4) related to biological goals and, (5) part of pattern of behavior (R. J. Richards, 1987, p. 530). Lorenz criticized older theories of instinct, especially William McDougall's version, for confusing subjective goals with biological functions whose effect was to create an overarching and vague view of instinctual action. Lorenz also identified the degenerative effects of domestication, a perspective he later applied to human societies as well.

Niko Tinbergen preferred ornithologists to U.S. psychologists, studying animals in their natural environment—as opposed to Lorenz who studied them at his home—and using terms like "nervous impulses" rather than "drives" (Burkhardt, 2005). He allied himself with T. C. Schneirla at the Museum of Natural History in New York, which gradually drew him away intellectually from Lorenz. He moved away from the notion that instinctive behavior and learned behavior were easily distinguished from each other and moved toward a more developmental, multilevel, integrated perspective (Burkhardt, 2005, p. 365). Some of this shift was influenced by the extensive criticism of Lorenz unleashed by Daniel Lehrman. Lehrman argued that instinctive behavior was not a single process in the nervous system, but operated at multiple levels of organization, a perspective obscured by intellectual dependence on the stale innate vs. acquired dichotomy and neglect of development (ibid., p. 365). Talk of "instincts" tended to compare behaviors on the basis of superficial resemblances as opposed to noticing fundamental differences in organization (Gottlieb, 1979, p. 167). He was especially troubled by Lorenz's belief in the degenerative effects of civilization, his hydraulic metaphors, and Lorenz's "purposive" language for talking about instinctual behavior. Finally, he criticized Lorenz's method of deprivation—observing behaviors that developed if animals were deprived of certain experiences; part of Lorenz's strategy for identifying instincts—and argued it was useful only as it could identify what was not innate.

Lorenz, unthwarted, responded to the growing criticism with *On Aggression*, a pessimistic look at the human species' inability to inhibit their powerful aggressive instincts. While they could be curbed through education, argued Lorenz (1966), they still needed to be discharged somehow (p. 243–246). This was a fairly unpopular position in the 1960s. Still, notions of instincts in one form or another popped up in the work of John Bowlby, Margaret Mahler, Abraham Maslow, and others. They mostly remained a background assumption, especially when it came to human behavior until the rise of sociobiology in the 1970s. The rapid developments in genetics over the 1950s and 1960s as well as a reaction against the liberalism and egalitarianism of the social programs and movements of the 1960s and 1970s helped to precipitate a shift toward "nature"-based explanations in psychology. There were many variants of this, but for now our focus will be on evolutionary psychology. Explaining social relationships using biological principles was fairly widespread in the nineteenth and early twentieth century (Bannister, 1979). In the United States, the dominance of environmentalist and behaviorist explanations as well as a reaction against the kind of eugenics advocated by the Nazis tended to discredit biological explanations for much of the middle third of the twentieth century, but by the 1970s this began to change.

The new paradigm took shape with the publication of Harvard entomologist E. O. Wilson's *Sociobiology: The New Synthesis* in 1975 and Richard Dawkins's *The Selfish Gene* a year later. Following a huge controversy over the political implications of their work—making the conservative argument that much of human life involved fixed adaptations—sociobiology gradually morphed into evolutionary psychology and returned to become more influential than ever by the 1990s. There were subtle differences between them, but both presented themselves as direct products of Darwinian thought—not so much the careful Darwin of the *Origin* but the more ambitious and careless Darwin of the *Descent of Man*. The evolutionary psychology of writers like Dan Sperber, Leda Cosmides, John Tooby, and Steven Pinker, among others, argued that domain-specific human thought processes or specialized "modules" were inherited, successful adaptations of human ancestors (Tooby and Cosmides, 2000). It wisely focused on the adaptive value of thought and behavior back when human bodies were evolving in the first place rather than their adaptive value in present society, which is fairly irrelevant with respect to explaining the origins of certain characteristics or behaviors. Humans, they argued cleverly, have stone-age minds. Many pop-science writers in this tradition have had much fun pointing out the ways in which psychological and social problems are related to the mismatch between stone-age minds and contemporary environments. They also stopped talking about behaviors being passed on through genes as this was recognized as too simplistic an explanation and instead talk of natural selection shaping the mind.

Evolutionary psychologists tend to describe natural selection as an active force or a mechanism when it is neither. At best, it is a passive filter. In essence, one is describing very specific interactions between an organism and its local environment in each and every generation. Over time these interactions can have long-term biological consequences, but they are not part of a broader process except to the evolutionary biologist who frames it this way (Dover, 2000, p. 61). Dawkins often refers to the "improbable perfection" of natural selection, sounding a lot more like the Natural Theology tradition Darwin rejected than Darwin. It's easy to describe evolutionary adaptations as perfect, but only in hindsight. Evolutionary psychologists tend to view selection as the exclusive mechanism for evolutionary change, but there is no way to really know this. It is taken as an article of faith (Gould, 2000, p. 112). Given that one can only study selection in a few species with short life spans (e.g., fruit flies) or in a few highly controlled natural settings, many sources of evidence require extensive interpretation. Even Darwin himself accepted that natural selection was the primary but not exclusive mechanism for speciation. This requires that every trait and behavior be viewed through the light of selection and adaptation. Every element of the human species must be adaptive, the logic goes, and it is the job of the evolutionary biologist to figure out how.

When this gets extended to human behavior and institutions, as evolutionary psychologists do, there is ample room for what Stephen J. Gould has called "just-so" stories or "guesswork in the cocktail party mode" (Gould, 2000, p. 119). All one needs to do is come up with a clever adaptationist narrative and one has explained origins. Too often these stories turn out to be genetically, neurophysiologically, or ecologically groundless. They uncritically take up conventional categories like "promiscuity" or "step-parenting" and project them onto biological history (Ruse, 2000). They focus on the adaptation of traits that are meaningful to them, rather than adaptation itself, which requires an understanding of ecology, biology, and psychology (Malik, 2000). Needless to say, we have too little evidence from the "Stone Age" to know for certain how certain behaviors might or might not have been adaptive. Much of the environment and most social relations do not fossilize. None of these elements are static, even during the "Stone Age," which when discussed like this seems lifted out of time. Moreover, in these narratives, one finds covert and not so covert notions of purpose. Judeo-Christian morality is simply replaced with an adaptationist morality. This comes through in terms like gene "for" trait X or behavior Y. Genes do not have a purpose; they are not "for" anything (Oyama, 1985). By naturalizing mind and behavior, these values are said to be part of nature and not society. Thus, they are value-free. Whatever role natural selection has played in the formation of human brains and body, when it comes to human society today, the forces of culture vastly supersede it. In the end, culture and nature are not distinct categories. What is relevant is that the ways in which "culture" achieves its effects that are different than those of "nature." The effects of culture are far more infectious and rapid, for example, and can be felt across great distances. Cultural change does not require generations to take hold, nor does it have to work within the kind of constraints that biological change does. Nor is it necessarily adaptive. Nor should it be regarded as "outside" a biological "inside."

3. STRUCTURE AND FUNCTION: GESTALT AND HOLISM

One way to make explicit the unique fusion of psychology, learning, and education in the United States is to look at how differently this played out in another context. In this section we will focus on Germany, where, in this same period, psychology continued to focus on the introspection of consciousness, leading it in a radically different direction. In rapidly industrializing Germany during the late nineteenth century, the state provided support for the development of the natural sciences, and the ideal of research was fully integrated into higher education. All the while, during this period, the natural sciences were seen as subservient to philosophy, especially when it came to education (Schnädelbach, 1984). German intellectuals valued the *geisteswissenschaften* over the *naturwissenschaften*. Rather than being led toward an exclusive study of behavior, as was the case in the United States, in Germany a series of experimental findings by those associated with the Gestalt school in the period after 1910 undermined some of the basic foundations of psychology as they had been laid out over the course of the nineteenth century. This was interpreted as a part of a broader "crisis" in science that dominated European thought and culture until World War II and questioned the role that science and technology had come to play in modern societies.

For most of the nineteenth century, philosophy dominated the German university. This was true not only because of the respect it accorded and its place in a developing sense of German nationalism, but also because the Prussian government required that all candidates for the state teacher's exam attend lectures in philosophy as a means of character development (*bildung*) and introduction to the spirit of science and research (*wissenschaft*). By the latter part of the nineteenth century, philosophy included an "experimental" component in the form of a laboratory psychology grounded in the method of introspection. It also included a disdainful attitude toward politics and applied knowledge (Ringer, 1969). One finds these attitudes in most of the German founders of psychology, especially Wundt who, during the 1870s, sought to bring the new experimental methods to the bastion of "purist" philosophy, the University of Leipzig (Ash, 1995, p. 24).

Wundt viewed psychological science as superior to the natural sciences because it was based in *unmittlebare* [immediate experience] as opposed to *mittlebare* [mediated experience], that is, the experiences of consciousness as opposed to the abstractions of post-Galilean science. The experimental methods turned psychology into an exact science, argued Wundt, as long as it remained focused on phenomena grounded in immediate experience like sensation, attention, and reaction-time. Wundt's focus was on psychical causality, which was distinct from physical causality and involved the study of subjectivity. It was certainly not the study of behavior as was evolving in the United States (Ash, 1995, p. 24). Nor could this study extend to the higher mental functions, a position that hardened in Wundt over time (Diamond, 2001, p. 32). Wundt was influenced by Dilthey's distinction between the natural and human sciences with psychology a key part of the latter. Although the next few generations of German psychologists—Ebbinghaus, Külpe, Stumpf, Meumann, Wertheimer, and Stern—would come to reject both Wundt's methodological limitations and disdain for application, the laboratory remained the principal space for the development of psychological knowledge. Within this context, a debate over perception played out which, though mostly ignored in the United States until much later, challenged some of the fundamental categories of psychological thinking.

Two key assumptions in psychology, and certainly in the psychology of the late nineteenth century, were the distinction between sensation and perception and the idea that sensations were composed of elementary units, which were the building blocks of thought. This distinction was a philosophical one, not a biological one, and reflected a key expression of Cartesianism in psychology. It mirrored the division between body, of which sensation was linked, and mind, a part of which perception was taken to be. The importance of sensation was a given in the associationist bias of early psychology, but one that was firmly challenged by the Würzburg School of Oswald Külpe in the early 1900s and more forcefully by the Gestalt School in Berlin after 1910. But for the most part, these challenges and the consequences of them have not been well integrated into contemporary psychology (Ash, 1995). Since the early 1900s, it has become clear that the distinction between sensation and perception is not tenable, yet it persists in most undergraduate psychology textbooks. These topics are important as they represent the focus of the original pioneers of psychology in the 1870s, 1880s, and 1890s, until the rise of behaviorism made the acquisition of knowledge less relevant.

The rise of experimentalism in German philosophy was fraught with tension and conflict. Many philosophers resented the intrusion of the experimental methods into their field as they had long regarded the natural sciences as an inferior form of knowing. They actively sought to prevent experimental psychologists from acquiring chairs in departments of philosophy, which was the only option for career advancement in a university without separate psychology departments (Ash, 1995, p. 47). They criticized "psychologism" or the tendency inherited from British philosophy to reduce logical and metaphysical problems to psychological ones. In other terms, they rejected the reduction of the question as to the nature of knowledge to the study of how the individual mind comes to know.

Late-nineteenth-century notions as to the nature of sensation were shaped by the thinking of Hermann Von Helmholtz and his Berlin School of physiology, which operated within the reflex tradition. Visual sensation was composed of a series of specific motions. Excitations resulting from external stimuli were transmitted by nerve fibers from cones on the retina through the optic nerve to the brain. The brain turned these excitations into representations of the world, though these replicas were never quite exact copies (Ash, 1995, pp. 31–32). Thus, the sensory organs provided the "data" for perception to organize. Helmholtz viewed the sense organs as operating mechanically and passively (Ash, 1995, pp. 56–57). Ewald Hering criticized this position for starting with stimulation from the object as opposed to what people actually saw. The job of psychology, argued Hering, was to focus on what was seen as opposed to the objects themselves, which was the job of the natural sciences. This led Hering assign some of the attributes to sensation that Helmholtz had reserved for perception (Lenoir, 1993). For instance, according to Hering, sense data were already organized by the retina. Hering insisted that psychological explanations rely on psychic causes not physiological ones. He believed psychology needed a new language to express this, one that was not so reliant on the sciences of physics and chemistry. This led him to criticize the work of Helmholtz and into a debate that played out during the 1850s, which, as we already reviewed, Helmholtz described as one between empiricism and nativism, a description that made Hering seem out of touch with recent science. This led to a sense that the distinction between sensation and perception was clear-cut.

Elementalist assumptions were also debated in the early development of psychology. For Wundt, for instance, the mind was experienced as a unity, thus simple sensations were never given in immediate consciousness but were the result of abstractions from it (Ash, 1995, p. 61). Some psychologists accepted the elementalism of physics and associationist philosophy, but most regarded the breakup of mind into elementary units as a methodological necessity but not a reflection of the way the mind really operates. For instance, Hermann Ebbinghaus, the first to extend the new experimental methods to a higher psychological function, defended elementalism by arguing that psychology must begin with an analysis of the components of mind before it could understand the mind as a totality. Such analysis was also required for assigning numerical values to processes like reaction time, a key part of making psychology a science (Ash, 1995, p. 67).

The founders of the Gestalt School in Berlin—Max Wertheimer, Kurt Koffka, and Wolfgang Kohler—were all students of Carl Stumpf, who in turn, developed his position from that of his teacher, Franz Brentano. In his *Psychology from an Empirical Standpoint* of 1874, Brentano sought to overcome the skepticism of Hume and limitations on knowledge set by Kant by arguing that one can grasp the truth of objects in the world through direct consciousness. Stumpf followed this line and, like Wundt, sought to make experiences given in consciousness the object of the science of psychology, as opposed to the reifications of experience taken up by the natural sciences (Ash, 1995, p. 36). The study of immediate consciousness was accomplished by an elite class of scientific observers, experimenters trained in the methods of introspection. For both Stumpf and Wundt, the goal of measurement and instruments were to support self-observation. They were not meant to be ends in themselves (Ash, 1995, p. 40). The purpose of this research was to ultimately address longstanding philosophical problems.

The experimental challenge to psychology's elementalism and absolute distinction between sensation and perception began with the study of "gestalt" qualities in the 1890s by another student of Brentano's, Christian von Ehrenfels. In his study of melody, von Ehrenfels realized that one could recognize two melodies as identical, despite their being played in different keys. This was because they had an additional quality beyond the sounds that made them up, a gestalt quality that could not be reduced to its component parts. This quality was not projected onto the sense data by the mind, but was inherent in the object itself. Soon, von Ehrenfels applied the notion of gestalt qualities to many different domains. In addition G. E. Müller took up a similar line. He identified certain factors that increased the degree of coherence between distinct stimuli (like nearness or expectations). This made the perception of them as unified wholes easier (Ash, 1995, p. 93). He also suggested that thought had a directional nature, something impossible in traditional associationism. By 1910, the study of gestalt qualities was a popular topic in German psychology. Finally, another challenge to elementalism and traditional psychological categories came from Würzburg and the controversy over "imageless" thought with Wundt. In some of the research of the Würzburg School published in the early 1900s, subjects described a thought that was not connected to any concrete image. This undermined the associationist assumption that the elementary units of mind were sensations. They named these "dispositions of consciousness." Later this finding was used to describe a general category of thought without content, what we might think of as a "sense" of something, a category that could not be accounted for in traditional sensationalist assumptions.

Max Wertheimer extended this criticism even further. Structured wholes [*gestalten*] were the primary units of mind, he argued. Few impressions were grasped as disordered elements but were instead perceived as structured wholes. In fact, argued Wertheimer, the whole was often grasped before the individual parts. Wertheimer used this to explain the phi phenomenon, a perceptual illusion where apparent motion could not be distinguished from real motion (Ash, 1995, p. 123–124). In 1913, his colleague in Berlin, Wolfgang Kohler, described the tendency to regard "perceptions and sensations as much as possible as unambiguously determined by peripheral stimulation" (Kohler, cited in Ash, 1995, p. 136) as a "constancy hypothesis" which he argued was untenable and had to be given up. He also rejected the simplistic distinction between the physiological and the psychological that he saw as common in psychology (Ash, 1995, p. 137). Any study that begins with stimulation commits a methodological error as it misses the experience as a whole. The same applied to motor activities, which were part of a whole process and not a bundle of reflexes. In one of the most famous examples of Gestalt research, Kohler studied problem solving among chimpanzees in Tenerife and found that traditional notions of trial and error as described by Thorndike did not account for what actually happened when chimps solved complex problems. Kohler noticed that they seemed to step back as if to study the problem and then in a moment of "insight" come up with a novel solution. Thorndike's animals learned by "chance" because the box limited their perceptual capacity (Ash, 1995, p. 160). When given a chance to behave intelligently, argued Kohler, chimpanzees did just that (Henle, 1992, p. 104). Kohler could never understand why American behaviorists were so focused on the most clumsy and least interesting forms of learning.

This focus on wholes fit nicely with broader sentiments that were developing in Germany during the interwar period. World War I had already allowed German psychology to move in more applied directions as it presented its usefulness to the military (Ash, 1995, p. 188). A new field of "psychotechnics" focused on solving practical problems. William Stern went as far as to argue that psychology must loosen its commitment to experimentalism (Ash, 1995, p. 204). This call made sense in a context where the value of laboratory science was called into question as part of a conflict between culture and civilization. Culture represented the aesthetic world of the German elite. It valued art, meaning, and German philosophical and cultural traditions. Civilization, on the other hand, represented the encroaching culture of the Franco-Anglo-American world. It valued science, technology, and the destruction of traditional values. For many Germans, Weimar culture itself reflected the dominance of civilization over culture and science over philosophy. Gestalt psychology spoke to a culture concerned with mourning the loss of meaning and value. Its rejection of sensationalism and elementalism reflected a broader rejection of a scientific spirit that only seemed able to view life in mechanical terms. Even defenders of application in psychology in Germany like William Stern addressed broader philosophical themes in their work.

These ideas made their way into German education in a tension between two approaches to school reform. Nineteenth-century German education was highly integrated into employment systems, which made it both very important as well as a reflection of social inequalities (Drewek, 2000). A minority of students were directed toward a university track, while the rest left school for work. A tension between the children of the traditional academic elite and those new classes produced by industrialization in the traditional *gymnasium* led to a more differentiated system with alternative paths to a university education. A second tension between the traditional German model of *bildung* and the needs of new categories of employment along with the demand for professionalization on the part of elementary school teachers, who were typically not integrated into the rest of German education, led to the emergence of new forms of reform pedagogies (Budde, 2012).

One of the new schools of pedagogy led by Ernst Meumann represented the extension of Wundtian experimentalism to education and focused on the introduction of psychological concepts into teacher training. Meumann also encouraged the use psychological aptitude tests for social selection, which would have broadened access to the *gymnasium* and further strained the already strained system. Wundt and others cast doubt on the validity of aptitude tests, arguing they were best suited for assessing physical functions exclusively (Drewek, 2000, p. 296). The second approach to school reform led by Eduard Spranger offered a humanist alterative to testing and attempted to modernize traditional notions of *bildung*. It focused on raising the standards of teacher education, turning teachers into defenders of traditional German culture as well as checking the threat of teacher radicalism. While Spranger's model of reform was more influential during the Weimer period, by the 1960s Meumann's model was viewed as the path to adapting German education to the needs of the twentieth century (Drewek, 2000, p. 300). The U.S. model proved victorious after all.

World War II freed German psychology from philosophy once and for all—quite literally as finally psychologists were allowed to establish their own departments—and moved the field to reconstruct itself along much more American lines, moving from the study of perception to the study of behavior. Yet, some of these ideas related to organized wholes eventually turned up in U.S. psychology through the influence of the Gestalt school as its founders immigrated to the United States as well as in the work of Karl Lashley, Donald Hebb, and J. J. Gibson or were imported into U.S. psychology through the influence of Piaget and European Phenomenology. Unlike the case with the United States, the Germans did not yet turn to mass testing to organize education, and so educational research tended to focus on individuals and be designed for use by teachers. In German schools, this holistic perspective better served teachers, and psychological research never became, at least in this period, a source of administrative data. Finally, the Gestalt turn in psychology helped to reconceive the relationship between structure and function. In a sense, American psychology had gone too far in its functionalism and abandoned all notion of organization. In other words, structure is not only a function of anatomy, but as the rationalist tradition in philosophy had long understood, it is an inherent component of mentality. The analytic approach of behavioral theories tended to ignore organization altogether and assume each component of behavior was acquired individually, making it impossible to consider higher-order organizational patterns. Gestalt psychology made it clear that this was a problem.

4. DESCRIPTION AND EXPLANATION: MENTALISM

Part of the point of the behavioral turn in psychology was to try to bring the field more in line with the methods of the more successful and established natural sciences. One of the most thorough attempts at this was that of critic of traditional behaviorism and likely most influential behaviorist of all, B. F. Skinner. Though he is often lumped together with traditional behaviorism, he did not see himself that way and many of his ideas sprang from the work of the radical empiricists of the late nineteenth century, which, as we have seen, pushed German psychology in a wholly different direction. On one hand, Skinner's reconfiguration of hedonistic conditioning exposed the problems with prior forms of learning theory, even though, as we shall see, much of Skinnerianism turns out to share some of the same problems. Skinner's warning to psychologists was that dependence on vague, poorly defined, and immaterial mental entities that may or may not have any independence outside of ways of measuring or talking about them was a problem that couldn't be resolved without turning to a functional analysis of behavior. Skinner's solution was quite radical and required purging psychology of most of its content. Although Skinner's system ultimately failed as an alternative psychology, his attempt to offer a distinct behavioral language to replace what Gilbert Ryle (1949) referred to as the ghost in the machine. Ryle's phrase for describing those mental forces that supposedly enervate behavior is still worth addressing. While substituting an exclusively behavioral language for a mentalist one might not be all that useful in the study of the psyche, at least it reminds psychologists to exercise caution as they depend on operationalized mental entities, especially when portraying them as agents with the power to change behavior as terms like "attitudes," "motives," and "schemas" tend to do. These entities are simply inferred from certain visible expressions. But caution is one thing, the complete repudiation of mentalist language is another. There is no psychology without mind, and as we suggested previously, the same is true of most of what we mean by learning. Before we elaborate further, a brief review of Skinner's work is warranted.

In *The Behavior of Organisms*, first published in 1938, Skinner introduced his version of what he later termed "radical" behaviorism. Radical behaviorism identified a functional analysis of behavior as opposed to the explanatory analysis of classical behaviorism. Classical Behaviorism or associational conditioning, what Skinner termed type "S" conditioning, was where the eliciting stimulus was known and the strength of the conditioning was measured by magnitude. It essentially tried to explain a response by referring to an eliciting stimulus; thus, it explained salivation by referencing its association with a bell. Pavlov believed he was doing more than just describing a particular situation where dogs salivated. He was explaining the cause of the salivation. Pavlov's lack of comfort with a psychological explanation ultimately led him to posit an underlying neurological one, but the same was not true of Watson or those influenced by him.

In Skinner's early work, he appeared to elicit pecking-of-bar behavior from pigeons. However, Skinner argued, the behavioral changes he witnessed were not elicited by a stimulus or an antecedent—pigeons do not spontaneously peck at keys—but had to be shaped gradually by him and were controlled by their consequences. This was once known as "hedonistic" conditioning, but Skinner termed it type "R" conditioning or operant conditioning. Here the stimulus is technically unknown, and the strength of the conditioning is measured by the response rate. Skinner rejected the practice of determining the strength of conditioning by looking at variance across individuals (i.e., average number of responses) or groups, but focused only on the responses of one individual over time (Hall, 1987). Skinner accepted that type S conditioning did happen, but attributed it to a physiological response (Skinner, 1953, p. 59). Most conditioning is operant conditioning.

The term "operant" referred to the organism's response. Operants were a type of behavior that could be manipulated by its consequences. Thus, its definition was a functional one. It was defined by what one can do to it. Operants were behaviors whose likelihood was controlled by reinforcers. Reinforcers were environmental contingencies that strengthened operants so that neither could be defined except as related to the other. Take the simple example of a reward. The reward is a type of reinforcer that strengthens particular operants. It might or might not cause the behavior, but we can never really know this. The focus on behavior is a means to an end, and the end is control via the modification of behavior. The functional analysis of behavior involved identifying two classes of variable: operants and reinforcers. There can be other "stimulants" in the environment (Skinner calls them discriminative stimuli), but these could not elicit operants for the analysis to work. Once behavior was broken down into its component parts in this way, it could be manipulated and predicted. Such analysis created a technology of behavior. This was the ultimate goal, not explanation. The assumption was that given similar conditions, the organism will behave in similar ways in future conditions. Thus one judged the validity of the analysis not in terms of whether the causes were identified but by whether it successfully predicted future behavior.

Skinner rejected all talk of neural or psychic causes and in fact rejected all mentalist explanations entirely. One cannot say, for instance, that the offering of a reward caused a subject to behave in a certain way or that the reward made the subject satisfied. All one can say is that with certain consequences the likelihood of a behavior was increased. It is not people that are reinforced but behavior. Operant conditioning works as the consequences of behavior feedback to the organism. This rejection applies to all causality-inferring terms like trial-and-error learning. All one witnessed, said Skinner, was that when certain consequences were contingent on behavior, the behavior increased in frequency. The experimenter cannot know anything about the subject's "trying" or "recognizing mistakes" which are mentalist categories. Even the term "response" was inappropriate given that one can never be sure that a single reinforcer was related to a specific operant. Similarly the organism has no "purpose" or "goals." In fact, the traditional distinction between associational and instrumental conditioning—the former was involuntary and the latter voluntary, a distinction that speaks to common sense—was also incorrect. It was simply the case that in the former, the connection was easier to observe; in the latter, however, the response was just as certain. Skinner's analysis was not causal in the "push-pull" causality of physics (Schnaitter, 1987, p. 59) but only in the sense that an organism's behavior "can and should be explained entirely in terms of what happens to it" (Hall, 1987, p. 54). It described a functional relationship between an independent variable and a dependent one. One of the problems with mentalist terms, argued

Skinner, was that they could not be manipulated and controlled and therefore could not be part of a technology of behavior. Skinner recognized that the control he developed in the laboratory was impossible out in the world. So, he used his findings in tightly controlled laboratory settings to "interpret" similar behavior in the world (Skinner, 1974, p. 228). These "interpretations" were valid not as explanatory or cause-effect analyses but only as sources of control. Much of Skinner's research focused on various patterns of differential reinforcement and their place in modifying behavior—famously recognizing, for example, that intermittent reinforcement actually increased response rates.

Through operant conditioning, the environment shaped the basic ways in which organisms behaved in the world. Because this was not always intentional, Skinner suggested that societies should be explicitly designed so that the contingencies offered end up modifying individual behaviors in ways that increased the common good. Skinner laid out this vision in his fictional best seller *Walden Two* (1962), which continues to inspire utopian experimental communities around the world. He later defended his vision from critics who accused him of authoritarianism and denying human agency and value in *Beyond Freedom and Dignity* (1971). Skinner regarded the view of humans as autonomous agents as flawed. In a sense, he was just extending the determinism of the natural sciences to the human sphere, which psychology had been doing implicitly for a century. Skinner was simply being really explicit about what that meant. Autonomy was a vestige of religious and philosophical theories of human nature, argued Skinner. It didn't belong in science.

Skinner's model of science was influenced by Ernst Mach and other figures in late-nineteenth-century positivism. Mach, like many in the nineteenth century, was struggling with the Kantian gap between subject and object. How can there be a science, if one has no access to the world in itself, if one has access only to "phenomena" and not "noumena"? The answer was to ground science in phenomena. Thus, for Mach, the proper activity of science was limited to observations and redescriptions of observations. Descriptions of the material world belonged to physics, and descriptions of the quality and intensity of sensations belonged to psychology (Robinson, 1992, p. 66). Science was the study of perceptual reality, argued the positivists who followed Mach, and there were no laws of mind or nature. This influence led Skinner to be wary of "theorizing" in science, and limit himself to description, prediction, and control. But, like his fellow positivists, Skinner refused to see that his descriptions were already theory-laden. Ironically, for Mach, psychology was the study of consciousness, and to ignore it or rule out its study a priori as Skinner did would have made little sense (Robinson, 1992, p. 67).

Skinner's critique of mentalism extended across much of his work. In essence, there were several basic problems with mentalism. First and most important, mental states could not be controlled predictably and thus could not be part of a technology of behavior. Second, Skinner's Machian vision of science was based in simplicity, since mental states had no immediate reference; they added unnecessary complexity to any account (Hall, 1987, p. 43). Because they were neither accessible to manipulation or observation, employing them as causes was meaningless or as Skinner put it, "mental explanations explain nothing" (Skinner, 1974, p. 224). They are reflections of a natural human tendency to invent explanations when none are obvious (Creel, 1987, p. 108). Third, mentalists, as Skinner called them, trivialized behavior by treating it as a direct consequence of mental states and ignored the relationship between the organism and its environment. Sometimes Skinner accepted that inner states mediated between stimulus and behavior and that there might even be lawful relations between them. At times he even implied that it was this lawfulness that allowed him to drop mental states out of a behavioral analysis (Schnaitter, 1987, p. 65). In other words, this attitude was simply a methodological tool. Other times Skinner went further and argued that there were no mental states and that reference to such states were really about behavior. This was a much stronger ontological point. He seemed to go back and forth between these positions.

Skinnerians tend to assume that all organisms learn in the same way. But we know this is incorrect. Different organisms have distinct learning mechanisms based on unique constitutional factors, contextual factors, and differential learning needs. For example, organisms with short life spans do not have much time to learn via association (Lerner, 2002). Thus, they tend to require more innate behavioral patterns. Organisms with longer life spans have plenty of time to spend on trial-and-error learning and can use this capacity to adapt to novel environments. Also, organisms with longer life spans tend to be better at integrating new associative learning into prior learning as well as transferring previous learned behavior or knowledge into new contexts. We therefore tend to describe them as more "intelligent." Also, Skinnerians tend to assume that the distinction between respondent and operant conditioning is always self-evident. But, this is a matter of interpretation. When pigeons press keys, for example, their behavior must be shaped so that their heads turn in certain directions (Hall, 1987). This is when the reward must be administered. But it is also possible to explain the repetition of this turn later in time as the result of an association between reward and behavior, even if the reward is no longer offered. This is what eighteenth century philosophers meant by habit. Thus, it is technically possible that operant conditioning is an amalgamation of associative responses that have been habitualized. It all depends on what one is looking for. This is exacerbated by technology as well. Thorndike's box allowed for minimal responses, Skinner's for more. Thus, Skinner's animals appeared to respond voluntarily, while Thorndike's did not. In neither case are any of these expectancies made explicit. In fact, Daniel Dennett (1978) puts it a bit more pointedly, "Skinner's experimental design is supposed to eliminate the intentional, but it merely masks it . . . because the highly reliable intentional predictions underlying his experimental situations . . . are disguised by leaving virtually no room in the environment for more than one bodily motion to be the appropriate action" (p. 15). In his quest to deny intelligence on the part of his subjects, Skinner simply built intelligence into his box.

Thus, critics of Skinner and the behaviorists who follow him argue that behaviorists assume that consequent conditions can explain behavioral outcomes because that is the only explanation they have available to them (Mills, 1998). They have no other alternative as they have rejected all talk of mental events. Instead they assign the environment the power of thought. They assume that because consequent conditions are correlated with outcomes in the laboratory, they are enough to explain the behavior. There is some truth to this criticism, although it is technically not correct. Skinner is not pointing to correlations exactly, but predictions, and in the process, subtly changing the criteria of what it means to be a cause. The more important question is whether those predictions have any relevance outside that context.

Naturally, identical outcomes can be produced in widely different contexts, and different outcomes can be produced in the same context. Most of these results are extensions via analogy. They explain nothing. There is a circular nature to Skinner's argument that is hard to miss, though Skinner assumed he was able to overcome it by focusing on predictions. It is similar to one behaviorists are happy to point out in Freud. The theory can never be falsified. If a specific reinforcer is not effective, it doesn't mean reinforcers do not work. Reinforcers always work. It also doesn't mean that operants cannot be controlled. All of this is built into the definition. Furthermore, the term "reinforcer" itself suggests that one has explained the source of the modification in behavior. But, this is deceptive. All one can say is that they witnessed an increase in response rates in a particular context, in a particular moment of time. One can offer a description of what they saw. But, when one uses the term "reinforce," a modification of the term enforce, literally to give strength, one is purporting to explain the cause of the behavioral change, something one has no justification for. In fact, in a new context or a later date, the same variable in the same set of conditions might or might not strengthen an operant. One has no idea. One is just describing the presumed "effects" of that variable in one moment of time, but subtly suggesting they have an explanation of what was witnessed.

Skinner, of course, was too smart to fall into this trap, and when he did, he quickly retreated, but many of those influenced by him do so all the time. Otherwise, if all Skinnerianism did was offer descriptions of specific behavioral changes in very particular contexts and moments of time, who cares?

The attractiveness of Skinnerianism is that it presumably explains the effects of the environment on behavior. Again, Skinner would disagree and say his goal is not explanation but prediction and control. But predicting the behavior of rats in situations where they have few options is one thing, predicting complex human behavior is another. This is why Skinner's "technology" works best in situations where control is the goal and subjects have few other options: laboratories, prisons, schools, mental institutions, etc. (Hall, 1987, p. 47). But, the layperson who hears talk of a predictable relationship between reinforcer and an operant thinks in cause-effect terms. This is why they assume that these reinforcers can generalize to different contexts.

Skinner's account, although not especially helpful as a means to explain human behavior, has certain plausibility because it seems to mirror that way we think about behavior anyway. Everybody knows if you offer a child ice cream to finish their homework, they probably will. If this applies to ice cream, it likely applies to other contexts. There is an elasticity to Skinnerian narratives that jibes with the everyday psychological and moral notion that actions have consequences (Hall, 1987, p. 48). Skinnerianism takes some fairly obvious observations and restates them in more technical language, again not unlike the archrival of behavioral theories, psychoanalysis. The problem is that nothing is really gained from this new language except some vague abstractions and the sense that one can control the behavior of certain species of animal.

And yet, Skinner's critique of mentalism is worth paying heed to. Naturally, psychologists tend to borrow some of the ways of framing the relationship between individuals and their behavior from everyday language. This language does suggest that certain types of mental entities have the power to cause certain actions. Thus a "feeling" of anger might cause a person to yell. Or a behavior might be caused by the "desire" to fight or the "motive" to undermine a relationship. There is a fairly overt Cartesianism here. Body and mind seem to be two distinct levels of activity that somehow interact with each other in a causal way. But, where exactly is this "feeling" or "motive"? Where are they being experienced? Are they entities inside the mind? Are they, as one might hear today, configurations of neural activity? By giving the capacity to feel or want to the mind or brain, we have simply begged the question. We return again to the homunculus fallacy. Most academic psychologists, like most who identify themselves as scientists, tend to be property dualists or eliminativists, thus they tend to view mental entities as a product of neural process that can or cannot be explained separately from those processes. For property dualists, physiological explanation and psychological explanations are two ways of talking about the same fundamental phenomenon. Viewing the psychological and the physiological as two distinct levels of describing the same phenomenon is useful except that it is unable to justify the basis of this distinct psychological level and its categories other than the fact that language presents them this way. If psychologists were simply describing the experience of immediate consciousness, as Wundt would have them do, then variants of these categories are clearly valid. We have the experience of a feeling, even sometimes, a motive, though they are likely not so easily distinguished. But most psychologists have rejected this approach for a "behavioral" one, that is, one that describes objects of consciousness outside of the experience of consciousness, in the third-person way the natural sciences do. Property dualists generally accept that psychological objects are not structures, as are those typically studied by the sciences of chemistry and physics, but functions. Thus, feelings and motives are not immaterial substances existing on an autonomous plane but functional categories, descriptions of what the mind does. But again, what is the basis for asserting that these are the most appropriate ones to rely on? The only resource is the first-person experience of immediate consciousness that psychologists do not wish to rely on or the ways in which such experiences are inscribed in language. Yes, we might experience a feeling or a motive as distinct from each other or we might retrospectively assign them to those categories in order to make sense of them, but on what basis can psychologists then say they are distinct processes and even localized differentially in the brain?

Of course, they cannot. They might try and say that the observable manifestations of these processes suggest they are different. Perhaps they lead to distinct behaviors but, finding these manifestations means that these categories exist before those observations. These categories are products of society and language although clearly involve physiology as well. This means that they change and that even the conscious experience of them changes. In Locke, for instance, thought and feelings were both types of ideas. With the spread of faculty psychology in the eighteenth century, they became distinct faculties. This is the sense in which Skinner's critique of mentalism is correct, much of which was prefigured in the later work of Ludwig Wittgenstein. Mental categories are products of language and convention, yet related to human physiology in mutually constitutive ways. They are human kinds yet easily create confusion that is exacerbated when one attributes power and agency to them or assumes an identity between them and what is seen as their behavioral or physiological manifestations. They can be, as Skinner noted, a substitute for saying we simply don't know the cause. Given the circularity of Skinnerian explanations, the same seems to be true of Skinner's alternative. Perhaps the lesson is that psychologists should stay away from explanations and instead focus more on where their descriptive categories come from in the first place.

5. DESCRIPTION AND EXPLANATION: WHAT IS LEARNING?

To be fair, behaviorism's dominance in psychology is long past, and psychologists since then have offered several alternative understandings of learning to educators. Some of these approaches came out of the rise of a cognitive paradigm in the 1960s, while others were generated by European psychologists much earlier in the century. In these cases, learning involved the acquisition and/or development of some type of cognitive structure: a mental map, a set of concepts, theory of mind, representations, or schema. Jean Piaget's work has been most influential here. In education, this is sometimes described as a "constructivist" approach in that learners need to create these structures themselves through everyday activity and practice. There are also intersubjective versions of this. Many, influenced by Lev Vygotsky, view these mental constructions as products of social relationships, whether they are "internalized" as Vygotsky thought, or more recently, offer opportunities for "participation," the latter recognizing that knowledge is distributed throughout various human and nonhuman entities in an interaction and is not located in individual's heads (Rogoff, 2003). For the most part, these more recent views have influenced early primary education in the United States, much more than middle, secondary, or college education where the prominence of standardized curricula and testing pushes teachers to focus on the facts and skills required to demonstrate student achievement. All this is valuable, but unfortunately, has been assimilated into the dominant paradigm far more often than it has modified it (Bereiter & Scardamalia, 1996).

In the end, though, the psychology of learning has been misguided from the start. Learning is not a mechanism, biological, or otherwise. Learning is not the modification of behavior. Nor frankly is it something done by minds, brains, or synapses. Only people learn. Learning is not a process but the outcome of many processes, each of which is determined by the relationship between a specific human person and that person's capacity for relating to the inherent organization of the thing to be learned in a particular context. Learning is not only species specific, but individual specific, task specific, and most importantly of all, context specific. There are no generalizable laws of learning. Moderns have gotten exceedingly good at offloading much of what they have to learn onto various technologies—books, computers, calculators, and so on—so good that it has become impossible to distinguish between what humans know and what the technology knows. This is often studied under the umbrella of "distributed" cognition wherein thinking is outsourced onto the environment. As we noted, learning need not involve internalization, as Vygotsky argued, but participation—there is no requirement for a hard distinction between inside and outside nor mind and body in learning (Lave & Wenger, 1991).

Learning involves entering into a situation, social or otherwise, and creating an experience, sometimes with other human persons, mediated through both those person's histories—including what we would term the cognitive, the emotional, the bodily, and the sensuous/perceptual—and integrated into such a way so that new versions of those human persons are created (Jarvis, 2005). Learning is an intimate activity, more like the soul-work described by Socrates than the adaptations described by Darwin, though adaptations are part of it. Learning sits on the boundary of what we call the interior and exterior, mind and body, and thinking and feeling. Learning can be gradual, as it is sometimes in the associative variety, but its more interesting varieties are sudden and insightful, wherein a new property or element is integrated into an existing whole or an entirely new whole is created through a reorganization of constitutive elements. This is the way both the Gestaltists and Piagetians understood learning. Learning is not a passive process of absorbing environmental cues, even in the associative variety; it requires the bringing to bear of specific sensory and motor modalities along with ways of organizing thinking and behavior—what we can also describe as a person's history—onto a specific situation so that the person-situation totality is transformed. Learning involves activity on the part of the person as they figure out which perceptual, bodily, and other types of external and internal elements are relevant and how they relate to each other. Often this involves imposing those relationships on various perceptual, conceptual, and bodily streams to create organization, including the reorganization of what has been already learned. But it also involves becoming attuned to the organization already present, even if it is not immediately obvious. Perhaps there are some associative links that must be constructed, as in behaviorist conceptions, but that is only one component of what is typically involved.

Finally, learning involves a mutually implicative relationship between biology and culture (Geertz, 2000). Behaviorists were correct that learning is a biological category; however it is not limited to a biological category. Learning can be constrained by biological organization, moderate its expression, or even transform biological activity into something novel. Another way of saying this is that learning takes place at multiple levels of human activity that interact with each other and lead to the creation of higher-order forms of organization. Again, this was the lesson of Gestalt psychology. Without a conception of multiple types and levels of structure, a conception that behavioral psychologies often lacked, we are limited to versions of stimulus-response psychology. We can go even further and try to develop a more critical conception of learning, which could then be applied to education. Olson and Bruner (1996, p. 22) describe a type of education they term "the management of "objective" knowledge," a pedagogy that focuses not on knowledge per se, but on the standards and sources of evidence used by a particular society or community to consider a proposition accepted knowledge in the first place. Olson and Bruner recommend doing this in the context of teaching children how to differentiate between "personal" and "objective" knowledge. But we can also relate this to the notion of "critique" as Kant used the term. What are the presuppositions that ground a particular claim to knowledge? In whose interests does such a claim serve? What is the history of this claim and what linguistic and narrative devices are used to make it convincing? This begs the question: How can schools reformulate the notion of education to capture a broader conception of learning? Does the category of "learning" have any value at all; are we not simply talking about experience? What are the roles for assessment, teachers, and schools in all this? They are likely much more limited than is the current practice, but we will leave this to future work to figure out.

Chapter Five

Biology, Brain, and Behavior

This chapter focuses on notions of brain, mind, and body in psychology as well as various related concepts that try to explain the relationship between mind and body more broadly. Can we explain mental activity by identifying underlying physiological processes? This has been a question that has vexed psychology since the nineteenth century and since then has mostly involved the search for mental activity in the neural pathways of the brain. This required laying out the relationship between body and mind, and more specifically between brain structure and psychological function. The metaphor of "underlying" is an important one and communicates much about the primacy given to physiological explanations. This question relates to the all the tensions we have discussed, those between inside and outside, structure and function, and description and explanation. It also relates to that between higher and lower, even in terms of which type of "explanation" is taken more seriously but also the idea of mind as a higher realm. Our focus, however, will be on the tension between structural and functional explanations in the study of the relationship between brain and mind. This is especially important in an age when many psychologists are turning to neuroscience to develop new conceptions of mental activity. For many, we are closer than we have ever been to explaining mind in physiological terms and establishing clearcut relationships between the brain and thought.

And yet, this is not the first time such progress seemed inevitable. The success of neurophysiology in the nineteenth century also made it appear possible that these pathways would eventually be identified. Yet if we look further back, we can identify several prior candidates for this physiological substrate. We can trace the search for the source of elements of soul in body back to the Greeks. One way to explain their relationship, articulated by Galen but fairly widespread until the eighteenth century, involved the notion that the soul operated through various vapors or spirits that traveled throughout the body. Roughly speaking, there were natural spirits produced in the liver and responsible for bodily functions, the finer vital spirits produced in in the heart and responsible for life, and animal spirits that traveled through the brain and nervous system and were responsible for sensation and motion. The term "spirit" comes from the Latin word for breath, a translation of the Greek term *pneuma*. In Greek, *pneuma* could mean either breath or soul, but was distinct from the term *psyche* (the Latin term is *anima*) that specifically referred to the soul. In more "religiously" oriented texts, the term blurred the distinction between soul and body, and in its medical usage it was the material that sustained consciousness. For Galen, it reflected the indissoluble unity of soul and body, though one must not go too far in reading this as a way to express the relationship of mind and body or we risk projecting modern concerns onto Greco-Roman thought.

Cartesianism separated the realm of mind from body while continuing to use some of the language of Galenic medicine. For Descartes, animal spirits belonged to the realm of the body and operated mechanically, were capable of stirring passions, and through the pineal gland create disturbances in the realm of mind. Descartes described one of the key mechanisms for the actions of animal spirits as involving a reflex. In the next generation, physician and founding member of the Royal Society, Thomas Willis, extended Descartes' reflex-mechanism to include many mechanical responses by the brain and body to sensory stimulation. As we already noted, in the nineteenth century, this became the basis for the reflex arc, which viewed some of the processes once attributed to the mind as a mechanical response to external stimulation. This became the basis for a new biological conception of learning. Descartes' critics argued that a sentient or vitalist principle must be present to explain living processes. This debate occupied the study of physiology throughout much of the seventeenth and eighteenth centuries until Luigi Galvani discovered the electrical nature of nerve impulses, which was only fully accepted in the nineteenth century. Thus animal electricity, which later became nerve impulses, was another possible source of mental activity. A final source, as laid out in the early nineteenth century by Gall's phrenology, was the structure of the brain itself, which as we shall see turned out to be a profoundly influential idea and have a lasting effect on the ways in which psychology conceives the relationship between body and mind.

The question of the relationship between body and mind only makes sense if one believes these are distinct substances that must "relate" to each other, and few individuals within academic psychology would still admit to this kind of blatant Cartesianism. Outside of academia, most people would describe the relationship causally starting with the body—that is, certain biological or brain structures cause certain mental states or behaviors, especially pathological ones. But as thinkers influenced by Wittgenstein have argued, much of this bias is built into language itself. Today, some might actually argue the reverse, that states of mind cause certain biological or brain activity, though this might seem too "new-age" to others. So either the cause of mental/behavioral processes like depression or learning can be traced back to the brain, or for some, depression or learning create changes in the structure of the brain, and in fact, the latter position is the message of the most recent neuroscience. For individuals outside the academy, one commonsensical way to talk about the power of body is to talk about the actions of genes, that is, to see genes as causing certain mental states or functions. The problem with this, as we shall see, is that it bears little relationship to what genes actually do.

Typically, psychologists are familiar enough with the idea that genes are pleiotropic and traits are polygenic; that, more often than not, they are careful not to link specific genes to mind and behavior and instead see brain structures (e.g., regions, networks, areas) as responsible for mental and behavioral activity. The one exception is still found in some variants of evolutionary psychology where genes are still regarded as the exclusive mechanism for the reproduction of ancestral adaptations, and therefore a gene or several genes are viewed as the source of various mental activities (e.g., language, higher-thinking, pathology) and behaviors (e.g., altruism, family structure, promiscuity) in individual members of a species, though still mediated through the brain. The problem with most of these variants is that they make little biological sense. Genes do not cause certain mental and/or behavioral activities or states, nor are certain behaviors/mental states a self-evident product of natural selection. Moreover, mental activities/behaviors are not products of brain activity, nor are they the cause of brain activity. In fact, the entire cause-effect framework used to explain these relationships is profoundly unhelpful in making sense of the kinds of emergent phenomena we are trying to understand. This is also probably true, in this context, of terms like "mind," "body," and "gene," which imply sharp divisions that may or may not exist in nature.

As noted, these problems are not new. The more carefully we examine neuropsychology, both contemporary and historical variations, the more difficulties arise with the assumption that we will one day know the precise neurological activities involved in key psychological activities like thinking, remembering, feeling, as well as broader psychological functions like language, pathology, selfhood, and the most mysterious of all, consciousness. Upon closer examination, we find several variants of this contemporary neuropsychological quest: (a) the first one, sometimes termed parallelism, looks to find correlates of mental activity in brain activity yet regards the brain and mind as involving two distinct sets of processes; (b) a second one, sometimes called property dualism, also looks for correlates between mental and brain activity but this time views them as two distinct levels of explanation of the same fundamental phenomenon; and (c) a final one, sometimes termed "eliminativism," ever gaining in popularity and influence, actually regards mental activity as simply the neural activity itself or some kind of after-effect of the neural activity and rejects that many of the categories used to describe mental activity have any relationship at all to brain activity but are simply vestiges of "folk" psychology (Ratcliffe, 2008).

Unfortunately, all of these positions bring with them certain conceptual problems. All except eliminativism seek to span the gap between the conventional language of psychological function and the specialist language of biological structure. The first and second positions never fully resolve the Cartesian problem of how the brain and mind are related to each other and eliminativism never explains how one thing, mental experience, can actually be another thing, brain structures or processes. It can't even begin to explain how mental experience emerges from neuronal activity but takes the thesis that they are identical on faith. It has to, given that it requires that one employ the explanatory framework of physics, a framework that is believed to be complete (Robinson, 2008, p. 15). Whatever one believes, it is hard to argue that people don't experience something akin to consciousness. One thing is certain, even if brain activity causes mind activity, brains standing alone can do nothing of the sort (Tallis, 2011, p. 92). More importantly, consciousness involves a unique set of experiences, unlike any other in the world of physics or chemistry (Davidson, 1974). Descriptions of firing neurons do not come close to capturing it. Nerve impulses are nothing like the qualia of experience (Davidson, 1974, p. 95).

Moreover, in an attempt to broaden the explanatory power of neuroscience, neuroscientists themselves borrow heavily from psychology, most of it fairly mechanical nineteenth-century psychology—conditioning, rewards, distinctions between higher and lower functions—as these tend to be the only variants susceptible to the kind of reductionism current neuroscience requires. We will return to these points later as we address some of the confusion in contemporary neuropsychology. But first, how and why did psychologists come to relate the brain to their work in the first place? And through what conceptual frameworks, some of which are still influential, have these relationships been understood?

1. STRUCTURE AND FUNCTION: THE REFLEX, LOCALIZATION, AND HIERARCHY

This section will explore the emergence of three central ideas in nineteenth-century neuropsychology: (1) the sensorimotor reflex, (2) the localization of function, and (3) the hierarchical organization of the nervous system. These went on to shape the way modern neuroscience and neuropsychology understand the relationship between brain, mind, and behavior. But first some background. Up until Homer, the heart, not brain, was regarded as the source of life, intelligence, and feelings. In the early 400s BC, Democritus moved intelligence to the brain or encephalon, but a cardio-centric bias persisted. Aristotle, for instance, believed the function of the brain was simply to cool the passions of the heart. Five centuries later, the Roman physician Galen demonstrated the role of the brain and peripheral nervous system in bodily movement by cutting spinal cords, and yet notions of the heart as the source of life and intelligence persisted until the eighteenth century. Galen divided the soul into motor, sensory, and rational parts—the rational was further divided into imagination, reason, and memory—an early model of localization. He distinguished between sensory and motor pathways, tracing sensory nerves to the cerebrum, which could better retain sensory impressions because it was softer and motor nerves to the cerebellum (Nordenskiöld, 1928). Galen believed that psychic-*pneuma*, the substance of life, passed through hollow nerves. Originally produced by the left ventricle of the heart and transported by arteries, these became vital spirits and allowed the brain to communicate with the organs of sense and movement. As we already noted, these spirits were central to Descartes' account of involuntary behavior. They were produced in the blood, responsible for bodily movement, and reflected in the brain—hence described by the term reflex—in contrast to voluntary behavior that required interaction with the rational soul. These spirits were described as "nervous fluid" and "animal electricity" in the eighteenth century. Galen's theories persisted until a great revolution in the study of the brain took place in experimental physiology over the course of the late eighteenth and early nineteenth centuries when several key frameworks for making sense of neurological activity emerged.

The first was the notion of a sensorimotor functional unit known as the reflex. We reviewed this in a prior chapter with respect to the psychology of learning, but here we will focus more explicitly on the physiology involved. The term was coined by physician Jean Astruc in 1736 but, as we noted, can be traced back to Descartes' reflexive mechanism a century earlier. In the middle of the eighteenth century, David Hartley, one of the more psychologically minded associationists, tried valiantly to unite the sensationalism of Locke with a theory of motor activity. While others in this British tradition had already sought the roots of morality in feelings of pleasure and pain, Hartley went further and sought to ground all knowledge in associations linked to pleasure and pain. As reviewed in a prior chapter, sensations, argued Hartley, were the result of vibrations of the nerves. They sometimes remained in the brain generating memories. These vibrations along with external sensations resulted in the ideas that made up thought. If two sensory-nerve vibrations repeatedly overlapped, they became associated with each other so that later vibrations in one triggered vibratory changes in the other.

Voluntary action was the result of a connection between an idea and a motor vibration. The model Hartley employed, linking sensation, brain, and behavior—ended up revolutionizing physiology and later psychology.

At around the same time, probably the greatest physiologist and anatomist of the eighteenth century, Albrecht von Haller, distinguished between "sensible" parts of animals, those that induced impressions in the mind, and "irritable" parts, those that contracted when touched (Nordenskiöld, 1928). He identified that nerves were sensible and muscles irritable, though this was later refigured as "excitability" for nerves and "contractibility" for muscles (Young, 1970, p. 65). In the 1820s, the founder of French experimental brain physiology, Jean Pierre Flourens, assigned the quality of "irritability" to nerves, meaning that they received impressions that gave rise to sensation and motion. He also noted that nerves needed to be connected to muscle tissue for motion and the brain for perception. In the 1830s, Francois Magendie verified the distinction between sensory and motor nerves in the spinal cord, termed the Bell-Magendie law—also named after Charles Bell, a Scottish neurologist who claimed he had discovered this distinction before Magendie and whose suggestive studies on emotional expression later influenced Darwin (Young, 1970, pp. 74–80). Both used new experimental methods (lesions, stimulation) to study the spinal roots of dogs. This led others to consider whether the brain itself could be divided into sensory and motor areas. Theodor Meynert, Freud's teacher and ardent defender of the neurological basis of psychiatric disorders, called this the first fundamental thesis of neurophysiology.

Finally, in 1832, the British physiologist Marshall Hall coined the term "reflex arc" wherein sensory and motor nerves, interacting via the spinal cord, formed multiple independent units that coordinated motor activity in response to sensory stimulation. The term stuck, and the reflex arc, the path from sensory nerves to spinal cord to motor nerves, became identified not only as the fundamental unit of neurological activity, but of all physiological activity. Hall, however, drew a sharp distinction between a mechanical and automatic "excito-motory" nervous system and a purposive "sensori-volitional" one. Like many of his generation, he was not ready to regard higher mental activity in such mechanical terms. Thus, reflex activity was limited to the spinal cord and did not extend to the brain. The designation "higher" as applied to the sensori-volitional nervous system was Hall's, and he meant it in two senses: it could control the lower, reflex-based system as well as was reflected in the spatial arrangement of the nervous system. This distinction was a way for Hall and many others in his generation to hold onto notions of human will and agency central to the Christian tradition as well as explain what made humans unique, all the while grounding their ideas in the latest science.

The distinction between a mechanical and volitional nervous system, however, proved untenable. The German physiologist Johannes Müller identified the reflex arc independently in his own research, but could not accept Hall's exclusion of the brain from this mechanism. In the 1840s, the founder of German somatic psychiatry, Wilhelm Griesinger, argued that there were no grounds to separate an excito-motor nervous system from a sensori-volitional one (Clarke & Jacyna, 1992, p. 127). In Britain, the concept of the cerebral reflex undermined Hall's sharp dualism between mind and body as well. William Carpenter, for example, was influenced by the idea of the unity of nature from German Romanticism. This perspective prefigured evolutionary explanations and suggested that similar mechanisms were found across nature along an increasingly complex scale. Thus, the precursors of the reflex were found in the capacity of simple organisms to adapt to their environment, instincts in animals, and more psychic variants in humans (ibid., p. 139–40). Carpenter developed these ideas through his reading of Lamarck, and his ideas influenced a young Herbert Spencer who translated them directly into psychology.

Another British physiologist, Thomas Laycock, went even further and rejected what he called the European principle "that no animal besides man is endowed with soul or mind; and that, consequently, the phenomena of mind are not to be studied in inferior animals, but in the phenomena of humans exclusively" (Laycock, 1860, cited in Clarke & Jacyna, 1992, p. 142). Needless to say, when first developed in the 1840s, these ideas were still quite radical. What Laycock accomplished in the end was to break down the rigid dichotomy between mental and physiological functions that others would exploit more fully (ibid., p. 146). Laycock's student, John Hughlings Jackson, argued that all thought was composed of reflexive or sensorimotor activity including the so-called higher processes, thus extending the Bell-Magendie Law to all neurological activity. Herbert Spencer had previously suggested this idea. As we will discuss in the next chapter, the idea of a developmental link between sensorimotor and cognitive activity became very influential in genetic psychology. And yet, the path from stimulation to action was not always so simple. The founder of Russian physiology, Ivan Sechenov, introduced the idea of inhibition to explain why stimuli do not always lead to responses. With few exceptions, as the paradigm was extended to psychological activity, American psychologists tended to focus on the excitatory nature of reflex activity rather than the inhibitory one. This was less true of European psychology, though this is still the case in much contemporary neuroscience, especially those variants taken up by psychology, which seems to focus exclusively on excitatory activity and only in special cases turn to inhibition, which has proven to be much more prevalent (Hergenhahn, 2005, p. 415).

A second key notion for making sense of the brain that emerged during this period was the idea of localization—that is, different functions are housed in different parts of the brain. While the origins of localization can be traced back to the Greeks—they believed mind was made up of innate faculties localized in hollow ventricles of the brain: sensation and imagination in the anterior, reason in the center, and memory in the posterior—it was not until the influence of Franz Joseph Gall's phrenology in the 1820s that the idea of distinct, innate localized faculties reemerged. In fact, even the very idea that the brain was the organ of mind was still debatable before Gall (Young, 1970, p. 3). Phrenology was the first popular and practical psychology, science of individual differences, and well-known form of psychological therapy. It established the ground for both the study of personality and intelligence as well as psychotherapy later in the century. Its adherents at times ranged from Herbert Spencer to Queen Victoria, the reverend Henry Ward Beecher and the writer Edgar Allen Poe. It was also the first empirical brain science. Gall convinced his generation that the brain was the organ of the mind, could be studied via observation, and that there was continuity between human and animals brains—all this a half a century before Darwin made this latter idea respectable (Young, 1970, pp. 3–5).

Gall rejected the traditional faculties of mind as laid out by Aristotelianism and medieval philosophy as well as the dominant sensationalism of Locke and British philosophy (Young, 1970, pp. 16–18). Instead, he sought to identify the innate faculties that contributed to human variation and personality via observation. Some of these faculties, according to Gall, included cautiousness, acquisitiveness, destructiveness, language, number, sight, and comparison. There were twenty-seven all together. This internal organization was revealed externally in the shape of the head, not unlike the ways in which internal conflicts are manifested as external symptoms in psychoanalysis. The brain, argued Gall, was a composition of organs that corresponded to these functions. Human variation was not a product of experience as the sensationalists had argued, but innate, inherited instincts transmitted through the physiological structures of the brain itself (Young, 1970, p. 21). This is an idea that, in modified form, is still contained in current notions of chemical imbalances in brains, which are said to cause psychopathology.

After phrenology, faculty psychology became a biological rather than philosophical problem, many decades before Darwinism made all this fully acceptable to his scientific-gentlemen class (Young, 1970). The importance of this shift cannot be overemphasized. Gall moved psychology away from understanding mind as an autonomous substance and instead viewed it as a composition of physiologically based functions. Notions of animal spirits as the cause of behavior were replaced by the notion of mechanical organs guided toward particular functions paving the way for evolutionary explanations later in the century. As phrenology became disreputable (probably more due to its popularization and supposed atheistic implications than anything else), so too did the idea of cerebral localization. For instance, although Flourens was able to demonstrate experimentally that in a broad sense, different parts of the brain were associated with different functions—using ablation in animals, he identified the cerebrum as necessary for perception and judgment, the cerebellum for motor coordination, and the medulla for vital functions that maintained life—he saw his research as a repudiation of Gall's claims of more specialized localization in the cerebral cortex. This was because he was able to remove parts of the cerebral lobe without concurrent loss of function (Young, 1970, p. 61).

Still others continued to regard the brain as a whole. For instance, Müller attributed an indivisible whole to organic life, a part of his broader vitalism, which set limits on what physical laws were able to explain. There was a broader sociopolitical element to this debate as well; older conservatives who generally opposed phrenology also opposed localization as it seemed to suggest that all of mind was amenable to scientific explanation, which they saw as leading to materialism, atheism, and social unrest. This was the case until the 1860s when Paul Broca localized the lesion involved in the loss of speech (aphasia) in his patient Monsieur Leborgne, known as the case of "Tan," and provided convincing evidence of the localization of language functions. He succeeded in finally divorcing notions of localization from phrenology and also changing the conception of language from a purely motor activity into a psychological one. By the 1870s, Scottish neurologist David Ferrier localized the senses and muscular motions in the cortex and identified the frontal lobes with "higher" mental processes. Localization allowed these psychological functions to become material (Young, 1970, p. 241). John Hughlings Jackson warned that the localization of symptom and the localization of function were not the same thing, meaning the identification of brain damage in an area and subsequent loss of function did not necessarily require that that area was responsible for the function. It was an important point, but the warning was ignored, and the debate over localization was mostly over, with some notable holdouts, like Karl Lashley who argued in the 1920s that maze learning required the dynamic organization of the entire cerebral system and not localized functions, described as equipotentiality. It is also interesting to note that others failed in this quest. Neither Charcot nor Freud could find lesions associated with psychic abnormality and subsequently rejected this approach for a more psychological one.

The third and final key notion we will review in this section is the conception of a hierarchically organized nervous system along evolutionary lines, formally laid out by John Hughlings Jackson in the 1870s but already implied in eighteenth-century notions of a great chain of being. For most of the nineteenth century, the need to allow for free will and human agency as well as human uniqueness led most neurophysiologists to distinguish between "lower" animal-like reflexes and "higher" mental functions like thought and language. This logic can be traced back to Aristotle's nutritive, sensory, and rational souls that were also hierarchically organized as well as a general distinction between a lower realm of animal/body and a higher realm of human/reason in Greco-Roman thought as well as Christianity. John Hughlings Jackson proposed that the nervous system was composed of three levels: a lower one where automatic movements were represented in the least complex form (medulla, spinal cord), a middle level associated with voluntary movements as well as the motor area of the cortex, and the highest centers found in the prefrontal cortex associated with volitional activity and thought as well as the inhibition of the lower centers. He also asserted that disease could precipitate decline in inhibitory capacity, a concern of European states throughout the nineteenth century who feared an "uninhibited" poor. For Hughlings Jackson, behavior resulted from sensorimotor connections at all levels as the higher and lower levels differed only in degree—with the exception that the higher levels were more easily modified by experience (Young, 1970, p. 205).

With the spread of evolutionary ideas, the notion that the nervous system was organized hierarchically starting from the most basic reflex responses in the spinal cord to the higher mental activities of the cortex made perfect sense. In a sense, the passage from lower to higher in the brain, especially as these areas emerged in individual development, repeated the evolutionary history of the species. This is one of the variants of recapitulationism that influenced late-nineteenth-century thought. The traditional version of recapitulationism held that the sequence of embryological development repeated the evolutionary history of adult members of the species, and it is usually associated with Ernst Haeckel. But the broader idea that individual development repeats in some form the history of the species influenced most developmental thinkers, even to this day, ranging from Piaget and Vygotsky to Freud, as we shall review in a later chapter.

In Hughlings Jackson's version, evolutionary history was inscribed onto the brain itself from the inner and mid primitive brain structures that humans shared with the animal world to the outer advanced ones, which were more developed in humans alone, and likely most developed by some humans in particular. There was usually a racialized dimension to this—that is, certain groups had more developed brains than others. In addition, the notion that the "advanced" inhibits the "primitive" was widely accepted in nineteenth-century thought, ranging from the idea that the upper classes must control the animalistic impulses of the poor to Freud's superego which, in a properly civilized individual, must inhibit the impulses of the id. As Roger Smith (1992) notes, inhibition represented a causal process and a functional relationship in an integrated organism as well as the Christian category of the Will.

This evolutionary logic exerted a powerful influence on anthropology as well where various versions of the cultural history of the species — typically a passage from savagery and barbarism to civilized—were repeated by various societies as they made their way to the pinnacle of the civilized, white, bourgeois, European society. From the nineteenth century on, the study of the brain was always more than simply anatomy. In an obvious sense, it represented the encroachment of a materialist perspective in a typically spiritualist sphere, as would also be the case of psychology. But it also became a way of talking about human character, illness, and a broader moral order. The study of the brain in the context of evolutionary thought allowed talk of purpose and value through the language of biological structure. Moral categories like good and evil were reconstructed through the quasi-biological language of lower and higher functions.

These three frames—the sensorimotor reflex, cortical localization, and evolution-based hierarchical organization—remain the foundation of twenty-first-century neuroscience, and in a broad sense they are all correct. Like most productive conceptual frameworks, however, they can also result in certain limits in understanding. In the case of neuropsychology, they can easily become dogma and make it difficult to see where they limit our understanding of the brain and its organization. Take the example of the sensorimotor reflex. In a basic sense, the idea that nerve cells receive input from the environment via sensory nerves and produce outputs which control behavior through motor nerves is correct, except that the process in humans is never quite so linear and unambiguous. John Dewey made this point in 1896 in his masterful "The Reflex Arc Concept in Psychology." With the exception of a few simple organisms, it is difficult to actually follow this path as so much else is going on (S. Rose, 2005, p. 149). What counts as "input" and "output" in the brain depends on the context, which relationships are the focus and which are ignored, and the way a problem is framed. It requires that we abstract a particular neural "arc" from the context of all the other neural "arcs" it is nested in, many related in nonlinear fashions, and describe it independently in such a way as to give the appearance of linearity. Not to mention that this also ignores that the role of neural relationships often involves inhibiting responses. Most importantly, however, focusing exclusively on the sensorimotor character of nerve transmission often loses sight of higher-order organizational dynamics, part of why many have become convinced that thoughts can be reduced to specific neural impulses rather than more complex neuro-psychological relationships. Such reduction can be a useful methodological tool, but only when part of a broader approach. While most working neuroscientists understand this, as the findings of neuroscience are popularized or imported into psychology, this complexity is easily lost.

A prominent example of this has made its way into the media and especially educational circles where it is argued early learning creates new relationships among neural pathways in the brain, eventually modifying the brain permanently (Zull, 2002). Yes, this is correct in a very trivial sense and usually goes along with the very sensible idea of improving early education for poor children. And yet, the idea of identifying clear-cut relationships between environmental stimuli, brain activity, and long-term brain changes is reductive at best and more likely just plain impossible. The way we understand what constitutes a stimulus or a response and how we mark them off from the rest of experience is more about linguistic categories than neurological ones. Social and language categories cannot simply be mapped onto neurological ones.

The case is similar with localization. Again it is correct that certain mental functions can be related to certain structures in the brain. But, by giving function materiality, the distinction between the conventional language of psychological functions and the structural language of biology is easily elided. Typically, certain psychological functions are correlated with measured activity in specific parts of the brain. In most cases this tells us much less than it seems, as we will see in the next section. By the time this insight makes its way into psychology and popular neuroscience, it is presented as if a certain part of the brain causes or controls a specific function or, worse still, the function is reduced to the neurological activity itself.

There are several problems with this. First, many different parts of the brain are involved with specific psychological functions, regardless of what "lights" up on a functional magnetic resonance image (fMRI). It is important to remember that there is a conventionality, even an occasional arbitrariness, to certain functional distinctions in psychology and it is hard to imagine that they map perfectly onto the brain. For example, there seems to be no question in today's neuroscience that emotion (or at least emotional behavior) and thought are fundamentally distinct functions that are differentially localized in the brain. But, how can we be so convinced by the naturalness of this distinction? It certainly has a long history in post-Platonic philosophy as well seems to us in the West to be intuitively correct. It is clearly built into language. We can also describe this distinction as a political one, offering certain folks (usually white, European males) the opportunity to transcend their emotions and ascend to a plane of pure thought, with the privilege that comes with that capacity, while others (women, nonwhites) forever remain prisoners of their passions.

Yes, it is true there is an experiential dimension to this distinction—thinking and feeling are experienced differently—but there is also an obviously social one as well as one stemming from language. How can we possibly disentangle all this? Some elements of this distinction appear universal, which incidentally does not mean it is inscribed into the brain, but finding universality depends on how we define these categories in the first place. An emotional expression of behavior is not the same thing as experiencing particular feelings. Further, several different parts of the brain can be involved in a single function. This can change in different contexts and different moments of an organism's history. How can we say that certain parts of the brain are responsible for emotions or for learning when there are so many different ways in which emotions and learning can be defined and experienced?

Finally, we can be fairly certain that the brain has certain hierarchical relationships, and yet, when we use terms like higher/lower or primitive/advanced to describe them, we are adding a moral framework to them that exceeds biology. For example, we risk forgetting that "advanced" is relative, to a specific species, a particular context, and even a specific function. This does not mean that one should not use a term like "higher" to describe that certain structures/functions in the brain can supplant or control others, and thus are hierarchically related. But such a limited sense of the term "higher" quickly expands when we shift from talk of brain functions to mental functions. We prefer to describe characteristics that humans uniquely possess as advanced, likely a vestige of a Judeo-Christian heritage that gave humans mastery over nature. From an evolutionary perspective, all one really knows is that these characteristics are still around. We cannot even be sure they were necessarily advantageous. They could just as easily be vestiges of other characteristics that are no longer recognized as important. There is hardly any reason to describe them as "higher" or "advanced" except that it confirms the values we already possess. The danger is, as psychology increasingly looks to neuroscience to find a materialist ground, these assumptions are naively imported into psychology.

2. STRUCTURE AND FUNCTION: THE AGE OF THE SYNAPSE

If nineteenth-century neuropsychology revolved around the concept of the reflex, twentieth-century neuropsychology revolved around that of the synapse. The term was first coined in 1897 by Michael Foster and Charles Sherrington and is from the Greek word for conjunction. It was seen as supporting Santiago Ramon y Cajal's "neuron doctrine" or his proposal that neurons are not continuous with each other yet still communicate "signals" using electrical and chemical means (Shepard, 2010). The importance of synapses to the study of the brain became much clearer after the 1950s when the individual agents of chemical transmission, or neurotransmitters, were fully identified, cataloged, and synthesized. Using the new technology of the electron microscope, brain researchers distinguished between noradrenergic, dopaminergic, and serotonergic systems and developed synthetic chemicals to modify these systems. Acetylcholine and glutamate were identified as the major excitatory neurotransmitters while GABA and the amino acid glycine

were regarded as the major inhibitory ones. These synthetic chemicals became part of a pharmacological revolution that fundamentally altered the
treatment of mental illness. The monoamine hypothesis of depression and the
dopaminergic hypothesis of schizophrenia, that both conditions are related to
brain levels of serotonin and dopamine respectively, transformed the modern
understanding of psychopathology. Mental illness was no longer the result of
a poor upbringing or a vaguely "degenerate" brain but an actual neurological
state at the molecular level that could be witnessed via visualization technology.

Another important finding of the 1950s was the identification of the limbic system (hippocampus/amygdala/basal ganglia) and its link with emotional expression associated with the work of Paul D. MacLean. In 1932, the
American neurophysiologist James Papez noted that lesions attached to what
MacLean later termed the "limbic" system resulted in major emotional disturbances. MacLean (1990) distinguished between the structures involved in
primitive emotional expression and those involved in the subjective experience of emotion. The latter, he argued, required the cortex and ended up
being ignored by the neuroscientific study of emotions, which found emotional expression to be more amenable to laboratory study. MacLean believed the limbic system was the seat of the Freudian id as well as key to the
body's "flight or fight" response.

Following Hughlings Jackson, MacLean included the limbic system in his
model of a "triune" brain: a primitive or "reptilian" brain controlling basic
functions and instincts, a limbic system or "old mammalian" brain related to
emotion and reproduction, and a "new mammalian" brain, the neocortex,
which controlled language and thought. The limbic system came to be
viewed as part of the brain's "pleasure center" identified in the work of
James Olds and Peter Milner in the 1950s. In this research, rats with
electrodes attached to this part of the brain repeatedly pressed a lever, stimu-
lating it at the expense of eating and drinking, eventually dying of exhaus-
tion. Today certain limbic system stimulation is regarded as explaining addiction and sexual pleasure.

A final key idea that came out of mid-twentieth century brain science was
a neuropsychological conception of learning. In *The Organization of Behavior* published in 1949, Donald Hebb gave new life to associationism as a
model for brain activity by describing learning as an increased strength in the
relationship between two neurons as a result of firing together. Thus, learning involved establishing novel neural relationships in the brain, relationships that became part of the broader networks that made up thinking. Similar notions can be found throughout the eighteenth and nineteenth centuries
in the work of David Hartley, Alexander Bain, Ramon Santiago y Cajal,
William James, and Sigmund Freud. In the 1960s, Eric Kandel (2007) extended this model to the study of memory, which he described as stored

through modifications in synaptic connections between neurons. He also focused on "learning" in simple organisms: habituation, sensitization, classical, and operant conditioning. Specifically, he identified a form of presynaptic potentiation that corresponded with simple forms of learning. This became the model for the study of all learning/memory in neuroscience, which hereafter focused on changes in synaptic activity. Thus, modifications in synaptic connection became the general ground "underlying" psychological processes.

All this has created a shared space where neuroscientists can do psychology and psychologists can later borrow these findings. Take the example of Joseph Ledoux. His *Synaptic Self* offers a new way to talk about selfhood; people are their synapses. Ledoux's work follows in the tradition of MacLean. LeDoux studies emotions, or at least "emotional behavior," and their neural correlates (Ledoux, 2002, p. 206). While he rejects the idea of a singular "limbic system"—these functions are much more distributed throughout the brain—he too views emotions as controlled by the amygdala. Some of his better-known research focuses on fear conditioning in rats. Rats freeze in response to predators, but they also freeze if they hear a sound that previously preceded an aversive stimulus. In his terms, an evolutionary advantageous response—predators usually hunt by detecting motion, so freezing is adaptive—has been extended to novel stimuli by the associative means described by Pavlov. Thus, says Ledoux, learning via experience has taken place (Ledoux, 2002, pp. 134–173). This suggests an explanation for some of the irrational anxiety and phobias psychotherapists treat today: selective responses are extended too far. Furthermore, damage to the amygdala eliminates the tendency of rats to freeze to either predators or novel stimuli associated with aversive ones.

This is described as a fear "circuit," a group of neurons linked together by synaptic connections or "system," a complex circuit that performs a specialized function like fear. The precise pathways or "wiring" looks something like this: information about the outside world is delivered to the amygdala which controls responses that act back on the world via synaptic outputs; that is, information that danger exists elicits responses like freezing, changes in blood pressure, and the release of hormones or can also inhibit responses by filtering out random excitatory inputs. While much of this was already understood, Ledoux's contribution is that this fear system originally designed to respond to one kind of stimulus can "learn" and apply to others—this involves modifications at the synaptic level or changes in "wiring." Nature and nurture, mind and behavior, says Ledoux (2002) over and over again, are two ways of "wiring up synapses" (p. 5).

More broadly, argues Ledoux, our knowledge of who we are is learned through experience, accessible through memory, and stored via synaptic modification. Ledoux is answering the question that troubled both Wundt and James about memory given their "process" view of the mind: how could a changing mind store fixed memories? These processes are "unconscious"—not quite in the Freudian sense, there is no active repression here—and this lack of awareness on the part of consciousness is the rule rather than the exception. Ledoux also supports the idea that this process involves less actual creation of new synaptic connections but selection from initial, intrinsically established synaptic connections, not so much "learning" as "pruning" and described by the term neural Darwinism. In general, explains Ledoux (2002), today's neuroscience is skeptical of learning as the transfer of information from the environment instead viewing it as mechanisms of transmission that involve internal selection (p. 73). These modifications can also involve the cortex, in which case they require more connections and longer processing times, what Ledoux terms the higher route, or can simply involve changes in connectivity with the thalamus, an evolutionarily older route and generating "cruder" representations and responses. Once again, we find the division between advanced and primitive central to contemporary neurological thought.

All these ideas are supported by new technologies of seeing, what William Lyons (1986) cleverly terms mechanized introspectionism. Today's visual technology allows researchers to "see" brains at the level of function, not simply structure. They make visible the neurological correlates of brain activity. As critic of the sometimes brash claims of contemporary neuroscience Nikolas Rose (2013) helpfully lays out, today's neuroscience rests on several basic principles:

(a) The brain is an organ like any other.
(b) Neural processes are conserved by evolution.
(c) The brain is best studied at the molecular level.
(d) Key processes revolve around neural transmission.
(e) This centers on the synapse and its neurotransmitters.
(f) But it can also involve other entities including transporters, receptors, modulators, and hormones.
(g) Different parts of the brain have different neurotransmitters and evolved independently.
(h) All mental processes reside in the brain and have neural correlates.
(i) Thus all mental and behavioral states have a relation to observable organic activity.

We can add a few others:

(j) Neural activity can be understood through the terms of stimulus-response relationships organized hierarchically.
(k) Neural activity can be adequately captured by various technologies like PET scans and fMRIs.

(l) Synaptic activity involves the creation of certain nerve pathways and networks that remain highly plastic throughout life ("soft" rather than "hard" wired).

(m) These networks or circuits are function-specific or "modular."

(n) They typically have differential responses to different stimuli.

(o) "Learning" can be understood as the creation of "associations" between nerve cells and networks active at the same time in the tradition of Pavlov—what fires together, wires together.

This list helps us understand why those familiar with today's neuroscience believe that the gap between mind and body has finally been bridged. Psychological causes and agents still exist, but they work exclusively through neural mechanisms. Some of what is on this list one can be fairly sure about. Other assumptions, however, are more tenuous. Let's start with technology. With the electron microscope, developed in the 1930s, the stability of images was achieved through a chemical process that, as Nikolas Rose (2013) puts it, was much more like a fossil than a snapshot. The technology seeks to isolate elements in order to offer a view into functions, yet ignores that those elements involve interrelationships with many other functions and structures removed from view in the interest of clarity. More recently, fMRI technology, developed in the 1990s, generates images of the brain in which certain areas are lit up or displayed in certain colors. This is intended to indicate activity with respect to a particular function. But the images that we are viewing are not photographs of actual brains or brain activity but representations of brain activity. These images represent movements of highly oxygenated blood, which is supposed to connote an active or stimulated state, but can get tricky when dealing with multiple functions. Some of the original relationships in the "raw" data are overlooked in favor of the "cooked" ones, and correlational relationships are framed as causal ones. A lot of this kind of neuroscience involves post-hoc explanations. We see what "lights up," assign that locale a function, and then explain why this is necessarily so.

Much confusion also revolves around language. The study of the brain has employed various metaphors since its nineteenth-century roots. Some of the old nineteenth-century metaphors are gone—mental energy, reflex arcs—while some still persist—associations, connections, inputs, outputs, and primitiveness. And as we saw in the case of Ledoux, there are a whole host of new ones—circuits, pleasure centers, wiring, firing, pruning, signals, processing, just to name a few. Naturally, there is nothing wrong with relying on metaphors, except when one forgets that they are metaphors and confuse them with reality. There is no "wiring" in the brain. Neural impulses do not "fire." Neurons do not form "networks" or "circuits." And neurons do not communicate through "signals." But the brain at times acts as if it was wired.

Neural impulses at times act like they were fired. Neurons at times behave as if they were joined in a circuit or are communicating via signals. These distinctions are not trivial. If neurons truly "fired," then we might wonder by whom or what? The idea of a "fired," impulse neglects that the "impulse" is actually composed of chemical changes in the nerve cell itself, not something distinct traveling thru nerve cells. Moreover, how can the brain use "signals" when there is no consciousness or "central processor" to interpret them? A signal, by its very definition, is something that conveys information about a phenomenon. But to convey information, one needs something capable of receiving it. In other words, we are back to the homunculus fallacy. These metaphors function to explain processes that we just don't understand.

This metaphorical language allows one to explain the properties of brain activity in certain limited contexts, but then neglect the ways in which brain activity resists these explanations. When I "wire" my house, that wiring is fixed until I modify it. Not so with the brain. Neural pathways are constantly in flux, something not often captured by static, decontextualized images of them. My brain of five minutes ago is not the brain I have now, nor will it be my brain five minutes from now. Moreover, modifying the wiring in my home requires consciousness. There needs to be thinking, acting, experiencing me to do this work. In the case of the brain, no consciousness is required. It's as if the wiring were doing the wiring! By using terms like "wiring," we are left with, in Gilbert Ryle's famous phrase, a ghost in the machine. At the other extreme, Ledoux is emptying psychology of all its content. Fear is not simply a fear response, nor is it an increase in amygdala activity, even though such categorical confusion makes it easier for neuroscience to study it. Addiction is not simply a response to triggered pleasure centers, as addiction is not simply a behavioral response. It's a way of being in the world. More importantly, we are not our synapses. Synapses are simply the wrong unit of analysis for making sense of minds, let alone people (Noe, 2009, p. 48).

The self is not some after-effect of brain processes. If anything it is the other way around. In the seventeenth century we created a language for talking about the world as if it was divorced from consciousness, as if the experience of it did not involve purpose, meaning, and intentionality. Today, we have forgotten that it is this scientific language that is the illusion—a wonderfully useful illusion no doubt, but still an illusion. If anything, the brain is the product and human consciousness is the producer! This might sound like the suggestion that world is created by consciousness, and of course this is not the case. It is the language for talking about the world and the categories for making sense of the world that are created by consciousness. The problem is that the world and the categories for making sense of the world cannot so easily be distinguished from each other, especially since they interact with each other (Hacking, 1999). Sometimes this radically limits what we can know. As neuroscientist David Gaffan writes,

The idea that mental activity is brain activity has retarded research in neuroscience. We have gone into the brain expecting to find such things as memories and percepts waiting there to be discovered, and systems for attention . . . all corresponding to traditional mental events. . . . The better we understand the brain processes we study, however, the clearer it becomes that they do not correspond in any sense to mental activities (194). (cited in Leahey, 2005, p. 194)

He goes on to give the example of "attention," an intuitive label perhaps, but whose study requires going well beyond what we associate with attention. Searching for an "attention system" hinders efforts to understand it. The case is similar with memory. In the end, the problem with all this is that brain activity and mental activity are not the same. Brain activity can often be adequately described using material and mechanical language, but mental activity requires that we use "people" language. It is correct to say that a person thinks or feels. It is incorrect to say that a brain thinks or feels, as thinking and feeling require consciousness. Actually, they require an entire organism. The human experience of depression is not the same thing as the brain state of depleted serotonin, just as the brain state of associated neural pathways is not the same as the human experience of having learned something. The human state requires consciousness to recognize and name it or more than one consciousness as the case may be. Of course, the brain state also requires consciousness to recognize and name it on some level. And consciousness in turn requires a body. In fact, consciousness requires the joint operation of brain, body, and world (Noe, 2009).

As Raymond Tallis (2011) notes, the same problem exists with one key metaphor of today's neuroscience, information (pp. 199–208). This is the supposed substance acquired by sensory nerves and processed by the brain. It is the substance contained in those neural impulses traveling along neural networks and crossing synapses. It is a metaphor for what was once termed a "signal." But how can information exist without a human that is being "informed"? At best what is traveling along these paths is potential information that will become realized information only when it comes into contact with consciousness. Some in neuroscience go as far as to try and explain the relationship between neurological activity and consciousness, a problem that has bedeviled the study of the brain since its inception, as a conceptual error. Christopher Frith (2007), for instance, argues that the brain creates the illusion that we have direct contact with the world. Conscious experience is simply an illusion created by neurological activity. Whether or not such a perspective makes sense in neuroscience is one thing, but turning consciousness into an illusion seems to lose sight of the point of the study of psychology. Similar assumptions allow psychologists to persist in the quest to study psychological processes divorced from the conscious experience of those properties. What is learning without the conscious experience of having learned something, or memory without the conscious experience of remembering? Today's neuropsychology is mired in linguistic confusion attributing properties and activities that require persons to brains and other material entities. This hardly seems a solid foundation for contemporary psychology.

3. INSIDE AND OUTSIDE: THE ALL-POWERFUL GENE

Over the past few decades a new narrative that includes both academic and popular manifestations has developed to explain the centrality of biology in explaining human thought and behavior and once again reconfigures the relationship between inside and outside as well as structure and function. It is, in one sense, a return to a pre-evolutionary view that regards the inside as determining the outside and function as following structure. It is grounded in the postwar discoveries of James Watson and Francis Crick (Watson, 1968) related to the structure and operations of DNA molecules as well as the more recent trend to locate the sources of human variation—particularly ones regarded as pathological—in biological abnormalities, a trend exacerbated by the influence of psychotropic medicine in psychiatry. It is a way of talking about heredity and family influence as well as a broader cultural and political discourse for making sense of identity, rights, and responsibility. We can term this narrative "genetic determinism." Evelyn Fox-Keller (1996) uses the expression "the discourse of gene action." Either way, it's a narrative that seems grounded in biology, but actually has very little sense of how bodies work. It's also a narrative that preexisted the discovery of the actual physiological structures. It also offers another example of the tension between structure and function, this time the seemingly perennial confusion between the precise structural organization of DNA and the slightly more ambiguous functional category of the gene (Griffiths & Stotz, 2007).

Like much of what we are looking at in this chapter, it's a narrative that first emerged at the very end of the nineteenth century. One figure vital to this new way of thinking about inheritance was August Weismann. By the 1890s, most biologists accepted the basic evolutionary framework of Darwin, but could not accept the idea that the principal mechanism for evolutionary change was natural selection. Instead, they turned to the thought of Herbert Spencer who, influenced by Lamarck, argued that evolutionary change was the result of novel responses to the environment during an organism's lifetime passed on to future descendants, what was known as use-inheritance or the inheritance of acquired characteristics (Gould, 2002). This solution also proved more optimistic than Darwin's, suggesting that organisms can learn during their lifetime and pass those results onto future generations, generating evolutionary progress. Natural selection, they argued, was best only for weeding out the unfit. Darwinism's most ardent supporter, German biologist

August Weismann, challenged this. Weismann defended natural selection's role as the principal mechanism of evolutionary transformation. He found himself involved in a public debate with Herbert Spencer in 1893 after Spencer published an article denying natural selection the importance Neo-Darwinians like Weismann gave it. While selection was important, Spencer argued, the inheritance of acquired characteristics was more important for the generation of biological novelty. Weismann responded in a paper entitled "The All-Sufficiency of Natural Selection" offering the classic pan-selectionist position. Selection, he argued, was the exclusive mechanism for evolutionary change.

At this time, Neo-Darwinism was identified with the students of Francis Galton and the school of biometry who sought to use statistics to describe variation in populations. They studied continuous variation (Mayr, 1982). Weismann's work introduced a key distinction, that between an "immortal" germ plasm and a limited soma-plasm—the latter constructed via the information contained in the former. This offered a framework for the soon-to-be-rediscovered genetic theory of Gregor Mendel who would definitively prove the erroneous nature of conceptions of "blended" inheritance and explained theoretically why use-inheritance was impossible. The path of information from gene to organism went in one and only one direction. Once use-inheritance was seen as impossible, natural selection became the only viable candidate for evolutionary change. In fact, Weismann argued, selection need not operate at the level of the organism à la Darwin. It could operate at the level of the germ—germinal selection. Thus what might appear like the product of "soft" or use-inheritance was actually an expression of an already-selected form of germ plasm. While variation might appear to be directed when seen on the level of the organism, argued Weismann, on the level of the germ plasm, it was not. Selection remained as "random" as Darwin had described.

This was a reformulation of the position of classical Darwinism, which viewed selection as taking place on the level of the individual organism and gave the germ plasm, soon to be renamed the "gene," a lot of importance. Many critics of Weismann argued that this new understanding of selection was simply trying to salvage its importance, one that most scientists had already come to reject. However, as Ernst Mayr (1982) pointed out decades later, Weismann was prescient in the sense that he recognized that the key to variability lay in genetics not habit. Mayr calls Weismann the most important nineteenth-century evolutionist after Darwin. Weismann reinvigorated the study of instincts in the 1890s, which were regarded as key to managing behavior and promoting social order.

Weismann's work and the developing unidirectional model of inheritance made individual development or ontogenesis irrelevant. Adult bodies were simply expressions of genetic instructions. The intellectual framework for Watson and Crick's discovery of the double-helix was set well in advance, a discovery which explained this process in structural and functional terms. The ground had already been prepared earlier in the century as the disciplines of embryology and genetics began to diverge. As Evelyn Fox Keller (1996) perceptively notes, while the term "heredity" had originally referred to both transmission of potentialities during reproduction and the development of those particularities over the course of life, after the rediscovery of Mendel's work, the term was increasingly used to describe transmission exclusively. The new field of genetics explicitly renounced embryology. Because genes were regarded as autocatalytic, that is, able to replicate themselves independently, they did not require anything but their own "will" to transmit hereditary information. Again, Keller describes this way of thinking about genes as the discourse of gene action, a vocabulary that offers genes far more agency, autonomy, and causal responsibility than they actually have.

The only ones to recognize this problem were the embryologists, who were familiar with development and thus, the complexity of actual living organisms. They argued that the effects of genes on organisms like the effect of environments on organisms were emergent properties of developmental systems and did not exist before them. It was typically European embryologists who recognized the flaws with the Anglo-American–dominated discourse of gene action. One of these critics was Richard Goldschmidt who spoke of "gene activation" in complex systems rather than gene action. This framework threatened the very foundation of the embryologists' discipline, as the question of how a single cell developed into a multicellular organism, the question of differentiation, was superfluous. For the geneticist, there was no question of development. Genes simply directed the process. In the 1930s with the rise of Fascism, as embryology became associated with German science, it was further marginalized. When molecular biologists took up the study of protein synthesis in the 1950s and 1960s, they did so with simple organisms, working on the assumption, as Jacques Monod famously put it: what's true for E. coli is true for the elephant.

One figure critical of the discourse of gene action was geneticist Barbara McClintock. She had already pointed out in the early 1950s that genetic elements could move spontaneously from one site to another, even one chromosome to another, a phenomenon she referred to as transduction. The consequences of this were profoundly challenging to genetic orthodoxy. No longer could genetic information be regarded as coming from a static, fixed source, but instead the source was one that was dynamic and mobile. Geneticists ignored her work until the late 1960s when independent evidence for transduction emerged (Keller, 1983). The consequences of the divergence of embryology and genetics were evident in simplistic models of protein synthesis that ignored the rest of the intra- and extracellular contexts in which proteins were produced. This in turn led to the kind of genetic determinism that became popular from the 1970s on.

Molecular biologists had long suspected that the key to the transmission of hereditary information lay with proteins. The idea that genetic materials possess "information" and later "instructions" began as a metaphor, but gradually became more and more real in the minds and theories of biologists. Finally, Watson and Crick's discovery of the double helix codified and materialized the metaphor. The language of "information" emerged from developments in computing during and immediately following World War II, and more broadly, through its circulation in the military-industrial complex of the Cold War era. Because information could be divorced from its content, it supplied molecular biology with a language to talk about genetic transmission without necessarily having any sense of what was being transmitted. Biologist Jacques Monod, seeking to move the French away from Neo-Lamarckism, characterized heredity as nothing but information, message, and code (Monod, 1971).

While the "information" discourse helped provide a language for Watson and Crick's discovery, the Rockefeller Foundation helped provide the funding. Warren Weaver, the director of Rockefeller's natural science division, first coined the term "molecular biology" in 1938 (Kay, 1996, p. 49). While Rockefeller's first forays into biology came with its popular Eugenics programs of the 1920s (including a program for sterilization of the feeble-minded), the Nazi's infamous use of eugenics language made those kinds of project politically nonviable. Moreover, as biologists realized that most traits were polygenetic and most genes were pleiotropic, breeding for distinct traits or behaviors was seen as not feasible. As a result, Rockefeller shifted its focus. No longer would biology be concerned with rooting out the "genetically unfit," but would instead master genetic technology. Still, the basic paradigm of human engineering through technology remained at the core of the program. Naturally, a unidirectional and reductionist model of genetic inheritance worked well with the project, leaving only one necessary site of intervention, the gene. In fact, Rockefeller refused to fund attempts by J. D. Bernal, Joseph Needham, and others to study the problem of biological organization from an antireductionist and whole-organism perspective (Kay, 1996).

The only problem was that, at this point, the gene was still largely an abstraction. It was a placeholder for describing the biological unit of inheritance, although the actual structures had yet to be discovered. Rockefeller's "Sciences of Man" program, inaugurated in 1933, hoped to change that. The new molecular biology was not to be "pure" science, but would be, in its essence, application oriented and dependent on the technology available—technology like electron microscopes, ultracentrifuges, and X-ray diffraction. It involved teams of researchers working together to solve puzzles, creating a new industrial model for biological research in the United States that required extensive funding. As it became more and more like physics, it was taken up in various elite universities across the country, particularly at Caltech. By focusing on the "molecular" level, expensive technology became necessary for biology to advance. After the war, the Rockefeller program promoted its programs to the public by highlighting the possibility of medical advance as it had made its most public advances in immunology research during the war. The new genetics, the program promised, would cure disease and improve the human condition.

The new biology required the gradual rejection of the idea that proteins alone controlled heredity. The process moved forward in the 1930s as biochemists began to involve themselves in the project. Biochemistry was a subset of biology that had long studied the metabolic pathways and cycles of the body and now sought to elucidate the structure of proteins. In the 1940s, the research began to focus on nucleic acids, of which DNA is one, although they had been discovered and identified in the nineteenth century. The idea of protein inheritance had a long history, and most geneticists accepted that proteins were responsible for reproduction, growth, and regulation. T. H. Morgan, the influential geneticist studying Drosophila, postulated the existence of hereditary material in the nucleus of cells long before any materiality was ascribed to genes. He went as far as describing cytoplasmic activity as irrelevant to heredity, not surprising given the distaste most geneticists felt for embryology and development.

Furthermore, the developing model of genetic transmission was affected by the organisms studied—mostly *Drosophila*, *Neurospora spores*, *E. coli*, and other unicellular organisms. They accepted that one could extrapolate what one discovered about these processes to multicellular organisms like humans. Naturally, this led to models of reduced complexity. Regardless of whether genes exist or not, Morgan insisted, we must act as if they do. Whatever the gene was, it could be associated with a specific location on a chromosome. The actual process of genetic reproduction and transmission remained a mystery. Thus, the role of genes in the body was well accepted decades before anyone knew much about the material form or function of genes. It was, for all practical purposes, a given. Another given was that the genetic substance, whatever it was, was able to reproduce itself or autocatalytic. Thus, by the time Watson and Crick came along, they simply had to devise a genetic structure that fit with the assumptions of unidirectionality, autocatalytic reproduction, and basic independence from the rest of the cell's activity.

By 1953, the year of Watson and Crick's discovery, several "observational" technologies were advanced enough—chromatography, the electron microscope and crystallography in particular, that the structure of DNA could be "seen"—using the term rather loosely. By 1951, there was some consensus among molecular biologists that DNA and proteins were functionally independent and that DNA was the source of genetic information. By

1952, the race to elucidate the structure of DNA was on. The story of the "discovery" is well known through Watson's personal account in *The Double Helix*. There, Watson admitted that all he had to do was to construct a set of molecular models and begin to play. Reading Watson's account, one sees just how much of the discovery was guesswork. Watson later admitted that he did not understand some of the basic aspects of helical theory even as he was devising models for a helix structure of DNA.

Watson and Crick presented their model at the 1953 Cold Harbor Symposium on viruses, and many participants recognized the revolutionary implications of their findings. In 1957, Crick referred to the idea that information can go from nucleic acid to protein but not the other way around as molecular biology's "central dogma." Ironically, Watson and Crick had not specified the solutions to the two most important questions that occupied geneticists: How did DNA reproduce itself? And how was it involved in the synthesis of proteins and therefore the transfer of hereditary information? Yet somehow, many molecular biologists accepted Watson and Crick's model because it seemed to point to the answer to these questions, leaving the presumption of unidirectionality intact. Also, the sequence of bases making up DNA could easily be read as a form of coded instructions for producing fully developed organisms. The sequences coded for specific proteins, and these were the building blocks of organisms, which acted according to the predetermined "instructions" of the DNA. By the 1960s, both these riddles were solved with further study of RNA. DNA had become the master molecule. The DNA was regarded as a "tape" and RNA as a "tape reader." Both were governed by the rules of information processing.

With the mystery of heredity "solved," it took years for developmental biologists to recognize some of the basic flaws of the gene-centered model of hereditary transmission. While most practicing molecular biologists probably know better, many others continue to describe genes as the primary agent behind organismic construction and development. One can easily find a myriad of examples of this discourse circulating in contemporary culture and even in mainstream psychology. The model was developed long before any knowledge of the structure or function of these processes was acquired (Griffiths & Stotz, 2007). This in of itself is not a problem, but in fact a useful technique. It does suggest, however, that this model might have just confirmed what was already believed. It allowed molecular biology to begin to "master" life as well as hinted that many of the social and economic relationships in U.S. society were biologically rather than culturally based. It was widely agreed that the function of DNA had to be related to its structure—the helical combination of the bases adenine, thymine, guanine, and cytosine—but the central dogma offered only one version of the process by which information on the DNA was communicated to the body.

Many thoughtful contemporary biologists disagree with the claim that DNA control protein synthesis or provide instructions for building bodies, except in a very distal and metaphorical sense. Watson and Crick's work and the work that followed on protein synthesis, while important, did not come close to proving that DNA controls the activities of cells. The discourse of gene action offers DNA as the "master molecule" endowing it with autonomy, agency, almost "thought," seemingly supported by the general consensus of the scientific community, but this is just bad biology and created the ultimate homunculus. The consensus is correct that the sequences of amino acid determine the structure (i.e., muscle) or function (i.e., enzymes) of proteins and that these sequences are directly related to the sequence of bases on the DNA strand. A change in the sequence of nucleotides can go as far as changing how proteins fold thus altering structure and function. In this sense, DNA provides "instructions" for bodies. But the "instruction" metaphor implies an intelligent reader to "follow" those instructions.

The real problem with this language is that it neglects all the other components involved, neglecting that other proteins determine where and when proteins are synthesized by activating certain gene sequences (Davies, 2014). The way these control signals are "interpreted" depends on the internal structure of the cell. For example, the fate of proteins is dependent on positional information. Other genes can also activate or inhibit gene action. RNA does not always faithfully reproduce DNA sequences as a result of phenomena like transduction and transposition; DNA sequences can change position on a genome. In complex biological systems, almost all causal factors are context dependent (Godfrey-Smith, 2007, p. 112). Finally, the discourse of gene action neglects the vagueness of the term gene itself. What is it that we mean by the term gene? A particular DNA sequence? A particular DNA sequence translated into a sometimes identical and sometimes not identical RNA sequence? The entire protein-producing machinery? The definition is an arbitrary one. Where exactly does "nature" end and "environment" begin? Outside the body? Outside the cell? Outside the nucleus? Outside a strand of DNA? Who can say? If one must have a dichotomy, a much more biologically relevant one is between specificity and plasticity, that is, between processes that have broader and narrower outcomes yet both are dependent on gene-environment-context interdependence (S. Rose, 2005, p. 64).

4. STRUCTURE AND FUNCTION: DEVELOPMENTAL BIOLOGY

Developmental biology introduces a more interdependent way to perceive the relationship between structure and function and is probably more useful to psychology than those approaches inherited from physics. One area of neuroscience that has value for psychologists as well as those trying to relate the structures of the brain to what we have historically associated with the functions of mind focuses on developing brain structures and functions rather than static ones. In fact, such focus reveals much about what is wrong with the picture of mind psychologists have developed over the past two centuries. In a general sense, much of what is described as static or prefixed turns out to be dynamic and highly contingent. And, ironically, some of what is described as variable turns out to be quite constrained. Nineteenth-century neurophysiology tended to view the brain through a language borrowed from eighteenth-century physics. This mechanistic approach was useful to a point, but in the past few decades it has become clear that a more complex understanding of the brain and nervous system comes when one studies its development, starting from a single cell at the start of life. Such study requires a different language and explanatory apparatus—one more focused on dynamic relationships, indeterminacy, and local interactions. Outside developmental neuroscience, people might be comfortable viewing genes as directing the development of the brain, but within the field it has long been recognized that this is not the case. There is no directing of the development of the brain, except in a very trivial sense.

To understand brain development, one must start at the very beginning or at least somewhere near the beginning. To start with, there is surprisingly little anatomical or chemical variation between human brains. The same basic structures are fairly universal across the species (Kagan, 2013, p. 27). And yet, the environment, at multiple levels, is integral to development from the moment of conception. Even identical twins will experience different environments given how they are positioned in the womb. Life, as Steven Rose (2005) puts it, is "about being and becoming, being one thing and simultaneously transforming into something else" (p. 62). Such transformations are not directed by a gene or an environment, but by the organism itself as novel properties emerge through the interaction of various components. A good question is: How does such a dynamic process lead to such a seemingly invariant brain? A related problem in developmental neuroscience has been the problem of differentiation: How do the few embryonic cells early in life know how to build an organism? This is why terms like genetic "instructions" or "blueprints" seem intuitively correct. But this language is very misleading. Genes are not blueprints, nor do they provide instructions to the body.

There are certain specialized genes that determine where in the embryo organs will develop (Wolpert, 2011). They do this by binding to sites on chromosomes, essentially making them active. This can determine which proteins are produced. These can, therefore, regulate the expression of other genes. They trigger identical genetic activities, with some slight variations, across the body. Such genes are conservative in this sense, and this explains why early embryogenesis in specific species tends to follow similar patterns.

They are sometimes described as "master" genes, but this language is misleading as it implies that they are not themselves regulated or would not respond differently in different contexts, which would be incorrect. They are better described as "micro-manager" genes (Roberts, 2004, p. 27). But, a better term still for all this is specificity.

And yet, if the growing blastula is placed into another organism, the organs developed will be those of the new organism not the original one. This is termed plasticity and means that genes must have additional sources of "information" when it comes to which proteins to produce. It turns out this information is present in the cytoplasm of the cell. Thus, the "information" is actually a function of the interaction between genes and genetic products in the cytoplasm. As J. A. Davies (2014) describes it, control is "nowhere and everywhere . . . No one is in charge" (p. 10). Unlike most interactions in the developing embryo, which tend to be local, the developing brain is capable of contact across great distances as its neural network spreads. It is thus able to integrate "information" from across the brain creating more variation in function. In other words, brain functions can take into account what is happening throughout the brain, incorporating them into an already organized system. As Terrence Deacon (1997) well describes it, the "whole is determining the parts."

This is essentially the problem with some of the new "modular" and localized accounts of cognitive functions—the brain is already highly integrated early in development, and it is unlikely that evolutionary changes in one part would not affect the others, which is what modular theorists often argue. As Deacon (1997) notes, this makes it almost impossible to describe the evolutionary origins of certain functions by describing how that specific function was likely adaptive in time passed as, from the get-go, that "function" was nested in a network of other functions (p. 351). This also means we need to be careful about what we identify as a "function." Because a distinction is important in the social world doesn't always mean it is important with respect to biological organization.

The development of the brain involves destructive processes alongside constructive ones. Neural cells, as well as synaptic connections between those cells, tend to be overproduced. There is a "competition" for targets in synapses. This is followed by a variant of natural selection wherein those cells compete for resources and many of them do not survive. Similarly, many connections between neurons end up atrophying. Thus, the cells do not require instructions up front, as the body has the opportunity to rid itself of less "adaptive" ones (S. Rose, 2005, p. 76). This is not quite what Darwin had in mind though; as it turns out, many cells end up dying after assisting other nerve cells reach their target, a process more cooperative than competitive. Connectivity is not preprogrammed either. It is a function of contingent, local properties of neurons including cell-surface adhesion, mechanical properties of tissues, and spatial patterns of attraction and repulsion. Otherwise, genes would have to carry far more "instructions" than they can code for especially given that gene size is constant across species. During this process of selective elimination, the brain adapts to the body it finds itself in. These adaptations are the result of locally determined interactions between DNA, RNA, cytoplasm, neurons, and their environment. As Darwin recognized, what looks like design need not have a designer.

Much of this continues well after birth. Weight increases in the brain are not due to the production of new neurons, but changes in the relationships between them. A major process in brain development during the first two years is the laying down of myelin lipid sheaths of the axons as well as the proliferation of glial cells—both required for conducting impulses across neural pathways. As the brain continues to change, different parts growing at different times and speeds, it is still able to retain a functional cohesion. There is no interruption in basic functions. A useful analogy is one of a plane that repairs itself in mid-flight. It becomes more and more difficult to match the growing structures of the brain with developing functions. One can make a few generalizations, however. Motor regions, particularly those associated with the upper body tend to mature before sensory regions, followed by the visual cortex. The infant in the first few weeks of life is a "subcortical" organism—that is, dependent on hindbrain and midbrain functions (e.g., respiration, digestion)—but by three months with the proliferation of glial cells and myelination, cortical neural regions are more active along with motor regions associated with hand, head, and feet movement. There appears to be a clear relationship between the disappearance of early reflexes associated with subcortical regions and the development of the cortex.

The human brain is well designed to learn to extract information from sensory inputs (S. Rose, 2005, p. 127). This requires organizing experience across multiple modalities—vision alone requires the linkage of motion to form along with the integration of color, distance, and direction. Just how this is accomplished remains a mystery, let alone how integration across multiple sensory modalities is accomplished or the eventual integration of perception, memory, and thought. Given this, it is clear just how little we know about the emergence and development of thought. There have been attempts to argue that there are so-called critical periods in brain development, but they almost always turn out to be wrong (Lerner, 2002). Over the first year, more and more bodily functions come under cortical control, but by this point it becomes difficult to make too many generalizations about the timing of specific functions, as they tend to be culturally and individually varying. The older the child, explains Steven Rose (2005), the greater the number of individual differences that can no longer be associated with changes in brain structure. Neurological development is nonlinear, the interaction of continuity and rapid change, therefore some of the results of prior development are integrated into future development. This is part of why predictions about specific outcomes are very difficult to make. At the same time, development tends to be highly redundant, ensuring that there are multiple pathways to the same outcome.

This model of neurological development suggests a few things. First, it is almost impossible to make predictions about brain structure or function given specific genes. This is even more so in the case of psychological functions, even though some of the language used in neuropsychology and contemporary medicine suggests otherwise. Second, it is also highly unlikely that we can relate certain psychological functions to brain structures, except in a fairly general sense. The more specific we try to get, the more likely the functions we describe are cultural artifacts as opposed to natural categories. There is the temptation to study some of these processes out of context. By holding the "environment" steady, causal narratives become easier to generate, but not only is the context a part of the process, but key higher-order relationships tend to be neglected (Roberts, 2004, p. 9). Not everything can be explained with terms like "genes" or "environment." The lure of neuroscientific reductionism remains powerful, yet it is unlikely that even those attracted to this paradigm would accept a similar reduction of the arrangement of symbols on a printed page to the chemistry involved with the paper and ink. The chemistry makes the arrangement possible, but in the end the organization of the page involves a different level of analysis.

Explaining brain processes relies on one language and psychological processes another. These are different levels of analyses regardless of whether they are focused on the same object. This is true even if some contemporary neuroscientists employ a neobehavioral framework that downplays this. Psychology is about people, not brains, even though there can be no people without brains, or brains without people for that matter. Psychological objects and processes are not products of the brain, they are not even, in less reductive terms, products of brains and bodies, but they are products of the activities of persons and worlds. This is often true of biological processes in general, but there is a case to be made about the employment of this kind of reductionism in the biological sciences given its fruitfulness. In psychology, not only does it not yield the same value, but also it does not reveal much about human psychology, which is the very point of this study in the first place.

Chapter Six

On Developmental Thinking

The idea that children grow into adults, passing through some kind of fixed sequence of stages in the proper order that involves a movement from child-like characteristics to adult-like characteristics, a great march forward from the simple to the advanced, from immaturity to maturity, is a relatively recent one as are the ideas that development is a gradual process and that the culmination of development involves autonomy and freedom from adult authority. A bit older is the idea that early experiences are preserved in some form throughout development. Observing children over time, it is hard not to see that they "develop"—or at least that they change over time in similar ways, or so one assumes given how much developmental thinking has become a part of the way we make sense of childhood. Metaphors like "stages" and "maturity," the latter related to the Latin for ripe, seem like neutral descriptions of reality. It takes a real stretch of imagination to go back to a time, only a few centuries ago, when things did not appear to fundamentally change, and if they did, those changes were regarded as trivial compared with a basic essence that remained the same. Thus, developmental thinking offers yet another opportunity to consider the relationship between structure and function, between being and becoming, as well as how the resulting ideas translate into certain cultural assumptions and practices. And, as we shall see, the more interesting variants tend to look more to biology than physics to try and make sense of these tensions.

Conceptions of childhood in general are normative as children typically end up being the ground upon which societies project moral values. They are also teleological. Developmental thinking is no exception. Development is a passage toward the good (White, 1983, p. 73). After 1860 and the spread of evolutionism, "genetic" psychology offered a new way to think about individual history and childhood. Quite literally, children became father to "mankind," as their nature resembled that of human ancestors, all this in the context of massive changes in terms of the place of children in Western society. Philippe Ariès' magisterial *Centuries of Childhood* (1962), the first to take childhood seriously as an important historical subject, has dominated scholarship on the history of childhood (Fass, 2013). The crux of the work revolved around the idea that childhood emerged in the sixteenth century with the spread of markets, literacy, and schooling. Medieval Europe, Aries declared famously, had no children. Furthermore, because of high infant mortality, parents dulled their affective ties with their children. Decades of historical scholarship since then has undermined both of these premises except the general idea that a new conception of childhood emerged in the West in the sixteenth century but only became dominant in the nineteenth century. By 1900, it made sense for Swedish author Ellen Key (1909) to predict that the twentieth century would be the "century of the child."

What can be said is that modern conceptions of childhood tend to take root in wealthier societies or among wealthier members of a society because first and foremost it means removing children from the workforce as well as informal family-based work and sending them to school. Childhood, therefore, is a mark of economic privilege. What emerged in the sixteenth century were the very beginnings of the economic conditions that made this possible (Fass, 2013, p. 9). These emerging conditions were magnified by eighteenth century Romanticism, which viewed the child as the exemplification of the pure and the good and of a human nature uncorrupted by civilization, a stark contrast with certain strands of post-Reformation Christianity that viewed children as sinful and corrupt. Still, even Greco-Roman thinkers recognized that the early years of life were especially malleable, and therefore a vital time to shape character. Plato assumed it in his model of education in the *Republic,* as did Quintilian, and this was even more true of Christian education. With the spread of literacy in the sixteenth century, especially in Protestant societies influenced by the idea that everyone should have access to God's word, more and more children went to school, even if briefly, which helped to further develop the idea that children were distinct from adults and had their own nature (Postman, 1994). Children's differential nature was made explicit by Rousseau (1762), complaining that people always look for the man in the child without thinking about what he was before becoming a man (p. 3). Rousseau's interest in children was certainly moral, as had been the case for a long time in the West, but was also medical. While others had already began to argue against the practice of swaddling, for example, Rousseau linked his rejection of swaddling with broader themes related to freedom and autonomy (Fass, 2013, p. 80). It became a metaphor for a pedagogy that extended children's innocence for as long as possible and liberated children from the shackles of authority and civilization, allowing them to develop independent minds. Even Fredrick the Great was moved by these new sentiments as to the importance of childhood and instituted the first compulsory education regime in Prussia in 1763.

All this culminated in the nineteenth century that witnessed both material and psychological changes with respect to childhood, at least in Western Europe and the United States. For one, a new "intensive" style of childrearing emerged among the middle classes in which the raising of children was said to be the central job of mothers (Fass, 2013). This led to a more romantic view of mother love. With the spread of industrialization, as fathers left the home to work and the home became the domain of women, a new class of childrearing experts emerged to offer advice to women as they assumed primary responsibility for childcare (Fass, 2013). As would be the case with a feminized teaching profession during this period as well, this work was viewed as too important to be left exclusively in women's hands. The nation-state, growing increasingly powerful, became more involved in children's issues through various child welfare movements as well as through the institutionalization of compulsory schooling. Medicine in particular operated through normalization, which is a doctrine that laid out the conditions for raising healthy children and posed moral issues in medical terms (N. Rose, 1990, p. 128).

Because an education for industrial jobs required a more differentiated curriculum—at the minimum there would be managers and workers—with different skills, chronological age, and later mental age, as it became associated with individual capacities, became one means by which to rationalize divergent educational tracks (Fass, 2013). Therefore, chronological age was increasingly viewed as tied to cognitive and social development. Genetic or "developmental" psychology began as part of the evolutionary project of studying human origins. With the spread of technologies of measurement and assessment, the anecdotal studies of Charles Darwin, William Preyer, and T. Stanley Hall were gradually replaced by more systematic and laboratory-based ones. The development of the nursery school in particular allowed for the observation of large numbers of infants and the construction of developmental norms based around averages (N. Rose, 1990, p. 142). In the United States and Britain, such standardizing methods tended to downplay the role of theory and leave many hidden assumptions intact.

Conceptually, modern developmental thinking involves the convergence of a Judeo-Christian sense of history with new theories of progress that emerged with the eighteenth-century French Enlightenment and the German-based Nature-Philosophy [*naturphilosophie*]. The latter was a romantic reaction against the Enlightenment, which regarded change as essential to life, and from which nineteenth-century evolutionary ideas eventually sprang (Bury, 1921; Collingwood, 1946; Becker, 1932). One figure who sat in both of these traditions was Rousseau who, in his fairly contemporary sounding treatise on education *Emile*, described a trajectory from immature and irrational childlike thought to mature and rational adult thought. This was the path of development. It was also a path toward freedom, and in fact, these ideas greatly influenced Kant's linking of morality and autonomy. These ideas are still taken quite seriously in most liberal democratic societies. The world of the infant, said Rousseau, was one of pure sensation, dominated by pleasure and pain without memory, imagination, or consciousness. Only later was the capacity for representation and thinking acquired. This path corresponded to the progress of the human race itself. Rousseau's developmental trajectory influenced his many followers in education, especially his idea that the child's unique forms of thought must guide education. Education must be geared toward a child's capacity in the present as well as by the history of the species. Genetic psychology from the start contained a moral vision. These were embedded in various laws of development. Development necessarily proceeded toward the good—whether that was defined as maturity, logic, rationality, civilized, hierarchically organized, differentiated, specialized, reproductive heterosexuality, autonomy, correspondence with reality, internally driven, and so on.

With the spread of evolutionary ideas in the second half of the nineteenth century, particularly the work of Herbert Spencer, this passage from immaturity to maturity was framed in broader evolutionary terms. Especially influential was the notion that individual development repeated the sequence of species development—known by the phrase "ontogeny recapitulates phylogeny" or recapitulationism—variants of which have been much more influential in psychology than is often recognized today. This provided impetus to study children. They offered a window into human ancestry. A similar case was made for the study of "savages" and the "abnormal." The disciplines of genetic psychology, anthropology, and psychiatry emerged partly as a result of this. Recapitulationists suggested that there were unifying, underlying laws across development regardless of whether the context was the individual, nature, or society. This shaped the perspectives of the first few generations of influential child psychology theorists. Most of these developmental narratives were teleological—that is, advancement required moving toward some predefined end. There was no way the culmination of development for Piaget was not going to be logical thought and autonomy or for Freud, genital sexuality, and the sublimation of instinct.

Development required the passage through specific stages in the proper order, and none could be skipped as each presupposed prior ones. In psychology in particular, where participants were invested in the idea that interventions in social problems could herald long-term change, there was often a covert Lamarckianism at play—that is, the playing up of the importance of inherited habit or "learning" in evolution and the downplaying of selection. As previously discussed, this was especially true of American behaviorists who placed much faith in their capacity to transform human nature via transformations in the environment and were also confident they had discovered universal laws of learning that applied to all species. Darwin is often regarded as seminal in the establishment of modern developmental psychology, but it is just as reasonable to give this title to Herbert Spencer (Parke, et al. 1994). Regardless, evolutionism of all variants transformed childhood from an object of morality to an object of biology. Its influence led to the study of minds in all forms—adult, child, and animal—stressing continuity between them and, as Darwin said himself, differences of degree rather than kind. One area where Darwin saw wide-ranging continuity was with emotions. He took extensive notes while observing his son, William—as did almost every child development theorist we will discuss—but only published them in the journal *Mind* as "A Biographical Sketch of an Infant" in 1877 after Hippolyte Taine published a similar account of his own daughter (Sulloway, 1979, p. 244). His students developed new "behavioral" methods to study animal minds, and these methods eventually came to dominate all of psychology.

And yet, in Darwin's thinking in particular lay the germs of an alternative theory of development, one that depended on contingency, randomness, and context, and one whose end was not prescribed from the start. It viewed biological properties as emergent rather than predetermined. It viewed development as the result of the coming together of autonomous parts into a novel whole. As Robert Richards (2002) explains, Darwin did not think of natural selection as a mechanism, as it has become, but a self-organizing structure. As we shall consider, this approach offers psychology a novel way to consider the relationship between structure and function, one mostly ignored by twentieth-century psychologists, especially in the United States. But even Darwin himself had difficulty abandoning a teleological view, finding it hard not to accept that humans were the culmination of evolution.

For psychology, biology rather than physics is a better place to look for concepts and organizing metaphors. Yet, this is not true of all biology. The various biological sciences since Darwin have vacillated between mechanical and organic approaches to making sense of life. These can be related in a loose sense to the tension between structural and functional approaches. In recent decades, as natural selection has come to be described as a "mechanism" for speciation and biological change, it is easy to forget that this is not always how Darwin described it. Let's start by understanding what is meant by mechanism. The basic principle is that the laws governing natural events apply to organic life (Lerner, 2002, pp. 50–53). The universe is understood as like a machine in several senses. It is composed of distinct parts. These form basic reality which complex phenomena can be reduced to. Forces are applied, typically from outside but not always, which result in a discrete, chain-like series of events that are related to each other as cause and effect. All motion has an immediate cause. If one knows this as well as the state of the organism, prediction is possible. Development can be multidirectional; identical elements can be added or subtracted. This was essentially the framework of Newtonian physics. This was also the language of nineteenth-century S-R psychology and American Behaviorism. To be clear, identifying a biological mechanism is not the same as a mechanical approach to biology. Many biological processes operate in a mechanical way, yet cannot be understood without a conception of the whole or of purpose.

The problem with this framework, Richard Lerner (2002) explains, is that one cannot understand more complex levels of activity from these more basic ones (p. 57). Even if you can "break down" those complex activities into simpler ones—study molecules rather than cells—you certainly cannot "add up" those simple parts and understand much about more complex levels. Organic life might contain mechanisms but the organism as a whole is not a mechanism. The issue is that new properties emerge at different levels—the cell is much more than an aggregation of molecules, and an organ is much more than an aggregation of cells. The same is true of an organism, and the same is true of the environment the organism operates in. The organic framework makes the essence of phenomena activity rather than atoms (Pepper, 1942). The whole is not simply the sum of its parts but is presupposed by them. In other words, each part operates in relation to the whole, and it is the whole that gives it purpose. Thus, the organic framework by necessity is teleological in a general sense. The activities of the parts/whole are moving toward an end, and formal causes trump efficient ones. In the Aristotelian version, what Lerner terms "predetermined epigenesis," the end is known from the start, but in "probabilistic epigenesis," higher levels of organization and activity result in the emergence of novel properties that cannot necessarily be predicted in advance (Lerner, 2002, p. 67). Thus reduction to some more basic level is impossible. This makes development unidirectional.

It does not, however, mean that anything is possible. There are constraints. Novel properties must emerge from existing ones, even though changes can be qualitative. Canalization, or the narrowing of possibilities as a result of experience, often occurs as well. Furthermore, these processes cannot be abstracted from their context, as context is a part of the process. The organism and its environment blend into each other. In fact, the distinction between organism and environment is an arbitrary one, as the organism is constantly taking in its environment and the "environment" only has meaning in relation to the organism. Finally, in development, causality is not linear or straightforward. Sometimes it is more realistic to talk of agents involved in the process rather than causes (Lewontin, 2002). It is more appropriate to understand the components as a series of relationships rather than as a collection of independent entities, relationships that come together to form spontaneous, organized patterns or structures.

While ideally developmental analysis privileges an organic view, late-nineteenth-century developmentalists were often quite mechanical in their concern with fixed sequences operating on a singular and linear plane, many reducible to reflex-like mechanisms. In any developmental analyses, therefore, there are hidden assumptions that preexist any "empirical" study. Sometimes these assumptions can make it difficult to understand the true complexity of change, especially when it seems to assume a single expected outcome. This becomes evident when we examine the idea of development in psychology historically. Yet, as we shall see, when developmental thinking is rejected altogether, as is happening in some quarters of recent infant psychology, the complexity of psychological change is lost altogether.

1. HIGHER AND LOWER: ADAPTATION AND PROGRESS

Eighteenth- and nineteenth-century theories of development piggybacked on two themes that had been immanent in the Judeo-Christian tradition prior to this—notions of history and progress. These were integrated into Greek notions of form and function as form was regarded as the product of function over time. Starting with the Renaissance and continuing with the Enlightenment, European thinkers became more interested in investigating the past, particularly the worlds of ancient Greece and Rome. The *philosophes*—the rationalist philosophers of the French Enlightenment—were very much concerned with human history as part of their conception of a world that could be improved upon by science and reason. Man is the place from which everything must refer, said Denis Diderot in his *Encyclopédie* published with Jean Baptuted d'Alembert. They were especially confident about Locke's physics of the soul and saw in sensationalism and the power of the environment to shape human nature the path to progress. Trying to rid themselves of Christianity, but not yet ready to let go of the idea of a divine, cosmic drama, they saw a golden age to come where reason would help bring humans to perfection (Passmore, 1969; Becker, 1932). This gave history a renewed significance, just as Christianity had done centuries earlier. For them, history became the progressive unfolding of reason rather than God's plan.

Notions of biological history became more commonplace among some Enlightenment thinkers as well, anticipating much of nineteenth-century evolutionary thought. For instance, Comte de Buffon's *Histoire Naturelle* of 1749 rejected the authority of the old taxonomic tradition wherein species were regarded as perfect creations of God, recently revived by Carl Linnaeus, and found an evolving nature. Buffon rejected the clear-cut distinctions between species and believed that nature operated along a trial-and-error basis, creating some "monsters" doomed to extinction and others able to survive because they were better adapted to their environment. Although Buffon was not a transformist—that is, could not accept that species transform into another—he was an evolutionist. Diderot, too, saw evolution in the animal world, arguing that the adaptation of life to environment was the result of natural processes. In his *Telliamed* of 1748, Benoit de Maillet suggested that animals transmute into each other but was ridiculed by Voltaire. Out of this tradition, Pierre Louis de Maupertuis came closest to prefiguring nineteenth-century evolution, describing a process in which traits were passed on to offspring by both parents and chance deviations, all of which led to the transformation and mutability of species. Slowly, a new conception of the history of life was developing.

Progressive notions of evolution, especially Spencer and hence developmental psychology, owe a great deal to the much maligned and much misunderstood turn-of-the-nineteenth-century French biologist Jean Baptiste Lamarck. Lamarck was part of a broader romantic reaction against the mechanism of Newton and the British empiricist tradition. For him, nature was not a passive force but a creative one seeking perfection. He rejected the notion of species, viewing them as arbitrary. In nature, there were only individuals. Changes in the environment, argued Lamarck, led to new habits and structures. It was not organs that led to habits in the traditional sense of formalist biology, but habits that led to organs—that is, form followed function. Because organisms actively changed their habits in response to their changing environments, they could affect the direction of evolution.

However, there was always much more to Lamarck than this. In fact, he was quite different from those neo-Lamarckians who followed him and emphasized his mechanism of the inheritance of acquired characteristics exclusively. They missed that, for Lamarck, this was not the principal mechanism of evolutionary change. In Lamarck there were two forces at play. The first and real vehicle for evolutionary change was an innate complexifying force in living beings that led to development. Lamarck located this force in the interactions of internal fluids (R. J. Richards, 1987, p. 54). The second force, adaptations resulting from changes in habits leading to changes in internal structures, was simply a deviation of the more basic evolutionary force. The adaptations resulting from inherited use and disuse, argued Lamarck, were not a source of progress but were disruptions of that progress. Contrasting most contemporary readers of Lamarck, adaptations interrupted nature's march forward (Young, 1983, p. 75). Many neo-Lamarckians ignored this in order to make the case that individual organisms can shape the direction of evolution. But, human will had no role in evolutionary change. This was not Lamarck's point. Darwin and his allies rejected the idea of an innate force leading to development, yet heartily endorsed the idea of a wholly naturalistic process like inherited use and disuse. That Lamarckianism has become synonymous with inherited use and disuse is testament to the power of Darwinism in shaping the conversation about evolution, limiting it to the question of adaptation. The resurgence of Lamarckianism at the end of the nineteenth century was a function of skepticism around natural selection but also related to the sense that Darwinian selection had little insight into the purpose of nature, which after all, had long been the goal of the study of nature in the first place (Gillispie, 1979).

By the 1830s, a growing number of British naturalists began to reject teleology although they did not question the idea of perfect adaptation. Adaptation came, they argued, not from direct intervention by God, but from the establishment of natural law. Natural law was responsible for the perfect fit between organism and environment. As many British biologists began to accept that new species arose over the course of history, they attributed this to a direct result of changes in environmental conditions (Ospovat, 1981). Charles Lyell, whose *Principles of Geology*, published between 1830 and 1833, helped shape Darwin's views on gradualism, went as far as to say that every environment calls into existence a perfectly suited form. Lyell could not see how this led to directional development. By the 1840s, many British naturalists accepted that new species were introduced as a result of natural law and secondary causes, rejected teleology, and yet remained committed to the idea that the universe offers evidence of a divine order. Gradually the language of efficient causes developed in physics was applied to biology. This new work privileged function over structure and focused on the variability of adaptation. Both those that accepted and those that rejected transmutation of species accepted the principle of perfect adaptation (Ospovat, 1981, p. 9). The problem for evolutionists who sought to rely on naturalistic explanations was this: if adaptations were perfect, why would species ever change? Darwin began to question that idea of perfect adaptation and the harmonious view of nature it suggested after he read Malthus. Eventually, he rejected the idea of perfect adaptation so that there would be room for a species to improve. In other words, for Darwin, adaptations were not perfect, but simply better in a specific context (Ospovat, 1981, p. 37).

Darwin was looking for a term to describe this force for change in nature, not unlike the forces Newton had described over a century earlier. He chose the term "natural selection." Of course, for Darwin, the term natural selection was simply a metaphor meant for brevity. It was a process that appeared to work like artificial selection wherein breeders chose their fittest stock for reproduction. Nature acted like a breeder. However, the term left open the possibility that there might be an agent who does the selecting. In Darwin, there was a tension between two visions of natural selection. The first regarded it as a passive filter that works in conjunction with ecological factors. Organisms were simply trying to survive in a changing environment and ended up modifying species in the direction of adaptive traits. The second sense regarded it as a much more active force. Here organisms were competing with other organisms to produce surviving offspring and actively trying to pass on their "fittest" traits. Selection does the work, and the environment is less important. Darwin vacillated between these two senses. At times, when Darwin discussed selection, he made it sound almost divine-like as he did in *The Origin of Species* when he characterized it with terms like "scrutinizing," "rejecting," and "acting" (Young, 1983, p. 94). As we noted in a previous chapter, today this deified vision of selection often comes up in popular accounts based on evolutionary psychology, yet another functional homunculus upon which gets assigned intelligence. Likewise, the idea of a "struggle for existence" was also a metaphor. It simply reflected that some species were better adapted to their environments than others. The "struggle" is simply to survive and a reflection of the scarcity of resources not an actual competition between organisms. Not surprisingly, though, the idea of a literal struggle between organisms or even groups made sense to many in late-nineteenth-century society, as it still does today, though today the struggle is sometimes said to be between gene pools. Was Darwin's less than careful use of language an accident or was it a vestige of Darwin's own ambivalence about a wholly mechanistic naturalism, especially given that he could not account for the source of variation? We will never know how "Darwinian" Darwin really was.

Darwin accepted Lyell's uniformitarianism and devoted much of *The Origin of Species* to providing evidence for gradualism. He could not see that his gradualist thesis—one that still remains dominant in developmental thought and seems to shy away from "revolutionary" changes—was an unchallenged presupposition in his work and not a product of the evidence. His gradualism did, however, align his work with previous generations' natural history, making it easier to harmonize Darwinism with existing scientific thought. Darwin rejected Lyell's supposition that gradualism was incompatible with evolution as it depended on repetition and that a struggle in nature could never be creative. Darwin instead took up the evidence from geology, which traditionally had been read as evidence for "catastrophist" progressivism—progress due to biblical-like floods—and instead read it in the light of gradualist progressivism. Darwin made the case that natural selection was nature's primary tool for creativity. He sought to demonstrate how gradual, nonpurposeful adaptations could look like design as they were selected and accumulated over vast expanses of time. Although many critics would later describe these adaptations as "random," for Darwin, the key was that they were not in accordance with any direction of evolutionary change and not that they were generated by "chance." Darwin was much too influenced by nineteenth-century morphology to think that biological forms could simply change at random, a position that seems more Lockean than biological. If these adaptations were somehow teleological—that is, in the direction of evolutionary change—as they were for Lamarck and Spencer, then natural selection became superfluous. Darwin suspected the ways in which his critics would respond to his work. The absence of transitional forms, argued Darwin, was not a legitimate test of his theory. Neither was the fact that he could not explain how particular variations arose. The cause of variation, argued Darwin, was not relevant, only that it offered the "raw materials" for selection to operate with. Many of his critics struggled with the notion that variations could be so fortuitous, though they tended to approve of selection as a winnowing force.

Darwin's "methodological" separation between heredity/variation (genetics) and evolution (the study of environment and selection) shapes the organization of evolutionary biology up to the present day. What was important was that these variations did not guide evolutionary change, as some mutationalists, saltationalists, and neo-Lamarckians would later argue, because that was the work of natural selection. It was, ultimately, the environment that made the decision, so to speak, about the adaptive value of a particular trait. Not all behaviors, however, were adaptive. To explain certain aspects of nonadaptive human behavior, Darwin introduced the idea of sexual selection—a competition among males to attract mates and reproduce. When his fellow evolutionists were convinced selection could not explain moral nature, Darwin responded with *The Descent of Man* of 1871 (Richards, 1992). In this work, moral judgments were grounded in spontaneous social instincts—described by later writers as "reciprocal altruism"—as opposed to the hedonism of the utilitarians (Richards, 2009). Sexual selection, a special case of natural selection in which organisms reproduced successfully because they were better at attracting mates, was used by Darwin to explain, among other things, why certain women had large backsides as well as why capitalism and private property were superior economic systems. In other words, Darwin himself set the precedence for using selection to make judgments about human societies, what is sometimes termed "Social Darwinism" and today one finds in evolutionary psychology.

Charles Lyell gave the term "evolution" its contemporary usage as he described the work of Lamarck. The term was generally used by Spencerians for their progressive and cosmic variant of transmutation and was reluctantly taken up by Darwin. In the *Origins* he generally preferred "descent with modification," as the term evolution was connected to an older embryological and teleological tradition. This tradition went all the way back to Aristotle and had been revived by German *naturphilosophie*, many of them embryologists, for whom evolution implied an unfolding of intrinsic patterns. The term evolution itself came from the Latin word *ēvolvere,* which means to unfold, as in the unfolding of a scroll (Richards, 1992). Over the early part of the nineteenth century, it began to refer to both embryogenesis and species transformation. And yet, by using embryological models, Darwin seemed to imply that organisms have an internal tendency toward change, albeit molded by an external agent. Darwin was clearly of two minds about directionality in evolution, no matter that some contemporary readers of Darwin insist otherwise, perhaps to distance him from Social Darwinism. As Darwinism became more and more influential, the environment gradually became more important as a source of progress.

Before Darwin, progress in nature was read as a sign of the Divine. In fact, until Darwin, the idea of progressive succession was used to support the reality of a great flood and the Genesis narrative. Helping to secularize progressive change was yet another of Darwin's great contributions. The idea of progress in biology resonated with many Christians and non-Christians alike. While it is correct to say that evolutionary theory was limited to a conception of relative progress—only the fittest in a particular environment survived—when one looked back at the sweep of evolutionary history, it was difficult not to see progress. Evolutionary ideas were so influential in the latter years of the nineteenth century because they helped to confirm the "advanced" nature of the world of that time. Furthermore, as science began to fulfill some of the cultural role once accorded to religion, some looked to nature as described by evolutionary science for moral principles. For instance, many in late-nineteenth-century American society found justification in nature for the inequities of the Gilded Age and the principles of free-market economics and competition. That many saw evolution as inherently progressive is clear when one considers Darwin's adoption of Spencer's phrase "survival of the fittest." Technically, of course, it is "survival of the fit" as those that survive are only "fit" in a particular context. The term "fittest" implies that those that survive are somehow ideally suited for survival (Mandelbaum, 1974). Natural selection, which only operates in a particular context, seems to be "selecting" by some sort of universal or absolute category of viability.

Although Darwin rejected the idea of an innate progressive force in nature, he never seriously doubted progress in nature (R. J. Richards, 1987, p. 87). He was careful to play down the idea of necessary progress because he could not explain the precise mechanisms that made it necessary without relying on a Lamarckian or Spencerian cosmic force (Ospovat, 1981). Darwin was also careful with terms like "higher" when describing species because he believed there was no precise way to define them, though he occasionally used the term anyway and accepted zoological definitions of organic progress including increased differentiation and specialization (Ospovat, 1981, p. 216). He could not help but see progress in the evidence from morphology and embryology. What he did reject in order to make selection "natural" was any innate tendency for progress. This was the real problem with Lamarck. Progress had to be almost an accidental consequence of selection. The key was that adaptation had to remain primary, otherwise the progressive force was responsible for evolutionary change and not natural selection.

For Spencer, on the other hand, all of evolution was the progressive manifestation of an unknowable power. Spencer offered his readers still invested in Christianity a variant of evolution dependent on unbreakable cosmic laws, thus retaining notions of providential progress, providential law, and a protected place for God in the natural world. He offered a vision of evolution that was both easily reconciled with Christianity as well as grounded in biological and sociological principles. This process was universal and grounded in necessary and natural causal relations. It could be no other way. For humans, this meant the passage from savage to civilized was an inevitable one. This made his doctrine an optimistic one. However, it also meant that there was little room for human agency and will. Human will only disrupted natural law. Hence, government intervention in society was a problem.

Spencer offered a unique synthesis of sensorimotor neurophysiology, British Associationism, utilitarianism, the evolutionary ideas of Lamarck, phrenology, embryology, and Romantic biology. Like the British tradition, he insisted that the principle of utility, or adaptation, underlay everything. All life was a product of adaptation. He also accepted the principle of continuity—natural laws applied to all domains of life. He borrowed the notion of progressive individuation from Samuel Coleridge, laws of development from Karl Von Baer (development was a passage from less to increased differentiation), organic transformation from Lamarck, psychic reflexes from William Carpenter, and a division of labor from Mile Edwards, which he applied to physiology as the law of specialized functions. His work was truly synthetic. He took the faculties of phrenology and turned them into hereditary instincts. This also helped him make the case for the continuity of mind between humans and animals.

Mental development began with reflexes that he conceived as chained serial reactions to external stimuli. As adjustment to the environment continued, these became more complex instincts and eventually intelligent responses to that environment. All life was a progressive tendency toward individuation as greater individualizing and specialization of parts in organisms was inherently progressive. Like Gall, he stressed the relationship between organism and environment, mind and life. Both mind and culture were reflections of past adaptations. Spencer described a process of continuous adjustment of internal relations to external conditions. He rejected sensationalism in the simple sense that the environment simply imposed itself on the organism. With his integration of the notion of developmental laws—progression from simple to complex, less to more differentiated—he retained the centrality of adaptation while saving the formalist conception of hierarchical organization. He proposed biological studies with different foci—the relation between the mental and conditions of life, comparing higher and lower races, observing development and comparing various grades of animals and humans (Young, 1970, p. 185). All these were integrated into the work of psychology by the end of the century, as psychology became a biological science of adaptation.

Also like Gall's phrenology, Spencerian evolution promised to explain change and social problems (Bannister, 1979). In his *Social Statics* of 1850, Spencer sought to derive a theory of ethics from biology. Spencer called for natural rights and the principles of *laissez-faire* as ethical standards. This led him to reject the Benthamite stress on using legislation to bring about social reform and oppose all forms of government intervention. People must be free to pursue their own interests. Echoing Calvin, Spencer insisted that some people were "elected" for success, not by God but by nature. By identifying the laws of evolution that governed natural and human societies, reformers could make decisions about concrete political matters. These laws tended to be interpreted differently depending on political orientation; however, all strains accepted some version of the inevitability of progress.

For liberals, a more Lamarckian version was the grounds for a new social order based in progress and competition. It was, as Richard Hofstadter described, a kind of naturalistic Calvinism stressing the difficulties of life, suffering, and the importance of individual responsibility (Hofstadter, 1944). This strain resulted in the development of the social gospel of Washington Gladden and eventually, the Progressive Movement in the United States. For conservatives, a more Malthusian version of these doctrines rationalized the prevailing social order by suggesting that those who were the most successful were the "fittest," and thus sanctioned to thrive by natural law. This was the case with Spencer as well as one of his most influential American followers, William Graham Sumner. Spencerian evolution dominated American science and society long after the British had already begun to reject it. It was simply too attractive to a society obsessed with individualism, liberty, and free enterprise as well as one that well believed in the power of the environment to shape human character. It helped to establish "Social Darwinism" as one of the leading strains of American conservative thought.

3. STRUCTURE AND FUNCTION: THE RECAPITULATIONISTS

Intimately tied with notions of progressive development were notions of the repetition of ancestral forms in both species and individual development. There were really three variants of recapitulationism in the late eighteenth and nineteenth centuries. The first was the most narrow and disputed and was associated with Lorenz Oken and later Ernst Haeckel. It argued that embryogenesis involved a repetition of the adult forms of ancestors. The second position, associated with critic of the first position Ernst Von Baer, but widely accepted in some form, was that embryogenesis involved a repetition of the embryological forms of ancestors followed by increased differentiation in newer forms. The third position was the broadest one: ontogenesis in general involved a repetition of ancestral forms and was parallel across differing contexts. Sometimes this was conceived as an analogy and other times it was conceived as a causal process. The third version exerted the most influence on psychological thought, especially attempts to explain development in infancy and childhood (Morss, 1990). In all of these variants, the assumption that there were only a few paths from simple cells to complex forms meant that similar transitions had to involve similar paths. These were regarded as developmental laws.

The notion of a relationship between the development of individual organisms and species had been noted since the Greeks. In a sense, Aristotle's system implied a kind of recapitulation. Higher souls entered the embryo during development—first the plantlike nutritive soul, then the animal-like sensitive soul, and finally, the human-like rational soul. But these were meant as analogies not causal relationships. In the eighteenth century, those that studied embryogenesis still relied on notions of vitalism or mystical properties to explain the process by which an embryo was turned into an infant. The only alternative was the performatism of Charles Bonnett. This was actually regarded as the more mechanistic and scientific explanation. Performatism is often caricatured with images of little adults inside embryos, but it was a reasonable position given the context. It described adult forms enclosed inside an embryo and simply required the shedding of an outer layer and expansion of parts. Its influence ended with the development of better microscopes and new frames for understanding biology.

Nineteenth-century recapitulationism was more directly related to German *naturphilosophie*, particularly that of Lorenz Oken and J. F. Meckel. Inspired by Kant's conception of an archetype or *bauplan* and understanding of biology as teleological, Oken saw the progressive unfolding of form in the natural world. All organisms strove toward perfection, and there was therefore a single direction to organic development. This involved better coordination and specialization of parts. Thus, all organisms must, at some point, repeat the same sequence, as there was only one path to perfection, requiring that ontogenesis involve a repetition of simpler to more complex forms (R. J. Richards, 2004). It also meant that higher forms could easily be compared to lower forms. Due to the unity of nature and its laws, this necessary repetition also included humans. Although not a particularly empirically minded movement—though Oken was a meticulous embryologist—this helped to inspire the mechanical study of nature in the nineteenth century.

The great critic of this form of recapitulationist thought was the founder of modern embryology and first substantive theorist of development, Ernst Von Baer. His extensive research led him to discover the mammalian ovum and, most importantly, that the embryos of higher and lower forms resemble each other. As embryogenesis progressed, those of the higher forms became more distinct. There was not, according to Von Baer, a single passage from lower to higher forms, as development seemed to be constrained by type. Von Baer was the first to replace the idea of a single line of development with a branching tree, a metaphor Darwin took up thereafter (Richards, 1992). The key difference between lower and higher forms was that higher embryological forms became more differentiated as they proceeded from a more generalized state to a more specialized one. This was the path of embryogenesis and, later for Spencer, the path of evolution in general. This idea that development moves from the general to the specialized profoundly influenced developmental thinking. Less influential though perhaps more important was the idea that differentiation takes place within boundaries imposed by type—certainly few American behaviorists ever considered this—which embedded a notion of structure in the process. Today this is described by the term biological constraints. The final influential figure, Ernst Haeckel, was well known for defending evolutionary ideas in Germany in the latter part of the nineteenth century. His well-known biogenic principle stated that ontogeny was the rapid repetition of phylogeny. This was not an analogy but a causal and mechanical process. Later evolutionary forms were simply added on to embryological development—actually making a good case for the inheritance of acquired characteristics (Richards, 2004). Because it was hard to accept that embryogenesis repeated the entire sequence of evolutionary history, Haeckel introduced an acceleration principle wherein the process was speeded up by skipping certain ancestral forms.

Three research programs emerged from evolutionary thought: the first concerned the workings of variation and inheritance, the second studied the emergence of new species through environmental pressure—a program which tended to be relegated to museums of natural history—and the third traced ancestry via the principle of common descent (Bowler, 1996). Developmental psychology emerged from the third program. The study of childhood became a vehicle for studying the past and the passage to the present. Darwin's gradualism set the pace for developmental change. The continuity between the animal and human mind allowed the methods of comparative psychology to be used for study of childhood as well. Darwin understood the importance of his work for a new psychology of mind, but never took it up himself, instead giving his notes on mind to George Romanes. When it came to psychology, he tended to defer to Spencer, although he clearly understood the radical implications of animal-human continuity (Young, 1983, p. 59).

One common error in Darwin's reasoning ended up influencing a nascent genetic psychology. Darwin read characteristic human capacities onto animal nature and then used this to confirm continuity (Malik, 2000). His study of emotional expressions, an example of this reasoning, focused on the correlation of behavior with muscle movements and offered a model for studying purposive behavior without reference to minds or higher faculties. Darwin made Rousseau's trajectory from child to adult thought and all the various versions of it that abounded—prelogical to logical, immature to mature, savagery to civilized, primitive to advanced, religion to science, and so on—appear rational, even obvious. Furthermore, the value of Darwinism for psychology was that explanation did not have to be reduced to physics or chemistry, thus a "holistic" and more organic science was possible. Unlike associationism, it took the notion of structure seriously, but viewed it as the product of biological functions. Ironically, it also meant that physiological specificities could be set aside, at least until the rise of genetics. All of this required the development of theory, not simple induction. Darwin himself made the study of childhood important to science when he stressed that the young were particularly malleable and thus more susceptible to the environment and changes in habit. His focus on variation and inheritance gave the field two foci, the former focusing on individual differences (e.g., intelligence, personality) and the latter on determining which characteristics were acquired and which constitutional, both major themes in twentieth-century developmental psychology.

4. STRUCTURE AND FUNCTION: THE DEVELOPMENTAL PSYCHOLOGISTS

The new post-Darwinian science of development depended on several shared assumptions—the term "developmental psychology" was not used till later in the twentieth century, a more historically accurate term is "genetic" psychology.

1. As children grow, gradual changes can be identified in thought and behavior.
2. Latter development is built on earlier, more influential experiences and an invariant nature.
3. Hidden structures are preserved over time.
4. Development involves better correspondence between thought and the world.
5. Development involves a passage from the concrete to the symbolic and/or abstract.
6. Individual development is analogous to species or societal development.
7. Children are simply an occasion to study laws of development in general.
8. The rejection of mechanical metaphors in favor of organic ones (sometimes).

9. Understanding development requires theoretical development, not simply experiment or induction.
10. Development is a passage from a "worse" state to a "better" one—it contains a vision of the good.

These assumptions were neither correct nor incorrect, but they simply shaped the way psychologists viewed children and change. Like all assumptions, however, they had their limits, limits that often went unrecognized. We will take up the issue of limits a bit later. One can find many of these assumptions in most of the influential thinkers on child development from the 1870s until the 1970s. They include Wilhelm Preyer, James Sully, George Romanes, G. Stanley Hall, Arnold Gesell, James Mark Baldwin, Sigmund Freud, William Stern, Karl and Charlotte Bühler, Heinz Werner, Jean Piaget, and Lev Vygotsky. The rise of a new paradigm in cognitive psychology following a return to a nativist approach in the work of Noam Chomsky and his students marks the end of this period and perhaps the end of a developmental perspective entirely. As can be easily inferred from this list, most of these thinkers represent a "European" approach to child development, a more "theoretical" approach that sat uneasily alongside the non-developmental and "empirical" behavioral approach that remained dominant in U.S. psychology during most of this period. The cross-Atlantic migrations and displacements during and after World War II allowed many of these thinkers to influence American psychology in ways that they would have not been able to earlier in the century.

Before the nineteenth century, child "development" was understood through the sensationalist tradition. Children's thought and behavior or "habits" changed as a result of changes in the environment. Whether complex ideas emerged as a consequence of associations or behavior emerged as a consequence of pleasure and pain, which when repeated enough, became habits. Children were passively shaped by the environment in the same way as adults only perhaps they were more "impressionable." In the middle of the nineteenth century, Alexander Bain's synthesis of associationism and physiology offered a new and influential path to describe developmental change. Over the course of infancy, argued Bain, voluntary control was established over spontaneous activity through trial-and-error learning. Although the notion of spontaneous activity was rejected by most nineteenth-century physiologists after 1850 and replaced with the notion of a reflex, this path from involuntary to voluntary remained central to later work. For Bain, the infant was active rather than passive, and feelings of pleasure and pain allowed it to adjust means towards ends. Describing the infant as active was key for Bain, as it protected the role of the will. This became known as the Spencer-Bain principle. The key principle of mind was not association but discrimination. Bain distinguished between reflexes and spontaneous activity, which was the basis for voluntary action. Spencer, unlike Bain, saw these along a single line of development of increasing complexity: development (an intrinsic force) along with associations (the environment) led reflexes to become instincts—which could be inherited à la Lamarck—memory and finally reason-based behavior.

In *The Descent of Man*, Darwin seemed to accept Spencer's premise of a single line of development when it came to mind. His branching tree was neglected in favor of a more traditional linear scale of nature when it came to human thought (Boakes, 1984). Like Spencer, he accepted that various muscular movements followed by success were likely to be repeated. Repetitive movements, for Spencer, were key to the organization of the nervous system. Spencer and Darwin both noted the resemblance between instincts and learned movements that had become habitual, hence the term "second" nature. Darwin also saw parallels between the acquisition of language by individuals and the origin of language in general—for instance, both began with expressive cries and imitation (Shuttleworth, 2010, p. 284). This allowed for comparisons across species, a view strenuously objected to by the leading philologist of the time Max Müller, who insisted only humans possess language.

The first substantive text of the new post-Darwinian developmental psychology was William Preyer's *The Mind of the Child* published in 1882. The original German title used the term *seele* or soul, not mind, the preferred term in the English version. Preyer was a Darwinist, and like Darwin, developed some of his ideas by studying his own children. He tried to systematize child observation and was an early figure in the turn-of-the-century child-study movement along with Sully and Hall (Cairns & Ornstein, 1979). For Preyer, the newborn was capable of direct sensation but no organized perception. Movement was involuntary. He observed innate instincts present at birth (White, 1983). Preyer followed Darwin here and compared them with those of animals. He identified four types of early movement: the "impulsive" or the accumulations of motor impulses, the "reflexive" or adaptations to the environment, the "instinctive" or the repetition of ancestral habits, and the "imitative" or the mimicking of the behavior of others. This account of impulse, reflex, instinct, and imitation was still widely accepted in the early twentieth century. His depiction of the development of mind was more active than Spencer's, more German than English. As an evolutionist, Preyer regarded heredity as key in the development of mind, but he also acknowledged that experience expanded inherited capacities. The world of the infant began as an empiricist-associational one, a blur of sensory images, but resulted in a rationalist one through recapitulation. Preyer argued that children recapitulated ancient events through memory wherein "vibrations" influenced the germ plasm and could be passed on from one generation to the next (Morss, 1990, p. 21). When it came to education, Preyer advocated following a natural course: from the senses, to feelings, will, and finally intelligence and language.

James Sully's *The Teacher's Handbook of Psychology* published in 1886 and his *Studies in Childhood* published a decade later also represented the early work of child development, though his work was regarded as less innovative than Preyer's. Sully was an acquaintance of Darwin and the founder of the child study movement in England. Sully explicitly compared children to savages. He saw several child behaviors—fear of strangers, for instance—as products of ancestral experience (Morss, 1990, p. 22). Dreams too referred to ancient impulses. Sully followed Spencer's sensationalist vision of the development of mind as opposed to Preyer's more active one and described development as a passage from sensation through perception, imagination, and abstract knowing. Like many in his time, he regarded the development of species, individuals, and societies along a single track, as part of an advancing scale of nature (Morss, 1990, p. 23). Sully used this understanding of development to explain the acquisition of language, which he argued, following Preyer, was independent of the acquisition of thought and the development of self-consciousness (Shuttleworth, 2010, p. 284). He accepted, following Hughlings Jackson, that higher inhibitory neural centers overlay lower ones and that these forms of inhibitory activity emerged over the course of development as well as evolution and the history of societies. This was to be another common theme, development as the growth of the power of inhibition.

Recapitulationism, often given a neo-Lamarckian twist, introduced the idea of periodicity in development by referring to various phases and cycles that were repeated across contexts. These became "stages" in many developmental theories. They involved movement toward a predefined end and an in-built directionality. Progress was typically built into the mechanism itself, that is, a new stage was somehow more satisfying or necessary. As John Morss (1990) recognizes, evolutionary ideas often gave structure and legitimacy to vague formulations, especially if they were progressive. Developmentalists had a lot of leeway in defining the high point of development—sometimes seven or fourteen, both related to entering school but also religious doctrines. By the turn of the century, Spencer and Preyer's slightly distinct visions of early development tended to frame the ways development was conceived. It was broadly accepted that child and adult thought were different. Prefiguring Piaget and Mahler, Eugen Bleuler described a kind of "autistic" thinking in the schizophrenic that was normal in children. His student Carl Jung made a similar distinction this time between archaic and reality thinking, and for Freud, the pivotal distinction was between primary and secondary processes.

The other influential early figure in this tradition was George Romanes, the first in the post-Darwinian tradition of comparative anatomy. Romanes had focused mostly on finding mind in animals and was often criticized for his flagrant anthropomorphism. He believed that mind could be recognized through its outward manifestations and frequently relied on over-the-top analogies to explain this. Romanes introduced a new sense of the term "intelligence." Behaviors and thoughts that showed the beneficial effect of past actions—that is, the capacity to adapt to changing circumstances—were intelligent.

Romanes rejected Spencer's notion of instinct as simply a compound reflex. Instincts were a type of reflex, but they also involved a mental perception that took account of stimulus specifics. This made the process more active and made cognitive faculties necessary for inheritance, ideas rejected by later comparative psychologists. He described "combinatorial speech"— the beginnings of sign use—emerging at around two and regarded imitation as a key part of perfecting instincts; this lead to reason, which was not based in reflex as Spencer argued, but perception. For him, mind involved discrimination and classification as well as the capacity to create symbols. All this he found in the minds of animals—with the exception of conceptual thought which was the exclusive province of human adults.

Romanes subscribed to a form of dualism wherein the evolutionary path of mind and that of body were distinct. Mental abilities were viewed along a hierarchical scale from lower to higher. There was a natural ordering of forms of thought that was repeated in ontogenesis: associations gave rise to precepts followed by recepts, preconcepts, concepts, propositions, and syllogisms (Romanes, 1888). This related to a natural ordering of development involving seventeen steps that went from protoplasmic movements and non-nervous adjustments to tool use. This was associated with a progressive scale from protoplasmic organisms at the bottom to primates and dogs at the top. Humans, argued Romanes, reached this point at around fifteen months and fully transcended their "bruteness" at three with the emergence of self-consciousness, an idea he borrowed from James Sully who noted that children generally refer to themselves in speech by this time.

Yet, another influential recapitulationist of the time was the American psychologist G. Stanley Hall. Hall argued that education be reformed by responding to the needs of the child, specifically it should account for "development" by focusing on where in the repetition process children were—for example, reading and writing should be put off till a child turns eight (Morss, 1990, p. 33). As was typical, Hall regarded earlier, lower mental functions as mechanical and higher, later ones as self-willed and autonomous (White, 1983). For him, repressing a child's natural urge to savagery led to disaster. The goal of education should no longer be simply the shaping of individual character but the "progress of mankind" (Ross, 1972). Hall's passion for psychology took hold after reading Spencer and Wundt in the 1870s. He studied with William James and was awarded the first doctorate in psychology at Harvard. As part of the reform of education, Hall argued, one needed facts about child development. To accomplish this, he started the child study movement in the United States. His interest in it, however, did not last long. By 1899, he complained the child-study had become too "sissified," that is, in his view, invaded by women's groups with their focus on health and hygiene, and in his disillusionment he turned to the study of adolescence. Hall turned recapitulation and development into such general terms—he applied them to animals, children, "savages," "defectives," and sexual "perverts"—that they lost much of their meaning (Morss, 1990, p. 36). He listed at least fifty vestiges of phylogeny in children. American child study researchers tended to be skeptical of broad theories like recapitulation anyway, preferring to gather facts about children instead.

By 1899, Hall distinguished between two psychologies: the comparative and the individual. Child-study was part of the former. Its goal was to determine the contents of mind at various ages as well as discover which behaviors were part of a child's original nature and which were the result of adaptation or learning. While the focus on learning and adaptation stuck, Hall's "questionnaire" method and recapitulationism did not. Hall's enduring influence was felt through his student Arnold Gesell, the leading infant researcher of the early twentieth century. He was also the one most responsible for turning developmental psychologists toward descriptions rather than explanations. He rejected the dominant experimentalism and focused on "natural" development instead. Gesell accepted what he termed that "supreme genetic law"—present growth hinges on past growth (Morss, 1990, p. 54). Like his mentor, he stressed the importance of maturational readiness. Gesell's focus on maturation led him to conceive development as unfolding in fixed sequences organized into patterns. These forces were so powerful that children could regulate their own development including feeding, sleeping, and wakeful cycles. He became one of the most influential writers on childhood in the early twentieth century known for his stress on "milestones" of developmental growth—products of internal forces and not the environment. His "leave babies alone" approach was quite a contrast from Watson's.

The most significant work of child development in the nineteenth century was James Mark Baldwin's *Mental Development in the Child and Race* published in 1895. For various reasons, Baldwin's work has gone unnoticed by many contemporary developmental psychologists, which is surprising given that his focus on the social nature of development prefigured many themes that would only become familiar when taken up by followers of Vygotsky in the last decades of the twentieth century. Like many in his generation, James Mark Baldwin developed his ideas by studying his own children. This led him to a synthesis between evolutionary thought and socialization, or the process by which children become members of society. Following Gabriel Tarde—who developed French social psychology around what he saw as an instinct for imitation—Baldwin stressed the centrality of imitation in the growth of the mind. He viewed psychological growth as the process by which a biological individual became a social person and viewed social transmission as central, noting that social creatures adapt to social pressures ("social heredity") not only environmental ones. In fact, through conscious imitation and intercourse with others, the self was attained. As the child develops, argued Baldwin, it made external relations into internal ones; a world of mind that begins as a re-creation of the external world eventually acquires its own life.

Development involved habit and accommodation. Habits involved repeating what was worth repeating, thus were conservative (White, 1983). Accommodations were repetitions with slight variations or "circular reactions," a term Piaget later borrowed to describe the development of voluntary and outcome-based activity as well as the source of change. Both of these were integrated into imitative action. Baldwin's trajectory followed the path of the development of imitation—from "physiological suggestion" or the passive receipt of images, which were integrated with reflexes to "sensorimotor suggestion" or the active assumption of perceptions and conscious motor activity, to "ideomotor suggestion," a mature state where children conceive the world as distinct from themselves (R. J. Richards, 1987, p. 463). In this view, development involved better coordination between thinking and reality as imitation was transformed into volition. These ideas influenced generations of developmental psychologists. Baldwin introduced the idea of organic selection, also known as the "Baldwin Effect," which explained the directional nature of development. This was true of both the individual and the species. Unlike natural selection, which worked with spontaneous variations, organic selection worked with learned adaptations that supplement an already existing congenital endowment (coincident variations). This supplied an amplifying effect, which gave the appearance of the inheritance of acquired characteristics.

After leaving the United States, Baldwin worked with Pierre Janet and through him influenced a young Jean Piaget. In fact, it was less than two decades after the publication of Baldwin's work that Piaget's teacher, Édouard Claparède, founded the Institute Jean-Jacques Rousseau in Geneva, which Piaget later directed, and took a functionalist approach to children's problem solving. Claparède had children talk through their processes including failure, a method that eventually led Piaget to describe what he witnessed as "egocentric thought." During his early work in the 1910s, Piaget was explicit about the homology between phylogenetic and ontogenetic development as well as his Lamarckianism (Morss, 1990, p. 63). There was a not-so-subtle moral lesson here: children must go from lower through progressively higher and higher prior forms of civilization to achieve, perhaps even to deserve to achieve, formal operational intelligence.

This early work on children's failure helped Piaget see that rational thought emerged gradually as children tried to avoid contradiction, culminating at around seven. Piaget learned this from Janet. Piaget had a host of adjectives to describe prerational thought available to him by this point—distorted immediate perception, savage, impervious to experience, prelogical, animistic, egocentric, and so on. Rationality involved the separation of the internal and the external allowing thought to transcend the subjective and better adjust to reality, although awareness of subjectivity always had to come first. As John Morss (1990) points out, both Freud and Piaget shared the assumption that development was a process of detaching from adult intellectual authority. Both saw this in biological and evolutionary terms repeated in ontogenesis (p. 43). For Freud, the male authority exerted by the father in the Oedipal Complex was a product of evolution—more neo-Lamarckian than Darwinian—a story Freud told in vivid detail in *Totem and Taboo*. The Oedipal complex is not, as is often read in the United States, a result of experience or a certain type of parenting. Even though these early phases of phylogeny were repressed, they remeerged in the neurotic. For Piaget, primitives were like children, trapped in adult constraints. The cultural implications of all this are fairly straightforward, both identifying maturity with the individualized, autonomous subject of Western modernity.

Piaget borrowed Claude Bernard's notions of dynamic equilibrium and extended it to the realm of thought. External disturbances of equilibrium, what Piaget later termed "dis-equilibrations," were the motor of development and what led to adaptation. This was not the trial-and-error learning of behaviorists, as it required thought and planning. Piaget would not accept the sensationalist view that cognitive mechanisms submit to reality by copying its features. To know an object, Piaget insisted, was to act on it (White, 1983). All later forms of rationality find their origins in these early prerational forms—for instance, notions of time begin restricted by infant action until they develop a representative character, notions of space as a disorganized mass, notions of causality as "phenomenolism" (or events occurring closely in time and viewed as causally linked), as well as other forms of "magical thinking." Intellectual operations in general had their origins in sensorimotor activity.

Animism is a great example of changes in the qualitative character of thought via development. Animism, according to Piaget, developed from assigning life to anything that effects people, to assigning life to anything that is mobile, to assigning life to anything that moves spontaneously, to finally, in concrete operational intelligence, assigning life exclusively to living things (Piaget, 1929). Yet another example of this trajectory is Piaget's view of language that moves from being primarily egocentric and imitative to socialized and representational, a view that has been mostly rejected today. The basic "motors" of development for Piaget were the so-called functional invariants: adaptation, leading to repetition and change, and organization, leading to consolidation and stasis. Both expressed the purpose and direction of development. These eventually led to changes in intellectual structures, which were conceived as abstract patterns of organization underlying cognition. Unlike the case with American behaviorists, these cognitive structures could be inferred from experience and studied through the case study—the primary method of French psychology given its basis in clinical psychiatry. Yet, these structures were constructed and not given in the organization of the world itself as the Gestaltists argued.

These changes in structure were understood as involving a passage through stages, which for Piaget were natural groupings. They involved a qualitative change, a culturally invariant sequence, and inclusion of conceptual structures of prior stages as well as integration into a larger whole. While early moments in a stage tended to have a rough and "intuitive" character, thinking gradually became more rigorous and flexible. As an aside, it is important to note that for Piaget, thinking passes through states and not children. These were not meant to be normative measures of a child's development, which was often how they were interpreted in the United States. This along with an obsession with learning and speeding up development, which Piaget insisted was constrained by biology, Piaget dismissively called the "American" question. Piaget's real interest was not in children per se but "genetic epistemology," the origins and structure of knowledge itself. Ontogenesis was simply an ideal venue to study this, the only substitute to a genuinely historical analysis of changes in the structure of knowledge over time.

The other influential work of child development during the early part of the twentieth century was William Stern's *The Psychology of Early Childhood* of 1914. Although critical of Preyer and recapitulation, Stern still accepted the idea of development through a fixed sequence. The original state of a child's thinking was diffuse and global, gradually becoming more differentiated as order emerged from chaos. Stern focused on the active role the growing infant played in organizing perception. He also became interested in individual personality and tried to relate dispositions to specific psychological functions. In education, Stern focused on the problem of the selection of students, trying to identify vocational talents and intelligence, which he viewed as the capacity to adapt to new tasks related to conditions of life and purpose. His best-known student, Heinz Werner, took these ideas up as well in his "orthogenetic principle" wherein development moved from undifferentiated global states to increasingly differentiated ones that were hierarchically integrated (Werner, 1957). These notions were borrowed directly from recapitulationist sources. Werner acknowledged his debt to them and insisted that the parallels exist because development follows certain rules, though he tried not to take the analogy too literally. Werner went beyond the traditional

notion of the unidirectionality of development, however, and introduced notions of de-differentiation and de-hierarchicazation. Werner's particular area
of research focused on perception. He linked acts of perception to motor acts
and distinguished between physiognomic perception—a more immediate and
emotional form—and objective-technical perception. He also studied symbol
formation that moved from motor-based to representation-based. For Werner, the developmentalist seeks to identify patterns at each developmental
level as well as the relationships between these levels. The focus was always
on the relationship of parts to whole, as the whole must retain primacy.
Without this recognition, Werner argued, developmentalists end up struggling to figure out the relationship between the organism, its constitutive
parts, and its environment. They are then forced to rely on invented causes
and vague "interactionist" principles to explain them. He described this as his
"organismic" as opposed to "mechanistic" orientation.

The other developmental thinker during these years focused on symbol
formation was the Soviet psychologist Lev Vygotsky, although he did not
influence the English-speaking world until much later. This was due to a ban
on his work after his death in 1934 for characterizing Russian peasants as
operating on a lower cultural level as well as suggesting education was
limited by genetic endowment. Vygotsky was absorbed in the same milieu
and developed similar ideas. He was influenced by Baldwin as well as Karl
Bühler, another influential German child psychologist, who started his career
at Würzburg under Külpe and published along with his wife Charlotte *The
Mental Development of the Child* in 1918. They viewed the development of
thinking as a passage from instincts to sensorimotor learning and finally
natural language-based thought and sought to apply these ideas to educational reform. Vygotsky was a critic of the dominance of Pavlovianism in Russian psychology and sought to develop his own recapitulationist trajectory
wherein animal-like "elementary processes" were gradually replaced by
higher sociocultural ones (Joravsky, 1987, p. 204). Vygotsky identified two
lines of development, thought and speech, which merged to form intelligence
and move the child from biological to sociohistorical development. Vygotsky's description of natural development in infancy essentially accepted the
findings of Baldwin and Bühler. The real transformation came with the introduction and eventual internalization of symbols. For example, in speech, the
child moved from speech based in perception to speech based in complexes
and pseudoconcepts to proper concepts. Speech was gradually internalized
and became "inner speech" which was used as a guide for action. Written
language played a part in this as well, allowing words to symbolize meaning
independent of spoken signs. This allowed thought to become more abstract.
True or scientific concepts, as opposed to spontaneous ones, required explicit
teaching argued Vygotsky, leading him to move away from the "bottom-up"

approach of the child-centered pedagogy typical of most developmental thinkers.

Many developmentalists during these years sought to develop a distinct language that avoided the mechanical language of physics. Their influence led to the rejection of stimulus/response and mechanistic metaphors for explaining development and the substitution of organic or biological ones. Metaphors like "drive" and "association" were replaced with ones like "structure" and "level." This was most explicit in the work of Heinz Werner. In comparative development, one of the most influential organic thinkers was curator of the New York City Natural History Museum and student of Karl Lashley, T. C. Schneirla. Schneirla recognized that the dynamism of organic ontogenesis made its study difficult—the traditional independent-dependent variable approach of S-R psychology would not do (Lerner, 2002). In development, the relationship between structure and function is a complex one. The same structure might perform different functions in different organisms and the same function could be performed by different structures. There was no way to generalize the relationship between structure/function across species or even sometimes across levels. Often it depended on the context. Even in a singular organism, different activities operate at different levels, and one must not only understand those levels independently but also the ways they are integrated with each other (Lerner, 2002, pp. 142–144). Any attempt to identify either nature or nurture as independent sources of these activities is meaningless.

Still, these descriptions are ideals. The distinction between "mechanical" and "organic" is never very precise in practice. Even biological processes can operate mechanically. Often, the methods of studying these phenomena tend to be fairly mechanical, typically lifting objects of study out of their context. Such decontextualization can be methodologically useful, up to a point. The language does, however, have a clear moral valence—the organic is clearly a stand-in for the good. This is also true for the concept of development in general. Neither can properly be said to be a product of induction or the study of children, as both are presuppositions that give sense and value to developmental study in the first place. Correct or not, this means much more than simply studying these phenomena over the course of time. It often means identifying the hidden structures that persist over development and identifying qualitative changes in which previous forms persist in some way. New stages emerge out of prior ones, typically containing some of the past but moving in a generally better direction. Jerome Kagan calls this the principle of "connectivity" (Kagan, 1983, p. 38). Piaget termed it "functional continuity," and Maurice Mandelbaum (1974) in his study of nineteenth-century thought calls it the "bias of historicism." Even Locke insisted that impressions acquired early in life have lasting consequences. There is nothing necessarily wrong with this assumption per se, as locating the origins and reviewing the history of a phenomenon helps to understand it. And yet, there is not always such a self-evident relationship between past and present. Sometimes, the evidence is all in the way one tells the story.

This is most clearly evidenced in the case of psychodynamic therapies where childhood traumas are said to exert an all-powerful influence on persons. There is really no way to know this, and the fact that this type of explanation has been so influential suggests that it confirms what is already believed about the power of the past. At least since Augustine, there has been a tradition in the West of constructing autobiographical narratives wherein the past leads to the present in some necessary way. Americans in particular tend see the past this way, despite the fact that they also love to reinvent themselves. Psychoanalyst Selma Fraiberg summed this up when she famously insisted that in every act of love in maturity, there is a prologue that originated in the first years of life. The same can be said of developmental narratives in general. People are already fairly sure they progress with age, both as individuals and a society, and that is what these narratives confirm. Not surprisingly, few developmental narratives talk about what is lost in the transition from childhood to adulthood or what remains exactly the same. Depending on how one defines it, it's fairly easy to find "simplicity" in infancy: sensations, reflexes, instincts, pleasure seeking, irrationality, confusion, autism, egocentrism, and innate conspecifics. They are all there to find. And yet, the developmental trajectories laid out in the theories we reviewed are remarkably similar: a passage from simple animal (instinct/reflexes) through more complex animal (associations) to humanness (volition/reason). Regardless of whether the structures of the earliest stage are viewed as reflexes, which could be automatic or externally triggered, or instincts, which tended to be regarded as more complex behaviorally and almost always internally triggered—these are the actions of the so-called lower forms of life. They reflect the absence of autonomy, volition, and thought as well as the absence of other advanced designations like differentiated, hierarchically organized, or socialized. Only the most "savage" humans live exclusively through instinct. Infants only do this for a short period. What is it that moves children forward? This was not always clear. For Aristotle and those who follow him it was the pull of final cause. For Lamarck, a progressive force was inherent in life itself. For Piaget and Freud it was contradiction and psychic conflict respectively. Most developmentalists assume some combination of these along with the assumption that the individual is an active agent in their own development. Most nondevelopmentalists assume that the forward momentum comes from some internal or external source.

At some point in these narratives children become associationists. It is true that the environment-triggered learning described by Locke and Hartley is a force in development; it is simply a biologically lower capacity than they had originally understood. Even animals have the capacity for this type of thought. Perhaps such form is ideal for young children who need managing and training, but for the fully developed Euro-American adult, thinking cannot be as mechanical and passive as associative learning suggests. Technically, some distinguish between the very passive formation of associations and the slightly less passive shaping of behavior through consequences. Many species are capable of learning via association, fewer learn via consequences. For the neo-Lamarckian, this identifies a possible mechanism for evolutionary progress. Some of these learned behaviors can be passed down to future generations. Aside from figures like Baldwin and Vygotsky, it was not always recognized how much the capacity for "higher" thought depends on language. But, it is during this time that the child becomes fully human, developing a capacity that is not present anywhere else in the animal world. Finally, the culmination of this process reflects where development has been heading all along. Depending on the theorist, different elements of these forms of thought determine its advanced nature—logical and abstract for Piaget, resigned to reality for Freud, syllogistic for Romanes, and volitional for Baldwin. Whatever the end, there seems to be only a single path to get there, a consequence of Darwin's narrower vision when it came to the development of mind as well as the tendency to confuse a logical progression with a developmental one.

As we have been suggesting, development psychology is a study of morality hidden in a study of the laws of development hidden in a study of children. The passages to reality, symbolism, abstraction—all are reflections of our own values. Take reality. As mentioned previously, for both Piaget and Freud, development culminates in the aligning of thought with reality. The real moral failure of early childhood is the inability to transcend the self. The all-powerful childhood ego prevents the young from seeing things as they actually are and not as they want them to be. The same can be said of abstraction. The child is trapped in the local and cannot transcend to that universal plane that Westerners had been trying to get to since Plato. Perhaps only Vygotsky fully understood how much access to this plane is related to the spread of literacy. Outsourcing memory in the way literate societies do allows thought to move further and further away from the everyday. One can build abstract taxonomies upon abstract taxonomies and never worry about forgetting it all. Language creates a kind of distance from reality that the spoken word can never really reproduce. It allows humans to better separate symbol from reality and representation from the world itself, giving them the opportunity to reflect on the adequacy of those representations. There is nothing "natural" about abstraction being the culmination of thought. As we shall see in the next section, some in contemporary psychology have forgotten this, convinced that such representations are "wired" into the brain and thus precede the acquisition of language. In psychiatry and psychotherapy too little alignment with reality is a symptom of severe psychopathology. The shamans and prophets of previous societies have become today's schizo-phrenics. Perhaps this makes sense. Given the complex institutional struc-tures and ambiguous social relationships that must be navigated, moderns need to be much more "reality" based than ever.

Developmental psychology is about telling stories, and most of these assumptions help to tell better stories. The process involves selecting certain events in childhood—after all there are an awful lot to choose from—and representing them in such a way that relate them to each other. This is the explanation (Kagan, 1983), or better still, this is the description disguised as an explanation. Sometimes, this is represented in mechanistic terms with effects related to clearly spelled-out causes. Sometimes it is represented in organic terms with agents helping to direct development toward certain ends. As Jerome Kagan (1983) notes, Westerners prefer to view significant events as having long histories—even though, ironically, discontinuity is more evi-dent when one looks at the evidence from morphology and biology. Things don't slowly turn into other things—such changes tend to be quite rapid and out of the blue. Sometimes, change doesn't happen at all. People tend to remain the same in some fundamental ways over the course of their lives, although storytelling conventions might lead us to believe otherwise.

Again, these "biases" are not wrong and do not distort some natural object. One cannot "discover" development in nature, as it is an artifact of a way of talking about nature. As we suggest in the first section, however, there are other ways to tell these stories. These alternative narratives can be found occasionally in the work of Darwin, Baldwin, Werner, Vygotsky, and even Piaget. They stress contingency and emergence rather than necessity and directionality. They are more akin to what we have described as probab-ilistic epigenesis rather than determined epigenesis. They sometimes de-scribe development as "self-organizing" or "nonlinear," and they understand all development frameworks have a purposive and moral character. We will develop such an alternate narrative in more detail in a later section. For all its problems, developmental thinking in general is far more sophisticated than what comes next in child psychology, the collapse of developmental thinking and the return to Platonic idealism.

5. INSIDE AND OUTSIDE: THE SCIENTIST IN THE CRIB

In the 1990s, evolutionary psychology and deterministic models of gene action were fused to offer a new framework for explaining the genesis of infant thought. A new variant of faculty psychology emerged using meta-phors like "modular" and "innately-specified" to explain findings that infants and young children were more capable than Piaget had believed. Some of these new faculties included innate understandings of physical objects, biological objects, pattern recognition, essences, people and behavior, number, quantity, probability, cause/effect, and most important of all, language. These findings made an important point. There is no question that infant capacities have long been underestimated by psychology, some of which was due to the dominance of empiricism and nineteenth-century evolutionism. Influenced by Locke and Rousseau, depictions of infancy and early childhood ranged from the relatively blank slates of behaviorism, the automata of drive theory, the polymorphously perverse creatures of psychoanalysis, and the egocentrics of Jean Piaget to the autistics of Margret Mahler. The new nativism was a response to several trends in psychology: (a) the influence of cognitive science and computing metaphors in making sense of the functions of mind; (b) the growing influence of gene-directed models in making sense of development; (c) the collapse of Piagetian structuralism, particularly the idea of general intelligence and the age-graded norms associated with stages; and (d) a general conservative shift in U.S. culture coinciding with the election of Ronald Reagan that made evolutionary metaphors more acceptable and pharmacological rather than social interventions more common, thus locating more and more human properties in biology.

The so-called cognitive revolution in psychology marked the end of behaviorist dominance. Rats were out, and computers were in. New computing-related metaphors allowed psychologists to talk of mind in ways that were initially disconnected from physiological properties. Particularly important was the distinction between structure and function. While computers clearly had a structure—the hardware—one could also study their data-processing functions—software—without knowing much about that hardware. The same was true with mind. The mind was reborn as an information-processing machine wherein information was inputted (stimulus), processed by a central processor (thinking), and then outputted to the body (response). It didn't take long to recognize that the new psychology was not that different from the old one. S-R psychology survived in cognitivism. The search for the universal laws of thought simply replaced the search for the universal laws of behavior.

A subtle difference was the focus on processing, though Edward Tolman had already developed an early version of this model in the 1930s. A new language, mostly borrowed from computing, but some of which can be traced back to Kant, was developed to identify what the mind contained— representations, schemata, symbols—and what functions it engaged in—coding, storing, retrieving, metaprocessing (Gardner, 1987). None of this necessarily required a turn to nativism. This "computer" could easily have been regarded as a product of development, as it was, for instance, in Piaget. But as new functions were "discovered," the notion of innate, specialized, autonomous "processors" emerged. This was opposed with the notion of a single general processor, which is more akin with the traditional Empiricist conception of mind. Thus a turn to nativism tended to follow from this new specialized version. The inspiration for the new turn to nativism came mostly from Noam Chomsky. The basic model offered by Chomsky was that of a specialized faculty for language that was "hard-wired" into the human brain and a product of natural selection. Not surprisingly, Chomsky did not bother with the physiology of all this, but as luck would have it, the idea of cerebral localization was gaining traction once again in neuroscience. New findings appeared to correspond with the idea of autonomous regions with specialized functions built into the brain. It was fairly easy to extend this to cognition and Chomsky himself suggested it. Thought was a product of autonomous modules with specialized functions, often framed in traditional stimulus-response terms. For example, one of the pioneers of this approach, Dan Sperber, described a three-tiered mind: a single layer of "input" modules, a complex network of first-order conceptual modules, and a set of second-order meta-representational modules for "culture" and "experience" (Sperber, 1996).

At the same time, readings of experimental evidence in infancy research appeared to confirm this shift as well. By linking various stages of thinking with particular ages, American Piagetians had set themselves up for a barrage of studies seeking to identify whether children could perform Piagetian tasks earlier than he would have predicted. And that was precisely what these studies found (Donaldson, 1979). Some of these findings were an artifact of the research—creating new tasks appropriate for younger children with different linguistic and motor skills but insisting they measured the same underlying structure—but most of the findings were a consequence of the failure of the theory itself. By generalizing "stages" across contexts, essentially making context irrelevant, Piaget was forced to distinguish between "having" a stage (competence) and "doing" a stage (performance). Typically, performance was indicative of competence but not always. Piagetians frequently referred to the problem of horizontal dècalage—showing evidence of advanced forms of thought in one context but not another, a problem that was presumably resolved once children mastered the advanced forms and generalized them to all contexts.

And yet, if one found contexts where those structures could not be generalized, or better yet, found that children employed those intellectual structures in isolated contexts much earlier than anticipated, one has undermined Piaget's notion of a general, formal intelligence and suggested that intelligence might be domain specific. And this is precisely what happened. The confusion here is the arbitrary distinction between having a stage and performing it. Competence is a consequence of performance. It has no autonomous reality. This is the same mistake that the practice of standardized testing makes in education: the test measures the capacity to take the test and not some independent capacity that exists outside of the performance. Obviously, this is a flaw in much non-Piagetian psychology as well that believes its objects of study are independent of the methods used to measure them.

This was the problem operationalization was supposed to solve. What Piagetians were actually testing was the performance of a particular child on a particular problem, interpreted by the child in a particular way, in a particular context, in a particular relationship with a particular experimenter, in a particular moment of time. Piaget must have known this given the historical importance of his clinical method in French psychiatry, but his American students did not. Ironically, the neo-nativists went on to make these same mistakes.

Much of the new nativism came out of infancy research. A new methodological paradigm was developed to study infants that no longer relied exclusively on observation but instead made use of the phenomenon of habituation (Kagan, 2013). This paradigm included violation of expectations (VOE) research and habituation research. Essentially, the method worked with the fact that infants tend to acclimate or habituate to stimuli fairly quickly. They usually become distracted a few seconds after noticing something and shift their attention elsewhere. However, if that stimulus changes and the infants do not return their focus to it, that tells us—defenders of this approach argue—that infants cannot discriminate between the original stimulus and the modified one. For instance, in dozens and dozens of versions of this study, fairly young infants were habituated to various images of scrambled faces. At some point, an image of a properly organized human face was shown, and the infants appeared to attend to it (Slater & Quinn, 2001). Other times this was measured in units of time, that is, the infants looked longer at the image of a properly organized human face than the other images. This was interpreted as evidence, not only that infants can discriminate between images of correctly organized human faces and other images (reasonable), but that infants are born with the capacity to recognize human faces, a face-recognition module (less reasonable). They therefore "prefer" them and this preference was innate (least reasonable). This is especially confusing given that infants were looking at representations of human faces, not actual human faces.

Sometimes this was described as controlled by a genetic program or hardwired into the brain and a product of natural selection that increased the likelihood of survival by bonding infants to their caregivers. Sometimes all this was just assumed with some brief mention of the importance of an environment as a trigger. And yet, nobody here studies the operations of genes, brains, or evolution. In recent years defenders of this paradigm just use the term "innate" to mean that experience is not needed for this capacity to emerge and are wisely more coy about the biology involved. However, the inference that because a trait or behavior appears early in life means it is innate is a seemingly reasonable but incorrect one. However one defines "experience," it begins from the moment of conception. There is also an assumption that the refocusing of attention or longer stares on the part of an infant is a sign of preference. So, researchers describe infants as "preferring" properly organized human faces. Similar preferences were found for a range of stimuli including mother's native language. But it is not clear why the variable "time staring" should be translated into the conscious state of preferring (Kagan, 2013, p. 34).

Another series of VOE studies demonstrated, its proponents claim, that infants are born with basic knowledge of the physical universe (Spelke et al., 1995). This time infants were shown a demonstration that seemed to violate basic laws of physics, for instance, one solid object passing through another. Infants stared longer at the conditions that violated physical relations than those that did not. This time, staring was not interpreted as a sign of preference but as a sign of surprise. Younger and younger infants seemed to demonstrate that they expected inanimate objects to behave in certain ways, and when those expectations were violated, they noticed. Again, it is not clear why staring longer means surprise rather than for example "I like something about the way these objects move." In similar research, infants at seven months or so recognize that these same expectations should not apply to humans because they can move in all sorts of ways inanimate objects cannot—suggesting they have mastered the distinction between animate and inanimate far earlier than Piaget had believed (Gelman et al., 1995; Gelman, 2003). Again, all this was said to reflect the existence of innate, specialized, domain-specific modules designed to provide knowledge of basic physics, in this case, knowledge of constraints on object motion. Researchers in this paradigm did not always agree on the specific frame for expressing these findings. Interpretations ranged from the notion that infants possessed these capacities at the start of life (e.g., Spelke et al., 1995) to the notion that initial simpler versions are progressively elaborated over the first year of life (e.g., Baillargeon et al., 1995), but most were fairly confident that experience was not required for these capacities to operate.

The architects of this research see this work as resolving the nature-vs.-nurture question (Premack & Premack, 2002). Needless to say, most of them believe that much human knowledge and capacity is rooted in biology, whose effects can be distinguished from the effects of experience. That is what is meant by the term innate: the structures of these cognitive functions are independent of experience. They tend not to be all that precise about what kinds of experiences they are referring to (intra-organismic, extra-organismic, intracellular, extracellular, in utero, post-birth, etc.). For these psychologists, experience seems to be a singular, distinct source of influence they can control for. The same seems to be true for context. As was the case for Piaget, performance in a particular context is said to reflect an underlying competence across contexts. Since the only alternative explanation for VOE researchers tends to be a vague conception of experience, which typically means learning as conceived by behaviorists or Piagetian generalism, they are left with nativist explanations exclusively.

Furthermore, VOE research has little regard for variation. If the number of infants performing the task successfully has statistical significance, the competence is a universal one. There is little analysis of the development of these competencies. They are simply there. These new modules are just as static as Piagetian structures, but at least Piaget understood that his structures had to develop. In the new nativism there is no mention of development at all. They seem to believe that taking one measure, in one context, at one moment of time says all this. Is it possible that the infant's attention is not about what they know or what they prefer but about what they perceive? Perhaps this is more a perceptual phenomenon than a cognitive one? How can we be certain the findings are about physics or faces? Jerome Kagan (2013) suggests humans have a tendency, appearing very early in life, to notice objects or events that violate expectations. This could be the case. Infants might be focused more on whether events are continuous or discontinuous than preference. Any of these interpretations are just as plausible. Maybe infants do develop expectations fairly early, and maybe a bit of life, even in the womb, is required to fill in what those expectations are? Or perhaps humans have specialized nerve cells in the visual cortex that attend to certain kinds of changes in patterns regardless of context? Either way, all of these interpretations far exceed what can be gleaned from these findings. Perhaps we can only say that Piaget tended to underestimate children and that most of his findings tended to be artifacts of the research itself.

VOE researchers believe that humans have innately-specified means for organizing knowledge of the natural world which they often extend to the social world as well. It is interesting that they take the opposite of Durkheim's approach, which has framed social thinking for much of the past century. Humans have categories developed to navigate through relationships with people, argued Durkheim in *The Elementary Forms of the Religious Life*, which are then extended to the natural world. Both use examples of the cross-cultural universality of certain categories to make their case. But this is faulty evidence. Universality, for instance, can be the product of certain stable features in human environments. It can also be an artifact of methods that divorce behaviors from what they mean to particular individuals in specific environments.

VOE researchers also ignore the clues adults provide children about the nature of certain categories of objects built into language itself. Take young children's tendency to classify things in rigid categories of kind. In other words, if someone is a boy, they must remain a boy and act a certain way. Is this a function of children's essentialism, an innate need to categorize which has not yet developed any flexibility as both Piagetians and VOE researchers argue? Or is this a function of specific categories of the social world imposed in alternate contexts? Or perhaps it is a function of the way we use nouns in language? Is it conceivable that the singularity of nouns is generalized into the singularity of kinds? Perhaps this explains the tendency of children to acquire many more noun-words than verb-words in the first few years of life, suggesting they are focused more on what things are than what they do (Clark, 2003). Patterns in language clue children into the notion that certain properties of things or persons are incidental and others are intrinsic. For example, one might say "the attractive female lawyer" but would not say "the female attractive lawyer." One property is incidental (attractive), one is intrinsic (female), and one is about a social role (lawyer). This says a lot about how we classify objects into kinds. Such clues are often language specific. For instance, English has many words for differing emotions, but unlike other languages, most of them don't convey the cause of those emotions. Might this suggest that very different emotional experiences, in very different contexts, belong to the same kind? Perhaps. The only way to identify the relationship between language and forms of thought in this way is to study how children's thinking changes, or does not change, in specific contexts as they acquire new language forms. In fact, this is precisely what Vygotsky and his school found and what is absent from research based in Chomskyan linguistics.

This is not to say that language is an independent variable and thought a dependent one, related as cause is to effect. Once children begin to acquire language, thought and language are inextricably linked in the larger enterprise of communication, meaning making, and getting on in the world. The acquisition of language is part of a broader pattern of conditions—entering school, acquiring new skills, more autonomy, and brain development—that can all be related to newly emerging forms of thinking and behaving. These conditions cannot be so easily distinguished from each other. Such study requires alternative methods to those borrowed from physics and used by S-R psychology. Ideally, such study yields insightful descriptions rather than explanations and is framed in terms of mutually interacting relationships between agents on many different levels rather than as the result of simple causes or something that happens inside the heads of children. Such study would yield, one imagines, that language is not a singular function—it involves a set of functions that develop independently, certain kinds of breathing, control over vocal cords, brain maturation, attending, sorting, symbol-use, representation, and interpretation—which come together, gradually, to form what we term the function of language. The same is true with specific forms of thought. They are not necessarily natural categories but analytic ones. Perhaps psychology can offer no more than some tentative descriptions of these relationships, which can still be useful in trying to make sense of the complex interrelationship between biology, thought, language, and social relations in day-to-day experience, at least as long as the focus is on acknowledging the discipline of psychology's own ground in a particular mode of knowing and experiencing.

6. STRUCTURE AND FUNCTION: LANGUAGE DEVELOPMENT

The case of language acquisition provides an illustrative example of how the pitting of inside against outside, nature against nurture, tells us little about the source of human capacities and how a complex developmental perspective including explicit attention to the relationship between structure and function can help provide a richer source of analysis. The science of language has its origins in the careful analysis and criticism of classical texts by Renaissance philologists. Modern linguistics was born in the 1780s when philologist William Jones noticed similarities in disparate languages and used this to make the case for a common source (Blumenthal, 1970). This allowed linguists to treat language with the same kinds of elaborate taxonomies used by eighteenth-century natural scientists to organize plants and animals. They used these to develop theories about the origins of various language families. Over the course of the nineteenth century, some students of language, the so-called neo-grammarians, dissatisfied by the focus on description and classification, sought to discover the underlying laws of phonetic change. They framed this in Darwinian terms and began to treat language like any other biological organ. The neo-grammarians studied children's language acquisition as a means by which to understand how language evolved in general. Some German psychologists focused on language acquisition, including Wundt, Preyer, and Bühler who viewed the study of language as a means to study thought. Debates raged on whether thought and language were extricable and whether animal cries were a precursor to language. Influenced by this, Piaget viewed delayed imitation as a precursor to language and focused on language performance as a means to distinguish between egocentric and socialized speech.

By the twentieth century "structuralist" linguistics began to analyze the underlying organization of language by studying it independent of speech. It became acceptable to talk of an underlying structure distinct from its appearance. Well before the 1950s some linguistics were already describing this underlying structure as involving transformational grammar, and this was the tradition that Chomsky extended. Before this, in the United States, Leonard Bloomfield dominated linguistics. He criticized structuralist linguistics and argued that language must be studied inductively. He gradually became more and more influenced by U.S. behaviorism and required that language study be conceived mechanistically. He repudiated all forms of mentalism. Influenced by Bloomfield, B. F. Skinner sought to describe the ontogenesis of language using the same behavioral framework he applied to all learning.

Language was simply a kind of behavior, he argued in *Verbal Behavior*, learned using the same kinds of external contingencies—reinforcement, punishment, shaping—used to acquire any other behavior. Chomsky's scathing review of Skinner's book in 1957 launched his career.

The behavioral approach to language is impossible, argued Chomsky, because of the poverty of stimuli—children are exposed to syntactically incorrect language, and parents do not bother to correct children's grammar. The environment cannot explain how children acquire the extensive syntax they do by the age of five. All this knowledge of syntax requires knowledge of the complex rules of transformation, which cannot be acquired inductively. Since they cannot possibly be learned via the environment, insisted Chomsky in a bit of forced reasoning that we have seen before, they must be innate. Humans are born with a specialized language module—Chomsky called this a "language acquisition device" or LAD—hardwired into the brain which possesses knowledge of a deep and universal syntax, what he called "generative grammar." This is a set of rules for combining words in all sorts of ways to create complex sentences. The meaning of words is limited to the "surface" structure of language, what Chomsky's most famous student, Steven Pinker, calls the "periphery" and acknowledges that this can involve learning (Pinker, 1994). The job of linguistics, said Chomsky, was to make the underlying structure of language explicit. This involved eschewing empirical data for deductive inference and formal rules, studying syntax independently of meaning and communication as well as viewing language-use as a mechanical process of following sets of rules. While not necessarily accepting his particular findings, a generation of cognitive psychologists influenced by his approach extended Chomsky's modular approach to psychological functions in general as was reviewed in the previous section.

Typically, Chomsky is viewed as the victor of this battle between nature and nurture. Perhaps there is some recognition of needing experience to fill in the content of language, but the premise is that the basic understanding of the structure of language is innate. This is further supported by the claim that certain parts of the brain are clearly involved in language function. Of course, one does not follow from the other. Resolving the developmental origins of language in this way leaves the basic premise of nature and nurture as distinct categories intact. Ontogenetic analysis, then, is left with, in the mode of Arnold Gesell, simply describing some of the major milestones in the acquisition of language.

Perhaps descriptive generalizations are the best thing psychology can offer, but such a path leaves too many of Chomsky's basic frames intact, most troubling of which is the hard distinction between the innate and the learned. In order to correct this bias, we need to establish some basic things about language, most of which the Chomskyan approach ignores. We can then use this as a vehicle to understand why, in any application we identify, the analytic distinction between nature and nurture is just not helpful in making sense of complex psychological phenomena. Once we move beyond this distinction, we can generate a less reductive language for talking about development in general. To start with, language is not simply syntax. It is part of broader communication practices that include utterances, gestures, movements, displays, facial expressions, memory, and emotion—essentially anything that contributes to a successful interaction. A successful interaction requires that the speaker convey their intended meanings to the listener. But language has additional functions as well. For instance, parents use language to regulate all kinds of behavior, helping to turn children into properly social-ized members of society. Children use language to get their needs met and eventually use language to develop more and more complex ways to repre-sent and reconceptualize their relationship to the world.

Speakers are typically not all that interested in syntax, unless they are English teachers. They are interested in communicating and, in the end, getting what they want or need out of an interaction. Syntax is part of this, no doubt, especially in its capacity for organizing and regularizing language, thus making it easier to construct and remember it. Children do develop the capacity for successful language-based interactions fairly quickly during the first few years of life, and it is not clear exactly why it happens when it does, but it is clear that certain environmental conditions help a lot. For instance, exposure to language is not enough. Children require opportunities for inter-actions revolving around language. This is why in general middle-class chil-dren tend to acquire language more rapidly than working-class children and both much more than children raised in extreme poverty. Middle-class par-ents tend to talk to their children more, exposing them to more words, as well as follow their children's lead on potential conversation topics. They also tend to follow up on them later, all of which induces middle-class children to talk even more. Eve Clark estimates that middle-class children hear about 2,100 words per hour, compared to about 600 per hour for children who grow up in extreme poverty (Clark, 2003, pp. 376–379). These differences can be mitigated, but they can also be exacerbated when these children enter schools with differing resources. Another helpful condition for language acquisition is the presence of child-directed speech, what is sometimes called "mothe-rese." Studies show that this kind of talk tends to be remarkably free of grammatical errors and well-tailored to its addressees (Clark, 2003). For instance, parents will lower the bar as to what counts as a response from infants so as to give them opportunities to develop turn-taking experiences in communication.

In fact, much conversation with children includes pragmatic instruction in conversation itself (Clark, 2003, p. 49). Parents also tend to focus on objects in view, making new words concrete, change pitch when talking to infants, as well as stress the syllables they want children to attend to. This is probably one of the reasons why many children can track adult attention and even redirect it by the end of the first year. Parents encourage children to notice what they are attending to, especially middle-class parents. Given how much interaction there is typically between infants and parents in the first years of life (e.g. feeding, dressing, diaper changing, comforting, playing, etc.), this is a lot of exposure to language, especially for middle-class children. Stimulation is not as impoverished as Chomsky imagined.

The problem with both the behavioral and Chomskyan approach to language development is they are still trying to explain how children acquire language. But, children do not acquire language at all, they create it. Language does not exist in the environment waiting to be absorbed by children, nor does it sit in modules in the brain waiting to be accessed. Language is created in the day-to-day, moment-to-moment practices of speaking and listening to others. Language-acquisition typically begins with ritualized gestures, neither shared nor a result of imitation, followed by deictics, gestures designed to direct another's attention, and finally symbolic gestures, those that represent something else (Tomasello, 2003, p. 35). Symbolic gestures are typically followed by a few words, usually holophrases or words that have multiple functions like "up" (Tomaseloo, 2003, p. 35). Children also quickly develop the ability to hear and process whole utterances, breaking them down and figuring out patterns and the functions of various parts. They experiment with different language forms, playing with them, altering them, and extending them into new contexts over and over again throughout early childhood. As educators have well known from the Greeks to Locke, repetition is an extremely effective way to develop a skill. A related problem with both of these approaches is some confusion as to what is actually involved with language acquisition. Acquiring language involves the acquisition of a rule-governed, symbol-based form of communication. This is correct, but there is much more to it.

What does acquiring language involve? Terrence Deacon (1997) offers an innovative answer combining a phylogenetic and ontogenetic perspective, and it is worth following his account closely. Deacon's account revolves around the development of the capacity to interpret meaning. One way to begin to answer this question, argues Deacon, is to look at some of the attempts to teach primates language. Primates cannot acquire language in the way humans can, and yet they are capable of communicating via signs and following rules. They can be taught the rules for using symbols, especially if those symbols do not involve vocalization (i.e., sign language), but they seem to be missing something that children are not, which prevents language mastery. Deacon (1997) terms the missing component the capacity for "symbolic reference," the capacity to interpret the meaning of symbols (p. 100).

Animals are capable of linking symbols to referents in the world. For example, a well-trained dog knows the behavior associated with a symbol like "sit" or the referent to a term like "treat." These are associative connections. But language use requires going beyond the associative level, giving up a focus on a specific sign and its referent and instead focusing on how that sign is related to an entire system of signs. This is true both syntactically—how that sign fits into structure of a sentence—as well as semantically—the meaning of that sign in relation to all other signs. The syntactic component is not necessarily the most challenging one. Syntax is just physical regularity, though a necessary regularity for interpreting words. But the latter component, what Deacon terms symbolic reference, makes it different from all other forms of communication. It is not committing associations to memory due to reinforcement, as behaviorists seem to think; nor is it a type of verbal behavior, as Skinner thought; nor is it the recalling of an underlying grammar as Chomsky argued; but language acquisition requires identifying those symbols that are relevant and figuring out how they are all related to each other. It involves taking symbols that one is already familiar with and reorganizing them into novel relationships.

By this point, children no longer acquire symbols one at a time, as they are now understood as part of a logically complete system of relationships. This requires, says Deacon (1997), a radical mental shift. One must move away from considering symbols individually as each relates to real-world referents, and focus on the internal relationship of symbols to each other (p. 95). These include combinatorial rules, which make the introduction of new symbols seamless without changing their basic organization. It also makes categorical generalizations and other forms of abstraction possible, allowing language to become a tool for certain forms of thought. This shift can be challenging given that prior associative relations might get in the way of new, broader ones. Yet, human children, unlike the case with primates, seem predisposed to doing precisely that by the end of the second year of life. Luckily, children do not have to adapt to language, as language has adapted to them. Current languages, as they evolved over centuries, are particularly suited to children's minds.

Acquiring language begins with what children already do spontaneously and is guided toward biases children already possess (Deacon, 1997, pp. 141–142). For example, Deacon suggests, underdeveloped neurological structures related to memory might make it easier for children to forget prior associative relations and focus on new broader ones. The support children require to acquire language comes from language itself. Languages evolved to be learned, that is how they survived. As languages were used over time, "grammaticalization" occurred, that is, patterns of use with meaningful constraints evolved to assist humans in acquisition (Tomasello, 2003). Languages are "parasitic," argues Deacon, in the sense that they use human brains and their preexisting capacities, as well as new capacities that come with language acquisition to survive. These biases relate to attention, memory, sound production, and automation. Language capacity is innate in the limited sense that almost all humans are capable of acquiring it but not innate as in already learned. Universals, often used as evidence for the innateness of certain linguistic categories, might be an example of language adapting to neurological biases. In fact, Deacon continues, it is almost impossible that these biases are related to deep syntax, as Chomsky would have it, because studies of brain damaged patients suggest language loss tends to revolve around "surface" properties of words—like loss of sense and meaning— rather than any deep grammatical structures, making them an unlikely category of knowledge for a brain organ (Tomasello, 2003, p. 333). It is far more likely that "syntax" is not a biological category but an analytic one invented by linguistics.

The attempt to link the function of language with neurological structures is often regarded as one of the success stories of nineteenth- and twentieth-century neuroscience (Tomasello, 2003, p. 283). Paul Broca and Carl Wernicke who correlated lesions in the brain in aphasia with loss of specific language functions are regarded as pioneers of cortical localization. Since then, it has become clear that language function is distributed in several specialized structures in the brain (Tomasello, 2003, p. 288). These discoveries have led to the claim that the brain is modular, with a myriad of specialized functions mapped onto certain neural structures. The same is true, it is argued, for cognitive functions. These, too, are mapped onto specialized neural structures. While this might be correct for certain perceptual and motor functions whose input/output relations in the brain are fairly easy to trace, given the integrated and multilevel state of cortical neural pathways, these types of relationships in complex mental activities are almost impossible to establish. We really have no way of knowing whether functional distinctions in psychology correspond with neural ones. In fact, language might prove to be a great example of how this is not the case. The brain does not have language "areas," as is typically argued, but areas that have been co-opted by language. These areas depend on structures and functions in other areas of the brain. Thus neural functions may or may not be modular, but it is highly unlikely that psychological ones are. With respect to the mind, the brain functions as a whole. Deacon describes the brain and language as undergoing a process of coevolution (Tomasello, 2003, p. 322). Language evolved to adapt to human neurology as the brain evolved as it used language. Deacon borrows this idea from James Mark Baldwin: the acquisition of language, over generations, biased natural selection to select for already existing variations that supported language. This in turn led to modifications in the environment adding new selection pressures to future generations. What looks like the work of use-inheritance—learning passed onto the next generation—is actually the work of selection. Other functions in the brain, particularly ones related to thought and memory, were able to amplify certain functions initially involved with language, eventually coming to be the advanced cognitive functions we associate with humans exclusively. Of course, it is just as likely that some of these cognitive skills evolved first for other reasons and language emerged as a result (Tomasello, 2003, p. 4). We will probably never know.

Some of these functions include the categorization of similar objects and events, the sharing of attention, sensorimotor patterns, and the ability to relate elements into more complex wholes (Tomasello, 2003, p. 4). And this is just a short list. Thus the development of language changed human nature in the ways described by Vygotsky. Vygotsky himself offered a great example: the acquisition of language allows humans to distance themselves from the contents of their own thoughts and reflect on them, as if they are external objects, not unlike a Cartesian theater. Thus the evolution of symbolic reference sits at the intersection of social and biological change (Deacon, 1997). The term "co-evolution" recognizes that one cannot easily distinguish between causes and their effects, especially given the complicated relations between structure and function in the nervous system. Again this does not mean that knowledge of language or certain types of cognition are hardwired into the brain, quite the opposite. The human brain has certain perceptual and motor biases—perhaps even learning and emotional ones—which makes us relatively good at language and thinking in certain contexts and especially with respect to thought that requires the manipulation of symbols. The human brain, says Deacon (1997), is likely overbuilt for symbol learning with an overdeveloped prefrontal cortex connected via vast and integrated neural networks across the brain (pp. 350–351). But only in hindsight do these appear like fully formed behaviors or characteristics which have been selected for. We will likely never know the original functions of these biases or even be able to catalog them in some systematic way. The best we can do is develop plausible accounts using what we know about behavioral ecology, human physiology, and already identified structural-functional relationships in the brain. Less useful is the development of plausible "just-so" stories that explain why a particular function was useful in the Pleistocene era (Deacon, 1997, p. 351). Trying to divide such an analysis into distinct categories like "nature" and "nurture" or even too rigid a distinction between structure and function, only makes it less likely that one will capture the complexity of language development in either phylogenetic or ontogenetic forms. The same is true with overly simplified, linear, and single-trajectory models of development. The same is true of all complex psychological activity.

Chapter Seven

The Cure of the Soul in the Age of the Therapeutic

This chapter focuses on the confluence of the fields of psychology, psycho-therapy, counseling, and psychiatry in creating new notions of psychological illness and cure. Together, we consider them the institutional and conceptual ground of the contemporary therapeutic sensibility. This chapter might seem a bit of a deviation from the previous ones, which focused more on topics more central to experimental psychology. For much of the twentieth century, a tension between experimentalists and clinicians has defined the discipline. Experimentalists have viewed clinicians as lacking the scientific gravitas of their own work and some clinicians have viewed experimentalists as narrow technicians missing much about what it means to be human. Yet ironically, to this day, those outside the field still have trouble distinguishing these groups from each other, made more difficult by the fact that a great majority of them refer to themselves as "psychologists" and describe what they do as "psychology" or as another "psy"-related activity including psychological counseling, psychotherapy, and psychiatry. Because the point of this mono-graph is to look at some of the conceptual themes that frame modern psychology, we need to set aside how people describe their vocation and instead focus on the underlying psychological themes in the work they do. In this case, it will involve going far beyond experimental psychology, even the university, and examining some of the psychological themes that have come to permeate everyday life in modern, Western societies.

We can point to some of the same tensions here that we identified in previous chapters, those between inside and outside, structure and function, higher and lower, and description and explanation. Many of these tensions have been well recognized. For instance, one way to describe twentieth-century views on illnesses of mind and their cures is as a struggle between a psychological/functional approach and a somatic/structural approach. While the psychological approach was dominant in U.S. psychiatry during the middle decades of the twentieth century, by the end of the century the somatic approach reasserted itself quite aggressively. Some of this was related to a move, exemplified through a revision of the The Diagnostic and Statistical Manual of Mental Disorders (DSM) in the late 1970s, from an explanatory approach to a descriptive one. Although typically an explanatory approach would be considered the more scientific one, given that medical diagnosis is organized around description, specifically the cataloging of symptoms, and the alternate explanatory approach derived mostly from psychoanalysis, in this case, a symptoms-based nosology with high reliability was considered a step forward. The authors of the new DSM-III made questions of reliability central to their revisions because, as they saw it, this would increase the scientific status of the field (Kirk & Kutchins, 1992). But also, as they well knew, by describing psychiatric illness in the same way as one described physiological illness, somatic explanations easily followed, which is what the authors of the revision really intended (Kirk & Kutchins, 1992, p. 14). The validity of the categories themselves was decided by consensus but over time has received "support" through talk of brain imbalances and genetic predispositions.

The idea of a therapeutic sensibility has its origins in the work of conservative sociologist Philip Rieff who described the emergence of a new type of human character, "psychological man." Psychological man, Rieff (1959) argued, has lost faith in the world, is too "modern" to make himself an object of faith, so he replaces faith with a sense of self-concern (p. 330). Psychological Man carefully keeps score of his satisfactions and dissatisfactions, appreciates insight, particularly into him, and is drawn into the psyche in an attempt to conquer inner life. Psychological man seeks salvation through contemplation, and his highest good is well-being, especially his own. He values feelings, authenticity, and tolerance. His devotion to an ideal is replaced by clarity about himself, and the guilt that held him responsible to others is replaced by a sense of guilt, which becomes the source of his suffering. He loves not from obligation but from self-realization. At his worst, he is amoral, selfish, and sees himself as victimized by others, and at his best he is "self-actualized." These ideas were further developed in the work of Christopher Lasch in the 1970s and Robert Bellah in the 1980s.

The dominance of a therapeutic sensibility reflects some broad changes in how individuals conceive their relationship to the world. Until the early nineteenth century, for the most part, the great majority of people on the planet related to the universe as had their ancestors for millennia. Most made a living off the land and viewed the world as part of a great cosmic drama organized by the divine. Their place in the world and experiences in life were all part of a larger sacred order within which they had a place. Rieff calls this character "religious man." Beginning with the Renaissance, Reformation, and especially the rise of experimental science, some European ideas began to undermine this worldview. Nature was reconceived through Galilean mechanics, not simply movements of inert matter. In a sense, it was the culmination of the Christian project of the radical transcendence of God and the complete removal of divinity from the natural world.

In concert with this new worldview was the Cartesian split between the immaterial substance that composed mind and the material one that composed body. The Greek soul, which gave form to the body in the Aristotelian sense, became the modern mind with vast inner resources. The solution as to the source of knowledge and certainty lay inward. A century later Rousseau and his romantic followers added that this mind was innately good, capable of generating its own moral order and knowing the truth of self. The intellectual stage was set for a paradigm that found freedom and dignity in an inner quest. Nature or scripture were no longer the ultimate source of morality and truth; we ourselves were (C. Taylor, 1989). For Rieff, these currents culminated in Freud who understood the problems that came with this new worldview. The problem is, Rieff argued, his progeny have not.

As we shall see, the psychoanalysis of turn-of-the-century Europe has been integrated into other psychological currents in American society and transformed into something else. It has become a way to make sense of self and other as well explain the source of the problems many individuals have as they make their way through life (Furedi, 2004, p. 12). Whether it is the media explaining current events in psychological terms or teachers charged with helping to protect their students' self-esteem or social workers "counseling" the poor as a condition for participating in social welfare programs, or the search to explain history by focusing on the inner lives of people involved, the United States is a society dominated by a psychotherapeutic sensibility. Moreover, U.S. culture and its institutions help to shape experience in such a way that individuals easily use this sensibility to make sense of their own lives. Psychoanalysis has transformed itself into psychotherapeutics, a program for life and a technology for permanent healing.

Freud's stoic self-mastery has been replaced by the simple pursuit of well-being. Freud believed that the traditional requirements for the renunciation of pleasure were creating more illness than solace in the form of guilt, but he did not seek to replace them with new forms of consolation (Rieff, 1966). If religion had long consoled individuals from the miseries of living, as Freud believed, the Freudian analysand was forced to live without such consolation. In the United States, with a general rise in living standards and expectations, therapy became more optimistic about what it could promise. Influenced by the "positive" psychologies of Abraham Maslow and Carl Rogers as well as the social movements of the 1960s, even the Self Psychology of Heinz Kohut, therapy promised to help its clients feel accepted, actualized, and content. Gone was the Augustinian view of human nature as inherently conflicted and unstable. Instead, conflict and instability were signs that something had gone wrong.

Therapeutics promised to restore individuals to the state of well-being which "bad" early childhood experiences, or of late, "bad" brain chemicals, robbed from them. In Freudian psychoanalysis, one must overcome conflicted instinctual passions in the service of an inner moral order. In therapeutics, reviving the spirit of Rousseau, human nature as naturally expressed is good, so there is nothing to overcome. Those moral agents who characterize these impulses—sexual, aggressive, self-seeking, and narcissistic—as bad are themselves the problem. Once these outmoded and restrictive forms of morality are replaced with more modern ones like medical and therapeutic reason, the seemingly inherent conflict between individuals and society disappears. Psychic stability, self-esteem, and happiness follow from accepting this authentic self (Cushman, 1995).

What exactly is involved with contemporary therapeutics? One can identify several basic propositions. The first involves a reconfiguration of the relationship between person and world wherein, for better or worse, the interior world is no longer made to serve the exterior one. Instead the exterior world must be redesigned to satisfy the needs of the inner world (Rieff, 1996). The great narrative of modernity views individuals as liberated from the authoritarianism of various collectives: the family, church, and state. This is part of the mythos of liberal democratic societies that promote the value of individual freedom on the political and economic plane. These types of societies also affect change on the level of the psyche. The psyche, too, is liberated from the bonds of community, especially its constrained moral order. One has the freedom to make choices with respect to vocation, lifestyle, values, feelings, and other aspects of life highly circumscribed in more traditional societies. But this "liberation" is a complex one.

Moderns experience themselves as free of others, yet in another sense, much more dependent on others than ever before. In an increasingly complex and technological society, moderns have become more and more divorced from the raw materials they require in order to survive and gratify needs. Moreover, those needs, which today are often wishes masquerading as needs, increasingly require them to depend on the work of others to whom they have little relationship—from the production of food and shelter to the latest styles and gadgets. When one becomes so dependent on distant others, those relationships as well as those with whom one is close can take on an increasingly unstable and frustrating character, leading to some of the conditions therapeutics will treat (Gellner, 1996, p. 33). Modern agents of therapeutics not only navigate between expectations for autonomy and the reality of dependency which modern societies are so good at straddling but help to create this tension in the first place (C. Taylor, 1989, p. 508). After all, therapeutics too requires that one seek out dependency to become autonomous.

A second tenet regards feelings as the cause of behavior, both normal and pathological, and the only source of truth (Luhrmann, 2000). As individuals turn inward, they find a new source of truth, value, and feelings. It is the individual's job, to use a popular metaphor, to "get in touch" with those feelings, as they are authentic expressions of self. The job of the "patient" or "client" is to scrutinize inner life, finding hidden or unexpressed feelings and express them. This is the path to healing. But, as Rieff noted, this in turn creates new illnesses—a kind of anxious and obsessive self-scrutiny leading to a turning away from others while becoming more concerned with identifying others' effects on self. In a therapeutic sensibility, to be dominated by one's feelings is a sign of immaturity perhaps even psychopathology. The same is the case with "bottling" them up. Certain expressions of emotion are valued—expressing emotions openly and spontaneously or talking about them rationally. One's job is to manage feelings and control their intensity or at least seek help if one cannot (Furedi, 2004, p. 34). But the difficulties in peoples' lives are directly related to the state of their emotions, always making them a potential source of disturbance.

A third tenet sees the primary end of life as increasing satisfaction that is precipitated by a strengthening of self and self-esteem. Today the end goal of this turn inward is no longer self-mastery as it was with Freud but the establishment of a sense of well-being. Gone is the pessimistic view of European psychoanalysis that argued that, at best, analysis could offer adjustment to society and less unhappiness. It could only promise better functioning in the spheres of work and love, Freud famously insisted. In the traditionally Freudian view, it was understood that human instincts are not easily shaped by the social. The agents of morality frequently fail. They can either become too powerful, overwhelming persons with neurotic guilt, or not powerful enough making them "perverts" or psychotics. But, in today's therapeutics, the conflict between the social and the individual and the instability that can follow is no longer an issue. Instead, the problem is an internal one.

The path to happiness and well-being follow from increasing self-esteem. Self-esteem comes from accepting an "authentic" self and ridding oneself of the protective masks that hide this self from others which were developed as a result of childhood pain. One of the most pervasive consequences of the therapeutic worldview is that various social institutions—medicine, education, law, and state—are charged with protecting this vital quality. Interestingly, this view misses the problem with traditional notions of character which psychoanalysis sought to modify: morality and esteem are built on a foundation of shame, guilt, and anxiety (Lasch, 1984). There is no "healthy" self-esteem only a less pervasive sense of its lack, a sense that doesn't prevent individuals from functioning in their lives. Such esteem was earned through struggle implied in traditional notions of character. In a therapeutic culture, self-esteem is something one is born with and entitled to. The focus of therapeutics shifts from generating esteem to protecting highly vulnerable people from those social agents that conspire to ruin it (Furedi, 2004).

A fourth tenet regards a class of therapeutic experts and practices as the only legitimate means to "heal" problems of self and feeling. Today versions of therapy can be managed by the psychiatrist, psychotherapist, social worker, and counselor, even if need be, by the life coach, politician, teacher, and talk show host. Over the course of the twentieth century, practitioners of therapeutics professionalized like their counterparts in medicine, law, and education. This offered them an opportunity to police the boundaries of the field by creating official educational organs to teach their craft and assist the aid of the state in removing amateurs from their ranks. These agents of the therapeutic are also evangelical. They seek to spread their notions of self-transformation and healing to the general public. Therapeutics also thrives through its agents in popular culture who are forever seeking to treat. These agents can infuse therapeutics with traditionally religious soul cures, Protestant values, New Age energetics, Eastern Thought, mind-cure, whatever works and sells. Here a degree is not required to heal. Popular therapeutic healers roam the bookstores and airwaves seeking to spread the therapeutic gospel. Adherents read books, watch television, and attend workshops and support groups. Like psychotherapy in general, these sources train patients in the art of narrative. Patients learn how to retell their life story, with a particular focus on how therapeutic agents changed their lives.

Today, therapeutics has allied itself with nineteenth-century somaticism, returned in a new form, particularly after the rise of the selective serotonin re-uptake inhibitors (SSRIs). Psychiatrists speak about psychopathology as akin to physiological pathology. The DSM describes mental disorders using the kind of descriptive, symptom-based approach one finds in medicine where talk of causes is sidelined and diagnosis is wholly separated from treatment. Psychological illness is cleansed of any moral value. As in physiological disease, this approach affirms that one is neither responsible for illness nor cure, only to seek help. Pharmacology then provides the corresponding physiological interventions, and insurance companies are expected to treat mental illness just like physiological illness. The psychiatrist's expertise, backed by elite journals, randomized trials, and medical authority, is no match for his or her "lay" patients. Reliance on medical metaphors pushes talk of feelings and self-esteem slightly to the margins, but make no mistake, the goal of treatment, perhaps even more so, is to help patients manage feelings, self, and behavior. It is only that the path to get there has changed.

The authors we have focused on are fairly critical of therapeutic sensibilities, especially the fact that it seems to generate self-obsession and personalize morality, but other analysts are more sympathetic to it. For example,

Mike Martin (2006) argues that the idea of a singular therapeutic sensibility is a myth and that there are many variants, some of which successfully navigate the tension between morality and medicine better than others. By focusing on its most superficial manifestations, Martin (2006) explains, critics of the therapeutics confuse self-absorption and selfishness with variants of self-actualization that stress service to others, fostering social change and living via higher ideals (p. 7). Some of these ideals can be traced to the United States' most innovative thinkers including William James and John Dewey. Be that as it may, what they all still share is the notion that the self and inner experience is the ground for all else. In his review, Martin (2006) lists the key virtues of contemporary therapeutic sensibilities. These include self-esteem and self-respect, integration and integrity, personal and moral autonomy, self-actualization and authenticity, coping and responsibility, as well as realistic cognition and truthfulness (pp. 29–36). It is fair to say that the values of integration, autonomy, coping, and reality extend across most modalities of the therapeutic. All four were central goals in Freud's vision of psychoanalysis, and "disintegration" as well as lack of grounding in reality, are often regarded as symptoms of psychoses. But what exactly does it mean to have a well-integrated and coherent self? What "version" of reality is one required to live with? Critics of the therapeutic sensibility Philip Rieff and Christopher Lasch believe that the problem with contemporary variants is that they undermine the distinction between inner and outer life, the psychic foundation of living in reality, what psychoanalysts term "ego strength." Most agree that a successful therapy involves taking "responsibility" for one's life, but deciding what that means involves making moral judgments disguised as medical ones.

The other important point is that these virtues, like the notion of mental illness itself, involve metaphor (Pickering, 2006). The anti-psychiatry movement of the 1960s, Thomas Szasz (1961) in particular, used the omnipresence of metaphors to argue that mental illness was a "myth." His argument depended on a seemingly self-evident divide between "real" organic illnesses and "socially constructed" psychological ones. Szasz argued that this myth was first perpetuated by the notion of "functional" disorders at the end of the nineteenth century. Instead, argued Szasz in the tradition of Wittgenstein and Ryle, the "psychological" is just a way of talking that mistakenly views mind as a substance, yet it has no independent existence outside of such language (Szasz, 1961). However, part of the project of psychology often involves separating the "natural" from the "social," inside from outside. The "organic" is no less conceptual, and the psychological is no less a product of biologically based organisms. This tension, while interesting historically, cannot tell us much about the origins or value of this way of thinking. Obviously, terms like "autonomy" and "integrated" are also metaphors, the first from politics, from the Greek for one who gives oneself law and is a key idea in Rousseau and Kant, and the latter from nineteenth-century biology, from the Latin meaning to make whole. The question is not whether these metaphors are correct or not, but rather how they shape modern conceptions of psychological disorders and the therapeutic, that is, what are the consequences of employing them?

Finally, the modern sciences of the disturbances and treatment of mind—psychiatry, social work, clinical psychology, psychoanalysis, neurology, psychotherapeutics, and so on—are built on narratives (Sadler, 2005). Since the days of Freud and Emil Kraepelin and before them, Philippe Pinel, psychiatrists have been generating stories about their patients, attempting to capture their "case." We can acknowledge this and remain neutral on the question of whether these stories represent deeper biological, psychological, or spiritual realities. Since the mid-eighteenth century, psychiatry has tended to vacillate between physiological and psychological explanations of these disturbances, but in either case the telling of the patient's story remained central. With the rise of variants of psychotherapy at the turn of the twentieth century, these narratives became even more important, but what changed really was that patients gradually became more and more responsible for creating these stories themselves, with the help of their therapist. Clearly, psychotherapy is not unique in this. Similar narratives have long played a role in medicine in general and certainly in religion as well. The psychotherapeutic narrative in particular typically has a redemptive quality. I was sick and I suffered, especially in childhood, I sought help through therapy, and now a new me has emerged. There are some clear culture-based assumptions in such narratives: these conditions belong to individuals not communities; they are of a secular nature, they can be treated in semi-egalitarian relationships; some of these conditions are of mind and some of body, which are distinct; the boundary between sane and insane is fluid—that is why we can get better; and whatever the source of these conditions, they are not to be viewed as moral failings (Sadler, 2005, p. 270). They all share some underlying assumptions, and one can easily make a case that these narratives both heal and hurt (Dawes, 1994).

Perhaps humans have some kind of constitutional need to create order even when none is there, or perhaps as psychoanalysts argue, the creation of order is an attempt to compensate for childhood uncertainties. Either way, humans, especially in the West, often fill in "blanks" to create a world that appears more orderly than it otherwise is. These biases, while efficient at some times, can lead people to make poor judgments from limited evidence (Kahneman et al. 1982). Such biases often come up in therapeutic logic, particularly about the relationship between past and present. Psychotherapy is about telling coherent stories to explain the genesis of self and pathology. While such "insights" might help a patient feel better, maybe a kind of placebo effect or maybe something more, they can also lock the patient into a narrow understanding of who they are. It's hard to know given that patients are typically not offered an alternate narrative to compare with the one generated in therapy. The more a patient believes psychotherapy works, the better it does (Frank, 1961). Because patients tend to enter therapy when they are feeling quite bad, worse than normal, after enough time has passed, one would expect them to revert back toward their "average" state. That is implied in the definition of an average. Outlier or extreme states are aberrations. Perhaps time does heal all wounds?

Determining whether therapy works or not is probably impossible, though not for lack of trying. With respect to psychoanalysis, two of the best-known examples involve the effectiveness of the cure and method. Hans Eysenck (1954) infamously offered a "meta-analysis" of prior research, which he claimed demonstrated that psychoanalysis was no more effective than spontaneous remission. And there have been many studies since trying to make the case that Freud's method of treatment—tracing symptoms back to unconscious wishes and bringing them into the patient's consciousness—does not actually get rid of those symptoms (Fisher & Greenberg, 1996). Ironically, this was something that Freud himself recognized; moving away from this idea with the development of his "structural theory," treatment was now about expanding the domain of the ego, a vague enough sentiment that made success almost impossible to measure. His 1938 paper, "Analysis Terminable and Interminable," was fairly bleak about the prospects of psychoanalytic cure. The other issue that came up in these criticisms was that psychoanalytic interpretations are hopelessly "contaminated" by suggestion on the part of the analyst, thus don't tell us much about the actual patient (Holt, 1989). It is hard to argue with this, and I don't think most thoughtful contemporary therapists would.

The results of the research into the effectiveness of psychoanalysis and psychotherapy in general have been mixed (Lubosky et al. 1975; Bergin, 1971; Roth and Fonagy, 2005). For instance, one meta-analysis of nearly five hundred studies found that that 85 percent of patients in therapy felt better than those on a waiting list (Smith, Glass, & Miller, 1980). But it is hard to know what to make of this given that measures were based on patient satisfaction. Even if correct, the effects of other variables including various placebo effects, the effects of simple empathic listening, and vagueness of what a successful therapy looks like could never be disentangled from the treatment itself in such a way as to make anything like experimental analysis possible (Mcmillan, 1996). People that undergo psychotherapy sometimes feel better, sometimes feel the same, and sometimes feel worse, and it's hard to say why. Likely the suggestive effects of therapeutic authority, faith in its effectiveness (by both therapist and patient), regression to the mean (people who come into treatment feeling terrible will end up feeling better over the course of time and attribute it to therapy), biased sampling (those who seek therapy want to get better), and the construction of new narratives around the self are primarily responsible for success, when there is success (Watters & Ofshe, 1999).

Freud understood the power of therapeutic suggestion—this is what he meant by transference—but until late in his career believed it could be "resolved." As Freud liked to put it, at the end of treatment, where there was once "id" now there shall be "ego." The goal of analysis was that one becomes the master of one's own impulses and moral prohibitions and learns to live within reality, tolerate frustration and ambiguity, delay gratification, and the like. Sympathetic critics of psychotherapy (Hubble, Duncan, & Miller, 1999) put the value of placebo/suggestion in precipitating successful outcomes at about 15 percent (attributing 30 percent to patient's personality and therapist relationship respectively and the final 15 percent to specific techniques); but it doesn't seem possible to disaggregate all the factors coming into play that easily not to mention how could one reliably measure or even capture outcomes like "integration" or "learning to live within reality?" Whether therapy works or not and whatever that might mean, notions of psychological therapy have become so pervasive in modern, Western societies, they are not typically required to prove themselves. Their value has become a given. The next few sections will seek to trace how this happened.

1. INSIDE AND OUTSIDE: THE SOMATIC AND THE PSYCHOLOGICAL

Historians of psychiatry describe three models as having competed with each other to explain the origins of disturbances of the mind in the West (Alexander and Selesnick, 1966). The first is most commonly found in traditional societies but also in Greek and Judeo-Christian thought: problems of the mind are due to the intervention of exterior forces. In Homer and the Greek playwrights, the gods altered the mental states of protagonists, sometimes for their own pleasure. In the Old Testament, madness was a punishment from God. Sometimes madness was read as evidence of demonic possession, as in medieval and post-Reformation Europe, and at other times, a sign of holiness or a special relationship with the divine, as was the case with the prophets of the Old Testament. Treatment typically involved an attempt to extricate those outside forces. The proper boundary between religious faith and madness has always been historically and contextually variable. Authorities in the West have typically looked suspiciously at various movements of religious enthusiasm, where groups of individuals become swept up in shared religious fervor and behavior that in another context would be characterized as madness. Some of this sense of possession is retained in today's dominant biomedical model of madness, especially popular accounts, as it purports to explain psychopathology through the invasion of persons by diseased forces foreign to the self, this time to be exorcised by medicine. Today's sociological theories of disturbances of the mind also borrow from this tradition, though it is not clear that these explanations are all that different than psychological ones if one sets aside notions of inside and outside.

The second model that has explained disturbances of the mind in the West is a philosophical/psychological one, which is the source of contemporary psychotherapeutics. This model regards problems of the mind as a result of a mind or soul turned against itself. It is dynamic and has various ways of describing this conflicted mind, but they all share the notion that the source of madness is internal. For instance, in Greek and medieval thought, a possible source of psychic instability or madness was a soul dominated by the lower passions. In post-Augustinian Christianity this was built into the very nature of human beings as a result of original sin, while in Freud, it was a sign of id run amok. For Freud, the higher passions or the superego can also be a source of psychic instability. Treatment involved restoring the dominance of reason, or in classically Freudian terms, strengthening the ego. This was the work of the philosopher, the priest, and later the psychiatrist and psychotherapist. The Stoics developed a technique of philosophical healing in which the principal treatment involved talking, and Philippe Pinel, the great reformer of post-revolutionary French psychiatry, used a version of this method in his moral therapy at Bicêtre.

The final model to explain disturbances of the mind is the medical one. Here, problems of the mind are due to illnesses of a mostly physiological nature and require the intervention of physicians. In Greco-Roman society this model was expressed in Hippocratic and Galenic medicine and competed with the other models until it became dominant in mid-nineteenth-century German psychiatry. With the exception of a few brief periods where psychoanalysis as well as sociological theories of psychopathology were embraced by psychiatry, this model has remained dominant ever since. One common metaphor for explaining these physiological disturbances involves imbalance, from the humoral imbalances of Hippocratic medicine to the brain imbalances of today's psychiatry. Other similar explanations involve the metaphors of "degeneration" and "sensitivity," both common in the late nineteenth century where modern life was supposed to have generated various conditions related to anxiety among those with highly sensitive nervous systems, typically bourgeois Europeans who had the money and time to visit sanitariums, spas, and neurologists for cure. For them treatment typically involved restoring the balance of internal forces, treating the degenerate organ, or simply rest. In the nineteenth century, with the rise of viral theories of infection, somatic psychiatry sought to identify and treat the brain lesions that they saw as the physiological source of mental disorders. The failure of this program led to the rise of "functional" disorders, which required psychological explanation and treatment. Today's psychiatry has come full circle and resumed the search for physical "lesions" whose treatment involves the use of various synthetic and natural remedies to compensate for these deficits.

While this division is not absolute and many psychiatric explanations actually belong to several of these categories, it is a useful heuristic. We should take care of accepting it too literally as it is easily adapted into the conventional narrative wherein the superstitious theories and practices of the classical and medieval world have been replaced by the reasonable and science-based practices of enlightened medicine. It is important to remember the line between superstitious and reasonable explanations of mental problems and cures is not only a historically variable one, but one drawn in such a way so to rationalize the dominant practices of the day. As is the case in science and philosophy in general, the thinkers associated with the Enlightenment were the first to characterize past societies as backward and irrational—they invented the term "dark ages" after all—and it is too easy to rely on this self-serving framework. Future societies will likely look back at certain contemporary medical and psychiatric practice and see superstition and unreason as well. The point is there are many ways to tell this story. We will focus on the tension between intellectualist and affective models of sicknesses of the mind along with the tension between psychological and somatic approaches, all in the context of the corporealization of psychological illness. At base, this version of the story is one in which a physiologically-based medical paradigm competed for dominance with various psychological ones, eventually culminating in a decades-long battle between somatic psychiatry and psychoanalysis at the start of the twentieth century, although some practitioners tried to bring them together, leading to an implicit parallelism between mind and body which still persists today.

In Greek medicine, persisting in some forms until the 1700s, serious problems of the mind were said to result from the dominance of black bile. While this humor was said to be related to a "melancholic" temperament, melancholy until fairly recent times meant something more akin to insanity as opposed to simply depression. The color black has long been associated with evil and the demonic, thus it is not surprising to find black bile associated with mental disturbance. As was said in the Middle Ages, the devil rejoices in the humor of black bile (Simon, 2008). Black bile was one of four fluids that were related to temperament. The others included yellow bile, phlegm, and blood—related to choleric, phlegmatic, and sanguine personalities respectively. These interacted with the three spirits—vital, natural, and animal—and the four qualities—cold, heat, dryness, and moisture—to create temperament and illness (Drinka, 1984). The Greek term *melaina chole* was translated into Latin as *atrabilis* and later into English as "black bile" (Jackson, 2008, p. 444). As an aside, the term "depression," was not used until the

1700s and comes from the Latin *"deprimere,"* which translates as "to press down" (Jackson, 2008, p. 444). It was used to refer to one of the possible mood states associated with melancholia and only replaced the term melancholia in the twentieth century, as the condition became a disturbance in emotion rather than reason. In fact, and this is one of the key historical shifts, mental disturbances were often viewed as violations against God-given intellect and reason, making them just as much a sign of sin than sickness. The French developed a more affect-driven understanding of mental disturbances in the nineteenth century, and this is where our current sense of these as reflecting emotional problems comes from.

The notion of a relationship between bodily humors and psychic disturbance first emerged in Greek medicine in the fifth century BC and was developed further in Galenic medicine, but likely originated in older Indo-European thought (Simon, 2008). One can find metaphors of balance in many global medical traditions including Ayurvedic, Chinese, and homeopathic. Alongside the notion of exterior possession, it is one of the most common everyday explanations for problems of soul and body, and one finds such themes in a global range of psychomedical traditions. While contemporary psychiatry looks back at medieval practices like bloodletting and trepanation as instances of superstition-based barbarism, given available explanations they were actually reasonable practices seen to correct imbalances of humoral fluids, not unlike some today regard the electrical therapies of the early twentieth century.

Similarly we can describe medieval exorcisms as instances of superstition and irrationality, but vestiges of the practice survive in the importance given to the release of feelings in the therapeutic context as well as other variants of catharsis including the Catholic confessional. As historian of psychiatry Bennett Simon (2008) points out, humoral theories functioned in several similar ways to today's theories of brain imbalances. They helped to professionalize medicine in that only trained medical experts understood how these fluids really worked. They also offered a guilt-free way to explain illness and treatment, likely part of what continues to make it a successful explanatory device. It convinced people that illness was not their fault. Greek and Roman therapies typically involved physical intervention—bleeding, diet, drugs—but also psychological ones, including dream interpretation, counseling, and incubation or "temple sleep" (Mora, 2008a). Most influential of all was Stoicism with its notions of *ataraxia* or freedom from perturbation and shifting one's perspective, likely sentiments borrowed from Indo-European traditions that have influenced contemporary cognitive approaches to therapy.

In medieval European thought, an intellectualist theory of madness developed wherein madness was said to involve a turning away from reason. Because God was the source of human reason, this also involved a turning away from God. Thus madness was associated with heresy and sin. Furthermore, the doctrine of original sin suggested that humans were especially vulnerable to this. The first hospitals emerged to take care of the sick, including the mad, after 1100, the most famous of which was Bethlem hospital in London. It opened outside the city walls in 1247 and limited itself to treating only the insane after 1407. Most of those regarded as mad in the medieval world were taken care of by their families, and private hospitals for care of the mad only emerged much later. There were some visible social roles available for the mad including the court jester and fool, memorialized in the plays of William Shakespeare, though some have suggested these figures were not mad but just good actors (Mora, 2008a, p. 231).

Another site for intervention into madness came with the persecution of certain women identified as witches, which increased after the Protestant Reformation and turned out to be important for the development of modern psychiatry. Part of the "enlightened" view that emerged in the seventeenth century involved recasting these women as sick rather than sinners. The new interpretation of witchcraft was first offered by Dutch physician and demonologist Johann Weyer in the 1540s as he was asked to advise on a court case involving a fortune-teller accused of witchcraft. He described those persecuted as melancholics, which made them especially vulnerable to the devil. Weyer also recorded in detail the verbalizations and behaviors of his patients (Alexander & Selesnick, 1966). Philippe Pinel's student, Jean-Etienne Dominique Esquirol, identified a condition he termed "demonomania," a religious form of melancholia that made one susceptible to religious superstition; thus the source of illness was superstition and not demons. In the late nineteenth century, Jean-Martin Charcot diagnosed witches as hysterics. In reality, the charge of witchcraft usually involved conflict between neighbors, antagonistic religious beliefs, or conflict between urban and rural dwellers, though many of the so-called witches often believed they were indeed witches (Mora, 2008a, pp. 237–238).

By the eighteenth century the state took a larger role in the treatment of madness mostly through the construction of institutions to house them. It was a period Michel Foucault (1964) famously described as the "great confinement." Gradually, this encouraged the idea that the insane were best treated under the eyes of watchful physicians and isolated from family and habitual pastimes (Dowbiggin, 2011). In fact, the development of psychiatry occurred in tandem with the growth of the state and the increased responsibility the state took on for managing the general welfare of the population ranging from regulating professions to compulsory education. This new spirit was also related to an emerging approach to disorders of the mind that developed over the course of the seventeenth and eighteenth centuries influenced by the spread of associationist philosophy. Insanity was regarded as a distortion of the intellect, perhaps an issue with forming proper associations. This suggested there was hope and that the insane could be guided back to reason, leading to an increase in new patients entering asylums and eventually pre-pared the way for asylum reform (Weiner, 2008a). Some of this increase was also related to commercialization and urbanization, bringing with them the spread of city-based psychoses like neurosyphilis and alcoholic psychoses (Shorter, 1997, p. 49).

The traditional tale of the birth of modern psychiatry begins with the iconic scene of French psychiatrist Philippe Pinel removing the chains of an inmate at Bicêtre Hospital just outside Paris following the French Revolution and the birth of a more humane treatment of the insane. This story is slightly distorted but not entirely false. It was Pinel's mentor Jean Baptiste Pussin who ordered the removal of chains from the inmate George Couthon, but Pinel later did so as well at Salpêtrière. Either way, similar reforms were being instituted all around Europe for a generation. Pinel's was a "psycho-moral" treatment, focused on instituting a regime of moral education through therapeutic conversation that stressed the values of order, discipline, and community. It also stressed the natural history of the condition, including documentation of the patient's case. He also noted the role of affect in treat-ment, ideas developed further by his successor Jean-Etienne Esquirol. In fact, the transformation of patients into "cases" was probably one of Pinel's most enduring legacies. Even so, before Pinel, careful observations of the insane as well as detailed case histories started to become more common and began to yield new diagnostic categories. Pinel divided madness into five types: mania, melancholy, dementia, idiotism, and "reasoning mania," a precursor of obsession.

Pinel's writings were read by every French student of psychiatry for generations as the idea that self-discipline was therapeutic spread (Weiner 2008a; Porter, 1999). The moral power of the doctor was seen as key in convincing patients to return to reason and made the figure of the doctor much more central to mental therapies, creating what Freud would later describe as transference. Pinel's writings were also permeated by a Rous-seauian sensibility that suggested that civilization itself had produced mental "alienation" and artificial passions. Treatment involved a "schooling" of the passions and restoring individuals to their true nature (Dowbiggin, 2011, p. 32). Thus Pinel's ideas were quite attractive in revolutionary France.

And yet, it was Pinel's rivals in Paris who turned to the pathological method of medicine and sought the source of mental disorders in brain in-flammation—and not Pinel whose clinical observations were a direct contin-uation of eighteenth-century reforms—who shaped a new somatic under-standing of disorders of the mind that came to dominate nineteenth-century psychiatry (Gach, 2008). In this approach, the seminal years are no longer the 1790s and the liberation of French asylum patients from degradation by Philippe Pinel, but the 1850s as Wilhelm Griesinger pioneered a new ap-proach to psychiatry in German medicine that not only required that all psychopathology have a physiological origin, but even more importantly, required that psychiatric education and practice include original research, turning psychiatrists from minders of asylums into respectable scientists. During the nineteenth century, psychomoral and somatic explanations of psychiatric disorders tended to compete with each other.

During these years, conceptions of milder and "treatable" forms of insanity were being developed as well. In England, the idea that disturbances of the mind could extend beyond the mad began to take root in the seventeenth century. Melancholia, a condition referenced often in the literature of the period, especially in Robert Burton's *The Anatomy of Melancholia* (1621), was described in 1733 by British doctor George Cheyne as the "British Malady" (Dowbiggin, 2011). In his writing, Cheyne introduced the notion of a personality marked by feeble and relaxed nerves, poor digestion, and sensitivity to temperature (Dowbiggin, 2013, p. 11). He linked this condition to England's emerging affluent classes blaming it on excesses in consumption and sedentary habits. At the close of the seventeenth century, one of the founding members of the Royal Society in Britain, Thomas Willis, coined the term "neurology" and developed detailed accounts of melancholia, mania, and idiocy. He distinguished the categories of "hypochondria" and "hysteria" from melancholia, which at the time was still a nebulous category that included all types of insanity (Jackson, 2008, p. 448). Willis also rejected the notion that melancholy was the result of black bile and instead suggested it was due to chemical disturbances in the body. Willis's distinctions set the stage for the continued identification of more treatable forms of mental disorders, to be distinguished from madness in general, which still remained a hopeless condition.

Willis's ideas were developed further in the 1760s as William Cullen, the leading medical authority in Britain in the mid-eighteenth century, developed an alternate nosology which introduced the term "neuroses" as diseases of the nervous system and hence not accompanied by fever or localized pathology. Cullen sought to rid medicine of the humoral theories, and he looked to physiological explanations. Neuroses, argued Cullen, were due to a tightening and loosening of nerves (Drinka, 1984, p. 34). One of his students, Benjamin Rush, went on to found somatic psychiatry in the United States. In 1764, Robert Whytt described a condition of nervous "sympathy" where sensations were carried inward through the nerves and outward to various parts of the body resulting in hysteria (Drinka, 1984, p. 35). This was a particularly acute problem for the well-to-do who had "sensitive" nervous systems. By the end of the eighteenth century, neuroses were viewed as distinct from psychoses or traditional madness. In France, "nerve" doctors began to focus on these conditions including the "vapors," a condition popularized by Pierre Pomme that could be treated with chicken soup and cold baths (Shorter, 1997, p. 25). During this period, psychiatry was dominated by a tension between the associationism of Pinel and the faculty psychology of the Germans, soon to be reworked by Gall. Typically, those who adopted more of a faculty psychology approach began to look to physiology to explain the source of the disturbances of mental faculties while those with an associationist approach looked to disturbed environmental conditions, usually in the family home. This was only the first modern version of a tension between biological and environmentalist theories that still persist today.

The success of psychiatry over the course of the nineteenth century, itself a remarkable story, from a small group treating only asylum patients to a respectable scientific and academic discipline, suggests that many in the West were open to new ways of thinking about disturbances of mind. The term "psychiatrist" was coined in 1808 by Johann Christian Reil, the father of German Romantic psychiatry, the leading force in psychiatry in the first half of the nineteenth century to replace the older term "alienist." Reil identified four principal disorders: fixed delusions, mania, folly, and idiocy (Marx, 2008). He described them as resulting from disturbances in the harmony of the nervous system and not brain lesions as would be the case in German psychiatry after 1850. His system contained some of the holistic and spiritual sensibilities of the *naturphilosophie*. For example, he rejected Gall's localization of brain functions, describing it as premature and regarded disorders as problems of the soul [he used the term *seele*] and a result of vital fluids (Weiner, 2008a, p. 291). His psychiatry promoted three types of treatment—surgical, medical, and psychological—and he helped to encourage psychiatrists to focus on alleviating the plight of the ill. Reil has been criticized for some of his crueler forms of treatment, including beatings, induced vomiting, and simulated drowning. He has also been extensively rebuked for citing the cases of others and not seeing many of his own patients, but there is no question of his influence in spreading a more psychological approach (Marx, 2008, pp. 318–322).

The other important figure in early-nineteenth-century Germany was Johann Christian August Heinroth. He regarded disorders of the mind as the result of the progressive abandonment of reason that generated guilt (Marx, 2008, p. 324). He focused less on the physiological origins of mental disorders and more on unhealthy mental lives and introduced the term "psychosomatic" into German medicine. He held individuals responsible for their illness. Heinroth also introduced the notion of intrapsychic conflict between instincts, ego, and conscience, an idea that Freud borrowed from many decades later. Like Pinel he treated certain melancholic symptoms as a disturbance of the passions, as opposed to most that were still influenced by the Greco-Roman view that treated it as a disturbance of intellect (Jackson, 1999). Heinroth's understanding of melancholia did not become widespread until the late nineteenth century but would provide a psychological alternative to the growing somatic perspective.

The towering figure of German psychiatry in the second half of the nineteenth century was Wilhelm Griesinger, who was determined to turn psychiatry into a science. He dominated psychiatry until it was transformed again by
Emil Kraepelin at the turn of the twentieth century. For Griesinger, turning
psychiatry into a science involved transforming it into a branch of medicine
and relying exclusively on physiological explanations of disorders. It also
involved moving away from simple asylum care and toward research. It was
to be based in universities. In 1822 physiological researchers discovered that
general paralysis was related to an inflammation of brain tissue, and a decade
later J. B. Friedreich declared that all mental disease had an organic source.
Griesinger turned this into orthodoxy with the publication of his *Pathologie
und Therapie* in 1845. He sought to remove all the vestiges of Reil's talk of
the soul and vital forces as the source of psychopathology (Gach, 2008, pp.
382–385).

Griesinger's work fit nicely with that of Helmholtz, who also dominated
this period, whose law of the conservation of energy required that all activity,
including mental activity, be reduced to their physical and chemical foundations. This created an abstract conception of energy that could be equally
applied to the physical and psychic realm. Griesinger also used the term
"states of mental depression" as a synonym for melancholia, turning it into a
condition caused by a diseased brain (Jackson, 2008). After this, the term
"depression" tended to refer quite narrowly to certain mood states associated
with melancholia until it replaced melancholia entirely in the early twentieth
century. This change was a sign that the mood state had become much more
important in making sense of the condition and that depression would no
longer belong exclusively to the category of psychosis.

The job of the psychiatrist in the new German model was to treat but also
to do further research, as was the case with all academic science in Germany.
Thus psychiatry moved into the university, where it adopted the methods of
the natural sciences. This new model of psychiatry began in Germany, but
soon spread to the rest of Europe and the United States. It ensured the
dominance of the somatic paradigm until the rise of psychoanalysis in the
next century. In this regard, Germany remained the leading force. French
psychiatry continued to focus on asylum care throughout the nineteenth century, and in the United States, even by 1900, less than 10 percent of psychiatrists went to medical school (Shorter, 1997).

Griesinger was succeeded at the University of Berlin by Carl Westphal.
Westphal fully integrated the neuroses into psychiatry. What he termed the
"psycho-neuroses" included homosexuality, phobia, and obsessions. Later
this would also include hysteria, the condition that was the focus of Freud's
early work, and the controversial diagnosis of "neurasthenia" from American
psychiatrist George M. Beard. These conditions were treated by neurologists
as they began to see wealthier patients in their own private practices. This

turned out to be an attractive option for those interested in research, but looking for a more economically lucrative option, a path followed by Freud when he was ready to marry. It also was an attractive option for wealthy patients who wanted to avoid entering an asylum and the stigma of madness (Shorter, 1997, p. 114). In the 1880s, one of Freud's teachers, Theodor Meynert, tried to reconcile the growing tension between physiochemical and psychological explanations by arguing that psychological activity was epiphenomenal and based in neural activity. Meynert also criticized German psychiatry for focusing too much on research and not enough on patients. Freud accepted Meynert's somaticism in his early work and tried to develop a physiologically sound model of the psychoneuroses integrating the notion of mental energy. His failure led him to accept the parallelism between psychic and mental activity and depend exclusively on psychological explanations, all the while still enjoying an extensive range of metaphors from physiology and physics.

Freud was not alone. The inability to pinpoint the physiological source of mental disease as well as limited treatment options led a growing number of neurologists to turn to psychological explanations and modes of treatment. Another key nineteenth-century theme in somatic psychiatry was the importance of heredity. The importance of heredity was stressed by Benedict August Morel in the 1850s. He used the term *degenerescence* in relation to insanity, which was thought to get worse with every generation. Morel tried to link various neurotic conditions to specific areas in the brain that were degenerating. He also introduced the term "dementia praecox," which referred to a type of loss of sanity specific to adolescence, in contrast to dementia later in life, a term later used by Kraeplin. He regarded dementia praecox as a condition in which those from the upper classes were more vulnerable (Gilman, 2008, pp. 463–464). The term "degeneration" spoke to broader social anxieties around cultural and economic change, the growing reach of science and technology and the increasing political influence of the lower economic classes (Dowbiggin, 2011). The popularity of Beard's diagnosis of "neurasthenia," a nervous condition related to sensitivities to the pace of modern life, spoke to similar cultural anxieties. The language of degeneration turned into an all-purpose form of social criticism couched in a medical framework: it explained the source of disorders of the mind for which no physiological lesion or brain pathology was discovered, but also a growing sense that changes of modern life were destroying human nature.

By the close of the nineteenth century several changes in psychiatric categories related to diagnosis and treatment were well established related to the dominance of the somatic paradigm. First was the transformation of the traditional categories of insanity (e.g., melancholia, mania) into collections of "symptoms," following a trend that was already developed in medicine in general (Berrios, 2008, p. 353). These were generated from clinical observations rather than from the imposition of a prefabricated theoretical framework, making them grounded in "empirical" research. Second, was a shift from intellectualist explanations to affective ones in the case of certain mental disorders. This was partially grounded in the Kantian notion of affect as a distinct faculty as well as highlights the growing importance of emotions as a result of the influence of romanticism.

One example is the case of "obsession." It was once a seemingly self-evident example of a disorder of thinking, but became a symptom of an anxiety neurosis by the end of the century (Berrios, 1996). Anxiety itself, which had once been a symptom of various disorders, was now a single class of disorders (Berrios, 1996, p. 265). The notion of disorders of affect was established by Morel's *delire emotif* (Berrios, 1996, p. 143) of which lympo-nia or depressive states, was a type, caused by, argued Morel, an unspecified brain lesion which related to a fixed idea of an affective nature. Janet took this up with his notion of the *idée fixe* that was the result of trauma, also termed dissociation. Psychiatry had begun the long process of turning away from depictions of pathology as diseases of the intellect and toward depictions of them as diseases of the affect, a key part of the contemporary therapeutic sensibility.

Disturbances in any of Kant's three faculties—intellect, affect, and will—became possible sources of various psychiatric conditions as a new faculty psychology, grounded in the notion of cerebral localization, and replaced associationism over the course of the nineteenth century. For instance, dementia praecox and paranoia were regarded as disorders of the intellect, mania and melancholia disorders of the affect and psychopathy a disorder of the will. The other influential disorders of the will in French psychiatry were impulsion and compulsion. The former, named monomanie by Esquirol involved the loss of control over the will, and the latter was eventually fused with obsession as a compromise with the German model that rejected disorders of the will and saw compulsions as simply the acting out of thought (Berrios, 1996, p. 141).

Other changes included the development of a distinction between hallucinations and delusions—the former disturbances in perception, the latter in thought. The category of hallucinations was first introduced by Esquirol in 1817 and tended to focus mostly on visual types, although it was later broadened to include all sensory modalities, and turned from a disorder of the senses into a psychological disorder (Berrios, 1996). Also, the content of symptoms, which had been mostly ignored in the first half of the nineteenth century, as opposed to the form or structure of them, was now seen as a resource for explaining the origins of various conditions. The past was increasingly viewed as a possible cause of particular symptoms. In French psychiatry in particular, the content of consciousness became an important focus. All these changes promoted a more psychological rather than somatic orientation.

A key source of the developing psychological orientation was leading French neurologist Jean Martin Charcot and his distinction between organic and functional disorders, the latter being used to describe cases when no physical lesions or pathology could be identified. As was described by a nineteenth-century neurologist, "Whatever the microscope cannot see, we call functional" (cited in Caplan, 1998, p. 3). This ended up moving certain organic conditions that had been lumped under neuroses into traditional medical categories. It also paved the way for the popularity of hypnotic cures (Berrios, 1996). Increasingly, diagnosis and treatment of the functional neuroses developed independently of the psychoses. Treatment of neurosis became the province of neurologists who treated them in their own private practices. Psychosis was treated by psychiatrists who still worked in institutional settings, particularly in the United States, and were regarded more as managers than purveyors of treatment.

This split led to one of the bitterest disputes in the history of U.S. medicine. After 1860, as the influence of Griesinger's somatic paradigm spread to the United States, asylum-based psychiatrists resisted its influence. Neurologists, who in general did adopt the new somatic paradigm, viewed themselves as carrying the banner of science and research to a backward and morality-infused psychiatry still stuck with the methods of Pinel from the last century. By this point, neurologists had greatly expanded their patient population, treating the types of patients privately that would have once been told by their doctors they were only suffering from "nerves" and sent home (E. Brown, 2008). The medicalization of neurology gave it increasing authority and influence.

During the 1870s and 1880s neurologists became increasingly vocal of their criticisms of asylum psychiatrists accusing them of barbaric practices and being out of touch with the latest developments in medicine, all in the name of protecting the insane. This along with well-publicized tales of abuses in mental asylums resulted in many years of back-and-forth criticism that grew quite bitter (E. Brown, 2008, pp. 522–523). By the 1890s, the conflict was over with the victory of the somatic paradigm and ironically, in the United States at least, the movement by psychiatrists out of asylums and into private practice, making the difference between neurology and psychiatry mute. While the neurological approach became the way forward, their somatic approach was not to dominate for long.

The close of the nineteenth century witnessed the most influential development of all, the formalization of changes from the prior decades into Emil Kraepelin's new symptom-based diagnostic model. Kraepelin was the director of the psychiatric clinic at Heidelberg University from 1891 to 1903. The mistake of psychiatry was to focus on etiology, Kraepelin argued, when it really needed to follow the course of a particular condition to understand it. His new nosological system changed in various incarnations of his text *Lehrbuch der Psychiatrie,* first published in 1893, but essentially reduced the categories of psychosis to two, manic depressive psychosis and dementia praecox, distinguished by their prognosis, whose diagnosis involved the identification of an organic source and the documentation of the clinical history of the patient (Berrios, 1996). Dementia praecox included paranoia and catatonia, which had once been separate conditions (Gilman, 2008). Kraepelin transformed Griesinger's somatic framework, which he termed "speculative anatomy," into a multistage and multicourse one, but whose basis still remained physiological and inherited (Decker, 2013). His nosology was a strictly empiricist one, he insisted, that posited a sharp line between normal and abnormal and would become the basis for the DSM a century later. Kraepelin's legacy included eloquent depictions of patients and their cases but also a psychiatry which focused more on maintaining consistency in diagnosis than on the unique qualities of individual patients (Decker, 2013, p. 48).

Eugen Bleuler, Jung's teacher in Zurich, later renamed dementia praecox "schizophrenia" or "groups of schizophrenia," recognizing that the category included several different conditions and offered a more psychological take on it, which reflected the influence of psychoanalysis on him by this point. Bleuler retained some of the old associationist sense as well by arguing that schizophrenia involves the associations of ideas that had lost their continuity (Berrios, 1996, p. 78). Sander Gilman makes the point that Bleuler chose the Greek derived terms "schizo" and "phrenia" or split mind, as opposed to the Latin derived "dementia praecox"—more linked to the notion of degeneration—partly as a tribute to Freud, partly to indicate cure was possible, and partly as a nationalist gesture to link German psychiatry with the more valued Greek rather than Roman heritage (Gilman, 2008, p. 465). The notion of the "splitting" of mind definitely gave it a more Freudian twist by describing a mind in conflict with itself.

Adolph Meyer, a student of Charcot, who emigrated to the United States in 1892 and became the leading voice in U.S. psychiatry for the first decades of the twentieth century, renamed it "paregasia" or incongruity of behavior, which never stuck, as well as used the term "schizophrenic reactions," which did stick, to highlight the role of external forces in creating the condition. Meyer's "environmentalism" paved the way for psychoanalytic-inspired accounts of psychosis, which traditionally had focused exclusively on neurotics, especially given that its patient population was made up of upper-middle-class functioning professionals seen in private practice. Eventually, this meant pointing more to the role of family dynamics. Meyer's perspective highlights the move toward environmental explanations in U.S. psychiatry by the 1910s and 1920s, which, as we shall see, helps to explain the growing influence of psychoanalysis (Hale, 1971). By the 1970s, as psychoanalytic explanations were on the wane and somatic ones on the rise again, U.S. psychiatry would again revive Kraepelin's nosology in its DSM-III published in 1980.

The postwar years were the heyday of psychoanalysis in U.S. psychiatry, but it was not to last. By the 1970s the pendulum was shifting away from psychological explanations and back toward somatic ones. Certainly the rise of psychotropic medications played a large part, as did the collapsing prestige of the profession as a result of the antipsychiatry movements of the 1960s and the sense that psychiatric diagnosis had low reliability. One place where the tension between the somatic and psychoanalytic approach played out was with the revision of the American Psychiatric Association's Diagnostic Statistical Manual (DSM) in the period from 1974 to 1980. The first DSM was produced in 1952 and was a small, spiral-bound pamphlet. DSM-II was released in 1968 and reflected a more psychoanalytic orientation. This meant both that it employed the language of psychoanalysis as well as adopted psychoanalytic etiology. Robert Spitzer, a trained analyst who was involved in the making of DSM-II was appointed chair of the committee to revise the DSM in 1974, though by this point his thinking was moving away from psychoanalytic accounts of psychopathology. As Hannah Decker (2013) explains, he was influenced by a group of psychiatrists from Washington University in St. Louis who sought to develop an "empiricist" approach to diagnosis that rejected conditions that had no observable referent. Decker calls them the neo-Kraepelinians.

Spitzer had already decided that intrapsychic conflict could not be a basis for diagnosis as all conditions had to be clearly observable or demonstrable and that he wished to get rid of the category of neurosis entirely (some of which ended up in Axis II-Personality Disorders). He appointed a committee that agreed with these goals. This invariably led to a showdown with the psychoanalysts. It took them a while to realize what was at stake. Spitzer had tried to appoint two analysts to his committee, but they declined. As Decker tells it, part of their lack of involvement was a reflection of arrogance and the assumption that the DSM was not all that important. Once psychoanalysts did get involved, most of the framework was already established. Spitzer developed the idea of a multiaxial system, partly to accommodate the objections of psychoanalysts. He at one point offered them their own axis—axis VI focused on etiology—but the rest of the committee rejected this.

The process lasted from 1974 until 1980, and the question as to the role of psychoanalysis was not the only one the committee worked through. In fact, reading Decker's account one sees just how much of the final document was arbitrary. For instance, Spitzer insisted that "subjective distress" be key to diagnoses, but his somatically minded colleagues argued that one did not have to be distressed to receive a diagnosis of cancer, thus the same was true with mental illness. One area that this came up was homosexuality. Since 1973 and the removal of homosexuality as a DSM category, various proposals surfaced to retain certain elements of it. In the end, Spitzer's notion of "ego-dystonic" homosexuality—that is, patients who were distressed about their sexuality—remained. Other debates surfaced over adult ADD, perversions—which became paraphilias—and whether Borderline Personality Disorder was a real condition. The new version of the DSM had higher reliability as a result of its "menu" model of diagnosis—users simply identified symptoms from a list—but lower validity in that it created hard lines between various conditions that did not represent what most psychiatrists saw in their practice (Decker, 2013, p. 325). The DSM-III was a huge moneymaker for the APA and offered health insurance companies a means to rationalize payments. While Axis-I conditions were typically reimbursed, Axis-II conditions were not. This encouraged psychiatrists to find anxiety and mood disorders at the expense of personality ones. One of the most successful of the newly created disorders was PTSD.

More recently, the new DSM-V has tried to move away from the firm categories of the biomedical model and toward a continuum model more akin to psychoanalytic diagnosis. Some of the changes in the DSM-V reflect a change in language and category: the term mental retardation is dropped in favor of intellectual disability; autism, Asperger's, pervasive developmental disorder, and childhood disintegrative disorder are combined into autism spectrum disorder (and those without repetitive behaviors are moved into the new category of social communication disorder); obsessive-compulsive disorder is no longer simply an anxiety disorder but its own class of disorders which include hoarding, skin-picking, and even certain forms of substance abuse. One of the most interesting changes has to do with the creation of a new category of conduct disorders, typically reserved for "difficult" children, and now includes a broadened conception of oppositional defiant disorder and a range of other disorders including impulse-control disorder, intermittent explosive disorder, and kleptomania.

Some changes are substantive: ADHD has been greatly expanded to include adults and is explicitly presented as a neurological condition; the different subtypes of schizophrenia have been dropped in favor of an approach that focuses on a person's capacity for functioning; the category of attachment disorder has been expanded; the fixed distinction between manic and depressive states in bipolar has been dulled, and the types of depressive disorders have been greatly expanded, including bereavement and premenstrual dysphoric disorder. As far as attachment, as we will discuss, it fits well with current therapeutic sensibilities, and so it should not be surprising that its range has been expanded. As far as the other changes, none are too surprising, especially the expansion of OCD, ADHD, bipolar, and depressive disorders, as that seems to be the way things were heading anyway in terms of the diagnostic categories most employed in psychiatric practice and in everyday life. This is likely related to a range of issues including insurance practices, available pharmacology, moral values around which conditions are okay and which are not, media representations including reality shows like "Hoarders" and "My Strange Addiction," and the increased tendency to explain failure in biological categories that feel less like moral judgments.

This is the case as well with gender dysphoria, which has been expanded as well as reframed in terms that view gender in a less dichotomous way, reflecting the influence of LGBTQ activism as well as a more fluid conception of gender in general. It is also true of paraphilia, what was once perversion, where care is made to distinguish the actual paraphilia, which is not an illness, from the distress caused by the paraphilia, a hard distinction to uphold in practice. For a long time, the DSM tried a similar fence-straddling strategy with homosexuality. Most recently all forms of pathology related to sexual identity were eventually dropped. Tracking changes in the DSM can be a useful tool for tracking broader cultural changes in values and attitudes as well as the rise and fall of various psychiatric paradigms. Will a new "psychological" paradigm rise to replace the current somatic one? If history is any guide, the answer is most likely yes.

2. STRUCTURE AND FUNCTION: THE NEW CURE OF THE SOULS

In the nineteenth century, psychotherapy meant using psychological measures to influence the mind, and that is as good as any place to start as far as a definition (Jackson, 1999, pp. 5–6). Some traditions focused more on intellect and insight, some on catharsis and affect, but as Jerome Frank's important study attests, in any variant there was always a relationship between healer and sufferer (Frank, 1961). The term was first used by Hippolyte Bernheim of the Nancy School in 1892 as well as by Daniel Tuke in the same year. Still, its principal techniques—confessing, confiding, catharsis, and suggestion—have been around for a long time, much of which can be attained by talking with a good listener. Precursors of psychotherapy include the religious and medical purification rituals of Ancient Greece, philosophical dialogue as a means to treat the sickness of the soul, and most famously, the Catholic confessional.

Modern psychotherapy has its immediate origins in eighteenth-century France and the movement begun by Viennese physician Anton Mesmer. Mesmerism was a synthesis of various medical and popular traditions including those of Paracelsus, medieval alchemy, astrology, electricity, Newtonianism, and astronomy, the combination of which made it seem familiar yet modern (Drinka, 1984). Mesmer was also influenced by the therapeutic healing techniques of priest and exorcist Johann Gassner who traveled northern

Europe healing in the name of the Church until the Vatican rebuked his work in the 1770s. According to Mesmer, the universe was pervaded by substances he termed "magnetic fluids," a secularized version of what Gassner described as the Holy Spirit. Adopting the metaphor of electricity, Mesmer described these fluids as moving throughout the universe in a mechanistic fashion, including creating currents in the human body called "magnetic attraction." Magnets were just one manifestation of this force. These currents that passed through the body could become blocked, and this was the source of disease. The job of the physician, or magnetic healer as Mesmer described him, was to alter the flow of these currents so that the body could heal itself. Originally, Mesmer accomplished this by running iron magnets over the surface of the body, but eventually decided that magnetic healers could manipulate these currents using their own magnetic attraction through touch.

During these sessions, Mesmer's patients experienced convulsions and bizarre states of consciousness, but would often end up feeling better after the session was complete. The process was so dramatic that as the influence of Mesmerism spread, these sessions were opened to the public, creating spectacular shows. For Mesmer specifically, though, most of his patients were seen privately, creating a model for later psychotherapeutic practice. As his ideas spread and generated controversy, Mesmer moved to Paris and found modest success. He was patronized by Mozart and Marie Antoinette. In the 1770s, the French government, concerned about its abuse, established a commission to study animal magnetism headed by Benjamin Franklin. The commission ultimately rejected the notion of a magnetic force, but did not reject the efficacy of the treatment nor find evidence of abuse. Mesmer left Paris humiliated that he did not receive official recognition and died in relative obscurity.

In the year the report was commissioned, Mesmer's student, the Marquis de Puységur published *Mémoires pour servir a l'historie et á l'etablissement du magnétisme animal* where he introduced the idea of magnetic sleep, which he termed "magnetic somnambulism," establishing it as a kind of sleepwalking. Puységur found the process worked better when he had his patients imagine pleasant things, which made convulsions less common and helped patients diagnose their own conditions. He also noted the importance of the rapport with the magnetizer and his suggestive influence. This "magnetic rapport," what would become transference in psychoanalysis, required goodwill and the employment of "sympathy" on the part of the magnetizer, given his or her influence, talk of which alleviated concern on the part of French authorities for abuse (Crabtree, 2008). As Puységur's version of magnetic sleep spread, it included the notion of a "second" consciousness which had access to traumatic secrets as well as that sexual feelings toward the magnetizer commonly arose in the process, again two themes that became prominent in early psychoanalytic thought (Caplan, 1998).

In 1846, Carl Gustav Carus's seminal *Psyche: On the Development of the Soul* developed and popularized these themes and argued that illness comes from this alternate consciousness. It contained all prior feelings and perceptions outside of awareness, and its access through mesmerism could cure hysteria and other neuroses. By this point, the popularity of magnetic somnambulism, what Scottish surgeon James Braid started to call "neuro hypnology"—Greek for "nervous sleep" and eventually simply "hypnosis"—had led it to fall into disrepute among European medical professionals. Braid's writing in the 1840s began a revival. The opposite was the case in the United States during the 1840s, as we shall review a bit later, where the spread of hypnotic and suggestive practices were creating a popular fusion of religion, self-improvement, and medicine known as mind-cure.

In Europe, the late-nineteenth-century tradition that produced psychoanalysis began with the work of Charcot during the 1880s. Unlike most neurologists who treated well-to-do patients, Charcot's patients were mostly from public hospitals and the poor, dispelling the notion that neurosis was an upper-class phenomenon (Micale, 2001). Charcot worked with patients diagnosed with hysteria, a condition that had long frustrated medical doctors who viewed most of the sufferers as "difficult" women. It was considered incurable. By 1882, Charcot had artificially produced and removed hysterical symptoms through hypnosis, helping to make hypnosis respectable again. It was suggested much later that his use of "hysterical" young women for photographs probably exacerbated their condition (Decker, 2008, p. 613). Charcot's position was that the capacity to be hypnotized was limited to those with hysteria, and not possible with the general population, a claim rejected by Freud. This would have set firm limits on the patient population of psychoanalysis.

Charcot was also not that interested in treatment and tended to focus on research and dramatic displays of symptom generation using "career" hysterics. What was interesting about hysteria to 1880s neurology was that it mimicked some of the symptoms one found in patients with brain lesions, although there were no identifiable physiological issues. While Charcot focused on hereditary disposition as the ultimate cause of hysteria, his use of hypnosis legitimated a psychological take on the condition, and he did accept that hysteria could be triggered by trauma. This was the start of the transformation of trauma from a physical injury to a psychological one, key to the Freudian tradition: external shocks became "nervous" ones (Decker, 2008, p. 123).

Charcot's critics in the Nancy School including Hippolyte Bernheim and his collaborator Augustine Ambrose Liébault extended these ideas further. Influenced by the Nancy School were Pierre Janet and Josef Breuer who also began to treat hysteria with hypnosis in the 1880s. Liébault was a rural physician who began to use hypnosis on his patients in the 1860s who later collaborated with Bernheim to create the Nancy School. Bernheim described hypnosis as a form of sleep. They distinguished themselves from Charcot in their focus on treatment as opposed to research and their position that the capacity to be hypnotized was not limited to those with "weak" nervous systems. Bernheim in particular, who published *Suggestive Therapeutics* in 1886, broadened his conception of hypnosis beyond magnetic induced sleep and focused on the importance of suggestion and developing a therapeutic rapport with patients. Freud visited Nancy in 1888 and adopted the technique of "suggestion" which he employed in his own practice, until he dropped it in 1896. The conflict between Charcot's school at the Salpêtrière and the Nancy School was celebrated in French intellectual circles, lasting from 1882 until 1893, and resulted in Charcot's humiliation.

Hypnosis was very much in the air during the 1870s and 1880s as was the idea of confessing pathogenic secrets, first introduced by neurologist Moritz Benedikt who was best known for his research into criminal brains (Ellenberger, 1970). Both ideas were taken up in the work of Pierre Janet who experimented with hypnosis to treat patients with "dissociative" personalities. He argued that there were two levels of self, the conscious and subconscious, and the latter kept track of post-hypnotic suggestions and explained why they were effective. The subconscious, according to Janet, lived a hidden life outside of conscious awareness, although its activities affected patient's lives in dramatic ways. Evidence for it was to be found in the phenomenon of "automatic counting" and "subconscious fixed ideas," both examples of a narrowing of consciousness and a kind of disaggregation or loss of the capacity for psychic synthesis (Ey, 1968). Like Charcot, Janet excluded healthy patients from susceptibility to hypnosis. Freud later renamed his notion of an alternative conscious the "unconscious" to distinguish his version from Janet's, as well as universalize it. He also termed his form of treatment "psychoanalysis" to distinguish it from Janet's "psychological analysis."

The other key figure in these developments was Josef Breuer the underappreciated mentor of Freud in the 1880s and early 1890s. Breuer, who was already well known for his physiological research into the semicircular canals of the inner ear, shared the details of his treatment of Anna O with Freud, whose case they later published in *Studies in Hysteria* in 1895. Anna O famously characterized Breuer's method as a "talking cure." Like Freud's later case of Dora, Anna O's illness developed as she was caring for her sick father, and in both cases, was interpreted as a revival of childhood sexual feelings toward their fathers (Freud, 1905). Anna developed several personalities and quite strange symptoms including the loss of ability to speak or understand any language aside from English and a hysterical pregnancy. Breuer claimed the treatment ended when he found that Anna was in "good health," but subsequent research shows that Anna was ill for many years after the treatment ended and Breuer likely terminated the treatment because he found her to be too difficult (Drinka, 1984, pp. 392–394). He reported to Freud that when Anna identified certain traumatic incidents, her symptoms abated and she reported feeling better. This, according to Breuer, was the result of catharsis as certain memories that had become inaccessible to consciousness were brought into awareness. Breuer used hypnosis to trigger this release. The patients were trapped in "hypnoid states" as a result of the splitting of mind due to an innate disposition. Freud accepted all this except rejected that hypnoid states were needed for this process, again making his variant of psychotherapeutics potentially available to all.

Freud argued that the hypnosis helped the patient reexperience the feelings associated with repressed trauma, a process Freud called abreaction, and this resulted in cure. By the 1890s, Freud realized he could trigger similar release without hypnosis, first turning to hand-pressing techniques, and eventually relying exclusively on free association. Janet came to abreaction independently of Freud and Breuer, though he termed it "treatment by mental liquidation" and "mental disinfection" (Jackson, 1999, p. 126). All these versions of psychotherapy accepted that illness was caused by an unreleased idea and treatment involved releasing it. Freud also emphasized an intellectual element in treatment, as was clear in his need to convince patients of his interpretations of their symptoms. This was eventually termed insight and was regarded as distinct from cathartic elements (Jackson, 1999, pp. 351–353). As he focused on dream interpretation, this became a more important treatment goal. This nineteenth-century model continues to resonate, as does its steam-related metaphors. By 1900, Freud had turned away from trauma as the source of neurosis and began to recast psychoanalysis from a simple medical cure to an explanation for all social and cultural activity (Decker, 2008). Freud distinguished his variant of therapy from others by the importance he placed on the interpretation of resistance and hostile transference. Therapy was not simply about insight but about "resolving" the transference, which Freud himself became less and less sure was possible toward the end of his life (Freud, 1937). Most of his critics dismissed these distinctions and regarded psychoanalysis as employing suggestive techniques. Austrian critics described Freud's system as too French, and ironically, French critics described it as too German. As Freud told it, Viennese medicine, resistant to his insistence on the sexual etiology of neurosis and belief that psychoanalysis was a "Jew" science, rejected his ideas.

In truth, Freud's unwillingness to participate in the academic life of Viennese medical societies, as well as his insistence that all members of his circle accept his official version of psychoanalysis probably contributed more to the skepticism he encountered from medicine (Decker, 2008). There was also a sense that Freud's notions of an unconscious and sexual energy harkened back to the days of prescientific, Romantic medicine, the days before the acceptance of the somatic paradigm. The other criticism of Freud was that he had gone too far in undermining the distinction between the sane and insane and held too firmly to a parallelism between mind and body. In Europe, Freudianism had its greatest success in 1920s Berlin, especially when it turned out to offer the only treatment for "shell shock" after World War I. Less than two decades later, the Nazi's essentially destroyed psychoanalysis in the German-speaking world.

The mind-cure movement set the stage for the influence of psychoanalysis in the United States. Mind-cure began when Phineas Parkhurst Quimby heard visiting mesmerists Charles Poyen and Robert Collyer lecturing in the United States during the 1830s. Taking some of what he learned from them, and combining them with Spiritualist and Swedenborgian notions already popular in the United States, Quimby created his own school of mental healing. Illness was the result of false beliefs, argued Quimby, and treatment involved correcting them. Quimby believed that his treatment produced actual chemical changes in the brain through simple changes in thought (Caplan, 1998, p. 68). Thus, words healed the sick. The point of treatment was to restore the body's "vital force." Other ideas related to mind-cure included that through the technique of "sympathy" the healer's mind could directly influence the mind of the sufferer (Caplan, 1998, p. 71) and that the traditional values of American religion—self-denial, hard work, and persistence—were not for salvation but for happiness. The postponing of happiness to the next life, Quimby insisted, was false and a form of idolatry. His new morality replaced self-denial with self-fulfillment (Moskowitz, 2008). Abundance and success came from changing one's beliefs, and the discovery of truth required a turn inward (Fuller, 1982). Quimby described all this as his "spiritual science" whose goal was to help people help themselves (Decker, 2005; Moskowitz, 2008).

By the 1860s, several mental healing schools were operating in the United States, mostly attended by women, who had long been responsible for issues of health in the family (Caplan, 1998). Happiness was the result of a psychological exploration, and patients were relieved to find that they had control over their unhappiness (Decker, 2005). Extreme self-consciousness was a method for protecting against sickness and sin, especially in marriage (Moskowitz, 2008). The most famous of these healers was Mary Baker Eddy, who created her own fusion of mind-cure and Christianity in her *Science and Health* of 1875, probably the most popular text of the movement. This became the foundation for the religion of Christian Science. Her religion sought to move away from the employment of fear and pessimism that characterized traditional American Protestantism and focus on prayer—a key part of healing—and fulfillment. The book sold over nine million copies, an astounding number in those days (Caplan, 1998, p. 74). Eddy argued that disease was caused by mind alone and out and out rejected the materialist worldview of science and medicine. Medicine's obsession with physiological causes, said

Eddy, was responsible for much suffering and death. The popularity of her ideas suggests that in the United States, many others felt the same way.

Other variants of mind-cure were more conciliatory toward science. The term "New Thought" was introduced in the 1880s to distinguish these ideas from those of Christian Science and other popular variants of mind-cure and spiritual science. Many American intellectuals were influenced by New Thought especially William James, who tended to see its roots in the Nancy School and Janet, rather than homegrown versions (Caplan, 1998). The key text was *Ideal Suggestion through Mental Photography* by Henry Wood published in 1893. Unlike mind-cure, New Thought was spread mostly to anonymous readers of books and periodicals. It was its self-help literature that made it so popular (Moskowitz, 2008, p. 18). Its message was that modern life required new forms of treatment, especially those directed at the mind and that traditional religion, with its basis in anxiety and fear, was little suited to this challenge.

This highbrow sentiment was also true of the Emmanuel Movement of the early twentieth century. The Emmanuel Movement was a joint venture between Boston physicians and the Episcopalian ministry that was popular with the educated and pillars of the establishment (Caplan, 1998, p. 118). The rector of the Emmanuel Church in Boston, Elwood Worcester, led it. He enlisted the support of leading American neurologist James Putnam and began to offer lectures for the public in 1906. By this point, psychiatrists had begun to respond aggressively against this nonmedicalized therapy. By 1910, Putnam had broken with the movement; even Freud criticized it, all arguing that such untrained healing put patient's mental health at risk. Best to leave it to the professionals, they insisted. And yet, the physicians never challenged the basic idea that talk cured—evidence for how much U.S. psychiatry had changed in a short period (Caplan, 1998, p. 148).

The mind-cure movement established a basic framework for a new therapeutic sensibility, which came to dominate U.S. society by the end of the twentieth century. As Eve Moskowitz (2008) notes in her study of mind-cure, it stressed three basic principles: (1) All in life is measured by whether it contributes to happiness; (2) human problems stem from psychological causes (and not social ones); and (3) the psychological problems that contribute to unhappiness are treatable, and all societies have a responsibility to address them (pp. 2–3). Unhappiness, many argued, had become an "epidemic." But mind-cure was also framed in the self-help tradition that had been popular in the United States for most of the nineteenth century. It affirmed the values of honesty, discipline, and hard work and especially the Victorian value of self-control. The widespread dissemination and acceptance of these ideas made psychoanalytic ones appear to be common sense by the time they appeared in the early 1900s (Gosling, 1987). European variants, still on some level concerned with the threat of revolution, generally sought to contain interior forces. In contrast, American versions, more concerned about the dangers of authority, increasingly sought to liberate them (Cushman, 1995).

Freudian psychoanalysis appeared on the American scene at just the right time. When Freud lectured at Clark University in 1909, he knew his audience well. He stressed the practicality, optimism, and simplicity of psychoanalysis including an extensive discussion of sublimation, that is, the directing of instincts into socially approved ends. Freud went as far as to suggest that conscious choice could eventually replace repression. He focused mostly on trauma, catharsis, dream interpretation, and the reform of sexual mores, all themes that would have appealed to his audience (Hale, 1971, pp. 6–16). He criticized the psychotherapy of Pierre Janet, which focused on the role of physiological degeneracy. Janet had already come to the United States in 1904 and focused on degeneracy and heredity, telling patients to live within their constitutional limits. Not surprisingly, Janet's message did not have the same impact.

Freud's timing was impeccable, as the leading figure in U.S. psychiatry, Adolph Meyer, had just called the dominant somatic style a "pile of rubbish." Americans were looking for a new approach to mental healing, and it turned out this new approach had much in common with some older ones. Mind-cure had already laid a foundation for psychoanalytic thought. Freudianism simply offered a version that professional psychiatrists could identify with. Two elements of the context are vital to understand. First is a crisis in civilized morality that Freud spoke to (Hale, 1971, p. 17). While this was much more of an issue in Europe where moral standards were far stricter, even in the United States the upper middle classes had long believed that hard work and the repression of sexuality distinguished them from the laziness of the aristocracy and poor. Freud's message of loosening sexual mores resonated. Second is the collapse of the somatic paradigm that had dominated psychiatry both in Europe and the United States from the 1870s until the early 1900s. By the 1890s, theories of brain localization were under attack, and American psychiatrists like James Jackson Putnam tended to describe the brain in holistic terms as a series of interlocking energy based functions, a position very much in line with both Freud and Janet. Adolph Meyer, likewise, began to adopt a similar language. American psychiatrists continued to distinguish between organic disorders, which were the purview of medicine and functional disorders that required the new therapeutic techniques. Another push came from Emil Kraepelin's new classifications, which also tended to stress the functional components of psychic disorders despite Kraepelin's belief that the sources of psychopathology were physiological.

By 1909, there were already several competing psychotherapies in the United States including those inspired by Janet, Freud, Christian Science, New Thought, and the Emmanuel Movement. Another influential version was that of the Boston school of James Putnam and Morton Prince, who along with William James, G. Stanley Hall, Adolph Meyer, and Boris Sidis, met regularly during the 1890s to consider the value of mental healing (Caplan, 1998). Prince combined the idea that thoughts can generate illness with the idea that, in the tradition of physiology, mental associations, and habits can explain nervous symptoms. His point was that the source of these symptoms was not degeneracy. Thus, habits could be unlearned, and healthy complexes could replace unhealthy ones. This also included talk of a dynamic subconscious as a source of pathology and the role of childhood and family environments. In fact Prince's book *The Dissociation of Personality* helped introduce American audiences to the idea of a subconscious. Both Prince and Putnam's therapy included hypnosis, suggestion, and a re-education that included techniques for self-healing. Putnam was less a behaviorist than Prince and regarded the goal of psychotherapy as establishing autonomy, dealing with the conflict between individual and society, and achieving emotional self-reliance, all themes that psychoanalysis stressed as well.

The conversion to psychoanalysis in U.S. psychiatry was remarkably rapid (Hale, 1971). Freud was already known among neurologists in the 1890s for his work treating hysteria and anxiety, and by the early 1900s, he was known for his "cathartic" cure. Putnam began to use catharsis without hypnosis or suggestion after 1906 and soon declared that Freud had provided him with the master key to the universe. Freudianism quickly spread to the popular media, especially women's magazines, and was sensationalized by journalists. They helped to bring psychoanalysis to the less educated for whom talk of a subliminal self with stored energies resonated. They warned of the dangers of suppressed desires. Conservatives feared Freudianism would subvert the social order by convincing people to stop restraining their antisocial instincts, but instead Freudianism simply adapted to its new surroundings, stressing the environment as the source of pathology, optimism, and social conformity. The latter reflected a new interpretation of the reality principle now described as "adjustment." The instincts, contra Freud's original vision, could be tamed. Freudianism spoke to a growing prosperous class interested in self-knowledge and soul searching (Shorter, 1997). Its alliance with medicine also helped spread its influence and its move toward a more conservative worldview. Yet concurrently, Freudianism was also embraced by political radicals (Hale, 1995). For them, Freud was a critic of bourgeois sensibilities. Part of the attraction to Freudianism seemed to be that one could find in it whatever one was looking for.

Professionally, the process of training analysts in the United States was institutionalized by 1927 (Hale, 1995). Training included a training analysis, supervision, and case seminars. And yet, there remained a large proportion of psychiatrists, especially those based in hospitals, who regarded the new psychotherapeutic ideas as not somatic enough. The biggest controversy in U.S psychoanalysis was that over the admission of so-called lay analysts, those without formal medical training. These battles on the part of psychiatrists to protect their exclusive right to treat patients became especially awkward in the 1930s as European analysts escaping the Nazis, some analyzed by Freud himself, were refused admission into leading psychoanalytic societies because they were not medical doctors. Freud himself tried to intervene in his "The Question of Lay Analysis" but to no avail. This began to change the nature of psychoanalytic training from the broadly humanist one found in European psychoanalytic institutes to a narrow focus on Freud's writing and classical techniques in U.S. institutes (Hale, 1995). As a result, the American analytic world became less engaged with developments in other fields and limited their "research" to confirmation of existing theories. Over the 1940s and 1950s, U.S. psychoanalysis moved away from Freud's focus on instincts and the unconscious and toward more practical concerns like strengthening the ego, anxiety, and superego-related guilt. Freud was transformed from a dangerous radical into a liberal sage. Influenced by logical positivism, the explanations employed by ego psychology in particular focused on causal relationships and the laws regulating mental activity, with the intent of generating testable hypotheses and addressing some of the traditional topics of experimental psychology including perception and intellect. At the same time, research by critics of psychoanalysis suggested that its effects were no better than spontaneous recovery (Eysenck, 1954). The insularity and elitism of the psychoanalytic community, the failure to marshal convincing evidence to demonstrate the validity of either the theory or treatment, along with the success of alternative pharmacology-based treatments spelled the end of psychoanalytic dominance over psychiatry (Lear, 1999). In fact, by the 1970s, the policy of excluding non-medical doctors from psychoanalytic training was reversed as institutes found themselves desperate to admit new candidates as a result of psychoanalysis' declining fortunes.

The other important development in the United States was the rise of clinical psychology and social work. They adopted variants of psychoanalysis in their own practice. Social work emerged as part of the mental hygiene movement and its focus on community-based mental health teams, all in an attempt to make psychiatry less isolated (Tomes, 2008). The movement combined a focus on psychological and social factors as to the source of mental illness. The social workers initially provided patients with support in aftercare programs designed to help them readjust to life, but gradually expanded their role to include counseling of the patient's family and dealing with the more practical sides of treatment.

Psychologists, who until World War II had mostly been involved in psychiatry through mental and personality testing, expanded the new specialty of clinical psychology as a way to meet the growing need for therapists to treat soldiers with war-related traumas. The new National Institute of Mental Health (NIMH) policies supported the expansion of clinical psychology as it was cheaper and quicker than medical school. This helped make the doctoral degree a requirement for advancement in psychology (Tomes, 2008, p. 668). Unlike the case with social work, psychiatrists responded to the growth of clinical psychology negatively and were more threatened by the capacity of psychologists to commercialize their work along with their advanced degrees (Tomes, 2008, p. 666). After the war, the APA established division twelve to focus on the issues of clinical psychologists, which culminated in the Boulder Conference of 1949 where new professional standards were set for clinical psychologists including doctoral level training and the requirement for original research. By the 1950s, psychiatrists, psychoanalysts, social workers, and clinical psychologists were all engaging in psychotherapy.

World War II was a boon to psychoanalysis, just as it was to psychology in general. By the 1950s, seeing an analyst was a mark of the elite, especially in New York, and some of the most influential books were psychoanalytic in orientation (Shorter, 1997). During these years, dramatic splits and revisionist movements within psychoanalysis itself, some of which had actually begun in the days of Freud, did not help the reputation of psychoanalysis. Some of the most famous of these included Alfred Adler, Carl Jung, Melanie Klein, Karen Horney, and Erik Erikson, many of whom started their own training institutes. Still others, like Herbert Marcuse and Norman Brown turned Freud into a radical critic of the Enlightenment (Rieber, 1998b). Christopher Lasch, on the other hand, used Freud to develop a highly conservative critique of 1960s counterculture, sexual liberation, and feminism. In the end, though, the seeming successes of somatic psychiatry in the form of psychotropic medication provided a cheaper, quicker, and more scientistic framework for treating psychopathology, and this, along with declining government support for public health, spelled the beginning of the end for psychoanalysis in psychiatry.

3. STRUCTURE AND FUNCTION: PSYCHOANALYSIS AND THE THERAPEUTIC

This section is about considering the emergence of and problems with a therapeutic sensibility from the perspective of psychoanalysis itself. We examine the therapeutic not so much as a mode of treatment as much as its role in creating the disease it purports to cure. As Ernst Gellner (1996) pointedly notes, psychoanalysis has always been better on the disease than the cure anyway (pp. 199–203). Getting a handle on psychoanalytic thought is not very easy. Within psychoanalysis itself, the field has moved away from Freud's drive theory, and various psychoanalytic orientations can conflict with each other to the point that it is difficult to get a sense of a general psychoanalytic position. Nancy McWilliams (1994), one of the few contemporary expositors of psychoanalytic thought, identifies four distinct schools of psychoanalysis: classical drive theory, ego psychology, object relations, and the more recent self-psychology of Heinz Kohut. The rise of the latter two approaches, both still fairly influential today, is yet another sign of the spread of a therapeutic sensibility. Their core concerns—self-coherence and the effects of early relationships—have become key concerns for this sensibility in general (Maloney, 2013, p. 14). As comprehensive as these categories are, they still leave out the so-called revisionist schools of Karen Horney, Erich Fromm, Wilhelm Reich, and others. Turning to academic psychology is no help either, as the dominant experimental paradigms have long found little value in the non-experimentally validated claims of Freud and his followers. At best, psychoanalysis is viewed as insightful but not very relevant anymore. Perhaps only practicing clinicians tend to be sympathetic to psychoanalytic categories, but even they are increasingly influenced by cognitive-behavioral techniques and pharmacological treatments.

Sympathetic critics of psychoanalysis argue that it makes no sense to get too caught up in whether or not psychoanalysis is a real science, whether or not its claims are falsifiable or whether its framework is capable of the kind of control and prediction valued by academic psychology today. Instead one should think of psychoanalysis as a science in the more of the eighteenth-century sense: concerned with description and the development of analytic categories rather than prediction and control (Spence, 1984). It depends more on pragmatic forms of validity—that is, does an idea ring true? Does it help illuminate aspects of experience previously hidden? Does it provide patients and others with a greater sense of agency and choice (Frosh, 1997)? There are, of course, problems with these sorts of validity, especially since such ideas can confirm things already believed. Yet, they are correct to say human behavior is not organized along the kinds of mechanical relationships experimentalism is oriented toward finding nor is it separated into the kind of distinct categories that allow for manipulation and control.

Freud himself made this mistake. Probably, the least helpful dogma of psychoanalysis is what Freud termed the "principle of psychic determinism." Contra Freud, all human behavior is not directly relatable to specific psychic causes. Not everything humans do is meaningful, even though it might make for some provocative insights into motivation and helps generate interesting narratives explaining behavior. In fact, there are no "psychic" causes, but there are reasons people do things even if they are not always aware of those reasons. Often people generate these reasons after the fact to feel they are more reasonable than they actually are. This was one of the most salient criticisms of Karen Horney and other revisionists: childhood experiences or feelings do not cause adult behavior or feelings. Because Westerners, Americans in particular, tend to believe early events disproportionately affect people for the rest of their lives, this was an easy case for Freud to make (Kagan, 2013). But, people do not simply reproduce childhood experiences mechanically. They make choices for certain reasons that they might or might not be aware of. Reasons are not causes; they are about assigning rationality. For this, they require language and someone to assign them. But more importantly, they are not predictable before the facts. Perhaps recognizing the effects of past relationships can allow us to make better choices. There is probably not any way to really know this, except to take it on faith.

To be fair to Freud, his thinking is not reflected in the "environmentalist," almost Locke-ian, interpretations which are common in the United States. Contra some contemporary pop interpretations of what Freud said, all is not the "fault" of parents. Ironically, Freud is sometimes turned into a full-blown nativist in European thought. Both extremes are incorrect. In fact, Freud's perspective was more sophisticated than either credits him for. As Freud (1912) himself put it,

> Psychoanalysis has warned us that we must give up the unfruitful contrast between external and internal factors, between experience and constitution, and has taught us that we shall invariably find the cause of the onset of neurotic illness in a particular psychological situation which can be brought about in a variety of ways. (p. 238)

The very structure of the psyche, argued Freud, precludes an easy distinction between internal and external which is why such a distinction is only precariously established with psychic maturity. No matter what Freud claimed, the psychoanalytic account is not a universal one. It is an account that attempts to describe and explain—and probably better on the former than the latter—the psychological condition of humans living in modern, Western, industrialized, and urbanized societies in highly value-laden terms. Philip Rieff was correct about Freud being a "moralist." And yet, up to this point in time, no other modern psychological framework seems to have come close to doing this as convincingly as psychoanalysis has, problems and all, if we take broad acceptance of its theses as evidence. There are two basic points about psychoanalysis that we will return to again and again: First, right or wrong, the influence of these ideas and practices on Western societies, especially the United States in the early twenty-first century remains astounding and is something that needs to be explained. Second, Freud excelled at creating experiences for his patients that validated his ideas, and the same can be said about his progeny, the contemporary agents of the therapeutic (G. Richards, 1992). There is power and danger in the therapeutic narrative. It establishes a new biography that links childhood to the present in cause/effect terms and typically culminates with crisis and the promise of redemption. Whether versions of those accounts are generated by cultural, religious, or psychotherapeutic sources, many humans seem to gravitate towards them.

Over the years, several lines of criticism of Freud have developed. We will take note of two. First, Freud was simply restating the obvious in his own obscure and mystifying language: this seems true of much of psychology but perhaps particularly true with Freud (Webster, 1996). Why invent a mental agency like the unconscious and assign it motives when one can simply say sometimes we do things without knowing why? Or why create a complex Oedipal story instead of saying that some children want to be like their fathers yet compete with them for maternal attention and end up resenting their authority? This becomes especially true when Freud simply renames objects that people have long taken note of. Why create a term like "superego" when one can use a term like "conscience?" So many of Freud's mental entities are vague, seem to be completely unrelated to any observable referent, and only make sense within Freud's very closed system. At times, psychoanalysis appears more like a thought-exercise out of biblical exegesis rather than a reflection of concrete psychological processes.

A more important criticism is that most of the basics of the Freudian framework were already around by the late nineteenth century and very much in the air as Freud came of age. Freud simply borrowed these ideas, renamed them, and brought them together in a unique way, all the while claiming to discover them. Obviously one of the big problems here is Freud's claim that most of psychoanalysis was arrived at inductively, from his own analysis and those of his patients. Actually, most were arrived at deductively. Freud was seeking to create a coherent system, including ideas that fit his preexisting assumptions and then ended up "finding" them in treatment. One cannot underestimate Freud's talent for creating the experiences in his patients that he required in order to validate his ideas.

Notions of an unconscious mind had been around since the eighteenth century and were quite fashionable by the 1870s. Johann Friedrich Herbart had advanced the idea that unconscious processes were repressed from consciousness and that one can view mental operations as conflicting forces. There was also a long tradition in the West accepting that ideas could influence bodily functions going back to the Greeks. While the advance of the germ theories of Pasteur and Koch made this less credible, such notions were still very much present in various hypnotic and suggestion-based treatments that were popular in the nineteenth century. Freud's original theory as to the cause of hysteria developed in the 1890s argued that an early sexual trauma had given rise to psychic energy that could not be discharged because of the sexual immaturity of the patient. Due to various conditions—the patient was in a "hypnoid" state, or the trauma was connected with an especially powerful emotion, or the excitement was especially at odds with consciousness—the energy was forced into the wrong channel, and the result was the symptom. In Freud's original mode of treatment catharsis or abreaction released the affect that was associated with that energy. And yet, through the years,

Freud was never really clear on what affect actually was; it was, at times, a descriptive category, a mechanism as well as a source of energy (Berrios, 1996).

As we already reviewed, by the 1880s, Bernheim was already using non-hypnotic suggestion in treatment, and the notion that hysteria was related to a sexual secret that could be cured by confession was well known. Soon after, Pierre Janet used catharsis to treat hysterics in psychotherapy and viewed trauma as the cause of those symptoms. Janet viewed the suggestive influence of the psychotherapist as key to cure. In 1887, the first psychotherapeutic clinic was established in Amsterdam and, given the influence of Janet, was widely practiced by neurologists in the 1890s. It is fair to say Freud was hardly alone. Freud's theory depended on his adoption of the idea of mental energy first made scientifically acceptable by Hermann Von Helmholtz and Gustav Fechner in the 1850s and a central idea in the work of Freud's teacher, Sigmund Exner. Fechner insisted on the lawful nature of these forces and that they operated along cause/effect lines. Freud studied with Brüke at the University of Vienna where he was exposed to the work of Helmholtz and Fechner. His first independent research in 1885 looked at the effects of cocaine on muscle strength. His lack of comfort with experimental work as well as his desire for more income led him to focus on clinical work in his postgraduate study under Meynert, Charcot, and Breuer (Rosenzweig, 1992, p. 141). Still, he continued to employ psychopsychical concepts in his clinical work. For instance, he described the libido as psychic energy which could not be increased or decreased but only converted or transformed, a description that remained quite close to Helmholtz and Fechner, though he broadened it into a general motivational principle (Rosenzweig, 1992, p. 146).

This influence along with his experimentalist sensibilities led Freud to the idea of psychic determinism. Key to all this was the notion that mental energy can be converted from energy in the environment, and also, the idea of the conservation of energy, meaning that if this mental energy was repressed, it had to go somewhere. This nineteenth-century biology certainly limited his framework, as even many of his sympathetic critics later argued, but also forced him, at least in his early work, to relate his speculative system to some physiological referents. The metaphor of mental energy was important because it seemed so rational to nineteenth-century sensibilities, especially given the role energy had played in transforming the world in their lifetime. It also offered Freud a scientific foundation based in biophysics. Given what we now understand about the nervous system, the idea of mental energy makes no sense but continues to play a role, even if explicitly rejected, in many dynamic models of psychotherapy, especially pop versions.

After 1896, Freud began to argue that these childhood seductions were actually fantasies and that the source of these fantasies was sexual instincts. Again, much of this was available to Freud already (Sulloway, 1979). In

1819, Schopenhauer had identified two instincts of the will: sexual and conservative. Darwin also identified two primary instincts: love and hunger.
Nietzsche linked satisfactions in life to basic instinctual drives as well as a
host of other ideas which eventually made their way into the Freudian framework including the role of trauma in the way individuals see things, the
aggressive nature of conscience, that instincts were realized through other
people, and the more noble the instinct seemed the more debased its foundation. Although Freud claimed not to have read Nietzsche, it is doubtful that a
well-educated middle-class neurologist like Freud would have not come
across many of these ideas in some form. Not to mention the influence of
sexologists who had been discussing childhood sexuality for over a decade.

Working closely with Wilhelm Fliess, who had already accepted the importance of infantile sexuality and the biogenetic notion that children recapit-
ulate in their own development the sexual development of the species including oral and anal tendencies, gave Freud further scientific ground for his
ideas: they were now part of a broader evolutionary discourse, of a mostly
Lamarckian nature, which accepted the homology between individual and
species development. Recapitulation later became the source for Freud of the
universality of the Oedipal complex. By the early 1900s, Freud had grounded
his notion of sexual and aggressive impulses and wishes in biology, arguing
they were determined by heredity—ironic, given that in the United States he
was read as a radical environmentalist. He, as did many others in the Victorian era, framed this as part of a great conflict between instinct and society,
one that made human happiness impossible.

The germs of the "superego" lay in the work of Freud's former teacher
Theodor Meynert who followed Hughlings-Jackson and identified a developmental progression from lower "impulsive" senses to emerging "higher" inhibitory ones. In Freud this was refigured as the move from primary to
secondary processes, pleasure to reality, id to superego, animal to civilized
impulses, and so on. These ideas became the foundation of Freud's notions
of psychological maturity, ideas that spoke well to an early-twentieth-century
Victorian audience anxious about the breakdown of civilized morality. Social
and moral authority now lay within all of us. To say that Freud brought
together these disparate ideas and integrated them into his variant of psychotherapy is by no means to suggest Freud was a "fraud" or charlatan. That is
often the work of science in the broadest sense. What it does is allow us to
identify some of Freud's key assumptions and the broader therapeutic framework that emerged.

Still, if psychotherapy has not been able to marshal extensive evidence as
to its success, how can anyone explain the quick embrace of Freudian ideas,
particularly in the United States, and their dissemination into popular culture,
so much so that we can now talk about a culture of the therapeutic? First,
there was clearly something about the particular variants of U.S. Protestant-

ism—a focus on scrutinizing individual consciousness, emphasis on feelings, conflicting moral forces—that made Americans particularly amenable to Freudian ideas. In fact, after European Protestantism had moved toward a more rationalist view of the self, various romantic reactions against this— including Methodism and the first and second Great Awakenings in the United States—sought to move it away from that rationalism. Forerunners of psychoanalysis had already made headway in nineteenth-century America. By the 1850s many Americans were already convinced that "bad" thoughts could make them sick. In the second half of the century, various nervous disorders were being treated by something like psychotherapy. Initially Freud offered neurology a weapon against amateur mind-curers, a scientifically grounded treatment. This assisted in the medicalization of psychiatry, allowing it to expand its services to respectable sites like industry and schools. Pathology was everywhere, and everyone needed the new analytic cure.

Freud eloquently combined a romantic view of human nature with an Enlightenment faith in a reason that could ultimately master that nature. He made freedom and autonomy, the great virtues of Rousseauian romanticism and Kantian rationalism, the culmination of a developmental passage from immaturity to maturity, a passage that mirrored, as turn-of-the-century Americans believed, the evolution of the species in general. For Freud and his American audience, too much authority and dependency was a sign of immaturity, even illness. By taking up some popular, science-related metaphors of nineteenth-century culture—instincts, energy, forces, determinism, primitive thought, and the like—and combining them with an intense focus on the self, which certainly would have appealed to a growing population of middle-class consumers, Freudian ideas were easily integrated into American consciousness. Plus, its reach was so wide psychoanalysis could be used to analyze art, literature, history, politics, and culture. It also spoke well to the childrearing needs of an urbanized and industrialized society that was anxious about the breakdown of traditional communal authority. Finally, Freudianism changed the way its adherents experienced their everyday lives, something its key competitor in psychology, behaviorism, was never able to do.

Quite rapidly in the period from 1910 to 1930, Freud's ideas became part of popular American culture though slightly modified for its new audience— the dominance of instincts was replaced by the dominance of parents and early experience. Freud's message was taken as: sexual repression was bad and sexual freedom was good. Rather than helping to reconcile individuals to the inherent conflicts that come with living in society as a result of human nature itself, psychoanalysis became a therapy of adjustment. It was made to explain human unhappiness in a way they spoke to early-twentieth-century Americans, and for better or worse, still speaks to many early-twenty-first-century Americans. Ironically, even contemporary neuroscience has incorporated quasi-Freudian notions of an unconscious, repression, and so-called "reward circuits" (i.e., pleasure principle) into its understanding of the brain.

4. INSIDE AND OUTSIDE: THE RISE OF POP PSYCHOLOGIES

Historically, academic psychologists have excelled at distinguishing themselves from debased popular variants, but as Graumann (1996) notes, one method to study this relationship is simply to examine the diffusion of new words from the university into everyday language. Here is just a short list of everyday words that originated in or were reformulated by academic psychologists: achievement, attachment, intelligence, motivation, subconscious, aggression, frustration, personality, learning disabled, authoritarian, conditioning, sociopath, stress, and self-esteem. The line between academic and popular psychology has always been unstable, with many leading psychologists writing for a popular audience including William James, John Dewey, John Watson, Arnold Gesell, B. F. Skinner, Sigmund Freud, and more recently Martin Seligman, Howard Gardner, Jerome Bruner, and Alison Gopnik among others. Early in the twentieth century, psychology was popularized by Joseph Jastrow, who sought to distinguish psychology from mind-cure and wrote articles entitled "Fact and Fable in Psychology" (Ward, 2002). Similar books about psychological myths and truths abound today. Jastrow also focused on keeping mentally fit in folksy articles like "Are You Too Big for Your Job?" combining the functions of country doctor and parish priest. Today's "positive" psychologists have a similar focus.

The first modern popular psychology was phrenology, and it influenced most forms of popular and academic psychology to this day. It was developed by the Austrian Franz Joseph Gall in the 1790s and dominated Anglo-American society for much of the nineteenth century. It began as part of a serious form of brain study, but morphed into something else under the influence of George Combe in Britain and the Fowler brothers in the United States. Gall borrowed many of his terms directly from Scottish faculty psychology and was influenced by the anatomical studies of Giovanni Morgagni in the 1740s and 1750s that indicated that diseases were related to particular organs (Alexander & Selesnick, 1966). Gall's nativism was in conflict with the dominance of sensationalism in France. After 1810, phrenology was spread by Gall's student, J. G. Spurzheim. Gall's influence led to the acceptance of some key principles that academic psychology still accepts today, including that (1) the brain is the organ of the mind, (2) and an aggregate of mental organs, (3) these organs are spatially distributed into specific functions, (4) external states can be used to identify internal ones, (5) mental actions are constrained by natural law, and most importantly (6) an understanding of mind can be used to help people adjust to life and properly organize society. The latter principle is the foundation of every popular psychology tradition since then including most psychotherapies.

In his study of this period, Cooter (1984) looks at social status among phrenologists and anti-phrenologists and found an underlying socioeconomic conflict. For the most part, critics of phrenology tended to be older and more established. At first, they regarded phrenology as too materialist in its implications but gradually adopted the position that it wasn't a real science, especially as it became more popular. Phrenologists tended to come from the new professionalizing fields, especially medicine, anxious about their lower social status in a society that did not yet accept education-related expertise or charging for professional services as more traditional class divisions still tended to dominate. This was especially true in Britain where young professionals hoped to create a society where success was linked to talent rather than inherited status and natural knowledge could offer a path to a society organized by utility and meritocracy. Phrenology promised this, especially in its focus on the head—the seat of reason. As phrenology grew in influence, its growing popularity among the working and lower middle classes made it less attractive to professionals, and they responded by trying to remove amateurs from their ranks. They accomplished this by establishing professional societies and journals—a path that would be followed by many variants of psychology—hoping to distinguish between a professional and common phrenology. By the 1840s, most of them had found the success of the previous generation and were ready to dismiss phrenology as quackery themselves.

In Britain, the spread of phrenology among the less educated classes was due to the writings and lectures of George Combe. Combe linked phrenology to a Methodist worldview, making it very attractive to mid-century lower-middle-class and working-class individuals. His *Constitution of Man* published in 1828 sold over 300,000 copies in the United States and Britain, far outselling Darwin's *The Origin of Species*, making it one of the biggest best sellers of the nineteenth century after the bible, *Pilgrims Progress*, and *Robinson Crusoe*. Combe argued that humans must adapt their lives to the laws of nature, a very attractive message to a society increasingly affected by scientific principles but not very clear about what they were. Such laws included traditional Methodist virtues like temperance, cleanliness, hard work, self-discipline, and property rights. Some were more novel, like the importance of occasional spicy foods and various strategies for maintaining physical health. The transgression of these laws had consequences, and poverty was the fault of the poor. If your failing in life was due to ignorance of your nature on the part of your parents or even bad heredity, they should be held responsible—echoes of future Freudianism. Its message of self-improvement couched in notions of science and natural law became a model for popular psychologies thereafter. After 1850, phrenology gradually set itself more and more against the educated elite, becoming more populist in tenor and focused mostly on self-help and self-healing until Darwinism, spiritualism, and later psychoanalysis replaced it.

In the United States, phrenology had to compete with homegrown self-help movements. Phrenology first appeared in the United States during the 1820s in its more middle-class form. Some of the early successes of "professional" phrenology were in Boston, where it even made it into the school curriculum. At the time, the United States had no scientific orthodoxy to police the boundaries of proper science. The establishment of the American Association for the Advancement of Science (AAAS) in 1847 changed this. A more populist version was established by the Fowler brothers whose Center for Phrenology in New York State focused much more on head reading. They developed a doctrine of self-improvement, the Fowlers claimed, grounded in the latest science. For them, phrenology explicated the "laws of life" in the way Newton had discovered the "laws of gravity."

As we discussed, the next popular U.S. psychology was mind-cure, which introduced ideas later taken up by psychiatry. The mind-cure movement began in Boston and gradually absorbed accepted insights from mesmerism, transcendentalism, and spiritualism as promoted by Quimby in the 1860s. This later turned into New Thought, whose influence was widespread. For instance, William James borrowed the notion of self-esteem from New Thought and used it in his *Principles of Psychology*. Much later, Abraham Maslow took up the idea as well (Ward, 2002). The most "scientific" of these homegrown popular psychological movements was the Emmanuel Movement, which most directly paved the way for the acceptance of psychoanalysis and also laid the foundation for Alcoholics Anonymous and other twelve-step programs (Dowbiggin, 2011). Unlike in Europe where psychoanalysis found success among the elite and cultural avant-garde, the rise of psychoanalysis in the United States introduced new versions of pop psychology (Dowbiggin, 2011, p. 90). Freud's message was simple: sexual repression was the source of illness, and so the less repressed one was the better. During the 1920s, French psychologist Emile Coué introduced Couesim, a do-it-yourself version of suggestion therapy whose essence involved the repetition of certain phrases on a daily basis usually replacing negative thoughts with positive ones. The media talked regularly of unmasking minds, hidden selves, and harnessing hidden mental powers (Burnham, 1998). Economic prosperity shifted concern away from the social problems that had been the focus of the progressives and toward the fulfillment of needs and desires. People became more attuned to their feelings as the state became more interested in supporting mental "hygiene," a term coined by Adolph Meyer (Dowbiggin, 2011). The experience of the war had also alerted people to the dangers of "primitive" aggressive instincts run amok, and commentators focused on civilizing these dangerous natural impulses. These instincts were reframed in this period from "bestial" ones as they had been regarded in the nineteenth century to "abnormal," and especially given the influence of Freudianism, "infantile" ones. This, along with Watsonian notions of child rearing and the mental hygiene movement contributed to the notion that pathology was everywhere (Burnham, 1998). Old forms of mind-cure still persisted in the writings of Dale Carnegie, Napolean Hill, and a bit later, the most successful of all, clergyman Norman Vincent Peale's *The Power of Positive Thinking*.

By the 1920s, most Americans exposed to popular culture were introduced to psychological explanations—both Freudian and non-Freudian—and this continued over the 1930s and 1940s so that when *Life* magazine began republishing in the 1950s, its first new issue declared "The Age of Psychology" was here. During the same decade, psychologist Joyce Brothers appeared on the television quiz show "The $64,000 Question." A few years later, she had her own show (Ward, 2002). Following the influence of humanism in academic psychology after World War II, particularly the work of Abraham Maslow, a new type of popular psychology emerged. It linked old mind-cure and psychoanalytic ideas with ones that stressed the expression of feelings, self-growth, and developing connections with others. This, along with the spread of some of these ideas in women's magazines in the 1950s, helped prepare the way for the social movements of the 1960s and the encounter groups of the 1970s (Moskowitz, 2008). Also after the war, William and Karl Menninger, the nation's most respected authorities on mental health and founders of the Menninger Clinic in Topeka, wrote best-selling books that helped spread the value of the psychiatric profession to the American public (Herman, 1995). Mothers especially took a beating as notions of a "refrigerator" mother were developed linking mothering practices with autism, schizophrenia, and at the other end of the spectrum, homosexuality. This jibed nicely with notions of "secure" attachments coming out of Britian, laying all of adult emotional well-being at the foot of mothers. Many of these ideas were integrated into practice during Lyndon Johnson's "War on Poverty," attempting to provide poor children with less emotionally and intellectually "deprived" environments.

Although the 1960s and 1970s witnessed a very public antipsychiatry movement, it also saw increases in the public's interest in self-help popular psychology. Popular psychology books in this later period included Thomas Harris's *I'm OK-You're OK*, which popularized the idea of the inferiority complex; Eric Berne's *Games People Play*, warning of the prevalence of dishonesty in interpersonal relations; and a bit later, Robin Norwood's huge 1985 best seller, *Women Who Love Too Much,* making the subversive case that too much subservience on the part of women was a symptom of pathology. Many of these included do-it-yourself psychological cures that didn't require an actual therapist or counselor. Even Jimmy Carter set up a national commission to study the state of mind of Americans and famously described a cultural malaise affecting the nation. This new therapeutic sensibility was spread in books, media, but also a new genre of television talk show where guests revealed personal struggles, a genre expertly crafted by Phil Donahue and Oprah Winfrey. The last decades of the twentieth century witnessed the therapeutic sensibility spread to all areas of life and society including the justice system, politics, government, religion, medicine, and education (Nolan, 1998; Cushman, 1995; Imber, 2004; Furedi, 2004). Its fundamental tenets were no longer up for debate.

5. HIGHER AND LOWER: THE CASE OF ATTACHMENT

The psychoanalytic framework has in fact translated itself into variants that do appeal to the sensibilities of the experimentalists in psychology, suggesting just how influential therapeutic notions have become. One such case is the theory of attachment, which one can find variants of in most child rearing books published in the past decade and is probably one of the most widely accepted psychological theories of today (Rholes & Simpson, 2004) and is even receiving support from the findings of neuroscience. Since Rousseau, Western romantics have made much of the importance of mother-love and the success of attachment theory in psychology—the idea that an infant's bond with mother affects the way in which that child will relate to others as well as predicts other psychological measures well into adulthood—speaks to this impulse (Kagan, 1998). Americans in particular have long believed that early experiences are key to the shaping of character and this manifests itself in many ways (Kagan, 2013, p. 126). In the nineteenth century it meant that schools had to shape the moral habits of the young through discipline and piety so that they grow up to be virtuous, God-fearing adults. In the twentieth century, two of the most successful psychological metatheories—psychoanalysis and behaviorism—both highlighted the importance of early experiences, and more recently, the findings of neuroscience promote the idea that early experiences are central in shaping the synaptic pathways of the brain, a position not so different from the early behaviorists.

Such a position tends to fit well with the liberal, optimistic, and egalitarian ethos in the United States where it is believed differences between peoples can be mitigated through public education and that character failure is often the result of a "bad" environment. It also fits nicely with the very romantic sentiment that love heals. Undoubtedly, theories of attachment speaks to all this. If one can discover "bad" mothering early enough, one can ameliorate social and emotional problems before they get out of hand. Or at least, psychologists can ameliorate these problems. It does put a lot of faith in psychology. In fact, the concept of attachment is so interesting because it both reflects a faith in therapeutic values as well as illustrates that vague ideas which speak to already formed assumptions about human nature can be easily dressed in the vocabularies of science and seem to say something more than they actually do. It also represents some basic confusion between structure and function as well as description and explanation.

The idea of attachment began with psychoanalyst John Bowlby's work with juvenile delinquents in postwar Britain. The states' concern over "dangerous" children was one of the issues in late-nineteenth-century Britain that helped to create the notion of a "healthy" childhood, and by the early twentieth century this problem was already framed in mostly psychological as opposed to judicial terms (N. Rose, 1990, pp. 152–153). After World War II, such children were increasingly viewed as a product of failed familial psychological relationships. The idea was that children's instinctual nature could only properly develop in the context of a normal family; without that, maladjustment results. As Nikolas Rose (1990) puts it, "love was no longer merely a moral duty or a romantic ideal, it was the element in which were produced normal and abnormal children . . . the group life of the family, its relational economy, the dependencies, frustrations, jealousies, attachments, rivalries, and frustrations that traversed it, became . . . the means of explanation of the troubles of childhood" (p. 156). The project of repairing the psychological damage of the abnormal family permitted the state to assert itself in the "private" sphere of the home as well as helped to rationalize the education of parents in therapeutic ideals by experts while they attended to the minutiae of mother-child relationships. Given the current popularity of theories of attachment in child rearing literature, we can make similar assumptions today.

Bowlby was concerned that British policy was too focused on meeting the physiological needs of children as opposed to on parent-child ties. He observed that disruptions in early mother-child relationships seemed to be a precursor of later psychopathology. In the short run, these disturbances manifested themselves as intense distress following separation, the children got angry followed by despair. He later termed this phenomenon insecure attachment. Bowlby was dissatisfied with the traditional psychoanalytic explanations for this phenomena—the children were distressed because they needed their mother to take care of unmet nutritional needs—and, after readings in ethology, control systems theory, and evolutionary biology, became convinced that human infants possessed innate attachment needs which required proximity to mother. This relationship promoted the stability of what he termed an "attachment system." Bowlby came across ethological studies, among them Harry Harlow's research demonstrating that infant monkeys prefer a cloth "mother" to a wire hanger one, even if the latter fed the infants. Extending this insight to humans, Bowlby introduced these ideas in a 1958 paper, "The Nature of the Child's Tie to His Mother" and later elaborated them in the series *Attachment and Loss*.

Bowlby gradually broadened attachment into a "behavior system," viewing many infant behaviors as part of proximity seeking. Part of what made Bowlby's ideas so attractive was that he seemed to ground them in systems theory and biology, a way that was much more acceptable than Freud's speculations on drives or universal Oedipal complexes, yet also relatable to observed behavior. Bowlby was able to make a simple case: the need for proximity to mother increased an infant's chance of survival and was thus subject to the forces of selection. He also extended the behavior through various contexts and situations in order to sustain its universality. The monkey's so-called preference for cloth "mothers"—of course, they are only "mothers" to us, it is likely monkeys can tell the difference and might be seeking something else—to infant's distress at separation, regardless if that separation takes place in a strange laboratory setting or in the home, which infants also experience very differently, and in more recent research, the primary school child's relations with others, are all examples of different manifestations of this same phenomenon.

In fact, the theory goes, the nature of that attachment can even be used to predict certain personality traits or patterns of relating to others later in life. So that what was once a description, how a child reacts to separation, becomes a cause of later descriptions, how one responds to a questionnaire or interview. As Bowlby's work grew in influence, it fed into larger social concerns around women working out of the home and changing norms of motherhood. The problem is not simply that attachment measures are poor predictors of psychological measures in grade school, high school, or adulthood, but that even if one found correlations between traits in toddlerhood and adulthood, the kinds of things being measured are part of the same semantic networks and thus are not independent of each other (Kagan, 2013). Maybe infants that are at ease with others turn out to be adults that are at ease with others; this doesn't mean that a lack of proper bonding with mother caused this, only that people don't change much.

Psychology is filled with concepts of this type: descriptions that become explanations because they confirm assumptions that we already have. Are there folks who grow up with "insecure" attachments who come out well on adult psychological outcome measures? Of course and vice versa. Can one control for all other variables and simply manipulate attachment style and predict how children will turn out? Of course not. Even longitudinal studies (see Rholes & Simpson, 2004) that show consistency in personality or emotional expression over time, mostly measured by self-report data, do nothing more than describe the basic idea that people stay the same. That is not to say psychology should not be descriptive. It does become a problem, however, when one loses sight of the origins of these descriptions and assumes they reside in nature. Turning them into explanations is meaningless. If one had to render a guess as to what can best predict a child's and adolescent's scores on various psychological outcomes including attachment, one should guess poverty before anything else, which by the way, given how we conceive psychological outcomes, are already highly correlated with family income (Kagan, 2013). Either way, the assumption of the importance of early mother-love is not falsifiable in any sense.

Mary Ainsworth went even further in her Baltimore studies of the "strange situation," observing toddlers responses to maternal separation and reunion. She saw this specific situation as revealing the nature of a particular mother-child attachment in general. Ainsworth focused not only on proximity but also on the availability and responsiveness of the mother, thus felt she was able to make further generalizations about the relationships she observed and what they might look like into adulthood. Would these children grow up to be "unavailable" in relationships? Too needy? Not surprisingly, the behaviors and characteristics associated with a "secure" attachment tend to be the kinds of things psychologists find morally acceptable: sensitivity, cooperation, acceptance, and autonomy, so that virtue begets virtue. Current attachment theorists see the continuity of childhood attachment and adult behaviors as measured by the Adult Attachment Interview (AAI) as near 82 percent. Secure attachments have been associated with behaviors ranging from superior social skills, self-esteem, and empathy to less hostility, at least for college students (Cassidy & Shaver, 2010). But what the AAI is actually doing— other than getting adults to generate narratives about their childhood—is identifying certain salient profiles and relating them to narratives about the past, hardly a real test of the predictive value of attachment theory.

The last point helps explain the success of attachment theory. It explains the source of relationship problems to an audience schooled in therapeutic ideals as it grounds those ideas in biology. In fact, many of Ainsworth's insights were "discovered" in primates including the fact that peer-raised primates, when compared to mother-raised ones, require more ketamine to be sedated and tend to consume more alcohol (Cassidy & Shaver, 2010). Today these findings are interpreted as due to deficiencies in serotonin, presumably because of lack of mother-love. These cause-effect narratives are strung together using correlational data that may or may not have any meaning other than they confirm what is already believed. These notions are already linked together in networks of meaning and are generalized well beyond the limited settings in which the data were collected. It is probably fair to say no one's maternal relationship can be summarized by a term like "avoidant attachment." In some sense, these are not all that different from the intricate Freudian narratives that many of these same psychologists likely disdain. Perhaps the only difference is this research gives the appearance of scientificity by taking place in university laboratories and using the more economic languages of physiology and biology. It also gives psychologists a lot of authority in fixing human nature when society corrupts it—all very Rousseauian.

A final problem with attachment theory is that it tends to downplay a fairly basic fact about infants—they do not come into the world all the same. What some psychologists have described as "temperament" is a key component of how one relates to others but also of how others relate to them. Stella Chess, for example, identifies several ways in which infants are temperamentally different from each other, most from the moment of birth: regularity in waking and sleep cycles, ease to comfort, levels of excitability, and so on (Chess & Thomas, 1977). Jerome Kagan (2013) boils this down to one distinction: more or less reactive (pp. 57–59). Such differences, especially if they mean something to caregivers, can shape the ways in which caregivers feel comfortable interacting with their infants, which in turn can magnify them. Critics of attachment theory describe this as "goodness of fit." Mothers with infants that refuse to be soothed for hours at a time might feel rejected on some level and distance themselves from those children. The children then might perceive their mother as inconsistently available, setting up the dynamics of an ambivalent attachment. This ignores all the other "contextual" factors that are part of the mix: socioeconomic status, culturally shaped expectations, gender roles, health, available housing and work, historical norms around good parenting, and so on. Attachment relationships are part of broader developmental and ecological systems that change in different contexts and different moments of time and cannot be isolated from the rest of what is going on.

Most of all, these factors depend on the meanings assigned to them by the children involved. The identical "avoiding" behavior viewed as evidence that my mother doesn't care for me as opposed to my mother is busy doing very important things to make sure I am cared for can be experienced very differently or maybe not, again depending on the particular child and the particular context. If it were important to identify the source of secure attachments, we could describe them as emergent properties of these relationships, but it is not clear that they are particularly important, other than for validating much of what we already believe about what is right and wrong in child rearing, virtue disguised as science, description disguised as explanation, and function disguised as structure.

Conclusion

STRUCTURE AND FUNCTION: SOME IMPLICATIONS FOR PSYCHOLOGY

The previous chapters have sought to identify some key conceptual tensions in psychology by focusing on four key areas: learning, the brain, development, and therapy. With respect to learning, psychologists were able to sustain a divide between inside and outside translated into a distinction between mind and behavior. The study of the outside offered a path to an unavailable inside via measurements, scales, and statistics. While the latter was typically descriptive, explanations were achieved through generalizations from animal experiments, language choice, that is, using terms that implied causality like "reflex" and "reinforcer," or by assuming underlying neurological activity. Similarly in the case of the study of the brain, an assumed functional parallelism allowed psychologists to attribute psychological functions to various neurological structures, and more broadly, assign human capacities to physiological entities, what we have described as the homunculus fallacy. It might be tempting to describe the brain as "thinking" or "learning," but this is typically a reflection of an absence of viable alternative explanations.

With respect to theories of development and psychological treatment, both fields are laden with assumptions about the good and both seek to offer paths for individuals to get there. These notions help to turn descriptions into explanations as they assume that individuals are constitutionally pulled toward the ends of maturity and health, with the exception of those that are ill in one sense or another and thus require expert intervention. Once again, functional parallelism, sometimes even full blown reductionism to physiological mechanisms generates an even more stable explanatory ground. We could have easily applied this approach to other subdisciplines within psychology whether we looked more closely at theories of cognition, person-ality, social dynamics like attitude formation and identity, motivation, or perceptual activity. All struggle with distinctions between inside and out-side—with most accepting a behavioral solution—description and explana-tion and higher and lower. It is not an accident in this therapeutic age that "self-actualization" sits at the top of Abraham Maslow's hierarchy of needs or that Paul Costa and Robert Mccrae's "Big Five" values virtues like "open-ness to experience" and "agreeableness." These are just some of the exam-ples of virtue in psychology.

However, in this final section we will approach the tension between struc-ture and function in psychology more directly and make some tentative sug-gestions as this can generate some of the subtler yet confusing conceptual and lexical problems for the field. As we have reviewed extensively, the spread of evolutionary naturalism offered psychology the scientific ground for a focus on psychological functions. This was attractive given the alterna-tives: an associationism that seemed to mirror neurological activity yet could not explain the emergence of complex psychological activity and a nativist faculty psychology that was closer to the everyday language that had evolved to talk about the psychological, yet with few exceptions, seemed to offer little physiological ground. For most of the twentieth century the solution was simple, focus on functional activity, preferably translated into behavioral activity, while assuming some unknown or vague relationship with physio-logical structure and activity. For some, this compromise began to break down in the closing years of the century, as neuroscience appeared to be developing a language of function, grounded in structure, which could re-place the language of psychological functions. Gall's vision seemed to be turning into a reality. Yet, as we have noted, the poverty of molecular lan-guage with respect to psychological activity is clear to anyone interested in describing complex psychological activity, and such activity is too much a part of the way modern Westerners have come to make sense of themselves and others to simply give up.

Within these paradigms, structure is typically framed anatomically, spe-cifically through the brain and its activities. This is one obvious expression of structure, but there are others. Structure in its essence is about organization. The traditional philosophical contest between rationalism and empiricism was about structure as well. Rationalists could not accept the contingent and fleeting notion of structure in empiricism. Galileo seemed to find structure in the universe, but Hume turned it into an accidental product of mind. From Kant forward, rationalists saw structure as a product of mind, perhaps more importantly, as the essence of mind in one sense or another. But it turned out, as post-Darwinian biology made clear, that structure existed in the biological world, that life required complex forms of organization operating at different levels of organismic activity. Moreover, these structures emerged from organismic activity. The psychological could now be recast as one of the many levels of organic activity.

The problem with behavioral theories of one sort or another was that they lacked a conception of structure or required that the environment impose structure on a passive organism. This seems to go against almost everything we know about organismic activity. It is active, creative, and "solution" oriented. When structure had to be accounted for, all was simply reduced to physiology. Such an approach tended to dominate in the United States, which still turns to anatomy for structure. It is clear that European psychology from the Gestaltists to Piaget and Werner retained a notion of structure, especially those with a more biology-based rather than physics-based sensibility. As behaviorism was replaced by a more cognitivist orientation, notions of structure were revived, yet the model for these structures was the computer, with its separation of hardware and software, not to mention that its structure was a product of human engineering. Other approaches looked to culture for structure but, as with cognitivism, struggled with the notion of integration across multiple levels of human activity or sometimes even regarded humans as copies of culture as in the associationist tradition.

As far as the source of structure it is not always clear. On one hand, organization already exists in the world to be discovered by humans, while on the other hand, humans tend to be skilled at identifying patterns and relationships whether they are "really" there or not. Thus the "structures" of psychology forever sit in a netherworld between description and explanation. There is much that psychologists will probably never fully understand about human experience. This is because norms of scientific work set limits on the types of answers scientists can accept. In psychology, given that we are not even entirely sure what the objects we study are, it seems a fair bet to say setting those boundaries in advance will leave out something important. Various homunculi have represented an easy way around this. By assigning certain properties to objects within those boundaries, psychologists did not need to turn to explanations of those properties themselves, which would likely exceed those boundaries. We simply cannot explain how mind arises from the nervous system. Now some of this is due to the fact that we limit the source of mind to the nervous system. A better question asks how mind arises from the relationship between person and environment, where person includes a nervous system, a body, as well as a history of meaningful experiences. But even if posed this way, the answer is still that we don't know. Terms like "emergent" and "self-organizing" are improvements on the mechanical metaphors of physiology that typically turn mind into an illusion, but even these biologically based metaphors cannot explain how thought emerges from the interaction of entities that cannot think. We do see similar types of emergence in biology that can be better explained, and this is why the metaphors are appropriate.

Human activity, whether behavioral or intellectual, is organized into meaningful patterns, and these patterns operate at many levels, often related to each other. The problem is that the work of psychology is also human activity, thus also seeking out meaningful patterns. Attachment, for instance, would constitute such a pattern. Yet, it is not clear whether this is a pattern that modifies psychological activity or is imposed on psychological activity by the discipline. In fact it is probably both, an example of what Ian Hacking calls a human kind. It is a description of an activity that, when given life in the worlds of child rearing, social welfare, and education, changes people's experience of the world. There is no problem with this, until it masks itself as an explanation and becomes the exclusive rationale for therapeutic intervention. Not necessarily that such interventions are ineffective—we will probably never really know—but that they are so caught up in a web of prior beliefs and assumptions, therapeutic norms, and institutional needs, it seems deceptive not to make all this explicit. Thus the key job of a descriptive psychology is to examine its own foundations and the conversion of its concepts into the practices of everyday human activity. This often involves identifying the "reasons" that things go in the direction they do. Thus, one must also acknowledge that psychological activity is grounded in consciousness, with or without a person's awareness. What is fairly relevant about a concept like personality or attachment is how it shapes conscious experiences of the world. This means that one cannot separate concepts from the meaning assigned to them by individuals and groups in different contexts. The structure and meaning of psychological activities cannot be separated from each other as well as are always undergoing transformation.

The disciplines that compose psychology must forever sit in a tension between academic and everyday psychology. There is certainly value in a psychology that seeks to de-naturalize everyday psychologizing, though perhaps the term "folk" psychology is a bit too disdainful. But given the back-and-forth relationship between these domains, academic psychologists must be extra critical of their own foundations. There is simply so much that goes unsaid and is assumed to be a reflection of nature rather than products of a back-and-forth relationship between humans and nature. It also means that psychologists must be able to synthesize diverse ways of making sense of human nature—physiological, intellectual, philosophical, historical, anthropological, linguistic, literary, and scientific. This requires an education designed to meet this. Maybe the *philosophes* were right about psychology being the "queen" of the sciences, just not in the way it is currently conceived.

Bibliography

Adler, H. E. (1998). Vicissitudes of Fechner's psychophysics in America. In R. Rieber and K. Salzinger (eds.), *Psychology Theoretical and Historical Perspectives*, 2nd ed. Washington D.C.: APA.

Alexander, F. G. and Selesnick, S. T. (1966). *The History of Psychiatry.* NY: Harper and Row.

Allport, G. (1937). *Personality: A Psychological Interpretation.* NY: H. Holt and Co.

Angell, J. R. (1907). The province of functional psychology. *Psychology Review,* 14, 61–91.

Anokhin, P. K. (1968). Ivan Pavlov and psychology. In B. Wolman (ed.), *Historical Roots of Contemporary Psychology.* NY: Harper and Row.

Appel, T. A. (1987). *The Cuvier-Geoffrey Debate.* NY: Oxford University Press.

Apperly, I. (2012). *Mindreaders.* NY: Psychology Press.

Aries, P. (1962). *Centuries of Childhood.* NY: Vintage.

Aronowitz, S. and Ausch, R. (2000). Critique of methodological reason. *Journal of Sociological Quarterly,* 41(4), 699–719.

Ash, M.G. (1995). *Gestalt Psychology in German Culture.* Cambridge: Cambridge University Press.

Baillargeon, R., Kotovsky, L., and Needham, A. (1995). The acquisition of physical knowledge in infancy. In D. Sperber, D. Premack, and A. J. Premack (eds.), *Causal Cognition.* Oxford: Clarendon Press.

Baldwin, J. M. (1894). *Mental Development in the Child and Race.* NY: Macmillan.

Bandura, A., Ross, D., and Ross, S. (1963). Imitation of film-mediated aggressive models. *Journal of Abnormal and Social Psychology,* 66, 3–11.

Bannister, R. C. (1979). *Social Darwinism.* PA: Temple University Press.

Beatty, B. (1996). Rethinking the historical role of psychology in educational reform. In D. R. Olson and N. Torrance (eds.), *The Handbook of Education and Human Development.* Cambridge: Blackwell Publishers.

Becker, C. (1932). *The Heavenly City of Eighteenth Century Philosophers.* CT: Yale University Press.

Beneke, E. (1845). *Textbook of Psychology as a Natural Science.* Second Edition. Berlin: Mittler [originally published in 1833].

Bereiter, C., and Scardamalia, M. (1996). Rethinking learning. In D. R. Olson and N. Torrance (eds.), *The Handbook of Education and Human Development.* Cambridge: Blackwell Publishers.

Bergin, A. (1971). The evaluation of therapeutic outcomes. In A. E. Bergin and S. Garfield (eds.), *Handbook of Psychotherapy and Behavior Change.* NY: Wiley and Sons.

Berrios, G. (1996). *The History of Mental Symptoms.* Cambridge: Cambridge University Press.

241

Binde, D. (1992). Motivation, the brain and psychological theory. In S. Koch and D. Leary (eds.), *A Century of Psychology as a Science.* Washington D.C.: APA.

Bloom, B. (1956). *Taxonomy of Educational Objectives.* NY: David Mckay Co.

Blumenthal, A. (1970). *Language and Psychology.* NY: Robert Krieger Publishing Co.

Blumenthal, A. (1975). A reappraisal of Wilhelm Wundt. *American Psychologist*, 30, 1081–1088.

Blumenthal, A. (1998). Why study Wundtian psychology. In R. Rieber and K. Salzinger (eds.), *Psychology Theoretical and Historical Perspectives*, 2nd ed. Washington D.C.: APA.

Boakes, R. (1984). *From Darwin to Behaviorism.* Cambridge: Cambridge University Press.

Boring, E. G. (1950). *A History of Experimental Psychology.* NJ: Prentice Hall.

Bouveresse, J. (1995). *Wittgenstein Reads Freud.* Princeton: Princeton University Press.

Bowlby, J. (1969). *Attachment and Loss.* NY: Basic Books.

Bowler, P. (1983). *Evolution: The History of an Idea.* CA: University of California Press.

Bowler, P. (1996). *Life's Splendid Drama.* IL: University of Chicago Press.

Brown, E. (2008). Neurology's influence on American psychiatry: 1865–1915. In E. R. Wallace and J. Gach (eds.), *History of Psychiatry.* NY: Springer.

Brown, N. (1959). *Life against Death.* CT: Wesleyan University Press.

Bruner, J. S. (1990). *Acts of Meaning.* MA: Harvard University Press.

Budde, G. (2012). From the '*zwergschule*' (one room schoolhouse) to the comprehensive school. In L. Brockliss and N. Sheldon (eds.), *Mass Education and the Limits of State Building.* London: Palgrave Mcmillan.

Burkhardt, R. W. (2005). *Patterns of Behavior.* IL: University of Chicago Press.

Burman, E. (1994). *Deconstructing Developmental Psychology.* London: Routledge.

Burnham, J. (1998). *Patterns into American Culture.* PA: Temple University Press.

Burtt, E. A. (1932). *The Metaphysical Foundations of Modern Science.* NY: Anchor.

Bury, J. B. (1921). *The Idea of Progress.* London: Macmillan.

Cairns, R., and Ornstein P., (1979). Developmental psychology. In E. Hearst (ed.), *The First Century of Experimental Psychology.* NJ: LEA.

Caplan, E. (1998). *Mind Games.* CA: University of California Press.

Cassidy, J., and Shaver, P. (2010). *Handbook of Attachment.* CT: The Guilford Press.

Cattell, J. M. (1890). Mental tests and measurements. *Mind*, 15, 373–381.

Chapman, P. D. (1988). *Schools as Sorters.* NY: NYU Press.

Clark, A. (1997). *Being There.* MA: Bradford Press.

Clark, E. (2003). *First Language Acquisition.* NY: Cambridge University Press.

Clarke, E., and Jacyna L. S. (1992). Nineteenth Century Origins of Neuroscientific Concepts. CA: University of California Press.

Collingwood, R. G. (1946). *The Idea of History.* UK: Oxford University Press.

Cooter, R. (1984). *The Cultural Meaning of Popular Science.* Cambridge: Cambridge University Press.

Costa, P., and Mccrae, R. R. (1986). Major contributions to the psychology of personality. In S. Modgil and C. Modgil (eds.). *Hans Eysenck.* UK: The Falmer Press.

Coulter, J., and Sharrock, W. (2007). *Brain, Mind and Human Behavior in Contemporary Cognitive Science.* NY: Edwin Mellen Press.

Crabtree, A. (2008). The transition to secular psychotherapy. In E. R. Wallace and J. Gach (eds.), *History of Psychiatry.* NY: Springer.

Creel, R. (1987). Skinner on science. In S. Modgil and C. Modgil (eds.), *B. F. Skinner.* UK: Falmer Press.

Curti, M. (1980). *Human Nature in American Thought.* WI: University of Wisconsin Press.

Cushman, P., (1995). *Constructing the Self, Constructing America.* MA: Addison-Wesley.

Danziger, K. (1990). *Constructing the Subject.* NY: Cambridge University Press.

Danziger, K. (1997). *Naming the Mind.* London: Sage Publications.

Danziger, K. (2001). Wundt and the temptations of psychology. In R. W. Rieber and D. K. Robinson (eds.), *Wilhelm Wundt in History.* NY: Plenum.

Darwin, C. (1859). *On the Origin of Species.* London: John Murray.

Darwin, C. (1871). *The Descent of Man.* London: John Murray.

Darwin, C. (1872). *The Expression of the Emotions.* London: John Murray.

Daston, L. (1994). Baconian facts, academic civility, and the prehistory of objectivity. In A. Megill (ed.), *Rethinking Objectivity*. NC: Duke Uinversity Press.

Davidson, D. (1974). Psychology as philosophy. In S. C. Brown (ed.), *Philosophy of Psychology*. NY: Barnes and Noble Books.

Davies, J. A. (2014). *Life Unfolding*. Oxford: Oxford University Press.

Dawes, R. (1996). *House of Cards*. NY: The Free Press.

Dawkins, R. (1976). *The Selfish Gene*. UK: Oxford University Press.

Deacon, T. W. (1997). *The Symbolic Species*. NY: W. W. Norton and Co.

Deacon, T. W. (2012). *Incomplete Nature*. NY: W. W. Norton and Co.

Decker, H. S. (1991). *Freud, Dora and Vienna 1900*. NY: The Free Press.

Decker, H. S. (2008). Psychoanalysis in central Europe. In E. R. Wallace and J. Gach (eds.), *History of Psychiatry*. NY: Springer.

Decker, H. S. (2013). *The Making of the DSM-III*. Oxford: Oxford University Press.

Dennett, D. (1978). How is mechanism conceivable? In M. Grene (ed.), *Interpretations of Life and Mind*. NY: Humanities Press.

Dennett, D. (1981). *Brainstorms*. MA: MIT Press.

Dennett, D. (1993). *Consciousness Explained*. NY: Penguin.

Denzin, N. K. and Lincoln, Y. S. (2007). *Strategies of Qualitative Inquiry*. NY: Sage.

Dewey, J. (1899). *The School and Society*. IL: University of Chicago Press.

Dewey, J. (1915). *Democracy and Education*. NY: Macmillan.

Dewey, J. (1929). *The Sources of a Science of Education*. NY: Horace Liveright.

Diamond, S. (1998). *Francis Galton and American Psychology*. In R. Rieber and K. Salzinger (eds.), *Psychology Theoretical and Historical Perspectives*, 2nd ed. Washington D.C.: APA.

Diamond, S. (2001). Wundt before Leipzig. In R. W. Rieber and D. K. Robinson (eds.), *Wilhelm Wundt in History*. NY: Plenum.

Donaldson, M. (1979). *Children's Minds*. NY: W. W. Norton and Co.

Dover, G. (2000). Anti-Dawkins. In Rose, H., and Rose, S. (eds.), *Alas Poor Darwin*. NY: Harmony Books.

Dowbiggin, I. (2011). *The Quest for Mental Health*. NY: Cambridge University Press.

Drewek, P. (2000). The educational system, social reproduction, and educational theory in imperial Germany. In T. S. Popkewitz (ed.), *Educational Knowledge*. NY: SUNY Press.

Drinka, G. (1984). *The Birth of the Neurosis*. NY: Simon and Schuster.

Durkheim, E. (1915). *The Elementary Forms of the Religious Life*. London: George Allen.

Ellenberger, H. (1970). *The Discovery of the Unconscious*. NY: Basic Books.

Ey, H. (1968). Pierre Janet. In B. Wolman (ed.), *Historical Roots of Contemporary Psychology*. NY: Harper and Row.

Eysenck, H. J. (1952). The effects of psychotherapy: an evaluation. *Journal of Consulting Psychology*, 16, 319–324.

Eysenck, H. J. (1954). *The Uses and Abuses of Psychology*: MD: Penguin.

Fass, P. S. (2013). Is there a story in the history of childhood? In P. S. Fass (ed.), *The Routledge History of Childhood in the Western World*. London: Routledge.

Fisher, S., and Greenberg, R. (1996). *Freud Scientifically Reappraised*. NY: John Wiley.

Forrest, D. W. (1974). *Francis Galton*. NY: Taplinger.

Foucault, M. (1964). Madness and Civilization. NY: Vintage

Fox, D. R., Prilleltensky, I., and Austin, S. (2009). *Critical Psychology*. NY: Sage.

Frank, J. (1961). *Persuasion and Healing*. MD: John Hopkins Press.

Freire, P. (1968). *Pedagogy of the Oppressed*. NY: Herder and Herder.

Freud, S. (1905). A Fragment of a Case of Hysteria. *Standard Edition*. Vol. 7, pp. 1–122.

Freud, S. (1912). *Collected Papers*, Vol. 2. NY: Basic Books.

Freud, S. (1926). The Question of Lay Analysis. *Standard Edition*. Vol. 20, pp. 177–258.

Freud, S. (1937). Analysis Terminable Interminable. *Standard Edition*. Vol. 23, pp. 255–269.

Frith, C. (2007). *Making up the Mind*. UK: Wiley-Blackwell.

Frosh, S. (1997). *For and Against Psychoanalysis*. London: Routledge.

Fuchs, A. H. (2002). Contributions of American mental philosophers to psychology in the United States. In W. E. Pickren and D. A. Dewsbury (eds.), *Evolving Perspectives on the History of Psychology*. Washington D.C.: APA Press.

Fuller, R. (1982*). Mesmerism and the Cure of Souls*. PA: University of Pennsylvania Press.
Furedi, F. (2004). *Therapy Culture*. London: Routledge.
Gach, J. (2008). Biological psychiatry in the 19th and 20th centuries. In E. R. Wallace and J. Gach (eds.), *History of Psychiatry*. NY: Springer.
Gardner, H. (1987). *The Mind's New Science*. NY: Basic.
Gaukroger, S. (1995). *Descartes: An Intellectual Biography*. NY: Oxford University Press.
Gaukroger, S. (2012). *Objectivity*. NY: Oxford University Press.
Geertz, C. (2000). *Available Light*. NJ: Princeton University Press.
Gellner, E. (1996). *The Psychoanalytic Movement*. IL: Northwestern University Press.
Gelman, R. (2003). *The Essential Child*. NY: Oxford University Press.
Gelman, R., Durgin, F., and Kaufman, L. (1995). Distinguishing between animates and inanimates: Not by motion alone. In D. Sperber, D. Premack, and A. J. Premack (eds.), *Causal Cognition*. Oxford: Clarendon Press.
Geuter, U. (1987). German psychology during the Nazi period. In M. G. Ash and W. R. Woodward (eds.), *Psychology in Twentieth-Century Thought and Society*. Cambridge: Cambridge University Press.
Gibson, H. B. (1981). *Hans Eysenck*. London: Peter Owen.
Gillispie, N. (1979). Charles Darwin and the problem of creation. IL: University of Chicago Press
Gilman, S. (2008). Constructing schizophrenia as a category of mental illness. In E. R. Wallace and J. Gach (eds.), *History of Psychiatry*. NY: Springer.
Giordano, G. (2005). *How Testing Came to Dominate American Schools*. NY: Peter Lang.
Godfrey-Smith, P. (2007). Information in biology. In D. L. Hull and M. Ruse (eds.), *The Cambridge Companion to the Philosophy of Biology*. Cambridge: Cambridge University Press.
Gosling, F. G. (1987). *Before Freud*. IL: University of Illinois Press.
Gould, S. J. (2000). More things in heaven and Earth. In Rose, H., and Rose, S. (eds.), *Alas Poor Darwin*. NY: Harmony Books.
Gould, S. J. (2002). *The Structure of Evolutionary Theory*. MA: Harvard University Press.
Graumann, C. F. (1996). Psyche and her descendants. In C. F. Graumann and K. J. Gergen (eds.), *Historical Dimensions of Psychological Discourse*. Cambridge: Cambridge University Press.
Griffiths, P. E., and Stotz, K. (2007). Gene. In D. L. Hull & M. Ruse (eds.). *The Cambridge Companion to the Philosophy of Biology*. Cambridge: Cambridge University Press.
Hacking, I. (1995). *Rewriting the Soul*. Princeton: Princeton University Press.
Hacking, I. (1999). *The Social Construction of What?* Cambridge: Harvard University Press.
Hale, N. G. (1971). *Freud and the Americans*. NY: Oxford University Press.
Hale, N. G. (1995). *The Rise and Crisis of Psychoanalysis in the United States*. NY: Oxford University Press.
Hall, G. (1987). The implications of radical behaviorism. In S. Modgil and C. Modgil (eds.), *B. F. Skinner*. NY: Falmer Press.
Hall, G. S. (1893). *The Contents of Children's Minds upon Entering School*. NY: E. L. Kellogg & Co.
Harlow, H. F. (1958). The nature of love. *American Psychologist*, 13, pp. 673–685.
Harre, R. (2005). The relevance of the philosophy of psychology to a science of psychology. In C. E. Erneling and D. M. Johnson (eds.), *The Mind as a Scientific Object*. NY: Oxford University Press.
Harris, R. (2003). *Saussure and His Interpreters*. Edinburgh: Edinburgh University Press.
Hartley, D. (1749). *Observations on Man*. London. Samuel Richardson.
Hearnshaw, L. S. (1964). *A Short History of British Psychology*. London: Methuen.
Hearst, E. (1979). *The First Century of Experimental Psychology*. NJ: LEA.
Hebb, D. (1949). *The Organization of Behavior*. NY: John Wiley and Sons.
Hempel, C. G., and Oppenheim, P. (1948). Studies in the logic of explanation. *Philosophy of Science*, 15, pp. 135–175.
Henle, M. (1992). Rediscovering gestalt psychology. In S. Koch and D. Leary (eds.), *A Century of Psychology as a Science*. Washington D.C.: APA.

Henriques, J., Hollway, W., Urwin, C., Venn, C., and Walkerdine, V. (1998). *Changing the Subject.* London: Routledge.

Hergenhahn, B. R. (2005). An Introduction to theories of Learning. NY: Pearson Prentice Hall.

Herman, E. (1995). *The Romance of American Psychology.* CA: University of California Press.

Himon, R., (1979). Social and intellectual origins of experimental psychology. In E. Hearst (ed.), *The First Century of Experimental Psychology.* NJ: LEA.

Hofstadter, R. (1944). *Social Darwinism in American Thought.* PA: University of Pennsylvania Press.

Holt, R. (1989). *Freud Reappraised.* NY: The Guilford Press.

Houghton, W. (1957). *The Victorian Frame of Mind.* CT: Yale University Press.

Hubble, M., Duncan, B., and Miller, S. (1999). *Heart and Soul of Change.* Washington D.C.: APA.

Hull, C. (1943). *Principles of Behavior.* NY: Appleton.

Imber, J. (2004). *Therapeutic Culture.* New Brunswick: Transaction Publishers.

Jackson, S. (1999). *Care of the Psyche.* New Haven: Yale University Press.

Jackson, S. (2008). A history of melancholia and depression. In E. R. Wallace and J. Gach (eds.), *History of Psychiatry.* NY: Springer.

Jahoda, G. (2007). *A History of Social Psychology.* Cambridge: Cambridge University Press.

James, W. (1890). *The Principles of Psychology.* NY: Holt.

James, W. (1912). *Essays in Radical Empiricism.* NY: Longman Green and Co.

Jarvis, P. (2005). Towards a philosophy of human learning. In P. Jarvis and S. Parker (eds.), *Human Learning.* London: Routledge.

Joncich, G. (1968). *The Sane Positivist.* CT: Wesleyan University Press.

Jopling, D. A. (2008). *Talking Cures and Placebo Effects.* Oxford. Oxford University Press.

Joravsky, D. (1987). L. S. Vygotskii: The muffled deity of Soviet psychology. In M. G. Ash and W. R. Woodward (eds.), *Psychology in Twentieth-Century Thought and Society.* Cambridge: Cambridge University Press.

Kagan, J. (1983). Developmental categories and the premise of connectivity. In R. Lerner, (ed.), *Developmental Psychology.* NJ: LEA.

Kagan, J. (1998). *Three Seductive Ideas.* Cambridge: Harvard University Press.

Kagan, J. (2013). *The Human Spark.* NY: Basic Books.

Kandel, E. R. (2007). *In Search of Memory.* NY: W.W. Norton.

Kahneman, D., Slovak, P., and Tversky, A. (1982). *Judgment under Uncertainty.* Cambridge: Cambridge University Press.

Kay, L. (1996). *The Molecular Vision of Life.* NY: Oxford University Press.

Kay, L. (2000). *Who Wrote the Book of Life.* CA: Stanford University Press.

Keller, E. F. (1983). *A Feeling for the Organism.* NY: Time Books.

Keller, E. F. (1996). *Refiguring Life.* NY: Columbia University Press.

Kendler, H. (1992). Behaviorism and Psychology. In S. Koch and D. Leary (eds.), *A Century of Psychology as a Science.* Washington D.C. APA.

Kenny, A. (1971). The homunculus fallacy. In M. Grene (ed.), *Interpretations of Life and Mind.* NY: Humanities Press.

Key, E. (1909). *The Century of the Child.* NY: G. P. Putnam & Sons.

Kirk, S., and Kutchins, H. (1992). *The Selling of DSM.* NY: Aldine de Gruyter.

Kitto, H. D .F. (1950). *The Greeks.* NY: Penguin.

Koch, S. and Leary, D. (1992). Preface. In S. Koch and D. Leary (eds.). *A Century of Psychology as a Science.* Washington D.C.: APA.

Kohn, A. (1993). *Punished by Rewards.* Boston: Houghton Mifflin.

Kohut, (1971). *The Analysis of the Self.* NY: International Universities Press.

Kuhn, T. (1962). The Structure of Scientific Revolutions. Il: University of Chicago Press.

Lamiell, J. T. (2003). *Beyond Individual and Group Differences.* CA: Sage.

Langemann, E. C. (2002). An Elusive Science. IL: University of Chicago Press.

Lasch, C. (1979). *The Culture of Narcissism.* NY: W. W. Norton and Co.

Lasch, C. (1984). *The Minimal Self.* NY: W. W. Norton and Co.

Lave, J., and Wenger, E. (1991). *Situated Learning.* NY: Cambridge University Press.

Leahey, T. H. (1992). The mythical revolutions of American psychology. *American Psychologist*, 47(2), pp. 308–318.

Leahey, T. H. (2005). Mind as a Scientific Object. In C. E. Erneling and D. M. Johnson (eds.), *The Mind as a Scientific Object*. NY: Oxford University Press.

Lear, J. (1999). The shrink is in. In R. Prince (ed.), *The Death of Psychoanalysis*. NJ: Aronson.

Leary, D. E. (1990). Psyche's muse: The role of metaphor in the history of psychology. In Leary, D. E. (ed.), *Metaphors in the History of Psychology*. Cambridge: Cambridge University Press.

LeDoux, J. (2002). *The Synaptic Self*. NY: Penguin Books.

Lenoir, T. (1993). Eye as mathematician. In D. Cahan (ed.), *Hermann Von Helmholtz and the Founders of Nineteenth Century Science*. CA: University of California Press.

Lerner, R. M. (2002). *Concepts and Theories of Human Development*. Third Edition. NJ: LEA.

Lewontin, R. (2002). *The Triple Helix*. MA: Harvard University Press.

Lloyd Morgan, C. (1894). *An Introduction to Comparative Psychology*. London: Routledge.

Lorenz, K. (1970). *Studies in Human and Animal Behavior*. MA: Harvard University Press.

Lorenz, K. (1966). *On Aggression*. NY: Harcourt Brace and World.

Luborsky, L., Singer, B., and Luborsky, L. (1975). Is it true that everyone has one and all must have prizes? *Archives of General Psychology*, 32, pp. 995–1008.

Luhrmann, T. (2000). *Of Two Minds*. NY: Knopf.

Lyons, W. (1986). *The Disappearance of Introspection*. Cambridge: MIT Press.

McLean, P. D. (1990). *The Triune Brain in Evolution*. NY: Plenum Press.

Malik, K. (2000). *Man, Beast and Zombie*. NJ: Rutgers University Press.

Maloney, P. (2013). *The Therapy Industry*. London: Pluto Books.

Mandelbaum, M. (1974). *History, Man and Reason*. MD: The Johns Hopkins University Press.

Mandler, G. (2007). *A History of Modern Experimental Psychology*. MA: MIT Press.

Martin, M. W. (2006). *From Morality to Mental Health*. NY: Oxford University Press.

Marx, O. (2008). German Romantic Psychiatry. In E. R. Wallace and J. Gach (eds.), *History of Psychiatry*. NY: Springer.

Mayr, E. (1982). *The Growth of Biological Thought*. NY: Belknap Press.

McCurdy, H. G. (1968). William McDougall. In B. Wolman (ed.), *Historical Roots of Contemporary Psychology*. NY: Harper and Row.

Mcmillan, M. (1996). *Freud Evaluated*. MA: MIT Press.

McWilliams, N. (1994). *Psychoanalytic Diagnosis*. NY: The Guilford Press

Megill, A. (1994). Introduction. In A. Megill (ed.), *Rethinking Objectivity*. NC: Duke University Press.

Micale, M. (2001). *Jean-Martin Charcot and les Névroses Truamatiques*. In M. Micale and P. Lerner (eds.), *Traumatic Pasts*. Cambridge: Cambridge University Press.

Mills, J. (1998). *Control*. NY: NYU Press.

Monod, J. (1971). *Chance and Necessity*. NY: Knopf.

Mora, G. (2008a). Mental disturbances, unusual mental states and their interpretation during the Middle Ages. In E. R. Wallace and J. Gach (eds.), *History of Psychiatry*. NY: Springer.

Mora, G. (2008b). Renaissance conceptions and treatments of madness. In E. R. Wallace and J. Gach (eds.), *History of Psychiatry*. NY: Springer.

Morgan, C.L. (1894). An Introduction to Comparative Psychology. London: W. Scott.

Morss, J. R. (1990). *The Biologising of Childhood*. Hove: LEA Publishers.

Moskowitz, E. S. (2008). *In Therapy We Trust*. MD: The Johns Hopkins University Press.

Napoli, D. S. (1981). *Architects of Adjustment*. NY: Kennikat Press.

Nicholson, I. A. (2003). *Inventing Personality*. Washington D.C.: APA.

Noe, A. (2009). *Out of Our Heads*. NY: Hill and Wang.

Nolan, J. L., Jr. (1998). *The Therapeutic State*. NY: NYU Press.

Nordenskiöld, E. (1928). *History of Biology*. NY: Knopf.

Nye, M. J. (2011). *Michael Polanyi and His Generation*. IL: University of Chicago Press.

O'Donnell, J. M. (1979). The crisis in experimentalism in the 1920s. *American Psychologist*, 34, pp. 289–295.

O'Donnell, J. M. (1985). *The Origins of Behaviorism*. NY: NYU Press.

Olds, J., and Milner, P. (1954). Positive reinforcement produced by electrical stimulation of septal area and other regions of rat brain. *Journal of Comparative and Physiological Psychology*, 47(6), pp. 419–427.

Olson, D. R., and Bruner, J. S. (1996). Folk psychology and folk pedagogy. In D. R. Olson and N. Torrance (eds.), *The Handbook of Education and Human Development.* Cambridge: Blackwell Publishers.

Ospovat, D. (1981). *The Development of Darwin's Theory.* Cambridge: Cambridge University Press.

Outram, D. (1984). *George Cuvier.* UK: Manchester University Press.

Oyama, S. (1985). *The Ontogeny of Information.* NC: Duke University Press.

Parke, R. D., Ornstein, P. A., Rieser, J. J. and Zahn-Waxler, C. (1994). *A Century of Developmental Psychology.* Washington D.C.: APA Press.

Parker, I. (1989). *The Crisis in Modern Social Psychology.* London: Routledge.

Passmore, J. (1969). *The Perfectibility of Man.* ID: Liberty Fund.

Pavlov, I. P. (1928). *Lectures of Conditioned Reflexes.* London: Charles Griffin.

Penelhum, T. (1993). Hume's moral psychology. In D. F. Norton and J. Taylor (eds.), *The Cambridge Companion to Hume.* Cambridge: Cambridge University Press.

Pepper, S. C. (1942). *World Hypothesis.* CA: University of California Press.

Peters, D. P., and Ceci, S. J. (1982). Peer-Review Practices of Psychological Journals: The fate of published articles, submitted again. *The Behavioral and Brain Sciences*, 5, pp. 187–195.

Piaget, J. (1926). *The Language and Thought of the Child.* NY: Kegan.

Piaget, J. (1929). *The Child's Conception of the World.* NY: Rowman and Littlefield.

Piaget, J. (1971). *Genetic Epistemology.* NY: W. W. Norton.

Pickering, N. (2006). *The Metaphor of Mental Illness.* Oxford: Oxford University Press.

Pinker, S. (1994). *The Language Instinct.* NY: Penguin.

Polkinghorne, D. E. (1984). *Methodology for the Human Sciences.* NY: SUNY Press.

Porter, R. (1999). The Greatest Benefit to Mankind. NY: W. W. Norton.

Porter, R. (2003). *Madness: A Brief History.* Oxford: Oxford University Press.

Postman, N. (1994). *The Disappearance of Childhood.* NY: Vintage.

Premack, D., and Premack, A. (2002). *Original Intelligence.* NY: McGraw-Hill.

Premack, D., and Woodruff, G. (1978). Does the chimpanzee have a theory of mind. *Behavioral and Brain Sciences*, 1(4), pp. 515–526.

Preyer, W. T. (1882). *Die Seele des Kindes.* Translated in 1888. *The Mind of the Child.* NY: Arno.

Prince, M. (1906). *The Dissociation of Personality.* London: Longmans Green and Co.

Ratcliffe, M. (2008). *Rethinking Common Sense Psychology.* NY: Palgrave Macmillan.

Rholes, W. S., and Simpson, J. A. (2004). Attachment Theory. In W. Rholes and J. Simpson (eds.), *Adult Attachment.* NY: The Guilford Press.

Richards, G. (1992). *Mental Machinery.* MD: The Johns Hopkins University Press.

Richards, R. J. (1987). *Darwin and the Emergence of Evolutionary Theories of Mind and Behavior.* IL: University of Chicago Press.

Richards, R. J. (1992). *The Meaning of Evolution.* IL: University of Chicago Press.

Richards, R. J. (2004). *The Romantic Conception of Life.* IL: University of Chicago Press.

Richards, R. J. (2009). Darwin on mind, morals and emotions. In J. Hodge and G. Radick (eds.), *The Cambridge Companion to Darwin*, Second Edition. Cambridge: Cambridge University Press.

Rieber, R. (1998a). Americanization of psychology before William James. In R. Rieber and K. Salzinger (eds.), *Psychology Theoretical and Historical Perspectives*, 2nd ed. Washington D.C.: APA.

Rieber, R. W. (1998b). The assimilation of psychoanalysis in America. In R. Rieber and K. Salzinger (eds.), *Psychology Theoretical and Historical Perspectives*, 2nd ed. Washington D.C.: APA.

Rieff, P. (1959). *Freud: The Mind of a Moralist.* NY: Anchor.

Rieff, P. (1966). *The Triumph of the Therapeutic.* NY: Harper and Row Publishers.

Ringer, F. (1969). *The Decline of the German Mandarins.* MA: Harvard University Press.

Roberts, J. S. (2004). *Embryology, Epigenesis and Evolution*. Cambridge: Cambridge University Press.

Robinson, D. (1985). *Philosophy of Psychology*. NY: Columbia University Press.

Robinson, D. (1992). Science, psychology and explanation. In S. Koch and D. Leary (eds.), *A Century of Psychology as a Science*. Washington D.C.: APA.

Robinson, D. (1995). *An Intellectual History of Psychology*. WI: University of Wisconsin Press.

Robinson, D. (2008). *Consciousness and Mental Life*. NY: Columbia University Press.

Rogers, T. B. (1995). *The Psychological Testing Enterprise*. CA: Brooks/Cole Publishing.

Romanes, G. (1888). *Mental Evolution in Man*. London: Kegan Paul, Trench and Co.

Rorty, R. (1979). *Philosophy and the Mirror of Nature*. NJ: Princeton University Press.

Rosch, E. H. (1973). On the internal structure of perceptual and semantic categories. In T. Moore (ed.), *Cognitive Development and the Acquisition of Language*. NY: The Academic Press.

Rose, N. (1985). *The Psychological Complex*. London: Routledge.

Rose, N. (1990). *Governing the Soul*. London: Routledge.

Rose, N., and Abi-Rached, J. M. (2013). *Neuro: The New Brain Sciences and the Management of the Mind*. NJ: Princeton University Press.

Rose, S. (2005). *The Future of the Brain*. Oxford: Oxford University Press.

Rosenberg, A. (1988). *Philosophy of Social Science*. CO: Westview Press.

Rosenzweig, S. (1992). Freud and Experimental Psychology. In S. Koch and D. Leary (eds.), *A Century of Psychology as a Science*. Washington D.C.: APA.

Ross, D. (1972). *G. Stanley Hall*. IL: University of Chicago Press.

Roth, A., and Fonagy, P. (2005). *What Works for Whom?* NY: The Guilford Press.

Rousseau, J. J. (1762/1979). *Emile*. NY: Basic Books.

Rozenbaum. W. (1960). The fallacy of the null hypothesis significance test. *Psychological Bulletin*, 57, pp. 416–428.

Ruse, M. (2000). *The Evolutionary Wars*. CA: ABC-CLIO.

Russell, E. S. (1916/1982). *Form and Function*. IL: University of Chicago Press.

Rylance, R. (2000). *Victorian Psychology and British Culture*. NY: Oxford University Press.

Ryle, G. (1949). *The Concept of Mind*. London: Hutchinson.

Sadler, J. Z. (2005). *Values and Psychiatric Diagnosis*. Oxford: Oxford University Press.

Schnädelbach, H. (1984). *Philosophy in Germany*. Cambridge: Cambridge University Press.

Schnaitter, R. (1987). Knowledge as action. In S. Modgil and C. Modgil (eds.), *B. F. Skinner*. NY: Falmer Press.

Schneewind, J. B. (1998). *The Invention of Autonomy*. Cambridge: Cambridge University Press.

Searle, J. R. (1969). *Speech Acts*. Cambridge: Cambridge University Press.

Searle, J. R. (1995). *The Construction of Social Reality*. NY: The Free Press.

Searle, J. R. (2004). *Mind*. NY: Oxford University Press.

Segerstrale, U. (2000). *Defenders of the Truth*. NY: Oxford University Press.

Shapin, S., and Schaffer, S. (1985). *Leviathan and the Air Pump*. NJ: Princeton University Press.

Shepard, G. (2010). *Creating Modern Neuroscience*. NY: Oxford University Press.

Shorter, E. (1997). *A History of Psychiatry*. NY: John Wiley & Sons.

Shuttleworth, S. (2010). *The Mind of the Child*. Oxford: Oxford University Press.

Simon, B. (2008). Mind and Madness in Classical Antiquity. In E. R. Wallace and J. Gach (eds.), *History of Psychiatry*. NY: Springer.

Skinner, B. F. (1938). *The Behavior of Organisms*. Oxford: Appleton-Century.

Skinner, B. F. (1948/2005). *Walden Two*. NY: Hackett Pub. Co.

Skinner, B. F. (1953/1965). *Science and Human Behavior*. NY: The Free Press.

Skinner, B. F. (1957). *Verbal Behavior*. MA: Copley Publishing.

Skinner, B. F. (1972). *Beyond Freedom and Dignity*. NY: Bantam Vintage.

Skinner, B. F. (1974). *About Behaviorism*. NY: Vintage Books.

Slater, A., and Quinn, P. C. (2001). Face recognition in the newborn infant. *Infant and Child Development*, 10, pp. 21–24.

Smith, M., Glass, G., and Miller, T. (1980). *The Benefits of Psychotherapy.* MD: Johns Hopkins University Press.

Smith, R. (1992). *Inhibition.* CA: University of California Press.

Smith, R. (1997). *The Norton History of the Human Sciences.* NY: W. W. Norton.

Smith, R. (2013). *Between Mind and Nature.* London. Reaktion Books.

Snell, B. (1953/2011). *The Discovery of Mind.* NY: Dover.

Spelke, E. S., Phillips, A. and Woodward, A. L. (1995). Infant's knowledge of object motion and human action. In D. Sperber, D. Premack, and A. J. Premack (eds.), *Causal Cognition.* Oxford: Clarendon Press.

Spence, D. P. (1984). *Narrative Truth and Historical Truth.* NY: W. W. Norton & Co.

Sperber, D. (1996). *Explaining Culture.* NY: Blackwell.

Starbuck, W. (2006). *The Production of Knowledge.* NY: Oxford University Press.

Staum, M. S. (2011). *Nature and Nurture in French Social Sciences.* Quebec: Mcgill Queens University Press.

Sulloway, F. (1979). *Freud: Biologist of the Mind.* NY: Basic Books.

Szasz, T. (1961). *The Myth of Mental Illness.* NY: Harper and Row.

Tallis, R. (2011). *Aping Mankind.* NC: Acumen.

Taylor, C. (1971). How is mechanism conceivable? In M. Grene (ed.), *Interpretations of Life and Mind.* NY: Humanities Press.

Taylor, C. (1989). *Sources of the Self.* Cambridge: Harvard University Press.

Taylor, E. (1998). William James and the demise of positivism in American psychology. In R. Rieber and K. Salzinger (eds.), *Psychology Theoretical and Historical Perspectives*, 2nd ed. Washington D.C.: APA.

Teo, T. (2005). *The Critique of Psychology.* NY: Springer.

Thomas, A., and Chess, S. (1977). Temperament and Development. London: Brunner/Mazel.

Thompson, E. (2007). *Mind in Life.* MA: Belknap Press.

Thorndike, E. L. (1898). *Animal Intelligence.* NY: MacMillan.

Thorndike, E. L. (1901). *Notes on Child Study.* NY: Arno Press.

Thorndike, E. L. (1903). *Educational Psychology.* NY: The Science Press.

Thorndike, E. L. (1911). *Individuality.* MA: Houghton Mifflin.

Thorndike, E. L. (1912). *Education: A First Book.* NY: Macmillan

Thorndike, E. L. (1913). *Educational Psychology. Vol 1.* NY: Teachers College Press.

Thorndike, E. L. (1918). The nature, purposes and general methods of measurement of educational products. In S. A. Courtis (Ed.), *The Measure of Educational Products* (*17th Yearbook of the National Society for the Study of Education*, Pt. 2, pp. 16–24). IL: Public School.

Thorndike, E. L. (1912). *The Psychology of Arithmetic.* NY: Macmillan

Todes, D. P. (2001). *Pavlov's Physiological Factory.* MD: The John Hopkins University Press.

Tomasello, M. (2003). *Constructing a Language.* Cambridge: Harvard University Press.

Tomes, N. (2008). Development of Clinical Psychology, Social Work and Psychiatric Nursing. In E. R. Wallace and J. Gach (eds.), *History of Psychiatry.* NY: Springer.

Tooby, J., and Cosmides, L. (2000). *Evolutionary Psychology.* MA: MIT Press.

Toulmin, S. (1992). *Cosmopolis.* IL: University of Chicago Press.

Toulmin, S. and Leary, D. (1992). The Cult of Empiricism in Psychology and Beyond. In S. Koch and D. Leary (eds.), *A Century of Psychology as a Science.* Washington D.C.: APA.

Turner, R. S. (2014). *In the Mind's Eye.* NJ: Princeton University Press.

Uttal, W. R. (2007). *The Immeasurable Mind.* NY: Prometheus.

Vidal, F. (2011). *The Sciences of the Soul.* IL: University of Chicago Press.

Voneche, J. (1999). The origins of Piaget's ideas about genesis and development. In E. K. Scholnick, K. Nelson, S. Gelman, and P. H. Miller (eds.), *Conceptual Development.* NY: Psychology Press.

Walsh, R. T. G., Teo, T. and Baydala, A. (2014). *A Critical History and Philosophy of Psychology.* Cambridge: Cambridge University Press.

Ward, S. C. (2002). *Modernizing the Mind.* CT: Praeger.

Watters, E., and Ofshe, R. (1999). *Therapy's Delusions.* NY: Scribner.

Watson, J. (1968). *The Double Helix.* NY: Atheneum.

Watson, J. B. (1913). Psychology as the behaviorist views it. *Psychological Review*, 20, 158–177.

Watson, J. B. (1928). *Psychological Care of the Infant and Child*. NY: Norton.

Watson, J. B., and Raynor, R. (1920). Conditioned Emotional Reactions. *Journal of Experimental Psychology*, 3, pp. 1–14.

Weber, D. (2010). The limitations of a behavioral approach in most educational settings. In G. S. Goodman (ed.), *Educational Psychology Reader*. NY: Peter Lang.

Webster, R. (1995). *Why Freud Was Wrong*. NY: Basic Books.

Weiner, D. (2008a). The Madman in the Light of Reason. In E. R. Wallace and J. Gach (eds.), *History of Psychiatry*. NY: Springer.

Weiner, D. (2008b). The Madman in the Light of Reason. Part II. In E. R. Wallace and J. Gach (eds.), *History of Psychiatry*. NY: Springer.

Werner, H. (1957). *Comparative Psychology of Mental Development*. NY: International Universities Press.

White, S. (1983). The idea of Development in Developmental Psychology. In R. Lerner, (ed.), *Developmental Psychology*. NJ: LEA.

Williams, R. (1985). *Keywords*. NY: Oxford University Press.

Wilm, E. C. (1925). *The Theories of Instinct*. CT: Yale University Press.

Wilson, E. O. (1975). *Sociobiology: The New Synthesis*. MA: Harvard University Press.

Wolpert, L. (2011). *Developmental Biology*. Oxford: Oxford University Press.

Yaroshevski, M. G. (1968). I. M. Sechenov. In B. Wolman (ed.), *Historical Roots of Contemporary Psychology*. NY: Harper and Row.

Yates, F. (1951). The influence of statistical models for research workers on the development of a science of statistics. *Journal of the American Statistical Association*, 46, pp. 19–34.

Young, R. M. (1970). *Mind, Brain and Adaptation in the Nineteenth Century*. NY: Oxford University Press.

Young, R. M. (1983). *Darwin's Metaphor*. Cambridge: Cambridge University Press.

Ziman, J. (2000). *Real Science*. Cambridge: Cambridge University Press.

Zull, J. E. (2002). *The Art of Changing the Brain*. NY: Stylus Publishing.

Index

1879, 29, 40

Abel, Frederick, 32
adaptationism, 23, 77
Adler, Alfred, 221
Ainsworth, Mary, 235
Allport, Gordon, 54
Angell, James R., 29
Animal magnetism. *See* mesmerism
Anna O., 214
apperception, 21
Ariès, Philippe, 143
Aristotle, 12, 14–15, 15, 31, 54, 57, 74, 89, 116, 120, 121, 148, 157, 170
associationism, 5, 20, 32, 33. *See also* psychology, associationist
Astruc, Jean, 117, 126
attachment,—7.129 66, 233
Augustine, 22, 23, 170, 189
autonomy, 21, 22, 104, 145, 166, 170, 190, 192, 218
Avenarius, Richard, 55

Bain, Alexander, 21, 33, 42–43, 48, 54, 79, 126, 127, 160
Baldwin, James M., 160, 164–165, 168, 170, 172, 184; co-evolution, theory of, 184, 185. *See also* Deacon, Terrance
Bandura, Albert, 71
Beard, George M., 204, 205

behaviorism: origins of, 18, 30, 37, 42, 43, 47, 48, 50; history, 65, 67, 68, 72, 76, 78, 82, 91, 101–102, 105, 173; methodological, 68, 71, 76
Bell, Charles, 118
Bellah, Robert, 188
Benedikt, Moritz, 214
Beneke, Friedrich, 38
Berlin School, 38
Berne, Eric, 231
Bernheim, Hippolyte, 44, 211, 213, 225
bildung,1.35 4.74
Binet, Alfred, 29, 44, 83
blank slate, 20, 23
Bleuler, Eugen, 162, 207
Bloomfield, Leonard, 169
Boaz, Franz, 54
Bonnet, Charles, 31, 157
Boring, Edward G., 30, 34, 36, 37, 44, 50, 55
Boulder model, 220
Bowlby, John,—7.129 66, 93, 233
Boyle, Robert, 54
Braid, James, 213
brain, operations and development, 9, 140–142
Brentano, Franz, 55, 98
Breur, Josef, 214, 225
Bridgman Perry W., 56
British Malady. *See* Cheyene, George
Broca, Paul, 121, 184

Brown, Norman, 221
Brüke, Ernst W., 225
Bruner, Jerome, 228
Büller, Karl and Charlotte 6.49 6.68 6.91
Burton, Robert, 202

canalization, 148
Carnap, Rudolph, 56
Carnegie, Dale, 230
Carpenter, William, 43, 76, 119, 155
Cartesianism. *See* Descartes
Carus, Carl G., 213
Cattell, Raymond B., 50, 81
cerebral localization, 43
Charcot, Jean M., 29, 44, 121, 207, 208,
    213–214, 225
Chess, Stella, 236
Cheyene, George, 202
childhood: study of, 10, 22, 23, 27, 162,
    163, 164; emergence of, 144–145
Chomsky, Noam, 71, 160, 173, 179–180,
    182
Claparède, Édourd, 165
cognition: situated, 109; distributed, 109
cognitive science, influence of, 172, 173,
    239
Coleridge, Samuel T., 155
Combe, George, 228, 229
comparative psychology. *See* minds,
    animal
Comte, Auguste, 44
Condillac, Étienne B., 31
conditioning: classical, 71, 73, 74, 80, 102,
    103, 105; operant, 71, 102, 103, 105
consciousness, problem of, 66; psychology
    of, 4, 16, 20, 21, 40, 42, 240
Cosmidees, Leda, 93
Coué, Emil, 230
Crick, Frances H., 132, 133, 135–138
critical education, 110
critical periods, 141
Cullen, William, 202
cultural evolution, 94
culture of the therapeutic, 1, 3, 187, 188,
    189–192, 231, 232
Cuvier, George, 25

d'Alambert, Jean-Baptiste, 149

Darwin, Charles, 20, 23–27, 42, 44, 47, 49,
    71, 73, 75, 90, 94, 110, 118, 140, 145,
    146–147, 151–154, 157–158, 161, 170,
    172, 225, 229, 238; influence of, 5, 49,
    55, 93, 120, 143, 158, 161, 166; neural
    Darwinism, 127, 140; social
    Darwinism, 153–154, 156
Darwin, Erasmus, 75
Dawkins, Richard, 93, 94
Deacon, Terrance, 182–185
degeneracy, 205–206, 218
Democritus, 116
Descartes, René, 11, 15–18, 20, 23, 31, 89,
    90, 116, 117; Cartesianism, 4, 11, 12,
    16, 17, 66, 70, 75, 96, 107, 114, 189;
    Cartesian Theatre @ B02.9 1.17 1.20
    6.104
development: emergence of psychology of,
    145; stages, 143, 146, 159, 164, 165,
    166, 167, 172. *See also* Language
Dewey, John, 84–86, 123, 192, 228
Diagnostic Statistical Manual (DSM) 7.1
    7.52 7.55-7.60
Diderot, Denis, 149
Dilthey, Wilhelm, 59, 96
drive, 92
Du-Bois Reymond, Emil, 38
Durkheim, Emile, 177

Ebbinghaus, Hermann, 96, 98
Eddy, Mary B., 216
Education. *See* public education
Edwards, Miles, 155
Effectiveness, therapy, 194–196
Ehrenfels, Christian V., 98
elementalism, theory of, 107
embryology, history, 133, 134, 147, 148
emergence, theories of, 17, 36, 172, 236,
    238, 239
Emmanuel Movement, 217, 218
Erikson, Eric, 221
Esquirol, Jean-Étienne, 35, 200, 201, 206
Exner, Sigmund, 225
Eynsenck, Hans J., 195

faculty psychology. S*ee* psychology,
    faculty
Fechner, Gustav, 32, 36, 37, 38, 39
Ferrier, David, 121

Fliess, Wilhelm, 226
Flourens, Jean P., 118
fMRI, 128, 129
formalism, in biology, 13, 23, 24, 123
Foucault, Michel, 200
Fowler, Lorenzo and Orson, 225, 228, 230
free association, 215
Freud, Sigmund, 91, 114, 126, 160, 162, 166, 170–171, 189, 190, 191, 192, 195, 196, 197, 204, 205, 214–215, 217, 218–219, 221, 222, 223–227, 228, 229, 230, 231; concept of mind, 6, 20; influence of, 10, 13, 32; metaphor, 3; origins of thinking, 18
Friere, Paulo, 70
Fries, 32
Fromm, Eric, 221
functionalism: biology, 5, 7, 9, 23–25; disorders, functionalist, 197, 207, 218. *See also* psychology, functionalist

Galen, 13, 113, 116, 197
Galenic medicine. *See* Galen
Gall, Franz J., 32, 114, 120, 155, 202, 203, 228, 238
Galton, Francis, 29, 36, 47, 49–50, 81, 83, 88, 133
Galvani, Luigi, 114
Gardner, Howard, 228
Gassendi, Pierre,
Geertz, Clifford, 62
geisteswissenshcaften, 41, 58–59, 62, 63
genes, 88, 93, 114, 115; mechanisms, 88–89, 115, 138, 139; study of, 93, 132–138
Geoffray, Etienne St. H., 25
Gesell, Arnold, 160, 164, 180, 228
Gibson, James J., 217
Gladden, Washington, 156
Goethe, Johann W., 23
Goldshmidt, Richard, 134
Gopnick, Alison, 228
Gould Stephen J., 94
Griesenger, Wilhelm, 119, 201, 204, 207

habit, 18, 26, 38, 74–75, 79, 81, 90, 105, 146, 150, 160, 165, 170, 218
Haeckel, Ernst, 122, 156, 157

Hall, G. Stanley, 38, 40, 46, 81, 85, 159, 160, 163, 218
Hall, Marshall, 76, 118
Haller, Albrect V., 118
Hanson, Norwood, 57
Harlow, Harry, 93, 233
Harris, Thomas, 231
Hartley, David, 33, 75, 117, 170
Hebb, Donald, 101
Heinroth, Oskar, 92
Heinroth, 203
Helmholtz, Hermann V., 36, 37, 38, 39, 97, 204
Hempel, Carl G., 56
Herbart, Johann F., 32, 224
Herder, Johann G., 3,30
Hering, Ewald, 39; controversy with Helmholtz, 39, 97
heritability, 87, 88
hierarchy, in nervous system 5,28, 121, 123
Hill, Napolean, 230
Hobbes, Thomas, 8, 18, 19, 75
homunculus, problem of, 5, 18, 71, 107, 129, 239
Horney, Karen, 221, 222
Hughlings Jackson, John, 34, 119, 121, 122, 126, 162
Hull, Clark, 92
human kind, 63, 130
Humboldt, Alexander, 37
Hume, David, 15, 20, 57, 63, 238
humoral theories, 198, 199
Hutchenson, Francis, 35
Huxley, Thomas H., 35
hypnosis, 213–214. *See also* mesmerism
hysteria, 213, 224, 225

imitation 4,29 6,60 6,65
infancy: study of, 175–177, 236; theories of, 145
information processing, theories of, 173, 239
inheritance of acquired characteristics. *See* Lamarck, influence of
inhibition, 77
innate 4,43
instinct, 25, 26, 44, 47, 66, 69, 77, 78, 89, 90, 91, 92, 119, 133, 155, 161, 163,

170, 219, 225, 226, 227, 230
instrumental conditioning *see* conditioning, operant
intelligence, conceptions of, 47, 48, 50, 69, 70, 79, 105, 162, 165
introspectionism, 16, 22, 29, 37, 40, 47, 53, 55, 65, 68, 98

James, William, 6, 11, 29, 35, 36, 40, 42, 45–46, 77, 91, 126, 127, 163, 179, 192, 217, 218, 228, 230
Janet, Pierre, 44, 165, 166, 206, 214, 217, 218
Jastrow, Joseph, 228
Jung, Carl, 162, 221

Kandel, Eric, 126
Kant, Immanuel, 8, 11, 15, 20, 21, 32, 53, 54, 58, 66, 98, 110, 145, 173, 193, 205, 206, 238
Koch, Robert, 224
Koffka, Kurt, 98
Kohler, Kurt, 98, 99
Kohut, Heinz, 189
Kraeplin, Emil, 194, 204, 205, 207, 208, 218
Kuhn, Thomas, 29, 57
Kulpe, Oswald, 40, 96, 168

Lamarck, Jean B., 25; influence of, 43, 77, 119, 132, 146, 150, 152, 153, 154, 162, 165, 166, 170, 184, 226
language: development of, 178–180, 180–185; psychological, 2, 6, 7, 8, 9; socio-economics and, 181; structure, 177, 179, 182, 183, 185; study of, 179–180, 185. *See also* metaphor
Lasch, Christopher, 188, 192, 221
Lashley, Karl, 101, 121, 169
Lavater, Johann K., 32
Lavosier, Antoine, 57
Laycock, Thomas, 115
Lazarus, Moritz, 58
learning: definition, 1, 67, 68, 70, 71–72, 77, 78, 82, 85, 109–110, 126, 127, 129, 131; trial and error, 48, 79, 160, 162; types, 71–72; situated, 71
Ledoux, Joseph, 127, 129, 130
Lehrman, Daniel, 92

Leibniz, Gottfried W., 21
Liébault, Amboise-Auguste, 213
limbic system, 126
Linneus, Carl, 57, 149
Little Albert, 80
Lloyd Morgan, Conway, 48, 79
localization, cerebral, 114, 116, 120–121, 123, 124, 128, 218
Locke, John, 8, 18, 23, 35, 54, 71, 108, 117, 120, 169, 170, 182, 223
Loeb, Jacques, 78
logical positivism, 8, 56, 57, 104
Lorenz, Konrad, 92–93
Lyell, Charles, 151, 153

Mach, Ernst, 55, 56
MacLean, Paul 126
Mahler, Margaret, 93, 162, 172
de Maillett , Benoît, 149
Malthus, Thomas, 151
Marcuse, Herbert, 221
Maslow, Abraham, 189, 230, 237
de Maupetuis, Pierre-Louis, 149
McDougall, William, 82, 91, 92
Mclintock, Barbara, 134
measurement, in psychology, 38, 44, 49–50, 60–61, 81, 86, 145
mechanism, 26, 88, 147, 149, 159, 167, 169
Mekel, JT, 157
Melanchthon, Philip, 31
Mendel, Gregory, 133
Menninger, Karl and William, 231
mental testing, 49
mentalism, 9, 101, 103, 104, 107, 108
Mesmer, Anton, 211–212
mesmerism, 211–212, 230
metaphor, 2, 3, 7, 49, 65, 67, 87, 113, 129, 130, 143, 151, 159, 166, 169, 172, 191, 193, 225, 227, 239
Meyer, Adolph, 208, 230
Meynert Theodore, 118, 204, 225, 226
Mill, James, 21, 42
Mill, John S., 43, 55, 56
mind: animal, 31, 43, 47–48, 66, 71, 72, 78, 89–91, 92, 99, 170, 182–183; brain activity, as, 5; conceptions of, 1, 2, 6, 9, 10, 11, 31, 33, 65, 78, 82, 89, 107, 115, 116, 131, 134, 215, 237; Greek view,

12, 13; modular, 93, 140, 166, 172; separate from body, 4, 5, 96, 107, 110, 113, 114, 119, 163
mind-cure, 216–217, 226, 230
Morel, Bénédict, 205–206
Morgan, Thomas H., 136
Muemann, Ernst, 96, 100
Muller, Georg E., 98
Müller, Johannes P., 38, 42, 43, 76, 77, 119
Müller, Max F., 162
Munsterberg, Hugo, 40

Nancy School, 213, 217
narrative, 63, 107, 194, 222, 223
natural selection, 14, 66, 77, 94, 147, 151, 153, 165
natursphilosophie, 38, 145, 153, 155, 157, 203
neo-grammarians, 179
nerve transmission, 39, 75, 114, 116, 126, 128, 129
Neurath, Otto, 56
neurology, 202, 204, 207, 213, 226
neuroscience, findings, 9
neurosis, origins of, 202
New Thought, 217, 218, 230
Newtonianism, 54, 76, 147, 150, 151
Nietzsche, Friedrich, 91, 225
nineteenth century thought, effects of, 3, 6, 29, 30, 113, 116, 129, 138–140, 149, 215, 217, 224, 225, 226, 227. *See also* reflex
No Child Left Behind (NCLB) 4.7
Norwood, Robin, 231

objectivity, 53, 54
Ockham, William of, 74
Oken, Lorenz, 23, 156, 157
Operationism. *See* Bridgmann
organicism, 67, 147–148, 158, 159, 167, 169, 193

Paley, William, 24, 25
Pasteur, Louie, 224
Pavlov, Ivan, 42, 73–74, 75, 80, 102
Peale, Norman V., 230
Pearson, Karl, 29, 49
phenomenology, 55, 57
phrenology, 21, 43, 120, 155, 228–230

Piaget, Jean, 8, 109, 122, 160, 162, 165, 166–167, 170, 171, 172, 173–174, 176, 177, 179, 240
Pinel, Philippe, 35, 200, 201, 202, 203, 207
Pinker, Steven, 93
plasticity, 138, 140
Plato, 12, 13–14, 19, 23, 66, 71, 86, 88, 144, 171, 172
Polanyi, Michael, 57
Popper, Karl, 56, 60
Pragmatism, 157
Preyer, William, 159, 160, 161, 179
Protestantism, 13, 29, 31, 216, 226, 228
psyche , 12, 13, 113
psychiatry: models, 196–198, 201, 204, 205, 208; origins, 188–189, 200, 203
psychologism, 97
psychology: applied, 37, 46, 68, 78, 99, 106; American, history of, 35, 37, 45–46, 49, 50, 77, 78, 91, 93; associationist, 31, 33, 38, 40, 42, 44, 98, 105, 110, 117, 126, 155, 160, 170, 182–183, 200, 202, 218, 232, 238, 239; British, history of, 31, 33, 42, 47, 49, 76, 77; clinical, 220; cognitive, 2; common-sense, 35; critical, 4; definition, 2, 34, 35, 67; discipline status, 1, 2, 7, 62; everyday, 2, 7, 60, 70, 228, 238, 240; evolutionary, 93–94; faculty, 14, 21, 34, 82, 108, 120, 172, 202, 238; French, history of, 35, 44; functionalist, 5, 6, 14, 27, 30, 50, 77, 101, 102, 103, 104; German, history of, 32, 37, 95–97, 99–101; Gestalt, 95, 98–99, 101, 110, 166; hedonistic, 18, 79, 101, 102, 117; methodological patterns, 41, 60–61, 62, 63; moral discourse, as, 11, 94, 123, 143, 146, 160, 162, 165, 190, 192, 207, 223, 232–233, 237; neuro, 72, 87; rationalist, 14, 18, 21, 31; Russian, 77; science, as, 53–54, 55, 56, 57; sensorimotor, 38, 43, 119
psycho-physics. *See* Fechner
public education: Germany, 69; research, 68, 81, 82, 83, 85; United States, 9, 68, 69, 109; reform, 83, 86, 100
purpose. *See* teleological
Pussiń, Jean-Baptiste, 201

Putnam, James J., 218
Puysegur, Marquis 7.65

Quimby, Phinneus P., 216, 230
Quintilian, Marcus, 144

Ray, John, 143
recapitulation, 10, 122, 146, 156–158, 162, 163, 167, 226
reductionism, 142
reflex: metaphor of, 3, 18, 237; physiology, 17, 47–48, 73, 76, 91, 116–119, 122, 123, 141; psychic, 75–77, 81, 99, 160, 161, 163, 170
refrigerator mother, 231
Reich, Wilhelm, 221
Reid, Thomas, 35
Reiff, Philip, 188, 189, 191, 192, 223
Reil, Johann C., 203, 204
Reimarus, Herman S., 90, 91
Ribot, Theodule, 44
Rogers, Carl, 189
Romanes, George, 47, 48, 158, 160, 162–163
romanticism, 22, 119, 189, 203, 205; and developmental theories 1.12 6.2 6.5
Rorarius, Hieronymus, 90
Rousseau, Jean J., 8, 22, 23, 70, 84, 144, 145, 158, 172, 189, 190, 193, 227, 232, 235
Rush, Benjamin, 202
Ryle, Gilbert, 101, 130, 193

science, origins of,. (intro) 11, 23, 26
Schleirmacher, Friedrich, 59
Schneirla TC, 92, 169
Scripture, Edward W., 35, 36
Sechenov, Ivan, 73, 77
self-actualization, 188
Seligman, Martin, 228
Shaftsbury, Earl of, 36
Sherrington, Charles, 125
Schopenhauer, Arthur, 91
Sidis, Boris, 218
Skinner, Burrhus F., 20, 45, 68, 82, 101–108, 179, 182, 228
Skinnerianism. *See* Skinner
somaticism, 192, 197, 198, 201, 203–204, 207, 208, 219

specificity, 138, 139
Spencer, Herbert, 21, 26, 33, 35, 42, 43–44, 45, 47, 76, 119, 132, 146, 152, 153–156, 157, 158, 160–162, 163
Sperber, Dan, 93, 173
Spitzer, Robert, 209
Spranger, Eduard, 59, 100
Spurzheim, Johann, 228
Steinthal, Heymann, 58
Stern, William, 54, 96, 160, 167
Stumpf, Carl, 96, 98
Sully, James, 160, 162, 163
Sumner, William G., 156
Szasz, Thomas, 193

Taine, Hippolyte, 44, 146
Tarde, Gabriel, 164
teleological, 15, 18, 44
Terman, Louis, 44
therapeutic sensibility. *See* culture of the therapeutic
Thorndike, Edward G., 49, 78–85, 91, 99, 105
Tingbergen, Niko, 92
Titchner, Edward J., 29, 50
Tolman, Charles, 173
Tooby, John, 93
Toulmin, Stephen, 57
trauma, 213, 214, 215
Trembly, Jean 2.8
Tuke, Daniel, 211
twin studies, 49

understanding, 8, 58–59
Upham, Thomas, 35
utilitarianism, 24

versthen. See understanding
Vico, Giambattista, 58
Voltaire, 149
Von Baer, Karl E., 155, 156, 157
volkerpsychologie, 41
Vygotsky, Lev S., 109, 122, 160, 164, 168, 170–172, 177, 185

Watson, James, 132, 133, 135–138
Watson, John, 42, 49, 68, 78, 79, 80, 91, 228
Weber, Ernst H., 36, 38

Werner, Heinz, 160, 167, 172, 239
Wernicke, Carl, 184
Wertheimer, Max, 6, 96, 98
Westphal, Carl, 204
Weyer, Johann, 200
Willis, Thomas, 114, 202
Wilson, Edward O., 93
wissenschaft, 54
Wolff, Christian 1.29 2.6

Woodworth, Robert S., 92
Worcester, Elwood, 217
Wundt, Wilhelm, 6, 8, 11, 29, 34, 36, 38, 40–42, 45, 46, 55, 58, 78, 96, 98, 127, 163, 179
Wurzburg School, 96, 98, 168. *See also* Kulpe, Oswald

Yerkes, Robert, 80

About the Author

Robert Ausch received his doctorate from the CUNY Graduate Center in Developmental Psychology studying education in science. He also studied psychoanalysis at National Psychological Association for Psychoanalysis (NPAP). He has published on a range of topics, including social science methodology and the philosophy of psychology. He has worked in teacher education and currently teaches psychology at New York University and Pratt Institute.

CPSIA information can be obtained at www.ICGtesting.com
Printed in the USA
BVOW07*0340270415

397528BV00001B/1/P